A Gambler's Tale

by Stevie Thomas

Clink Street

Published by Clink Street Publishing 2023

First edition.

ISBN:
978-1-915785-11-4 - paperback
978-1-915785-12-1 - ebook

This book was written by Stevie between 2002 and 2005. We have tried to keep the tone of the book in the style that he wrote/dictated it in, so we didn't lose the essence of the colloquial nature it was written.

Everything in this book is 100% factual (as unbelievable as it may seem with some of the stories) and it is important to note that some of the sums mentioned in the stories are of even greater value in today's date due to inflation over the years.

We really hope you enjoy reading the book and in doing so hope the book will preserve a part of Stevie's memory with his unique character and exuberance with his family, friends and all who read it. If you had the honour and privilege of knowing Stevie Thomas, our ultimate goal was that you read this book and can hear him narrating it.

Thank you so much. His wife and sons:

Emma, Max and JJ x

I have always said that if I had a chance to write about gambling stories it would be a very intriguing and exciting book indeed. This book will include some of the experiences I have encountered on my travels. I have read a few books on gambling stories and I felt that I could write a book of my own! I will share these experiences with you but obviously I will change some of the names and some of the places to protect those concerned. Everything you will read in this book is true. If you have read any gambling books in the past you will find this book quite incredible.

I said to my wife some time ago, I would like to write a book on all these fascinating events that have taken place in my life and it was she who suggested that I should sit down and put pen to paper. What happened was, when we used to entertain at dinner parties, I used to always tell a story that I had experienced in my life about gambling and throughout the evening I used to tell one or two stories that were funny and my wife said to me, "You made everyone laugh tonight, you could write a book." So it was then that I decided to sit down and start. I said to her, "It would take a very long time indeed to start all my adventures, going back to when I was possibly four to five years old." She said, "Well you are in no rush!" So, I sat down, probably a couple of years ago now, probably about the year 2000. We then bought a PC and we found some software that you could dictate to as it would be a lot easier because I can't type. Well in the beginning it was great but then the software packed up halfway through and it started spelling certain things wrong and I decided to call it a day because everything was getting on top of me. Then my wife started typing a bit for me, my sister started typing a bit for me and then my niece started typing a bit for me but eventually everything faded out and we got nothing done.

It wasn't until by pure chance one day that I met a very nice chap called Dave English who gave me the number of a lady who would sit down and do the manuscript, and it seems now that we are finally going to get something done, so I am going full steam ahead to write this book.

I started at 39 years old, I'm already 41 and we still haven't got the final copy finished. This book will include stories of some of the biggest gambling cash games, even by todays standards. I know that the $10,000 Hold'em Event in Las Vegas is the biggest competition in the world and I know the prize money is probably $2 million now, which is about £1million but in a lot of my stories I am talking about 'hard cash' not tournament chips. The size of those games was well ahead of their time. Also there was a poker game that I was involved in, dealing, that was the biggest game to be known, but one slight thing, it was 35,000 ft up in the air, but I will tell you about that later on. Myself, I've played poker all around the world. UK, Australia, Hong Kong, Cyprus and many, many other places. Wherever there has been Five Card Stud and me knowing that there is a good straight open game, I want to get involved. I have also dealt in the biggest games in the world, for their time, and even in today's standard as I said, they would be considered very large indeed.

My stories will include some of the top Professional Five Stud poker players and then some other stories; will consist of some modest amateur very weak poker players. Both can be quite amusing! I suppose with a book, the only problem is where do you start. My wife said to me, "Well, why don't you start at the beginning" and I said to her "Where is the beginning?" She said, "The beginning of your gambling stories."

So I had to think quite hard and the harder I was thinking the younger I was getting. In my mind I kept thinking of experiences of when I was young and then younger and younger. Well I can tell you I ended up at five years old and that's when it all started.

My dad owned a casino in 1965. It was called the Wembley Spinner Club. It was a casino well ahead of its time. Wembley in those days was a very nice area with a large Jewish community. It was quite classy; I would probably say it was on a standard to Stanmore, Radlett or Elstree.

On the ground floor there were three roulette tables, a dice table and two blackjacks, on the first floor there was a poker room, & we always had buffet nights. Now it was my dad back in the 60s that introduced free drinks, free coffees and free buffets. The spread he used to put on was quite incredible. We still look at some of the Cine films today and are quite impressed. Once a week they used to hold a raffle and the first prize was a brand-new Escort car. Needless to say, on these special nights, the club used to get extremely busy. What with the complimentary drinks, food and a chance to win a car, can you imagine? In those days there were hundreds and hundreds of casinos dotted around the London area. It was quite easy to get a licence. It was not until 1969–70 the Gaming Board restricted the licences.

When I was five years old, my mum used to take my brother, sister and me into the casino on a Sunday afternoon and I remember until this day sitting on my dad's knee watching him play poker. I also remember a couple of the players at the time because I played with them 20 to 25 years later. Sonny,

French Alan, Italian Gino, to name a few, they all had nicknames. Dad also told me there was a very big Poker Player by the name of Kuros. Now Kuros has died but he owned a couple of restaurants in the West End and Kuros was a fearless poker player. Dad was telling me, he could possibly lose £10-15 grand in one night. Now you are talking about in the mid-60s. In those days a three or four bed-room house was about £6000.

They all used to play Five Card Stud Strip Deck. Five Card Stud is the mother of all poker games. It was played in the 30s, 40s and 50s back in America, but it soon died a death, because with 52 cards the action used to get a little slow and boring. When the game hit London in the mid-50s, the Cypriots and the Italians discarded the 2s, 3s and 4s and ended up with a 40-card deck. This used to give the game a little more action. It used to be a 'no limit game', which can be a very dangerous game indeed like the 'no limit game' they play in Las Vegas at the moment with Texas Hold'em. Players out there currently know that in this kind of game, you could put your entire cash at stake at any time. When the 60s came around that structure seemed to die off. What happened to the game next was that they took the 5s and the 6s out and left a 32-card deck & also changed the structure to a Pot Limit Game, so you could only bet the size of the pot, which definitely gave you a lot more action and you were able to 'buy' a lot more cards for your money in the course of the game. With this structure you could 'build' pots, knowing you could not lose all your money in one pot. Strip Deck, as is now known was born. The Americans have never played Strip Deck Poker; it never took off within the States. If you go to a couple of the card clubs in Los Angeles, you will find it in some of the rooms and they call it 'Asian Stud'. They still play it over there in the Asian Section, but they still play No Limit. I have played it in America for three or four years and I have made money. However, I feel that you have to play very tight indeed, but I will tell you about those stories later on in the book. There was still a lot of Five Card Stud Strip Deck right up until the mid-90s but the game died and Hold'em took over. Now it seems that Hold'em has died and is being taken over by Omaha Poker. Any Omaha player will tell you, that game has got a lot of action. I will argue with anybody out there that has played in a very good Five Card Stud Strip Deck game that Five Card Stud has just as much action as Omaha.

Now, I am going to begin with one of my stories. My dad told me this story many years after it actually happened. It's actually quite an amusing one, so I thought I should definitely share it with you.

When he had the casino between 1965–70, there used to be a customer who went there every single night of the week at 6 pm. He used to have a confectionary shop, a sweet shop. He would never leave the casino until he had lost every single penny. His sweetshop used to be around the corner and he used to walk into the casino with about £40–£50 every single night. Now you're talking about the mid-60s, and he would never ever win! One night my dad was at home with us and he rang the casino and spoke to the manager, whose name was Sollie and asked "Any Poker players in yet Sollie?" to which Sollie replied, "Not yet Max, but our first customer in tonight was the 'sweet-shop man' and he's winning a couple of hundred pounds." Dad said to the manager, "No problem, I'll call you in an hour and I'll find out roughly what time the poker will start," disregarding what Sollie said about the 'sweet-shop man'. Dad called him back in about an hour's time and before he asked any questions, Sollie informed Dad that the 'sweet-shop man' was now winning about £2000. My dad still replied to Sollie, "No problem Sollie, he'll be there all night." Don't forget in those days it was 24 hours. Dad knew that this guy was an out and out gambler and he would carry on gambling and gambling. Anyway dad told me that he was not too worried about it. He was more concerned about getting the poker started. About midnight that night, the phone rang home. It was Sollie. He said "Max, I think you had better come down." Dad said, "Why, has the poker begun?" "No Max! The 'sweet-shop man', he's winning about £8000." Now £8,000 as we said in the 60s, was a lot of money! Dad said, "I'm on my way, I'll be down in about 15 minutes." Well the story goes like this. This 'sweet-shop man' couldn't do anything wrong that night. He was playing roulette, he was hitting number after number after number. Anything he backed was coming up. Dad even raised the limit. In those days, you could do whatever you wanted. The maximum you could have on a number at the Wembley Spinner was £5–£10 a number. Dad raised the limit to £25 a number. Dad raised the limit to £50 a number, but sure enough this guy carried on hitting number after number. Dad told me, "They changed the dealer every 20 minutes, but to no avail. At six o'clock in the morning the 'sweet-shop man' had accumulated every single 'cash chip' in the casino. Notice that I say 'cash chip'. Cash chips are the chips that you can go and cash in. The normal coloured chips are the chips that you play at the table on the roulette. There is a reason I'm telling you this, it's because he had accumulated every single 'cash chip'. He then accumulated every single coloured chip on the three roulettes. At one stage the 'sweet-shop man' had gone delirious. He was having £4000 on black and £3000 on red. This we know is stupidity, but I think the guy had gone into oblivion, he started having £100 on a number which was a ludicrous limit in those days, but my dad being the gambler he is, just carried on raising the maximum. By 8.30 am the 'sweet-shop man' still couldn't do nothing wrong. Even Sollie the General Manager started spinning the ball, but it was no use. They estimated with the 'colour chips' (they put a different value on those ones) each one was valued from £5 to £100 a chip, plus all the cash chips in the casino, he was estimated at winning over £150,000. I mean, this is an unbelievable and incredible amount to be winning and this kind of money in the 60s could set you up for life. The magnificent ending to this story is this. By 7.30 pm the following evening, the 'sweet-shop man' left the casino – he went to his car and he brought out another £5 worth of change. He had lost every single chip back within the 24-hour period. The 'sweet-shop man' was never ever seen again at the casino. The casino was still to be open for the next three or four years. He disappeared without trace.

Dad laughs about the story now and obviously, if the man cashed in, he would have got paid, but it could have been the end of the Wembley Spinner Club, within the first year. You must be asking yourself, "How did he manage to win this kind of money, so effortlessly," but as I said, with my dad raising the limit and keeping on raising the limit, this was all possible.

There was another customer that used to go regularly to the Wembley Spinner Club, everybody used to call him 'Little Norman'. Well he used to go in day in and day out and lose his money and this went on for months and months. After about six or seven months Little Norman used to come in have his drinks and have his food and not play. Dad noticed this but didn't say anything. After all little Norman was a terrific customer. Well after nine months, Dad still didn't say anything but there was no action coming from 'Little Norman'. One night he wanted to meet Dad and he said, "Max, as you've seen I haven't been playing in the last nine months." Dad said, "I've noticed." He said, "Max, I've been coming in for the buffets and all the free food and all the free drink." Dad again said, "Yes! Norman I have noticed." He said, "I feel bad Max." So Dad said, "Look Norman, it's not a problem, come in and eat and drink whenever you like." Norman said, "I do feel bad Max because I haven't been playing, I'm not a good customer anymore, I've done all my money and I can't play anymore." Dad said, "Norman it's not a problem come and eat and drink whenever you like you're my guest."

Norman said, "I've got an idea." Dad said, "What is it?" Norman said, "Can you give me a job?" Dad said, "Are you kidding me?" He said, "No Max! I love the Wembley Spinner so much. I love your food here. I love your drink, I love the company and I love the Casino; I'm here every night, even though I'm not playing. I wanna job?" Within a week Norman was a dealer and a Croupier at the Wembley Spinner Club! One night, Dad told me Little Norman span the wheel and span 26, 26, 0, 0, 3333! Which is unbelievable because if you play roulette, you'll know they are all next to each other on the wheel!

One night when there weren't enough poker players to get a full game going, one of the players that were there challenged my dad to Heads Up Poker. He must have been a brave man, his name was 'Sonny'. A very experienced poker player at Five Card Stud and he is still on the circuit today. Dad said to him, "Let's get it on Sonny, if you want to play me Heads Up, I'll play you." As they were to begin the game, Dad realised that they were playing with 52 cards, a full deck. Sonny said to my dad, "Max, I'm not playing you Heads Up Strip Deck, because you are unbeatable, I want to play you Full Deck." To which my dad replied, "No problem Sonny, deal them." The game lasted three and half hours and my dad lost his money. Apparently, Sonny was a very good Five Card Stud Full Deck player and Dad, not knowing the mechanics of how to play Full Deck, told me that he was outclassed by Sonny. In the years gone he had played a 40-card deck with the 5s and 6s included, but this was a different ball game, Sonny had the beating of Dad. Well Sonny came in the next day and said, "Max you on for a game?" Dad said, "Let's go Sonny." The same result, Sonny won money off of my dad. The night after, guess what? Sonny turned up again. "Hey Max," he said, "Want to play again?" My Dad looked at him and said, "Sonny no more full deck with you, I will play you Strip Deck." To which Sonny replied, "Come on Max, Strip Deck you're too good!" Dad turned around and said, "Sonny full deck you're too good!" I've never ever played Five Card Stud with 52 cards, I thought it would be a very slow and boring game, but something was to happen very recently and I will tell you about that towards the end of the book that made me change my mind.

One night my dad popped into the Spinner early, it was quiet but he noticed that there was one customer standing all by himself at the bottom of the casino on the dice table. He walked over and he noticed it was Stan the minicab driver. They used to call him 'Stan the man'. Now Stan, was a regular punter at the Wembley Spinner Club, he was also the driver for the club, so any customers that wanted to be driven home he would drive them, get the cab fare and then come back and gamble. Dad noticed on this particular night that Stan wasn't gambling. Dad walked over to Stan and said, "How are you doing, are you winning or are you losing?" Stan replied, "Max I've lost my money tonight, I can't even have another bet, all I've got left is this 2/6 p chip [which is about 12.5 p in today's currency]." Now the minimum at the Wembley Spinner on the dice on the front line or the pass line was 5 shillings, which is 25 p so Stan is standing there with this 2/6 p chip in his hand and he can't even have a bet. My Dad said to Stan, "Stan put your 2/6 p chip on the front line and I'll tell the Croupier to match it, so that you can have a bet." Stan said, "That's very kind of you Max, because I've been losing my money a long time at the Wembley Spinner Club." Anyway Stan put his 2/6 p chip on the front line. Dad told the Croupier to put another 2/6 p chip on top and Stan picked up the dice. Stan made a couple of numbers and he had £3–£4 in front of him. Dad walked away and went up to the office to make a few phone calls to see who was coming in to play poker that night. About an hour later the manager Sollie phoned up the office, and said, "Max, Stan the man, has just left, he was telling everybody that you gave him an extra 2/6 p." Dad said, "That's right Sollie, not a problem." He said, "Well Max, that 5 shillings that he put on the front line has just won him £1800"! Dad said to Sollie, "Are you kidding me?" Sollie said, "No Max, he was throwing the dice for over an hour, anything he was betting was winning." Dad said, "I can't believe that." Sollie replied, "It's true, he has just walked out of the casino, winning £1800." Well Dad tells me that he didn't worry about it too much because as I said, Stan was the regular driver, and a regular customer. That night the story went around the casino and Dad was saying to Sollie during the night, "Don't worry, Stan the man will be back, it's probably a good thing that he has had a 'touch' and won that money." Well the following night came and yes Stan the man walked in at about 9 pm. He saw my dad and he said, "Max I've got to thank you very much." Dad said, "I know Stan, I heard all about it, we are going to get some action from you tonight." He looked up at Dad and said, "Max can you follow me outside please"? They walked outside the Wembley Spinner Club and as they got outside the front door Stan said, "I want to thank you Max, because without you I wouldn't have won that money." Dad replied, "Well I know that Stan, you are welcome." Stan said, "No, I also want to thank you Max, because not only did I win that money, I went out this morning and bought this lovely new Jaguar parked over there, so that I can do some executive minicab driving and because of that 2/6 p chip that you gave me, I was able to have that first bet, win that money and buy a lovely new car! I promise you Max, I will be the Wembley Spinner driver until the day it closes… but I don't know if I'm going to gamble any more!"

Now, I'm going to tell you a little bit about my father. My father is known in the gambling world as one of the most fearless poker players and also one of the strongest Five Card Stud players on the planet and that's no joke. In fact, his forte (his strongest point) is Heads Up (match poker). In fact very recently, Dad was playing Hold'em at the Vic, which is a casino in London and he was playing in a ten-handed game, and he was playing so aggressively that one of the Hendon Mob, Barney, emailed me the next day and said. "I tell you what, in a fight, I want your Dad on my side, because he just 'pounds' away at the pot!" Now when it's Heads Up you can afford to play very, very aggressively and believe you me, he will take on anybody head-to-head at Five Card Stud. In fact recently on the internet there was a challenge by four or five current professional poker players, challenging anybody in the world to any poker game of their choice, at any stake. This challenge was out over the internet, because of the Vienna Heads Up World Championship, which was a Heads Up Hold'em. I replied to all five professionals, that my father would play them one by one Heads Up Five Card Stud and a minimum stake of $10,000 and no limit maximum, but the game had to be Strip Deck Five Card Stud pot limit. All five declined the offer. One replied and he said, "He would play, but there was a small snag as he wanted to play also 'Heads Up Omaha'. The guy's name was Dave and is also known as 'The Devil Fish', a very strong Omaha player. A very, very good gambler doesn't play Five Card but the way he sees it, he would give it a bash. I'm sure he knows Five Card but his forte is Omaha. Well Dad declined the Omaha and wanted to play Five Card, but Dave declined the Five Card. I replied and said it was them who put the challenge over the internet. Nothing ever evolved and there was never a game. My dad's reputation is obviously world-renowned.

You see when he sits at a poker table he could have very, very big 'swings'. Some nights he could actually skin the table, take everybody's money one by one and on the nights if his cards are not going well, he could lose money. He could lose big money, but overall in the last 55 years of playing, his winnings at Five Card Stud outweigh big time the losses. His wins some nights are humongous and the losses could be big, but that's the style of his play. Me on the other hand, a lot of people say that I play a lot more carefully. My wins aren't as big on my winning nights as my dad, but my losses on the losing nights are usually very small. As a few people have said in the past, the difference between my dad and I at Five Card Stud is that you have more value with my dad, but the result is still the same. Whether it's father or son we win, you lose!

In the early 60s, Dad was telling me about when he was playing poker in North London; he had lost a considerable amount of money one night. He found out the next day that the cards had been marked and he was actually cheated out of that money. Now, the money he lost was 'Markers'. Markers means when you've got credit and you have to pay the next day or the day after. My Dad found out that the cards were marked, but just to let you know the gentleman my dad is, he went back the following day and paid them the money he had lost. You might ask why? And I also asked him why? He said, "If you lose money at poker and it's on credit and you go back the next day and say I'm not paying because I was cheated, it always sounds sour grapes. Be a man, pay your losses, wipe your mouth, you keep your name clean and afterwards you can also say, 'I didn't like the game,' but once you've paid, then they might get the message. That's just a little bit of the character of my dad.

Time for another small story. This time a short and funny onc. My dad had a small club and casino in Haringey, North London, it was called the Empress Club. He received a phone call at home, by the manager; his name was Dinos. They used to call him 'Mr Beans', because he was always lively. Someone was playing The Maximum on The First Dozen on the roulette. That means from number 1 to number 12. Then obviously, Dad told the manager to keep him updated on the action, because apparently, this customer was winning quite a lot of money. This guy couldn't stop winning on betting the first dozen. Dad went down to the Club to see what was going on, because the manager and the dealer mentioned that the first dozen was coming up quite regularly. My dad got down there and after about half an hour decided to stop the game and close the table. The whole roulette table was full of customers. So Dad wasn't a popular guy when he stopped the game in mid action and said, "This table is now closed." One of the guys was winning £7–8000. Mid-60s again! The table was closed and Dad paid the guy. After closing time, he then examined the roulette wheel and found many of the numbers had the gaps closed slightly, so the wheel was favouring the first dozen. This, we call in the gambling trade "The wheel was biased." This was another expensive lesson for my dad, in today's casinos all roulette wheels are balanced, checked and investigated so the wheel has no bias and they do this on a regular nightly basis.

There was another customer that used to go every single night to the Empress Club and he used to bet on red and black and for a long time he never lost. I'll tell you his system. He used to start off having £5 on red or black. If it lost, £10. If it lost, £20. If it lost, £40. If it lost, £80 etc. etc. This we know is a doubling up system. As any of you reading this, you will say, you will always lose your money at that system and the reason you will lose is that nowadays they have limits. Most limits on red and black is £10,000 and even with those kinds of limits if the red or black comes up consecutively 12 times on the trot, you would have lost a lot of money, in fact you would have reached the limit. This guy never, ever, lost, Dad was telling me. There was no limit on the red and black at the Empress Club. That's right, no limit on the 'even money' chances. I mean this in itself was ludicrous and I actually asked my dad recently why was there no limit. My Dad said, that back in the early 60s all the London casinos and there were many of them, used to have no limit on the even money chances. Obviously, this in unheard of nowadays. Well this young man used to walk in and play his doubling up system. Many nights, the young man used to walk out of the Empress winning between £50 and £100 without a problem. This went on for months and months until one night, Dinos (Mr Beans), the Croupier, who I've mentioned before, span 17 reds on the trot! That's right, 17 reds one after the other. The guy had done his entire cash flow all in one night and his entire winnings for the last six or seven months and when I say he lost the entire lot, this man used to walk in sometimes with £8–£10 grand. He'd lost the whole lot within the first 13 spins! That just goes to show you doubling up on the roulette is definitely not a good system. I know many gamblers that have tried it and many failed, except one, well I'll get to that later on.

There used to be regular poker games at the club in Haringey and just around the corner was where my grandfather and grandmother used to live. I'm telling you this for a reason, because my grandfather was very much against gambling. He accepted it with my dad because my dad always told him that it was his business but to tell you the truth he was dead against it. One night there was a very big game at the club and there came a pot between my dad and a guy named Tony and after the last card, Tony ended up with a possible straight and my dad had a pair of 10s on the show and it was my dad to bet. My dad checked to the possible straight and Tony bet the full pot £1150. This was a lot of money in the 60s and probably equivalent to £10-£12 grand in this day and age. Dad started thinking and as Dad glanced across the room, he saw my grandfather, who must have come in; just standing there watching this pot. Now Dad tells me he wanted to call Tony but he didn't want to do it in front of my grandfather, just in case Tony had the straight. To lose £1150, probably would have given my grandfather a heart attack! The Croupier said to my dad, "Are you calling or are you passing?" My dad said, "I'm thinking." He looked up again and my grandfather had now walked closer to the table to have a better look at this pot. So Dad said to him, "Father you couldn't make me a cup of coffee could you?" To which he replied, "Yes in a minute I will." Dad tells me my grandfather wouldn't move from the table until he had seen the end of this pot. He stood there and after a couple of minutes, my dad said to the Croupier, "Pass my cards, Tony you win." My grandfather then said to my dad, "I'll make you that coffee now," and he walked out of the room. My dad looked at Tony and he said to him. "Do you know what, if the 'old man' wasn't here, I swear to God, I'd call your £1150 bet because I think you were bluffing, but I didn't want to take a chance in front of the old man because if I'd called the bet and you'd had the straight, it would have killed him… and that's why you made this bet to me because you saw my father was in the room and you knew 99% that I wouldn't call you." Tony turned over his hole card and he said to my dad, "Your right Max, I was bluffing… thinking about what you've just said, maybe, just maybe I shouldn't play poker with you."

Back in 1969, we spent quite a lot of time in Plymouth, down in the south west. Dad had some very good friends down there. They had a casino, a hotel and a card club. All the family used to go down there for the summer holidays Dad popping down for three or four days at a time, as he was still running the two casinos in London.

When he used to get down to Plymouth, his friends always used to arrange a poker game, which sometimes used to continue throughout the next day. We used to go and see Dad at the Card Club, just as they were finishing the game the next day. There was a poker player, who when he used to see me, my brother and sister walking in, we're all about seven, eight or nine years old, he would slowly take three £5 notes from my dad's pile and he used to craftily give them to us, when my dad wasn't looking. I remember this quite vividly as we were only young and certain things always stick in your mind and £5 was a lot of money. A lady named Yanulla, who was a friend of my mums, whose husband was playing poker, said to my mum. "All those poker players, they are snakes in the grass, playing for two or three days at a time." Many poker games my dad has been in at the Wembley Spinner Club used to start on Friday night and finish on Sunday afternoons, many, many times. While we are on the subject of Plymouth, Dad used to go to Torquay, quite a lot, which was about 20 miles away. He used to play very big Heads Up poker, with a guy called John. Dad tells me he had four or five very big match 'Heads Up Poker' games with him and he never lost.

The reason I'm telling you this is, apparently many nights John used to host other poker games, where an English guy named Mike used to go on a regular basis. This Mike lost a small fortune. We don't know exactly how much he lost, but a lot of people said he lost his house and he lost his business, playing in these games in Torquay. Mike the English guy found out that the games were supposedly bent. He'd heard that he had been cheated. Now whether he was or whether he wasn't we'll never know, but one night I can tell you this. He got himself drunk in Plymouth and he jumped in his car and he was racing along the street. He saw one of my dad's best friends Gregory from Plymouth and Gregory said to him. "Mike! Where are you going? And Mike replied, "I'm going to kill John, I've heard, I've been cheated for the last six months." Gregory said. "Don't be silly Mike, you're crazy!" Gregory was by the side of the car. Mike pulled out a gun and he said, "Let me go Gregory! I'm going to kill him. Gregory run off and jumped back in his car and Mike sped off. The police on the motorway then stopped Mike. He obviously, was going well above the speed limit. As the policeman went up to the car, Mike shot the policeman dead. He jumped back in his car and he got to the casino. Mike walked into the casino and shot the manager dead and the Croupier. I know this is all true, because Mike is still in prison, as I write this book. My friend's uncle whose nickname was 'Ginger' was working at the casino at the very time this happened. He told us this story. He obviously, caught the end of the story and Gregory told me the beginning. Ginger told us the guy walked in, guns blazing, like a movie. Ginger dived under the table for cover. Needless to say, Mike was caught and sentenced to life imprisonment.

There was another casino in Torquay and it was owned by another Greek, named Babbis. Dad told me he went in there with Rocky and Gregory, his friends, one night and the very first number Dad backed was number 16 to the maximum. This was the first bet that Dad had at the Casino that night. The ball span and landed straight into number 16. Dad took his winnings and placed all of them, on and around number 16. The ball span again, and bang straight into number 16 repetition. Babbis came over to the roulette wheel and said, "This roulette table is now closed!" Dad said, "Why?" and Babbis repeated, "I said, this roulette table is now closed!" Dad cashed in and had won about £4000 in two spins and had walked out with Rocky and Gregory within five minutes of walking in. Even in today's casinos, floor managers are able to close any game at any time on the casino floor, if they think there is something wrong. There was nothing wrong that night, Dad was just lucky!

The year is 1969. Dad still had the Casino in Wembley and got involved in buying some greyhounds as the Wembley Spinner Club was quite close to Wembley Dog Track. I think this was meant to be a business venture and a bit of pleasure combined. I think Dad knew at the back of his mind, that the casino he had in Wembley, had to close by June or July 1970, as the Gaming Board sat around at that time and decided to close many casinos outside the centre of London. Dad invested quite a lot of money in buying a small litter. He then decided to call them after the Wembley Spinner Club. He named one dog, 'Spinners Club', another, 'Spinners Dice', the other 'Spinners Glory', 'Spinners Chance' etc. etc., the last one was my one. My brother, sister and I had one each. My one, his real name was Bobby, but he used to run under the name of 'Spinners Chance'. I remember that quite well, because on Sundays we used to go up to South Mimms Kennels and all of us used to spend Sunday afternoons walking the dogs for a bit of exercise. In fact we had a photo taken, which appeared in the *Sporting Life*. Anyway, I'll tell you about my dog, it was an absolute donkey! It never, ever won a single race. Not one I tell you. I mean we used to go to Wembley on Saturdays, Haringey, Mondays and Fridays. We used to go to the track on a regular basis and I always used to back, maybe 20 p, or maybe 30 p. At nine years old, betting on my dog and it always finished last! Maybe that's why I don't really gamble nowadays, because I remember the hurtful feeling when I lost my money on my dog. Knowing my dad, he probably used to lose as well. Now on the other hand 'Spinners Dice' which belonged to my sister, actually won some very good graded races. I think, to cut a long story short, with all these greyhounds, reading in between the lines, it was not a very good business at all. Dad has never told us to this day. I think he lost a small fortune, following those bloody dogs! I'm not too sure, but I can tell you this, we went out for dinner not so long ago with some very close friends. Peter, one of the guys that we were with wanted to buy a dog at Walthamstow, which was being auctioned. It was in a charity event and Dad in no uncertain terms, kept on saying to him, "Don't do it Peter, don't do it Peter, don't buy it, don't buy it." Peter was bidding and bidding and Dad was saying, "Leave it, leave it." Dad tried to put Peter off and thankfully Peter decided not to up his offer. Dad said to Peter, "I've had greyhounds in the past and it's not a very good idea." I think if you mention the idea of buying a greyhound to my dad, he seems to be very concerned indeed.

After Dad got rid of the dogs, he decided to have a share with a guy named Harry Bubbles at Hackney Wick dog track. Now Harry Bubbles had a pitch twice a week and he used to run a book. He was called Harry Bubbles because his main business was glass blowing and they used to call him 'Bubbles'. In fact, he was a very successful glass blower and he had made a lot of money. So the dogs to him, was a bit of a pastime. So anyway, Dad has 50–50 with Harry Bubbles. Now the problem here was that Harry Bubbles was a compulsive gambler, he wasn't really a bookie. Now he brings my dad in because, I think, he wasn't doing so well, but there you've got my dad who is a bookmaker and a very big gambler, and Bubbles an out and out gambler, what a combination! Well I'll tell you exactly what happens when you put that combination together. They used to stand up and take loads of money for the favourite. In fact Dad always used to go a bigger price than the rest of the bookmakers. If the favourite was evens, Dad would go 5/4. If the favourite was 7/4, Dad would go 2/1. You name it, Dad would lay bigger. Dad used to say, "Harry, lets lay this dog to the maximum." Harry used to say, "Let's do it Max." Well, that's OK but one slight thing here, they used to take all the money that they'd laid on the favourite for the race and give it to the bookmaker next door and back the second favourite! Well this as anybody in the gambling business will tell you is suicide. Dad being the bookmaker wanted to lay big and Harry being the out and out punter, wanted to bet big. This was definitely a recipe for disaster. Now sometimes in a race they didn't used to lay any favourite money. They used to lay the second favourite or the third favourite, so what did they used to do? They used to up the price and get as much money as they could for the second or third favourite and take all the money and back the favourite! The partnership with Harry and Dad, I think lasted three months. Dad pulled out after losing week after week. I think Harry lasted another six weeks and the pitch was again available at Hackney Wick, so we'll say no more on that subject.

Sure enough in 1970 the casino closed. Probably, 1970–71 was quite lean times for my dad. Not that we would ever know, because we always had everything we ever needed. He could probably write his own book and more, which could cover these times in much greater detail. In 1971 we saw the opening of the SP office in North London. He is now a bookmaker by trade and a property developer. He always had his Bookmaking Licence and I think he was one of the first, if not *the* first Cypriot legal bookmaker in London, if not the UK. Dad used to renew his Bookmaking Licence, since the early 60s, but he never used it. Once the casino closed and the greyhounds weren't winning, it was time to go into the 'bookmaking business'. My brother and I used to go up to the office every Saturday and watch the afternoon racing. I had seen enough of dogs and horses by the time I was ten years old to last me a lifetime!

1971 (at 10 years old), was a very big year for me, because this was the year that I had my first ever poker game. The games only lasted two weeks. What I didn't realise in the next 30 years, I have never been in a poker school that has lasted more than nine months and that's because I ended up the only winner in every school I've entered. The games in 1971 though were stopped for a very different reason completely. I'll tell you why and how. We used to go to Margate for our summer holidays. In those days Margate was the place to go. You were very lucky indeed if you found a space on the beach to place your deck chair. Well anyway, we used to stay with our auntie in a very nice house and our cousin used to come over. He still lives in Margate to this day, poor fella! His name was Dassos. One day it was raining, so instead of bringing his football to play with in the garden, he bought a deck of cards. He told us he was going to play poker and the game we were going to play was Five Card Stud. I had never played before, but it came to me like second nature. Maybe because I used to sit down and watch my dad and take in all the information without me even knowing it, but at the end of three or four sessions with our cousin, I had won a lot of money, which might have only been about £10–£15 at the time, but the games were stopped. Not because I was a winner, but because my auntie found out that we were gambling for real money. She took away the cards and she said that she was going to tell my dad. "As soon as he comes to Margate, I'm going to tell him," she said. (Meanwhile, during that summer he was involved with some very big games in London at the time and I'll tell you about them in a minute.) But anyway, Dad came down and my Auntie told him. He pulled my brother and me into the kitchen and he looked at both of us and he said in a very stern voice, "I heard you've been gambling," to which I replied cheekily as per usual, "Yeah! But I've been winning!" He then told both of us that, if he ever caught us playing cards again, he would make us eat the deck. Not hit the deck, eat the deck! I think those words definitely worked on my brother, because as it turned out he could never play poker. But with me, I'm afraid it had the opposite effect and it opened my appetite to play Five Card Stud for the rest of my life. Maybe it's because I was hungrier than my brother to be a good poker player. That tells you also something about gambling, people say it's learnt behaviour, I don't know, some people say it's genetic, we still don't know. I know poker players who I do play with, they could play for the next 20 years and they never improve. Their game is always the same. There are some that improve to a certain standard and then they stay still. I think this you can apply to any sport, whether it is poker, football or tennis. Anything you do, you improve to a certain standard and then if you have a gift you go further.

I did mention in the last story when I was on about Margate that Dad was involved in some very big games in 1971–72. They were in London and I'll tell you about them. They were in a casino club called The Pair of Shoes. They were playing Five Card Stud and the table stakes were £2000 minimum, a lot of money! Dad told me they were very, very good action games, and very big for their time. Dad wasn't playing in the early days, when the games had started, because of one thing and another and business commitments and what with the casino closing and other adventures he was doing. When I talk to Dad about those days, he caught the tail end of the games. He told me he was winning quite a lot of money at one stage. There was an Iranian guy over a period of a year that lost an absolute fortune. His estimated loss in one year in that game was one million pounds! His name was Hamir. Everybody on the table was winning every session twice a week. Apparently, he was an extremely open and aggressive poker player. He definitely went to the wrong table that year! He was playing against the top Five Card Stud poker players that have ever played the game. I'll tell you their names, Israeli Simon, French Alan, Maverick, just to name a few. But as I said when Dad came in at the tail end of the game, he was also winning a lot of money, but then there came one big night, it happened on the very last hand of the night. My dad was dealt an 'ace showing' and an American guy was showing 'a Queen' and Hamir was showing 'a 7'. So that was ace to my dad, Queen to the American and 7 to Hamir. The Ace, my dad opened for £50, the Queen raised £100, the 7 called £150. My dad re-raised the pot and the American guy and Hamir both called. There was already a couple of grand in the pot at this stage. Dad hit an 8, showing ace 8, the American guy hit a 9, showing Queen 9 and Hamir hit a King, showing 7, King. It was the ace 8 to bet. My Dad bet the full pot, about £2000. The American with the Queen 9 showing called. Hamir raised £8000 with the 7 King showing. Now to me this seems like Hamir has got a pair of Kings. When it came round to my dad, he re-raised the pot. Now I can tell you my dad had aces. Dad re-raised about £14,000. The American guy called "All in" and Hamir re-raised the rest of his money. There were two cards to come. My Dad hit an 8. Now he's showing Ace/8/8. The American guy hit a King, he's now has showing Queen/9/King and Hamir hit a Queen, he showed 7/King/Queen. It's obvious now before the last card, what everybody had. Dad had aces and 8s. The American guy only had two Queens and Hamir had two Kings. With already one King and Queen out, it was going to be very difficult for my dad to lose this massive pot. Well as you know this is going to be one of those 'bad beat' stories because Hamir hit the very last King on the very last card to win over a £90,000 pot! He had made three Kings with the last hand of the night. The games continued but one day Hamir disappeared. Reading in between the lines he had lost an absolute fortune at the poker table and also at the same time he was playing roulette. He has never been seen since.

In 1972–73, there were no longer these massive poker games, because any poker player will tell you, you always need a 'star' at the table. A 'star' means someone who is willing to throw his money away, and you always need one star. It isn't any good with seven or eight professionals sitting at a table because at the end of the day, no one will get the money; you need a star to feed the table. With the disappearance of Hamir, the games lost a lot of life, they continued for a while, but they were dead. The games did continue at the Curzon House, but in those couple of years, he never went, as he had opened another gambling club in Leyton. It was in Leyton High Road, in London. With me being only 11 or 12 years old at the time, I only went there a handful of times. Dad tells me there were some very good poker games there a couple of times a week, but they were definitely not in the same league as 'The Pair of Shoes'. Dad was with a guy called Mark (they were business partners). There used to be a full-sized snooker table on the ground floor. Apparently, Mark was a much better snooker player than my dad, when they used to play for nothing, which was very rarely the case. Mark would absolutely thrash my dad 'out of sight', but what they used to do, was play for £500 a game. Dad tells me, when they were playing for this kind of money, the game seemed to 'even up' a little bit. It just goes to show you, especially in gambling when the stakes get high, whether you are playing poker or any other sport, you might not be on top of your game when the pressure is really on. That's not taking anything away from Mark. Dad tells me he was a fantastic and terrific gambler, with 'a lot of bottle' as we say. He used to gamble on many things, but it so happened on the snooker table, with the stakes being so high, it used to be a level game.

In 1974, I remember watching the World Cup Final, Holland and West Germany. Mark and many others at the Club winning a small fortune with Germany winning the World Cup. The poker games were still going quite strong in Leyton and a small story here about my uncle. He used to deal in the poker games and get tips. As soon as he earn't enough money dealing, what did he used to do? He used to sit down and play. I heard this story from a guy called Rocky in Plymouth very recently. My Uncle Andy and my dad were involved in a big pot together and my dad made a £500 bet at the very end of the pot. My Uncle Andy was thinking and thinking and thinking. He picked up his money and he said to my dad, "Do you know if I call this bet and I lose, I'm not going to go on holiday tomorrow?" My dad, as cool as a cucumber, looked at him emotionless and said, "Andy! You can call or you can pass!" To which my Uncle Andy stood up at the table and repeated in a louder voice. "Do you know, if I call this bet and lose I'm not going on holiday tomorrow!" to which again my dad said emotionless, "Andy! You can call or you can pass!" To which my Uncle said, "I call the bet, I call the £500." My Dad looked at him and said…. "You're not going on holiday tomorrow! I've got a straight and I've got you beat!" If you knew my dad, he would play poker with anyone. There are no friends on the poker table. Needless to say, and may I hasten to add, my Uncle Andy still went on holiday the next day and I think it must have been because my dad, made sure he did, if you know what I mean.

There was another small story about my dad and my uncle at the poker table and this was on a different night when they were playing together. This time it was my uncle that made a big bet on the last card and this time it was my dad who was thinking whether to call or pass.

The story goes like this. My dad was thinking for a minute. He then got up and walked around the table to where my uncle was sitting. Slowly my dad placed his hand on my uncle's heart for a couple of moments. He then walked back to his seat and sat down and he said, "Andy, I pass, you've got me beat, I think you've got the winning hand, pass my cards," he said to the dealer. So, my Uncle Andy looked up and said, "Why did you pass? I was winning, why didn't you call the bet?" My dad replied, "Because your heart wasn't beating fast enough!" He continued to say, "If your heart was beating fast, when I felt it, then I would have thought you were bluffing, but it wasn't and you weren't!"

In the early 70s, around '73, '74 (around those years) Dad still had the lease for the Casino, which had now closed. He gave my uncle Ron a couple of nights to run as a nightclub. He used to run it as a disco, Thursday, Friday and Saturday nights. Never earn't a penny never could get it off the ground! Who's going to go to a disco in Wembley in the early 70s? Uncle Ron never knew what to do! Dad never knew what to do. Uncle Ron came up with a great idea. This idea he had, had never been done in London, especially in Wembley. He turned it into one of London's first Reggae Clubs. Twice a week Fridays and Saturdays were Reggae Nights. He used to tell me he got on with everybody. Everybody loved my Uncle Ron. They used to come in from South London, North London, and East London. All the people used to love the Reggae Nights with my Uncle Ron. My Uncle Ron got good DJs in and the nights all of a sudden, were 'kicking'. Many times there was trouble at the Club, my Uncle Ron was in the middle. He was the peacemaker. Any problems, see Uncle Ron! There was a bit of trouble one night, two guys had had an argument in the toilet of the club and one of the guys who wasn't known as a trouble-maker at all, said to my uncle Ron, "I'm going to kill that man tomorrow, he's upset me." That's all that was said. Apparently, as the story goes, the next day he walked into a betting shop in South London and stabbed the guy dead. There was frequently trouble at the Wembley Reggae Club and slowly, slowly I think Uncle Ron had had enough. It closed its doors for the last time. That was the end of the Wembley Spinner Casino and the Wembley Reggae Club.

In 1974, saw me going to a new school. It was in Swiss Cottage, in Eton Avenue. It was a very small school with approximately a couple of hundred pupils. I was 13 at the time and in lunchbreaks when it was raining, we used to have to stay in the classroom and entertain ourselves. Sometimes people used to go from class to class. I used to pop into the fifth year and I made a friend and his name was Hamid. What I did notice about the fifth-year pupils was that on their lunchbreaks, which they spent inside, they used to play cards. I used to watch them for five or ten minutes and I realised that they were playing Five Card Stud and it seemed to me that there was one girl in particular; her name was Michelle, who used to be a regular winner. I asked a couple of times, if I could sit down and play, but I was always refused because I was only a third year and 13 years old, they were 15 and 16. Sometimes they used to play six or seven handed and there used to be some very good games, with the pots going up to £10–£20 a time. This was a lot of money, as I was only getting £1.50 pocket money. I had to find an angle to get in the games. After a couple of months, I found a way. I asked Hamid to sit down, who by the way was a non-gambler and a non-poker player to play for about ten minutes. I then walked in, started watching as per usual, he would complain of a headache and suggested that I sit down and play for him. In fact it was my money and I was going to play for myself. Well this worked a treat. Hamid played for about 15 minutes. He was losing about £4–£5. I suggested that I play for Hamid. They weren't keen at first, but I said. "Hey! I've never played poker before, give me a chance." I lost £10 but this was not on purpose. I feel even today, even when I play poker that when I sit down with a new school, sometimes it takes me a couple of sessions to get the feel of the players. Not always, but sometimes. This can work big time in your favour and all poker players out there know this, if you go into a new poker school and you win all the money for the first few times, you won't be welcome.

Well, I'm going to tell you later on in the book, I've gone into a few poker games and maybe broke even or lost some money the first time, but this is not on purpose. This is genuine; you need to get the feel of the cards and the players. You know that in any poker schools, once you've lost a couple of times, they want you back. This always works out well and it's worked out financially very well for me in the last 30 years.

Now I was in the games at school. The games started taking place, every single afternoon, when we were meant to be out in the playground, we were inside playing poker. I started to win the money. I was always a better player than the others, but I really wanted to improve my game much further, so one day I decided to go to Tottenham Court Road into Foyle's bookshop and look for a book on Five Card Stud. Well needless to say, I couldn't find anything beneficial and today there is a very limited market. As we all know it's played on a very limited basis. Unlike today you can find books and software on Hold'em, Omaha, Seven Card Stud and the literature and information you can get is invaluable. I believe you could get any kid off the street today, who's half intelligent, give him some software, give him some books to read and I say after three weeks he could be an average poker player, this could never happen in our day. You would have to learn the hard way, but I was lucky enough to sit behind my dad in my younger years and get the book information and the software, by watching and learning. (Notice that I didn't say that you can get any kid off the street and he could become a strong player, but I did say average}.

I used to go home after school and I started to talk to my dad about poker and started asking him certain things. Now I had to be very careful, as poker was a touchy subject, if you remember what happened in Margate and I didn't want to eat any cards! He mentioned to me that he was still playing every Saturday, down the Empress Club in Haringey and if I wanted to pop down and watch him, I could, but I felt that this was never going to happen as the games used to start about mid-night. What I discovered was, they never used to finish until about 5–6 pm on the Sunday the next day. I used to get up on Sunday morning and walk down to the club and I remember thinking, "I hope the games are still continuing, I hope the action is still on." Sure enough, many Sundays at midday the games were in full flow. I used to sit behind my dad and really concentrate on what was going on. The players he used to get down there were very strong Five Card Stud players, so here I had found my own 'real live' software. Probably, something that no one could ever get the experience of. What I received in that year was invaluable. I was now going to school every day, winning most of the money, most of the time, and my game had dramatically improved. The players at school seemed to be getting weaker and weaker, but it was me who was improving tremendously. It was Monday to Friday, poker at school and 'Sunday lessons' with Dad down in Haringey. This went on easily for a couple of years.

I want to tell you that one time when I went down to the club – I walked in, Dad was sitting in seat number two and in seat number three, there was this big guy, with big hair and a big beard and he just seemed huge! He was massive in frame and he was scary to look at. In fact, he looked like one of those scary characters out of a horror movie. His eyes always used to pop out of his head when he used to play on the poker table. He was one of the most fearless gamblers that ever lived, who used to call any amounts of money, raise many pots and as many people know too fearless at poker means that you are going to lose. They might lose, but they sure will scare the hell out of you at some stage. Well that's how I felt about this man. His name was

Velli. Anyway, I walked into the club one Sunday and I sat behind my dad as per usual. As I said Velli was sitting on my dad's left and there came a pot of one of the biggest pots that I have ever seen, with my own eyes, with the cash on the table at that time. Velli was £25 blind and my dad was £50 over blind. Everybody passed. Velli called the £25 with a 10 showing. The blind card was a Jack to my dad. My dad raised the pot, which was £100, Velli called. Velli hit a 9 to give him showing 10/9. Dad hit a 10 to give him Jack/10. My dad bet the pot £300. Velli called. Now there was £900 in the middle with two cards to come. Velli hit an Ace to show 10/9/Ace and Dad hit a ten to give him showing Jack/10/10. Again my dad bet the pot £900. I remember Velli thinking some time about this bet, which was very unlike him because he was really the kind of player that never used to think more than two seconds! So I thought to myself, that Velli must have hit the Aces. He then called the £900. That put £2700 in the middle. The last card was now to come. Velli hit an 8, he now had showing 10/9/Ace/8. He had a possible bottom straight with a 7 in the 'hole' and Dad hit a Jack. So Dad ended up showing Jack/10/10/Jack. Even though I was sitting behind my dad, I had not seen my dad's hole card or closed card. I had no idea what my dad had. There was £2700.in the pot. My Dad looked at Velli, Velli looked at my dad. Velli had a possible straight, my dad had two pairs showing, but with a possible Full House. Dad said "Check Velli, check to your possible straight." Velli looked at my dad. His eyes were bulging, his beard and his hair were big, bushy and sweaty. He paused for a second. That was more like Velli. He then said in loud words. "I bet the pot," in a strange Turkish/Cypriot accent, £2700, I will never forget it. I started to get nervous, because Velli was an intimidating character for someone my age. Dad then looked right back in his eyes, stood up and said. "Call and raise the pot!" Now that's £7100. Velli stood up and he was glaring at my dad, I felt I wanted to leave! You had these two players standing up looking at each other. It was like out of a movie, but now there was about £14,000 in the pot and this was really happening! Velli was thinking about the last bet my dad had made. Velli started to slowly count the cash. In those days it was all cash. He said to the dealer. "I've got £5800 left, I call the bet." Velli slowly turned over his 'hole' card and it was a 7 of Clubs, he had the straight! He had the bottom straight. My Dad then slowly turned over his card. It was the Jack of Clubs, which made a 'Full House' and as everybody knows, a 'Full House' beats a straight at poker. My Dad had won over £17,000. My heart was beating fast. Velli then sat down and he slowly turned around and looked at me and he said in his very unusual broken Turkish/Cypriot/English accent "Hey boy! Do you play poker?" To which I replied, with a stutter "Um! Um! No! Mr Velli, I! I! Don't play poker." He then said with his eyes still bulging "One day you will play poker and I will skin you like your dad is skinning me." Dad said to him "Leave the boy alone Velli, leave the boy alone, I tell you!" I will never forget those words, because Velli and I were going to meet on the poker table some 11–12 years later, but I'll tell you that later on in the book. Dad used to play him in match poker, Heads Up, on many, many occasions and the game used to be very, very big. Dad told me that they played eight or nine times. Velli had only won once and I assure you that when they used to play Heads Up poker,they were massive games. It was not unusual for Velli to run out of cash, to be doing £10 grand and to make a phone call and a carrier bag would show up in the club with a person delivering it and there always used to be a minimum of £10 grand in there! Velli used to go to my dad's games on a Friday or a Saturday, that used to finish Sunday night, and my dad used to go to Velli's games on a Tuesday, which were down the road and they used to finish on a Wednesday. Sometimes the game used to go down to four, maybe three or even two players. Well I'll give you £100, if you can guess whom the two players were left at the table together! It was my dad and Velli and they used to always end up Heads Up.

Another time I went down to the club, I sat behind my dad as usual. The minimum opening bet used to be £5 or £10, maybe £20 blinds and then there used to be an over blind. There was this guy, who came in one time and he sat down with a couple of grand. He had a bunch of thirty to forty £1 notes in front of him, with the rest of his money. Every time he used to make his opening bet, he would open for £2 or £3. This made the game a lot smaller. So what my dad did, every time he got hold of the £1 notes in front of him, he used to slowly take them off the table and slip them to me behind him. This was great because I remember that day; I ended up with about £35 in £1 notes! This was a lot of money for me, but effectively what he used to do was make the game bigger. As there were not so many £1 notes on the table, so people had to open for £5. Or £10 and it certainly stopped this guy opening for £1 or £2.

Another Sunday, I got down there quite early in the morning and there was this guy who used to stand up and say "This is my last hand, I'm going to play, because I have a wedding to go to this afternoon." After the hand he used to sit back down, play the next hand and in 20 minutes, he used to get up and say, "This is my last hand, I've got a wedding to go to." Then he used to sit back down to carry on playing. Well this went on for a couple of hours and all we kept on hearing about was the wedding he had to go to. Finally, Dad looked up at him and said, "What's this wedding you've got to go to, it can't be that important"? He looked up and said. "It is very important, it's mine and I'm leaving in ten minutes!" Well needless to say he didn't leave after ten minutes, but I can tell you he left at 1pm in the afternoon. Whether he got to the church on time, I'll never know.

Meanwhile, poker was going fine at school and I built up a nice few quid in savings. The biggest problem that I now would face was getting regular games, they were slowing down. They weren't every afternoon like they used to be. We were lucky to get them twice a week and then after a while once a week. Over the next 18 months they died, no poker at school.

I'd played a couple of times Heads Up with a Spanish guy called Ricardo and after a while he got fed up losing his money and I think that was the final straw. He told everybody that I was too good and that they would never win. There was a girl named Julia, whose father was a very good Seven Card Stud poker player, who could also play Five Card Stud as he had done with my dad. He told Julia, "Your friends won't have a chance with that Steve, his father is a top Five Card Stud poker player and obviously, he has learnt a lot from his dad. So tell your friends at school to cut their losses while they can." This spread around the school and that was the final nail in the coffin for the poker games. The only game after all these events was with the maths teacher who decided to challenge me one day after school. We played four or five times and he ended up losing £100 and he even called it a day and that was the maths teacher.

So now, I faced a small dilemma, what to do at lunchbreaks? No poker, no action, no money coming in. I ended up going to the shops and buying a very small mini roulette wheel. It was one of those play roulettes, it was about five inches in diameter and it had a small spread with numbers on it, with a tiny ball, that used to spin around. To tell you the truth, the wheel used to go round so fast with the ball in it, you couldn't even see the number the ball landed in until you stopped the wheel! Anyway, I took it into school one day and I decided to give it a try at lunchbreaks. There was me spinning the roulette wheel at my desk and two or three pupils having some small bets. Within a couple of days, it really took off in a big way. The only problem we had was because they were all betting in small coins, pennies, ten-penny bits, sometimes there were arguments of, who had what, on which number, but we got it all sorted out. I used to lay them a maximum of 25 pence per number, which would take out about £9. And with five or six players playing sometimes the same number, sometimes the liability was quite big but everyone wanted to bet with me, because they always knew I was fair and that they always got paid. After about three or four months of Roulette every day, one morning, I went into school and the Roulette had disappeared. No one knew what had happened to it. It turned up back at my desk about three days later. I didn't think too much of it. I thought, maybe someone had borrowed it, used it, but what was about to happen, I wasn't really ready for… It was lunch time and I got the roulette out and I started spinning as usual, but what I did notice was that six or seven people wanted to play that day and they were all backing the number 17, one spin after another. After five spins, number seventeen came up, I ended up paying about £30/£40 out. After another 10 to 15 spins, 17 came up. I paid out again. After another five or ten spins 17 came up again. I smelt a rat. I stupidly increased the limit and the very next spin; there was about £7 straight up on number 17. Now if this came in, it comes to over £200. As I span the wheel the ball was flying round the roulette wheel. All of a sudden, the classroom door came flying open. Five teachers came running in. One grabbed the roulette wheel, one grabbed the layout, then one grabbed the money and one grabbed me. It was like a raid from the police. Except it was the Geography, Science, Maths and French teachers! They took me into the staff room and told me that I would be getting expelled for all my gambling activities as the Head Mistress had heard what had been going on for the last couple of years. I personally think that it was the maths teacher, as he had it in for me after he lost that £100! I was told that I had to go immediately to see our Head Mistress, who by the way was a minimum of 80 years old and her English wasn't that good as she always spoke to us in French. She wanted to see me straight away. I said to the maths teacher "Look, can I cut a deal?" He looked puzzled. I said, "Look, I'll give you back your £100 Sir! I'll even give £100 to 'Save The Children Fund', if you can save me from being expelled." He said he was unable to do that as it was the Head Mistress herself, who knew that I was the main instigator for the entire gambling going on in the school and I was responsible that most of the school were not doing their French homework! Sounds crazy doesn't it, but she was. I got into her office and she told me she was ringing my father and mother and she was going to arrange to see them in the next couple of days. I got home that night and I was a little bit scared, nothing was said. Got to school the next day, nothing was mentioned. Got home that night, again nothing was said. A couple of weeks went by and everything seemed to go quiet on the matter. Until one lunchbreak I was called to her office. I walked in, there sitting on the settee was my father. Now I knew that the heat was really on. She started telling my father and me that my French was appalling, my French homework was not being done and my attitude was very nonchalant. She was saying that I don't speak enough French, I don't read enough French, that when we were doing our French lessons I didn't pay attention. It was French, French, and French! She went on and on for one hour. I cannot believe right up until this day, that she never ever mentioned any of the gambling activities. When I got home that night, Dad spoke to me and told me that I had to buckle up and get some more work done if I wanted to be any good in life. Even now until reading this book, he didn't know what we got up to in school. When I got back to school, everything seemed back to normal. Nothing was ever mentioned about the gambling and the poker. Well I have to tell you a little bit about this Head Mistress. As I said earlier, she must have been about 85 years old, going on 100 and I can tell you she wouldn't even remember your name! In fact the secretary told me some time later, she had asked why she was seeing Steve's father and the secretary didn't even know, so that's how I got away with all this. I faced another problem; there was a new rule in school. Every single break everybody and I mean everybody had to be in the playground. There was a master that went round to every single classroom and made sure that everybody was out doors and no one was in the class. No exceptions bar none! This was obviously a problem for me as there was no way we could play poker outdoors. I came up with one idea, but before I go into that there was an Israeli guy called Ares, who finally told me what happened to my roulette wheel, on those couple of days it had disappeared. He said two pupils took it home, (I think he was one of them, but he didn't own up to that), they span it consistently over two days and they had found out that the roulette wheel had a 'bias', which means number 17 was favoured heavily. Hence, that's why I lost that money that day, just before the raid! This all made sense now.

Well once we were in the playground obviously, there was not too much that we could do. There was a guy named Villas, an Indian guy, he bought in a deck of cards one day and decided to play Draw Poker. Now, he said Draw Poker would be a good idea, as the cards didn't have to go down onto the floor, so they wouldn't get dirty. Well I played Draw Poker for about two days, I lost money and I never played again. I maintained in life that, if I lose two or three times at something, I give it up. If you can't make money then why play?! So I decided to go a little bit cool on Draw Poker, it wasn't my game. Then no one really wanted to play Draw Poker. They all wanted to play Stud, they wanted to play roulette but obviously, as you know all avenues were now blocked. The other idea that I had for the playground as we had a lot of pupils, that now liked to have a gamble, and were itching to have a bet, was out of the blue we decided to play Penny Up The Wall. Every lunchtime it was no longer poker or roulette but Penny Up. After three or four weeks of Penny Up, I was dead even. Not winning or losing. Now to me this is a waste of time. I therefore decided to place a small 'edge' to my action. I ran upstairs to the classroom for some chalk, I went back to the playground and drew a semicircle against the wall of about eight inches in radius. Next to it I drew a slightly smaller semicircle against the wall, about four inches, the third semicircle was even smaller. I put 'even money' on the largest one, 3/1 on the middle one and 5/1 on the smallest one. Now the name of the game was whoever came up with the money in their hand, had to nominate the circle they were going to throw into, and they would get the offered odds. All of a sudden there were queues of pupils lining up to bet! It was a new variation of Penny Up and it wasn't long before a lot of people had lost a lot of money over the next month. I arrived at school one day and I noticed that at the opposite end of the playground, two pupils Hans and Elliot were their names, had started up their own Penny Up corner, offering bigger and better odds. All of a sudden I had competition! I didn't complain, because I had been winning a lot of money over the last month, so I decided to go over to them and give them a 'spin'. I pulled out a 50 p piece and nominated their smaller circle, which was 10/1. I then threw the coin and it landed straight bang in the middle of the circle, as luck would have it. Their faces, I still remember to this day, were a picture and they had to pay me £5, which they did, all in tenpenny pieces! I think I wiped out all their cash and float for the next week. They weren't able to operate for the next two or three days, so I took over the action once more. After a while the game slowly died as no one was winning any money and my nick name became Mr Money Bags, as everybody could hear me walking along, as the change rattled in my school blazer!

We used to finish school about four o'clock and after school, there used to be a place in Swiss Cottage on the Finchley Road called Emmanuelle

Restaurant. Now I'll tell you about Emmanuelle Restaurant, it was an all night restaurant that used to open until 6 am. What I didn't find out until possibly 10–15 years later was that an Iranian guy, called Kuros owned it. Kuros was the same guy, who used to play poker at Wembley with my dad in the 60s. Anyway, at the back of Emmanuelle Restaurant there used to be a pool table. I was invited by a couple of pupils, who used to go there regularly. They used to play a couple of older guys, who worked in the Swiss Chalet pub down the road, and as I had a small snooker table at home, I wasn't all that bad for a 15 year old. I went along to play for maybe £1–£2 a game, but the 'grownups' wanted to play for £10 a game. That was a little bit steep for me because, if I lost a few games, I would be down £50–£60, and I didn't know how good they were. The first two games we played, I ended up winning £20. So from then on I decided to play on with my winnings and we regularly played four to five games every night after school, before I went home by tube. Over the next seven months I won about £300.

At around this time, I still used to visit the club down in Haringey. It seemed to me that even Dad's games were tailing off. Now this was a real big disappointment to me because my weekend pocket money seemed to be drying up as well. I asked my dad, what was happening to the games? He explained to me that usually in poker schools, the maximum the school usually stays together is a couple of years and then slowly what with one thing and another, there are winners, losers, some people leave and the games dry up. So this was a real bummer for me because Sunday mornings for me were like Sunday school.

When I was 15, I used to go Saturday night roller-skating at Pickets Lock and I used to make sure I was home for *Match Of The Day* on TV. At the time there was a Saturday Late Night Movie, and then nothing else to look forward to as there was now no poker on Sunday mornings. Well one Saturday night, I got home and after watching the movie, which used to finish around one o'clock in the morning, out of the blue, Dad said to me "Do you fancy going for a drive?" Now here's me thinking, where can we be going at one o'clock in the morning? Of course, I didn't refuse. He told me to wear my high heels, which were fashionable for men at that time, by the way! But I was still mystified. He told me to put my glasses on. I put my glasses on; I still didn't know where we were going. We were driving down the West End at about 1.15 am, well I'll tell you; we ended up at a casino called Charlie Chester's. Charlie Chester's casino was in Soho, it's now closed. It was one of the original casinos in the heart of the West End and it used to have 24-hour action, until 1970. After that, it closed at 4 am. It attracted people from all walks of life and it was a little bit of a dive. Here I am, at 15 years old with all this gambling going on. Now one thing with Charlie Chester's, it had to be closed by 2 am on Saturday nights. The other Casinos were 3. But inside certain areas some Casinos were still 2. So by the time we got down there, it was about 1.30. Dad only used to play roulette for half an hour. The maximum time he would play is an hour if we got down there earlier. Well I can tell you this, we went to this casino every week for the maximum an hour on a Saturday Night for ten months and not one Saturday we ever lost. We had 100% win record, which I still find unbelievable. Every week Dad used to go there and win between £500 and £2000! Every time my dad won, he used to give me between £20 and £50, a lot of money for me.

I think this is the main reason why I've never ever played in casinos throughout the years. Whenever I was a youngster or right up until my twenties, when I went to the casino with my dad and he used to win, he used to look after everybody who was with him that night. £50 for him, £100 for him, £25 for him, everybody got looked after when my dad won. When he used to lose, nobody got anything. So I thought, what's the point of playing? All I would want to do is funk for my dad to win, so we would all end up winners! So, why play myself? Sometimes I've spent £20 or £30, when I go outside London for fun, but I've never had the appetite to play roulette and sometimes when I lose that £20, I really get the hump.

Back at school for the last six months of my education, which was around 1977, there was nothing going on, and I mean nothing, except for lessons of course! One day we had a tip for the Miss World Contest. Someone came up to me and he wanted to back Miss Sweden and he said "I want £5 on Miss Sweden, to win at 16/1 in the Miss World Contest." Then another person came to me and said that he wanted to back £5 on Miss Sweden at 16/1. Then another person came and he wanted £2 and all of a sudden, everybody wanted to back Miss Sweden for the Miss World Contest! The only person that could take their bets was me! I took all the bets. The problem here was that I ended up with about £60 on Miss Sweden. It was 16/1. I then found out it was a tip that George Best was seeing her and she was going to win the Miss World Contest. I now wanted to pass some of the bet over to a bookmaker. Now the nearest betting shop, to my school in Eton Avenue, Swiss Cottage was the Joe Coral Shop, which is still there today on the Finchley Road, not far from the tube station. Now the problem was, how was I going to get into the shop and lay this bet off?! I did not look 18 years old. Now, as I said earlier, there was a Spanish guy that I used to play Heads Up poker with, his name was Ricardo, I gave him a couple of quid (he was a big guy, I'm sure he didn't look 18 but he definitely looked older than me.) I got him to run to the Coral Betting Shop and to put the bet on. He came back and said he got 18/1. Well I returned everybody 18/1 for their bets and I had a couple of pounds on for myself. Sure enough, that night, Miss Sweden won the Miss World Competition. All the 4th, 5th and 6th year pupils were really happy. I got them their bets on and I paid them their winnings and they were absolutely ecstatic. So, I was popular at school, after all.

During the summer holidays, we had eight weeks off. Four of those weeks, I used to go down to Margate to stay with my brother, who was living on the top of my dad's betting shop, in a flat. My brother used to run the shop in the day and at night times, many times, he used to take me out and we used to go to nightclubs. One of the nightclubs was named Crackers. He used to sneak me in through the back. We used to wear two white tee shirts, one named Steve and one named Mick and also Margate 'Kiss Me Quick' and 'Kiss Me Slowly' hats. It was the time of the number one single 'Young Hearts Run Free' by Candy Staton and it was 1977. This was fantastic for me, because no one knew what time I went to bed and no one knew what time I got up! During the days, me and a friend of mine, his name was Andy Florides (his family used to have a fish & chip shop there and I still keep in touch with him to this day) used to get to the bowling alley and play American pool. There used to be some Arabians studying in the town at the time. We used to play them for £5–£10 a game and it was quite easy for me to make £15–£20 a day beating them. My pool was getting quite good at the time and I was improving rapidly and this was to play a big part in the next couple of years of my gambling activities. I started work in the September of 1977 and opposite my dad's office in Haringey was a snooker hall. I left school in 1977; at the age of 16, but I must tell you about my 16th birthday.

We all went to a Greek Taverna in the West End and we had a big party. Dad had a friend named Mario who came over from Cyprus to join us. Now, we were all in this bouzouki place and Mario was drinking and drinking and every time he had a double scotch, he used to wrap up a £20 note and throw it at me across the room, to the end of the table where I was sitting and say "Happy birthday Stevie, happy birthday Stevie." I ended up with £360 in

£20 notes from Mario, so you can imagine the amount of scotch he drank that night! After we left the restaurant, everyone worse for wear, we decided to go to a leading London casino. We all ended up on the Dice table, with Dad and his friends playing. Well no one could 'make a number' that night and everybody was losing their money. As the dice came around to my dad, he said "I pass the dice." He then looked at me and said "Stevie, you throw them." I had never thrown dice before, so I was what they call a 'first timer'. I picked up the dice and I threw them. I hit number after number. I made 'pass after pass', which means 'a winner' in dice terms. I'd got to an 'eight-timer', which means I'd made eight numbers on the trot and everybody had absolutely thousands of pounds running on the next point, which was a ten. There was about £300 on the hard ten, which means you had to find two 5s on the dice. It seemed like 20 minutes I was looking for this ten and then boom! Two magical 5s came up. We all had won a fortune. I threw 13 passes that night, that means 13 good numbers. I was throwing the dice for an hour and 15 minutes. I can honestly say, that to this day, I've never thrown three passes since. If ever I go to Vegas I play dice for fun, I throw a number, then 7 loser, a number then 7 loser. This was an unforgettable and unbelievable 16th birthday for me because I ended up with about £700. Every time I picked up the dice that night and when I was going to throw with every throw all the table started singing "Happy Birthday to you, happy birthday to you!" It was like a comedy sketch.

This was the year that I was going to start work with my dad. He was a bookmaker and he had an office in Haringey. He said to me, "Before you start work in September, have a good summer holiday and be ready for work!" In the Credit Office or the SP Office, you have to be 16 years old. Before this, my mum, sister and I decided to take a holiday for the first time ever and go to Los Angeles. It was an eye-opening experience to go to America for the first time and see a whole different culture. When we got to LA, we did the usual tourist things. Disney, Universal, etc. While we were there mum arranged a Triangle Trip. Los Angeles, San Francisco, Las Vegas and back to LA. This was going to be the first of many trips that you will hear of my experiences in Las Vegas. The only problem that I knew that I would have, was that I was only 16 years old and for Vegas, 21 is the minimum age, but I was still getting very excited indeed. We got to Vegas and spent four nights in The Hilton, off The Strip. It's where Elvis used to perform and I do believe we missed him by a week or two, not knowing that we would never be able to see him again.

When we stepped out of the hotel, we didn't know where to go, so we flagged down a cab from outside and we told the cab driver, "We're from London, it's the first time we've been to Las Vegas, we want you to show us Vegas!" and he said "No problem! Buddy," in his American accent, "Is there anywhere in particular that you want to go?" I said, "No, anywhere!" Well he took us along the strip; he took us to see the 'Dunes' and the 'Sands' which are no longer there. The hotels were very impressive for their time. He also took us to see Caesars. The Strip was nowhere built up as it is today. This cab driver took us everywhere. He took us Down Town and when we went past the Nugget, they used to have $1,000,000 in cash in the front window, Yep! $1,000,000 in cash! Right in front of your eyes! That was a sight to see. Well this cab driver, took us everywhere. He took us to so many places, he even took us outside his old high school and he said "Hey folks! That's where I went to school," can you believe it? Well we were running around in this cab for maybe a couple of hours. The taxi bill came to about $70, but it was money well spent and we were very pleased with our 'tour guide'. Once we got back to the hotel, we managed to see Liberace, who was appearing at the hotel at the time. He was an extraordinary character. Now the thing for me being in Vegas was, how was I going to have a gamble? The law is 21 and they always ask for ID, but I had an angle. I gave my sister $5, who by the way was only 18 at the time and she used to go and play the slots. Well this was no good, because she would not stop when I wanted her to stop! And then I'm signalling her to change machines and she wouldn't change machines and slowly that system didn't work. She drove me mad! It caused an argument, so I thought what the hell! I'm going to have a go myself. What I didn't realise was that in the short term on the slots in Vegas, you are able to win. Some of them have a 98% return. I would never have believed that, I always thought, the slots were like Margate or Southend gambling slots, you never win, but in Vegas, you can win on slots in the short term. It's only in the long term that at the end of the day, the casino always gets your money. Some slots are 99.5% return and I think that's better than playing roulette or craps, except if you are playing craps 100 times the odds, but I'll go into that later on. I finished my first trip in Vegas about $140 dollars up. Maybe this was a sign of things to come. To go to Vegas for the first time and win was great. In fact, all of my trips to Las Vegas...... well I'll let you know later on, how I did. Vegas is a great place! Mind you, Vegas is a great place if you are winning! I know people who go to Vegas and hate it but they still keep on going back and they still keep losing. It was a fantastic experience for me to go to America, as I said, to see the way they live. I ended up living in Los Angeles for a couple of years later on in my life. Vegas was only 45 minutes away. By the time I got to LA in the 90s, a lot of Card Clubs had opened and a lot of them were playing Five Card Stud! Another subject that I'll go into later on.

A month later, I was back in London and work was to begin. Now as you know, or might not know, horse racing does not usually start until 2 pm in the summer and maybe 1 pm in the winter. Dad always wanted us in one hour before the first race, so this used to give me plenty of time to spend across the road at the snooker hall. I got to know a couple of people that used to go and spend a lot of time there. In the snooker hall there used to be a couple of fruit machines to gamble on. There was no way; I would ever go near those things, as it said in the small print, there was a 75% return, to me this was a bad bet. I'd been in Vegas and you could get 98–99%, but what I did do, not being a bad American Pool player, I started to practice my snooker. So when I started playing, within the first couple of months I improved rapidly. After two or three months, I was making 25–30 breaks. We used to play for a couple of pounds a game and if I used to play somebody better than me, I always used to receive a handicap, if I could get the fair handicap, I can get a fair bet on! I was playing snooker for three to four hours a day. A couple of hours before racing, a couple of hours after. One day out of the blue, I walked into the snooker hall about 6 pm, just after work, the regular faces were there, and they were playing cards. They asked me if I wanted to play, which I said, "Deal me in." The only problem was, they weren't playing poker, they were playing a game called Kalooki. Now I've never played this game before. They were playing 2/4/8. To me, I didn't understand this. I was told it was similar to Rummy. You got to put £2, £4 and £8 etc. I was going with the flow. Well going with the flow, cost me £100. They told me it was the same as rummy, but I realised that Kalooki was more than just rummy, I decided to call it a day. They wanted me to play on. I said I would, on one condition, if we could change the game to poker! Now poker was never played in the snooker hall, so a couple of players hadn't played it before, but a few had. Some agreed and some didn't, but within half an hour, with me not playing Kalooki, we changed the game to Five Card Stud Strip Deck Poker! We started to deal, we started opening for £2 and £5 and the game got rather big. Within a week the games got so regular day after day, there used to be no more seats for new players. It was Monday to Friday poker, just like the old days! I started to win money. My dad knew that I was spending more and more time in the snooker hall and he said to me, "I hope you are not playing those fruit machines, I'm telling you, you can't win on those machines " I said, "Dad I'm not playing those fruit machines, I'm playing snooker." What he didn't know was that we were playing poker, he didn't even know that I could play.

For the next six months, I was a regular winner at the games at 16 and a half years old. Slowly, slowly the games died. They died a death and after a while no one wanted to play poker anymore at the snooker hall. They went back to their Kalooki. "Uh! We don't want to play poker anymore," they all said, there seemed to be only one winner. Guess who that was? In fact, there was one other winner; his name was 'Dave The Roof'. When no one used to turn up, I used to end up playing Dave, not poker, but snooker! We used to play for a couple of hours. He used to give me 18 start, we might play for £5 a game. It used to be quite a level game, but I always fancied beating Dave the Roof with 18 start. After one of our regular sessions of snooker, one night with Dave, everyone was at the bar and they all said, "Steve, maybe can play poker, sure he's winning money at poker, but when he plays snooker and he's under pressure, he doesn't play the same game." Now a lot of people who gamble, usually, either they've got the 'bottle' or they don't, but one thing I can say at 43 years of age, I play many sports and I think bottle and confidence come with experience and age and when you're under pressure, sometimes you can crack. At poker I've never cracked, but on the snooker table, sometimes, I could crack, but that comes with experience. The conversation came up that if Steve played for big money, he would 'go to pieces'. I heard this conversation and I said I don't think I would. Now I thought I was talking a good fight, because if I played for big money I didn't really know what my game would be like. Dave turned around in front of everyone and said, "I'll give you 14 start, best of 21 frames. The first person to get to eleven frames gets £1000." The place went quiet. I really didn't know what to say to Dave. He said, "Steve, if you've got the bottle." Now you've got to read deeper into this, Dave The Roof, always had a little bit of the 'needle' with me. I always felt that he didn't really like me. As he said to me one day, and I'll never forget this, "Steve, I've got more bottle and more guts in my little finger than you've got in your whole body." That stuck in my mind, so three or four months later, he challenged me for £1000 in front of everybody. I said, "A 14 start Dave, what you don't want to give me 18?" He said, "No! I think with an 18 start, you could beat me, but at 14, I'll beat you for the

£1000." Now I'm going to be honest with you, this was a huge amount of money for me to bet at 16 years old. I didn't want to decline the offer, I said to him, "You're on!" This was around August/September 1977, but we set the date for January 14th 1978. I went home, I spoke to my dad about it and I told him about the challenge and exactly how it was laid down to me, in front of people. I said to my dad, "I can only put down £500." Dad replied to me, "No problem son, I'll put down the other £500, do you think you can beat him?" I replied, "Dad, it's going to be tough, but I think I can." The match was on. Everyone in the snooker hall started talking about the £1000 match. Meanwhile, I thought it would be a very good idea to get in some practice. I started practicing many hours by myself, because I figured out that if I could improve by 14 points within six months, I would have the beating of Dave.

One day someone went to go and see my dad and he told him, "Max I know your son is playing a lot of snooker. It would be very useful for him if he goes up to a snooker hall called Ronnie Gross's in Neasden." Dad said to me when I was in the office, "If you're not doing anything on Friday, I will take you up to this snooker hall." I said, "Why dad, what's so special about this snooker hall?" Dad replied, "I've been told that the top amateurs and a few professionals get up to this snooker hall." On the Friday, dad drove me up to Neasden and we went up the stairs and we were introduced to Ronnie Gross. Dad knew someone that knew him from Wembley Dogs. He recognised Dad also from the dog stadium. Ronnie was introduced to me and he was actually a very good amateur. He said, "Nice to meet you Steve, I'll get you a game straight away." Dad stayed up the first night. Ronnie called a young man over, who was about 18 or 19 and he said, "Tony you're knocking by yourself give Stevie here a game." Well, I was playing with this guy; I can only say to you he was one of the most gifted snooker players that has ever lived. His name was Tony Meo. We played about 12 games of snooker that night. I used to break, he used to move in and make an 80 break. We used to set the balls up again. He used to break and I used to make a small break, he used to go in and clear the table. Out of the 12 games we played that night, without exaggeration he must of made three 100s, a couple of 80s and the rest were 60s and 70s. I think out of all the professionals that were around in the late 70s and 80s Tony Meo was the most gifted professional. In my opinion the problem Tony had was that when it was the big tournaments and the cameras were there, he never seemed to reproduce that unbelievable magic he had. I started going up to Ronnie Gross's snooker hall very regularly. All day on a Sunday, I used to get up there from 10 am and I used to play for eight hours. My snooker was coming on really well. Steve Davis, the professional snooker player used to pop there from time to time. Neal Folds was a young boy at the time and a good amateur that later turned professional. Jeff Folds, his dad who was a top amateur. Ritchie Bert was a snooker coach and top amateur. There were 30 or 40 top amateur and professionals that used to get up there. One of the greatest players for the time was a guy called Patsy Fagan. He was a very good pro and had some very good wins to his name.

There was a handicap competition at the Ronnie Gross Snooker Centre one night up in Neasden, the prize money was £250 but I didn't manage to go. A week later I'd heard that there was some guy playing Tony Meo in the final. As I said before Tony Meo was a class player but the player that he was playing against couldn't really hold the cue! It worked out that Tony had to give him a 130 start! That's right 130 start! It was the best of three frames and the score stood at 1–1. The guy managed to pot a few reds but Tony was slowly taking red black, red, black one after the other. Well anyway, Tony played superbly. I mean to give someone 130 start, even if he can't hold the cue is a feat in itself, but the last game went to the black which meant it was a black ball game. Can you believe it, the guy that Tony was playing was two points still in front on the black?! The black ball was situated close to the pink spot and the white ball was up by the 'D'. Tony went for broke. He smashed the black ball, it flew straight into the corner pocket, but wait for it… the white came off three cushions and its gone 'in, off' the middle pocket, which meant he had lost the match! The guy had won the first prize. I was told Tony Meo sunk to his knees and he couldn't believe it!

It was while I was going to Ronnie Gross's snooker hall in Neasden that I heard that there was a very good snooker hall in Clapham in South London and it was called the Pot Black Centre and I heard that top players also used to go down there. I went down to the Pot Black snooker hall meeting all kinds of top players and playing against them. One day when the racing had been cancelled due to bad weather, I decided to go down and play snooker all day long. I got down there about 10.30 in the morning and there was one table going out of 30. I opened up a table and I decided to practise. After 20 minutes, I looked up and I saw a young boy, teenager standing by the bar, I recognised him instantly. His name was Jimmy White, the snooker player and legend. He'd won the Junior British Championships and I knew that this guy was one of the most talented players. I put down my cue on the snooker table and I walked up to him and I said, "Your name's Jimmy, do you fancy a couple of games?" He said, "I would play with you, but I haven't got my cue here, it's down at Wandsworth, if you'd like to pop down to Wandsworth, I'll give you a few games." Now this was an offer I couldn't refuse. Jimmy was a very good player. We went outside and jumped on a bus and went upstairs and I said to him. "Jim I've heard so much about you, one day you're going to be World Champion." He said to me, "I'd like to think so because a lot of people tell me that." I said, "I go up to Ronnie Gross's snooker hall and I see a close friend of yours, Tony Meo." He said, "Yes, Tony is a gifted player as well." We got off the bus and we walked into a church that had been converted into a snooker hall, there were about eight tables. Jimmy got his cue. I set the balls up. Jimmy came to the table and he broke, he started the game. With the very first shot I knocked in a 54 break. There were four or five people watching us at the time. Jimmy looked up at me after I'd missed the black to make a 61, Jimmy said, "I haven't seen you around here before." Someone looked at Jimmy and said, "Jimmy looks like you've met your match." Jimmy just chuckled. He then proceeded to clear the whole table. The next game I broke. Jimmy moved in and made a 92 break. The next game Jimmy broke, I didn't make a break and Jimmy moved in and made a 118 break. We had two or three more games with Jimmy knocking in 60s and 70s and he was only 16 years old! This man was the most talented snooker player that we'd ever seen on the planet. He is also without doubt the most talented person ever to be at a snooker table who has never won the World Championship. It's definitely too late for Jimmy now. I did bump into Jimmy White some 22 years later and I'll tell you what happened later on in the book.

Meanwhile back at the office, I used to go in one hour before the first race or thereabouts, but there was never a lot to do. In the small office next door, my dad had a roulette wheel; it was left over from the Wembley Spinner casino. So I'm practicing my snooker, going into the office an hour before the race, there's not a lot of work on, but I had to be in the office just in case a call came through. So for 45 minutes I used to spin the roulette wheel. I used to get some chips and there was a place mat where I'd place my bets. I can tell you now; I tried every single possible system for many hours to beat that wheel. I tried doubling up, increasing the amounts that I bet, decreasing the amounts, you name it I tried it. I really believed in those days when I used to spin this wheel I could beat it and when I say I tried every system, I tried it. I tried covering every number besides two numbers. I tried covering one number and doubling up. I even tried a system where there was no limit, which was ludicrous but eventually the roulette wheel always won. There are two reasons why I've never ever played roulette. The first reason was that after spinning so many spins on the roulette wheel, I got bored. The second reason, as I said earlier on, if I went with my dad, he always used to look after us when he won.

I'll tell you a little story. My dad had a friend. His name was Mr Nick. He used to love to play roulette three or four times a week. He popped up to see Dad at the office one day and Dad wasn't there. He saw the roulette wheel and I said to him, "Here, Mr Nick, come into the other room, I want to show you something and you've been playing roulette for how long?" He replied, "I've been playing roulette for 20 years." I said, "Mr Nick, roulette, I'm telling you, the croupiers can bring up any number they want!" He said "Oh Yeah? I can't believe that." I said, "Give me a number, Mr Nick" and he said, "Number 29." I said, "No problem!" Now I was a pretty good spinner at the roulette wheel, so it was usually a lovely crisp spin I used to throw around the wheel. I span the wheel and I said, "Mr Nick, you are going to see 29." The ball landed bang! Straight into 29. Mr Nick couldn't believe his eyes. He then used to say to my dad, "Max, I'm telling you the croupiers can do anything they want with that ball. It's incredible, your son said he's going to bring 29 and he brought 29. I'm never going to play roulette again." I'm telling you now, as you know, this was just pure luck! The croupiers cannot control the ball, the way the roulette wheels are nowadays, it's impossible to even bring sections. The grooves on the modern roulette wheels are shallow; the ball sometimes jumps in one number and finishes on the other side of the wheel, it's impossible to beat the wheel no matter who you are.

My brother used to go into the office a little bit earlier than me, as per usual. Sometimes he wanted to play roulette. I would spin and he would bet. One afternoon, my brother was losing £370 in fifty penny pieces, but the problem was I only gave him a maximum of fifty pence on a number that could return him £17.50. He started moaning, I should up the limit. "Up the limit," he said. I said, "No! We started at fifty pence a number; we're sticking to fifty pence a number." He then put fifty pence on 23, fifty pence splits, all the way round 23. He even put fifty pence on the corners. He started to back 23, any which way he could get at it. When I span the wheel, boom! It went in 23. Wow! He managed to win about £64 with the first spin. I span again and span slightly different this time. I fastened the wheel and span the ball in the opposite direction, as you can do. Bosh! It's 23 again! Incredible, two times 23! I paid him another 64 quid. He then said to me, "I want to put a pound on 23 and I want to put a pound splits and a pound corners." I replied to him, "Be my guest!" I changed the spin. I span the wheel really slowly and the ball really fast. Could you believe it, Bang! It's 23 again. I ended up paying him another £130. So now he had something like £260, with three spins. He then said to me, "Spin the ball again" and I said to him, "No! I want to quit while I'm ahead." He said, "That's not fair, spin the ball again! I'm still losing." Reluctantly, I span the wheel, I then span the wheel so fast and the ball so fast, that you could not see the ball going around the roulette wheel. He started shouting and screaming. "I can't see the numbers, I can't see the ball!" I said, "Unlucky, that's the way I'm spinning the ball." As the ball landed, the ball was getting thrown out of the number and back onto the roulette wheel because it was going round so fast. He was still shouting and screaming, "You can't spin like that! You can't spin like that!" I said to him, "I can spin any way I want." Well the ball landed and eventually it settled in a number. Well of course our heads were moving round and round because we couldn't see the number the ball was sitting in. I slowed the wheel down and I could not believe my eyes. It was number 23. I had spun 23 four times on the trot. Yes! Spun 23, 23, 23 and 23 and my brother had recovered all the money he'd lost. This little story just goes to show you that the roulette wheel, as my dad has said, has got a mind of its own, when your number wants to come up, there's nothing the dealer can do. The only thing we can do as punters and gamblers is control our staking of our bets and that's like any gambling game. Now I'll tell you a little fact, if every single person that went into the casino knew when to stop when they were winning or losing, there would be no casinos in six months and that's a fact. But you had to hear what I said, even if you were losing one night, you had to leave losing the minimum and when you're winning, you have to know how to win the maximum. Not an easy thing to do, but like every gambler out there on the planet, they've all got feelings and they know when their luck is in and they know when their luck is out but like 99.99%, they never know when to stop!

Christmas 1977. Well every Christmas Day, after lunch, we used to always play poker. Now my uncle Andy used to come round and play. So did my uncle Tom. We used to sit there with 100 chips each. What we used to do, was Dad used to lay a book on who would win all the chips, it was like a tournament. So many times, the book would look like this. Evens, my dad. 2/1 each the two, my uncle Andy and myself. 5/1, my uncle Tom, and 33/1, my brother Mick. Now, it wasn't because my brother was such a bad player at poker; that he was 33/1 it was because he has never won a penny at poker in his life! Now, the name of the game was, you had to have a bet on yourself and Dad being the Bookmaker, whoever ended up with all the chips, would get paid out to the relevant odds, subject to the amount of the money you put down. Looking back, they were bad odds that my dad was giving, except really my brother was good value at 33/1. My Uncle Andy and I got knocked out quite early, then followed by my uncle Tom and that left a heads up situation with my dad and the outsider, my brother. He had backed himself for £50 and he stood to win, just over £1700. Well, I can tell you now he was steam rolling all over my dad, and that was a hard thing to do. Pot after pot after pot my brother Mick was winning. We couldn't believe it; my brother Mick was on a high. He couldn't do nothing wrong. He bluffed Dad, Dad passed. He had many times the winning hand, Dad called! One pot, my brother made a big bet and my dad called, all the chips went into the pot. They turned over the cards and boom! My brother had won the pot. As he scooped the pot my dad realised that he had left one solitary chip in front of him, which was not in play in the last pot, because the chips were counted out and there was a certain amount of chips that went into the pot and it did not include the last chip that was resting by the front of my dad, towards the edge of the table. So just as my brother was shouting and jumping up and down "I've won! I've won!"… Dad said, "You haven't yet! It's not over." My brother said, "What do you mean, it's not over?" Dad said to him, "I've got one chip left." My brother looked at him in disbelief. He said, "Dad?" My Dad repeated, "I've got one chip left." Mickey said, "Stick it in the middle, and we'll draw five cards each and the highest hand takes the two chips, to give me the victory." This is what we call in poker, 'A Squeezy'. A Squeezy means, you put a certain amount of money in the pot, you draw five cards and the highest hand wins, as easy as that. Well Dad, won the first hand for two chips. My brother Mick then said, "No problem, stick the two chips in and we'll deal another, Squeezy." Dad won the second hand. Mick said, "Dad stick the four chips in and we'll have another Squeezy, Dad won the third hand. Now Dad had a total of eight chips, he'd won three hands on the trot. My brother still had 492 chips. Mickey said, "Stick the eight chips in." Dad said, "No! Let's play poker." Well in Five Card Stud Strip Deck, there are rounds of betting, so you don't have to bet all your money all the time. Slowly, slowly Dad built it up to about twenty chips. Mickey started to look worried. Well, I can tell you the unthinkable happened. If I wasn't there to see it with my own eyes, I'd say it was crooked, but I saw it happen. It took Dad 45 minutes to claw back every single chip against my brother Mick. My brother still talks about it today. I would love to know the odds of my dad winning when he went down to one chip?

January 1978 came around quite quickly and as you know, I had a big snooker match coming up with Dave the Roof for £1000 and it was in about a couple of weeks' time. I was practising every day, but I felt that I hadn't improved the way that I thought I was going to. Out of chance a guy came up to me in the snooker hall and said, "If you want to improve quickly in the next couple of weeks, go and see my friend Jack Karnem. Now Jack Karnem was an ex-professional snooker coach. Sometimes he used to commentate on the World Snooker Championships, with Ted Lowe. He was a very good snooker commentator. He was a well-respected professional snooker player, but he was never a top pro. However, his lessons were excellent. He lived in Palmers Green in North London. I went up to see him the next day and I booked in five or six lessons straight away. He noticed on the first lesson, that I had head movement on my shot, which was hindering my game. He put that right straight away. He also told me that when I hit the white ball at snooker onto the red or any other colour, my eyes should be firmly fixed on the object ball. Well I improved within the next three weeks; I would say at least 8-10 points. Now I really felt confident at beating Dave the Roof.

Sunday, the game was on, the second week of January, our match was to begin at 10 am. It was the first one to win eleven frames. There was a small crowd watching us, so I was quite nervous at first. I raced into a 2-0 lead. Dave came back to make it 2-2. I then took a 5-2 lead. He came back again to make it 5-5. He went on to lead at 5 pm in the afternoon 7-5. We broke for tea, me and 'Skinny George', 'Fat George', Jimmy and Andy 'Mole', close friends of mine, went up to the Wimpy in Haringey and they said to me, "Come on Steve, we know you can beat him." Now to be honest with you, a lot of people, except my close friends, gave me no chance in the snooker hall, but Dave had noticed that I was playing with a lot of confidence. I didn't think I could beat him, but when I first raced into a 2-0 lead, being in front in the match gave me a lot of confidence and even still to this day, whenever I gamble and I'm in front, I've got a lot of confidence. Now the break happened at 5 pm. I was

7-5 behind but I still felt good. People were expecting Dave to beat me 11-1, 11-2. So now, even if he wins the next four frames 11-5, I haven't done bad and that's what I was thinking. The second session began. Now it was jammed packed with spectators. This made me even more nervous. The match was finally balanced coming into the second session. I took the next four frames to lead 9-7. Out of all these frames that we played, there hadn't been some bad breaks. There were some 30 breaks, 35 breaks, maybe 40 breaks; I don't think any of us made a 50. I think the tension was getting quite a lot, but the funny thing is, when I was leading 9-7, it looked like Dave was under pressure, and I was two frames from victory. Now I knew I had done myself proud. The tension was building up, but I was feeling less and less pressure. I don't think to this day Dave could believe, how well I was playing. The match got to 10-8, with me needing one frame for victory for the £1000. Dave won the next two, it now made it 10-10. It couldn't be more exciting. There were so many people watching at the snooker hall. I honestly believe to this day, I didn't think that I could win the eleventh. It was a strange feeling; I felt no pressure because I'd done myself proud. Dave looked under pressure, but with so many people watching at 10-10 with one frame to go, I walked out of the snooker hall. Skinny George and Fat George, my friends, followed me and said, "Where are you going Steve?" I said, "I think it's getting a bit too much for me." They said to me, "You can't leave now, we stand to win £500. We started betting on you against Dave's friends!" I said, "I'm not leaving, I need some fresh air." I walked back into the snooker hall and a massive cheer went up for me. Dave looked tired. It was now 10.15 pm. We'd been playing nearly 12 hours, except for the break and there was one frame to go. In the final frame, I broke and I left the white ball right up against the bulk cushion. Everybody cheered. I can say that the final frame was a little bit of a mess, with a lot of safety play. Well, when we came down to the colours, I was leading by two points, with only four colours left on the table. The brown, blue, pink and black. Now, the blue, pink and black were right over the pockets, so whoever potted the brown, would win the match. But the brown needed quite a good shot using the 'rest', it was situated by the pink spot. Dave picked up the 'rest' and he got straight down and he hit the white ball onto the brown. From where I was sitting, the brown was going straight into the pocket. Now the table we were playing on, which was number seven, in the snooker hall in Haringey, had a very slight roll towards the black spot, but he hit it at a reasonably good speed and when he hit it, the ball was going straight in, but as luck would have it, it rattled and it stayed right on top of the lip of the pocket. I could not believe it. It seems a blur now, I ran over and I whacked the brown in, then the blue and then the pink to give me the match. It was an incredible victory, as during the day, I later heard, they were laying 5-1 against me winning. All my friends picked me up and carried me around the snooker hall, jumping with joy. We then went on to celebrate at Bumbles Nightclub for the rest of the night. I got to the office the next day and I said to my dad, "Dad! Dad! Did you see the final frame, did you see it?" He replied, "When you were leading 5-2 earlier on in the day, I popped up to see how you were doing, without you knowing and as you were breaking off the eighth frame, 'Ginger Gary' had £300 Dave to win the next frame, which he won. Then Ginger Gary had £600 for Dave to win the ninth frame, which Dave won. Then Ginger Gary had £1000 for Dave to win the tenth frame," and as you know, as I've already told you, the match went from 5-2, to 5-5. So, Ginger Gary had won £1,900 off my dad in those three frames without me even knowing. I said to my dad, "Why did you do that?" Dad looked at me and said, "That's gambling son, but the main thing is that you beat Dave the Roof and no one gave you a chance and you proved everybody wrong, there's your £500 winnings and there's an extra £500 for beating him from me." So it proved quite an expensive match for my dad, but he didn't mind being the gambler and man he is.

After the match of 1978, I was still playing snooker regularly. My top break in competition was a 93 and I actually missed the black for a 100 clearance. My real interest was still poker, but as I said the games at the snooker hall had died and there didn't seem to be much poker going on.

One night, I went out with Skinny George and Fat George and we ended up going back to Skinny George's house and playing poker all night. I ended up winning about £1800 off Skinny George and Fat George and as soon as the snooker hall opened in the morning we started playing for £300 a frame, but I lost it all back to them because I had to give them such a big handicap start. However, with them being quite close friends of mine, it was difficult to take that kind of money off them, number one because they were friends, and number two they didn't have it! Anyway, I'm now going to tell you how my dad found out that I was able to play poker!

One night, in 1978 we went out to a casino for dinner with a guy named Ali Karabina. Now 'Karabina' is a nickname for a guy that when he plays poker, he's very tight. Well this guy called Ali, 'God Bless His Soul' was a lovely guy but he was called Ali Karabina because when he sat down on the poker table, he used to play very tight but when he used to lose his money, he definitely wasn't a Karabina, he used to 'open up'. Anyway, we'd been out one night and Ali had come with us for dinner at a casino. We left early and when we got in the car, Ali said to my dad, "Max please come down to the Beach Club tonight because there's a game of poker there." Now let me explain something about the Beach Club. The Beach Club was in Soho. It was in the basement and they used to have Five Card Stud Strip Deck, every single night for 20 years. If anyone wanted to play Five Card Stud, you'd go to the Beach Club. The ironic thing was that the guy that owned the Beach Club, his name was Michael, would stay there night after night for 30 years. Eventually, his wife persuaded him to close the Beach Club and retire in Cyprus, which he did and then one day he was killed in a motor accident in Cyprus. So the moral of that story was, when your names on the card, your names on the card. Anyway, we got down to the Beach Club. It must have been about midnight. The game was in full flow. It wasn't a big game, it was £5 openers. Dad sat down, I sat behind Dad. After ten minutes, Dad said, "Deal me out and deal my son in," just like that. Then Dad said to me, "Do you know how to play?" I said, "Yeah! You get one down card and you get one up card." I played for about 30 minutes. Now I came up against a guy called Stavros. Stavros is one of the best Five Card Stud poker players there is. He's now playing Omaha at the Vic and Hold'em, but his Five Card Stud is very well respected. There came one pot with Stavros, as I said I think that it surprised Dad how I played the pot and lost the pot, but it was the way I played it. I won't go into any details, because it wasn't such a great pot. So after playing for about half an hour, I was even. Dad then dealt himself in and he started playing. On the way home, Dad said to me, "Where did you learn to play poker like that?" Obviously, I knew how to arrange the cards in a certain order, which I copied from the early days when I was a youngster watching my dad, but he was intrigued to find out how I knew how to play. I said, "Dad, I've been playing a while." That's all I said. I said "I didn't do bad, did I?" Dad replied, "You did alright," and for my dad to say you did all right, that must have meant, I did bloody good! Dad said to me, "Look, I tell you what you could do, Theo is now renting out the Empress Club in Haringey, why don't you go and see him and try to arrange with them to have poker on Sunday afternoons. It's the ideal time, Sunday at 2 pm, play poker. I couldn't believe what Dad was telling me. I remember 17 years previous to this; he was telling me that he was going to make me eat the cards! Now he's telling me, make a game! I didn't say anymore. The next day I went to go and see Theo. He said, "It was a great idea." Now this guy called Theo, 'God Rest His Soul As Well', was a very, very shrewd Cypriot man, but we decided, or should I say, I decided, I was going to give this a bash. Dad told me, "Look if you're going to play poker, one thing you've gotta do, they are a lot better than you down at the Club and they've all been playing for a minimum of 20 years, so if you start off with a £100 table you must sit there with a hundred and you must play Karabina! (As I said, Karabina means tight). If you lose the hundred, you can sit there with another hundred pounds and if you lose the second hundred you've got to stop, you've got to do this for a year." I said, "Dad, this is difficult." Dad said, "This will teach you control and this is like your apprenticeship, because after a year, if you can do this, you will soon learn the game properly." Well, I decided to do this and I kept to the rules. The interesting part about doing this was that I never used to lose my cool on the table, so maybe that's what held me in good stead for the future. But one thing I want to tell you is that some nights I was winning three/four/five hundred pounds and then Bosh! I used to lose all of it, plus my hundred in one pot. Now, this used to happen quite regularly. A couple of times I went to see my dad afterwards and said, "Dad I lost my hundred and I lost my second hundred, but I was very unlucky. I was winning four/five hundred pounds" and then I explained to him the pot that I lost it in. He said to me, "Be careful because they are very shrewd down there, maybe they 'cold decked' you! Now 'cold deck' means, they could have set up the cards, not marked, but they could of pre rearranged the cards so that you can lose your money. Always watch for a cut, make sure there is a player to cut the cards after a shuffle." The very next time I was winning three/four hundred pounds and the cards were changed for a new deck, sure enough I noticed that I was going to be 'cold decked' and I passed. When I passed and I didn't get involved in the pot, that I was meant to lose all my money in, I looked at Theo and I said to him, "I don't want to play this pot" and I winked at him. Theo then, never ever, cold decked me again.

After I'd finished doing one of the games with Theo at the Empress Club, it was late one night. I'd got home about 2.30 am in the morning and I was starving. I saw a small note, it was from my mum and it said, "You've missed your tea, but help yourself to anything that is in the fridge." I opened the fridge, I couldn't see a lot but I saw this very large tin. I pulled it out and I opened it. It didn't look very nice. It was like a thick black jam. I put my finger in and tasted it. It tasted quite nice, very salty so I thought lovely, I'll put some toast on and I'll make myself some sandwiches. I had two or three sandwiches because as I said, I was very hungry so I put all of this black stuff all over the toast, it was delicious and I didn't think anything of it. In the morning, I got up and Mum and Dad were in the kitchen. "Morning Mum!" "Morning Steve!" "Morning Dad!" Dad looked at me and he said to me, "Do you know what you ate last night?" I said, "Sorry Dad?" "Do you know what you ate last night?" I said, "Um! I had some toast and I had this black jam, um! I don't know." Dad looked at me and he said and I'll never forget it, "You ate a £1500 tin of caviar!" I said, "What!" "That's right," Dad said, "You ate a £1500 tin of caviar!" I said to my dad, "Well if that's what caviar tastes like, it weren't alf good." He was not amused and he wasn't wrong, I must have polished off near enough the tin. I do remember I did leave some at the bottom, after all Mum's note did say, "Help yourself to anything in the fridge." Even when we used to go out in the later years to the casinos for dinner and if there was any caviar ordered or any caviar left, my dad used to say to the waiter as a standing joke "Stevie, will have it, he will finish the caviar off!"

We used to get all kinds of faces down in the Empress Club. We used to get a guy called Kenny, they called him Kenny Icky Flicky (one of gambling's greatest characters), and with his brother Ramsey, we used to get some top class and hardcore players.

Now as I said in the early stages of my book, the experience I got from the club in the next year or two was invaluable, that no software could teach you. My Dad always said, "You have to pay to learn," and I can honestly say that I must have paid the minimum.

After one of the games at the Empress Club, my uncle Andy asked me if he could have a word with me. To which I said, "No problem Uncle, what's up?" He replied, "Stevie, I must tell you, you have got a big flaw in your game. In fact," he said, "you have got two flaws in your game." As I've always listened to free advice, I said, "Uncle tell me, what's the flaws I've got in my game, what's the mistakes I'm making?" He said, "There are two mistakes you always make [I'm actually only going to tell you one of them that he told me, because I don't want to give too much away]. The first one, my uncle was 100% correct. It was a certain way that I played certain cards and what I did. A little bit difficult for you to understand without me going into detail, but I understood it fully and he was dead right. The second mistake or flaw that he spotted in my early days was definitely a weakness; whenever I went behind on a poker table I always found it difficult to recover my money, which in a way is not a bad thing because I've never 'steamed' or 'chased' my money. Now that was an advantage because I've never lost big money, but if I was behind and losing on the night, I used to find it very difficult to get out of trouble, as we say. Uncle gave me two tips that I should do on the two mistakes that I was making on a regular basis, it definitely strengthened my game by at least 40–50%. That's one thing that you can never ever get from any kind of book.

A few of my friends used to come to the games and we decided one Sunday, we were going to have a private poker game around one of my friend's houses in Muswell Hill. His name was Tony S. Now Tony, when he played poker, he was a crazy guy, he used to always want to gamble, gamble and gamble. Anyway, the game was set. It was 1979 and the game was set for June of that year. It was a £1000 minimum to sit down. Now this was a big game, so realistically you had to go with a couple of thousand pounds. Well that game was one of the biggest games I've ever played in at 18 years old and I was winning about £4500. When Tony and I got involved in a pot together, Tony was £25 blind, everybody passed, I had a Queen showing and a Queen in the hole, so I had Queen's 'backed up'. The blind card was a 7. Tony didn't raise. The cards came out, 7 to me, Queen/7 showing and then Ace to Tony, 7/Ace showing. It was Tony to bet with the 7/Ace, he checked. I bet the pot, it was about £125. Tony called. The cards then came 10 to me, Queen, 7/10 showing and 8 to Tony, 7/Ace/8 showing, Tony checked. I bet the pot, £400. Tony flat called so now I knew that Tony didn't have the Aces, I put him on possibly a pair of 7s, maybe a pair of 8s but definitely 7s Aces. The last card came out, a 7 to me, Queen, 7, 10, 7, so now I had Queens and 7s. Then Tony hit a 10, 7, Ace, 8, and a 10 showing. It was the pair of 7s for me "to speak." There was £1200 in the pot and I saw that Tony had a possible straight with a 9. I really didn't fancy him with a straight, but me knowing Tony, he could have anything. However, I knew he didn't have the aces. I checked, Tony bet £1100. I decided to think. Deep down I knew I was going to call him. I thought for about five minutes. The dealer we had at the time said, "Steve you have to call or pass" and I remember exactly what I said to Tony. "Tony, if my dad was playing this pot, he would call… I call the bet." Then Tony showed his hole card, it was a 9! He had the straight. He found a middle pin ten at the end to hit me with the straight. Tony had won a pot of over £3000.

This was a gigantic pot to win. Anyway, at the end of the game I finished just behind. I had possibly been involved in the biggest game I'd ever played in and I had got outdrawn on one or two big pots. There was nothing you could do. We never ever had a return match. I think everyone was surprised that I lost my money that night, but it was one of the greatest poker games and Tony still talks about the pot that he beat me in.... 23 years later.

During 1979, the games were still taking place at the Empress. Now, I started to claw back some of my losses from that year, playing with these top class players and I felt within six months, I'd become a very confident and competent poker player of Five Card Stud. There was one little story I would like to tell you what happened that year. It was towards the end of '79. Friends of my dad had a horse. It was running at Newton Abbot, we knew that this horse was a very, very good horse indeed, but my Dad's friend used to give it a run in quite a strong field. Well one day we received a call at the office and it was my dad's friend from Plymouth saying, "Max, my horse today, it's 33/1 and I'm telling you now, it's running at 4.15, it will win the race." Well as soon as I heard that, I ran out of the office and I ran to every single betting shop I knew and started putting £30/£40/£50 first show. First show means, as soon as the horse opens up at a price, you can back the horse at that price. The horse opened up at 33/1. Now those of you who know Newton Abbott know it's not a strong market, so if there was a lot of money for this horse at the course, it will shorten quite rapidly, which it did. The horse ended up 5/2 joint favourite and it won by a distance. This was one of the greatest tips, I've ever had. I probably never backed another winner, except for the Grand Nationals of course and one other, but I'll tell you about that later on.

By the early 80s, there were no poker games in the snooker hall; even the poker games in the Club in Haringey had died. So it was a case of not doing much on the gambling scene. In the snooker hall they started to play backgammon. Now backgammon is not exactly one of my strength games, but at the time we were going to a casino called Aspinalls, where they were having some big poker games that my dad used to play in and they had four or five of the top backgammon players in world. Now when I say top, these guys used to go to Monte Carlo and they would always finish in the final ten of the Championship. So I used to watch them play, and pick up some tips but even then, I don't think I was a strong player. Well at the snooker hall, there was a lot of backgammon going on, so I'd play. We used to play maybe £2 or £5 a point. That means that the game can double up at any time. Well I'll tell you this little story because this turned into a very dangerous incident indeed. I was playing a guy named; Babs and he had me beat. The only way I could beat Babs in this particular game was to throw a double 6. Now meanwhile in front of us, there was a guy nicknamed 'Tank', his real name was Chris, but we nicknamed him Tank, because he was built like a tank and he could fight like a tank, he always went forward. He was playing snooker at £20 a game with a guy named Joe. So this game of snooker is continuing, while Babs and I were playing backgammon. As I said to you, I needed a double 6 to win the game. I rattled the dice and boom! I threw double 6, I laughed and I laughed. At the time of me laughing, Tank who was playing snooker with Joe, missed the black that was over the pocket and he looked up and shouted at me, "What are you f…. laughing at?!" to which I replied, "What?" He said, "You heard, what are you laughing at?" I said, "What are you talking about?" He turned around and said "Don't f…. laugh." I said, "Shut up, what are you talking about?" Then he picked up the black ball that was still in the jaws of the pocket which he had missed and he threw it as hard as he could in my direction. The black ball hit the back of the chair I was sitting on, splitting it into two. I had my back to Tank as we were arguing and only my head was turned. That black ball could have killed me. I jumped up and ran over to Tank. He ran over to me and we both ended up on the floor fighting. Then within three seconds, there were between eight to ten people pulling us apart. Well, needless to say we never spoke for about ten months. I've seen him recently, we're 'as good as gold' now, but even today he doesn't know why I was laughing.

I introduced another game at the snooker hall. It was meant to be played with just me and a couple of close friends but what was about to happen was to take the snooker hall by storm. The game was called 'Yaddis'. I'll explain the rules of the game, as it is a very simple game. It's a Greek game and it's meant to be played with the wishbone of a chicken. Two people are meant to pull the wishbone, both wish for a gift and the bet is on when the wishbone is broken. Now the way a player wins at the game is this: if any of the two players give each other any kind of object in their hand, as one hands it to the other, the receiving person has to say the words, "I remember," simple as that. If he forgets to say, "I remember," the other says "Yaddis." It's like saying, gotcha! A very simple game. I started playing Yaddis with one or two of my close friends, but we didn't have a wishbone, all we used to do was 'shake on it' and we started playing for £5 or £10 a time. Within three weeks of us playing Yaddis, 75% of the snooker hall were playing this game! I must have had eight games going at the same time and sometimes they were for £100 or £200 a time. Tank lost £500 on one bet with Yaddis to Jimmy Manchester one night at the snooker hall while Tank was already losing his money on the fruit machine. Tank had asked Jimmy to get him some change for the machine and as he gave Jimmy a £5 note, Jimmy, himself had forgotten to say the words "I remember!" So Tank could have got him there and then. When Jimmy got the change from behind the bar and was just about to give it to Tank, he now remembered that he'd forgotten to say "I remember," so when Tank took the change from his hand, Jimmy said to him "Yaddis!" Tank immediately dropped all the change on the floor and started shouting and swearing, "I'm doing my money on the machine and you've cost me an extra £500!" What annoyed Tank even more was that he'd forgot to get Jimmy out 30 seconds previously. Well I'll tell you a fact; I have only ever been beaten once in my life at Yaddis. In fact I would say I'm unbeaten and I've played the game thousands of times but I was beaten one night on a technicality and I'll tell you how. I was driving my car home and in the back were Luke, Jimmy and Andy Mole. Luke had asked me for a light, so I gave him a light from my cigarette lighter in the car and I passed it back to him while I was driving and then Luke said to me, "You can have the lighter back." I had my eyes fixed firmly on the road and the next thing I knew, I took the cigarette lighter and I heard the word Yaddis. Jimmy had got me out. Apparently, Luke had asked me for a light genuinely and he gave the lighter to Jimmy to light up Jimmy's cigarette and it was Jimmy that had given the lighter back to me. Well that was the first and only time I've ever been beaten at Yaddis and I still feel, even though legally I lost, it was a tough defeat to take under the suspicious circumstances but the game is, to keep your wits about you at all times when people give you objects. We were playing Yaddis for a whole year at the snooker hall and there were two people that made a lot of money and that was Jimmy and me. Me and Jimmy stand at one defeat each. I beat him once fairly and squarely and he's beaten me once questionably? Even to this day, if we ever give each other any objects in the hand, one of us will always say the words, "I remember" and there's not even a game going on!

Meanwhile, back in 1981, Dad opened a Gambling Club and it was called Inverness Terrace. They used to always play poker down there. There was some very big poker games and really you needed a minimum of £2,000–£3,000 to sit down. Well I'll tell you about one pot that Dad played because this is one of the great pots. Dad was £100 blind, everybody passed except for Billy F and he called with a King showing. The blind card was an 8, Dad didn't raise. The cards came out, Queen to Bill, King Queen showing and 9 to my dad showing 8, 9. Bill bet the full pot £300. Dad called. Third card came out, King to Bill, King, Queen, King showing and a 9 to my dad 8, 9, 9 showing. Again Bill bet the full pot £900. Dad thought for a second and called the £900 and raised the pot £2700. This put Bill on the back foot. He thought for maybe ten or twenty seconds and then he called. As he put the £2700 he was looking a little bit worried. I didn't know what Dad had, even though I was sitting behind him. I certainly didn't know what Bill had. The last card came out 7 to Bill, so he ended up showing King, Queen, King, 7; and 7 to my dad, he ended up showing 8, 9, 9, 7. Bill looked disappointed that he hit the 7 and he looked at Dad and said, "Check to you Max." Now, I remember this vividly, Dad looked at him, looked at his card, looked at Bill and must have thought for about 25 seconds, which is a long time on the poker table and Dad's words were to Bill, "I check as well Bill," so that means Bill didn't want to put any more money into the pot and nor did Dad. The Croupier turned over Dad's hole card. Dad had three 9s! He then turned over Bill's card and Bill had three Kings! Bill tried to trap my dad from one card out, but it never worked. The Croupier said to my dad, "This was fantastic play, Max, I can't believe how you never bet." Dad looked at him and didn't say anything. On the way home, I remember saying to Dad. "Dad, how comes you never bet on the end? What made you think he had three Kings?" Dad replied to me, "Just before the last card, when Bill bet the £900 and I raised £2700, I can only really raise with three 9s. So if I can only raise with three 9s, Bill should know, that I can only raise with three 9s, so in theory Bill can only call the £2700 with three Kings." Well this was a little bit advanced for me at the time, but it all makes perfect sense to me now. Dad continued to say, "When the last card came out and Bill looked disappointed, I thought, 95% he had the three Kings and he was trying to trap me, or he could have had Kings and Queens, but unlikely." So rather than invest any more money in this pot, Dad decided to slow it down, which he did, but he lost. It just goes to show you, the class of poker player that my dad was, he actually lost the minimum. This pot could have quite easily cost him £30,000.

Dad sometimes used to let me start the games at Inverness Terrace before he got down there. When I used to start the games Dad only used to let me play table stakes, so that means that I used to have to sit down with £1000,

I couldn't play any more money until he got down there. The greatest feeling I used to have is when Dad used to walk into the Card Club at Inverness Terrace, and say, "My son now plays, Call or Pass." When you play Call or Pass at a poker table in a private game that means you can call or pass any amount of bet unlimited. This is not played in the casinos today, because of credit limits. To be able to play Call or Pass or someone say to you, "You can play Call or Pass," this is a very great compliment that you are giving someone because you are actually giving them unlimited funds to play poker, especially for me at 20 years old!

One night I got down to Inverness Terrace and there was a big game taking place. It seemed to have gone on since the early afternoon. I got down there at about 11 pm. Dad was playing with a couple of others and then there was Stavros. Stavros was the guy that I played against at the Beach Club three or four years previously. I'm going to tell you about a pot my dad and Stavros played because it always comes to mind when I think about Inverness Terrace. Stavros opened with an Ace showing, there were a few callers in front and Dad raised the pot with a King showing. Stavros immediately re-raised the pot and everybody else passed but Dad called, it was Stavros and my dad in this pot. Stavros had an Ace showing, my dad had a King showing. The cards came out. King to my dad, two Kings on the show and Queen to Stavros showing Ace, Queen. My Dad immediately bet the pot, it was about £280. Stavros called the £280. Now at this point I was 99% sure that Stavros had Aces, if not even 100% sure. The next card came out, the one before the last, 7 to my dad, my dad now had King, King, 7 showing and Jack to Stavros, Ace, Queen, Jack. Dad bet the pot £840. Stavros thought for a second and then called. The last card came out. A 9 to my dad and my dad ended up showing King, King, 7, 9 and 10 to Stavros, showing Ace, Queen, Jack, 10, a possible straight. My Dad looked at his hole card and as he looked at his hole card, I actually peeked at it too as I was standing right behind him. Dad had the three Kings. Now for sure, my dad has now put Stavros on Aces from the beginning. My dad saw that Stavros had a possible straight, but he didn't fancy Stavros with the straight. He asked the dealer, "How much is in the pot?" The dealer replied, "£2500." My Dad said, "I bet the pot!" Right into Stavros's straight! I'll never forget it; Stavros looked up and said, "How much is the bet?" The dealer said, "£2500." Stavros said, "I call the £2500 and raise 'all in' another £800." (Stavros had no more money left in front of him to raise any more.) My dad immediately called the £800 and showed Stavros three

Kings. Stavros looked up and said, "That's good Max" and then turned over his hole card, it was a King! Stavros had made a straight. At the time when my dad had showing two Kings with two cards to come, Stavros had showing Ace, Queen with a King in the hole, it was very difficult for Stavros to win this pot. He was looking to hit the straight or possibly bluff it and if he had hit his 'bluffing card', he would have run into a lot of trouble. Stavros had won a pot of around £10,000. That's not taking anything away from Stavros, he's a great Five Card Stud player and later on towards the end of my book, I will build a table of the eight best Five Card Stud players there are and Stavros is definitely in the eight, he is a terrific gambler.

I used to pop down to the Inverness on many occasions and possibly the biggest game I've ever seen, was one night I walked in and I saw this young man, blond and tanned. His name was Paulo, they called him Italian Paulo. He was going £100 blind, Dad was going £200 over, Paulo was going £400 super blind! This is possibly the biggest game I've ever seen for 1981. The game got so big that night that the guy who used to run the games with Dad said to me, "Oh! I don't know, with your Dad and Paulo at the table, these games are getting out of hand. They are killing the games between the two of them. It's like a war out there, people that come are scared to play, the game has got too big!"

One day down the Inverness Club we were watching the World Snooker Championships. Steve Davis was playing Jimmy White and he needed to pot the blue, pink and black to win the frame. The blue was on its spot and the white ball was right behind the blue going into the middle pocket. It was a straight forward shot for Steve Davis to follow through or stun on to the pink. He looked at the blue and crouched down and I mean this was an easy pot. Two guys who were watching the snooker with me, one turned to the other one and said, "I want to bet £3300 to £100 that he pots this blue." The other guy looked up and said, "I'll lay you that." So the guy that's wanted the bet, laid out £3,300 could only win £100. That's what we call a 33/1-on chance, but this was a really simple pot. Anyone could have potted this ball. Steve Davis queued up and missed! He missed the blue from the spot and the guy lost £3,300!

Another time I went down to Inverness Terrace, there weren't enough poker players to get a game going, so they decided to play rummy. It's called 79 rummy, I won't go into too much of the mechanics of rummy but it's quite an easy game, when there are four players you can all put a certain amount of money down and you can bet on yourself. For example if there are four players playing 79 rummy and we all put £10 each, the winner of the game will take the £40 showing a profit of £30, quite easy! Well they started playing rummy one night and my dad was playing, Italian Gino and two others. They agreed on the stakes that they should all put £200 each, so that there was £800 in the middle. The first game my dad won, so he scooped the £800. The second game, they've all agreed to put £800 each, to which my dad won again, that was £3200. The third game, the two other players didn't want to put the £3200 which my dad wanted, but Italian Gino said to my dad, "I'll lay you Max, if you want the £3200 I'll lay you 3/1 that you don't win the next game." My dad put the £3200 on the next game of rummy and guess what? He won it! He won £9600 from £200 by winning three games of rummy on the trot. If I see Italian Gino nowadays, I always remind him about that treble that Dad did.

There was one time that I went down to Inverness with Dad and there was no game. We left early and Dad was with a guy named Fossis. As we left, we stood outside and Dad said to Fossis, "Let's go down to Mavericks' game, he's got poker on tonight." I said, "Dad, I'm coming with you!" He said, "Boy! You're going home because, you've got work in the morning, it's two o'clock in the morning, go home!" Well the reason I'm telling you this is because, I went home and when I woke up in the morning at about 10 am, Dad was just coming in home. I said, "Dad! Was it a good game?" He said, "No!" I said, "What do you mean?" He said, "Well! We started playing poker, and within ten minutes, there were a couple of guys standing around the poker table and the next thing I knew, Bosh! Twenty police came in and arrested us all and stopped the game. Well really, this was a first. I said to my dad, "It's a good job that I didn't come then, isn't it Dad?" He said, "You're right, I wish I never went myself!"

Around 1982, as I said, Dad used to go and play some big poker games in Aspinalls. They were big, you needed £5000 to sit down and the opening bets were £100 and it was usually £100 blind. This is a big game for today's standard, never mind 20-odd years ago! Well everybody used to sit there with a thousand and there was this little guy who used to walk in and he used to sit down with a hundred grand! His name was Taleef. Well, I can tell you something. When this little guy sat down, he opened the game up enormously. In fact, possibly the biggest pot I've seen at that time was £96,000, and £25,000 in the side pot. Involved were Taleef, Morat and my dad. Taleef won it. That night was one of the biggest games I've actually ever seen. In fact, Dad was losing that night and at 10 to 4 in the morning, he managed to recover all the money he'd lost and he was about even. Then there came a pot, which was very interesting between Dad and Taleef. Dad had showing, Ace, Queen, Jack and Dad had a 10 in the hole. The last card Dad hit was a 7, so all he had was Ace, Queen high. Taleef had showing Jack, 10, 9 and Taleef hit a Queen, so Taleef had a possible straight, but Dad had nothing. There was about £45,000 in the pot, so Dad checked to the possible straight because all Dad had was Ace, Queen high. Taleef bet the pot £45,000. Dad thought about it. I remembered thinking, sitting behind Dad, "What's Dad thinking about, he can't call."

I mean Dad had showing as I said, Ace, Queen, Jack, 7 with a 10 in the hole. Taleef had showing Jack, 10, 9 and he hit a Queen. Anything that Taleef had, would have beaten Dad. Dad nearly called him, which I couldn't believe, but he then decided to pass because it was 10 to 4. Taleef turned over his 'hole card' and he turned over a 7 and that means that all he had was Queen, Jack high and he was bluffing and Dad would have won a £130,000 pot, but that shows you, that's poker. Sometimes, it's not so much the money that you could lose, it's also, because Aspinalls used to close at four o'clock in the morning, it was a difficult call to make at that time of the evening. I forgot to mention this Taleef, who started playing poker with all the poker professionals at Aspinalls, used to always sit down as I said, with £100,000. Well in the other room was a couple of Arabic guys, and we later found out that Taleef was the driver / chauffeur for the Arabic brothers, that were playing roulette in the other room! One time we heard, when Dad didn't go in, Taleef sat down and won £80,000 on the poker table and he skinned everybody up within half an hour. Then Taleef himself went to the roulette table and lost the £80,000 in three spins! All the poker players had their tongues hanging out and couldn't believe it. But as I said, Dad wasn't there that night, so we never saw that, but we heard about it the next day.

For a while, Dad went through quite a losing patch at Aspinalls and on the way home, my brother Mick said to Dad, "Why don't you let Steve play?" My dad's words to my brother were, "If Steve plays, they will swallow him up, he won't have a chance, he can't play in that kind of game, it's too big." I said, "Dad give me the chance." Within the next month or two, Dad was still on a losing streak and just by chance, we were having dinner at Aspinalls one night, when my dad hadn't finished eating and the poker game was just about to start. Dad said to me, "Go and start with the boys, sit down with £5000 and play very carefully." Well I can say to you, by the time Dad came up after his dinner, I was winning about £8000, so Dad decided to let me play on that night. There came a pot with Simon, and me, which could be still debatable today. What was right and what was wrong? I feel I was right, he feels I was wrong. To cut the long story short, I ended up hitting three Jacks, two Jacks showing, one in the hole and Simon ended up hitting three 9s, two 9s showing, one in the hole. Now, I decided to think for about 5–10 seconds. The reason, I was thinking, I didn't think that Simon had three 9s so I then decided to check. He then bet the pot £2000. I called the £2000 and raised £6000 straight away. He immediately called me and showed me three 9s to which I then showed him three Jacks. He objected saying that I couldn't think and then check. This was a strangulation bet. Well there was a big "Hoo Ha!" at the table. I was told that I'd done wrong. Dad was called into the room and two or three people backed me up and two or three other people backed Simon up. There is such a thing as a strangulation bet, which can't really be done at poker, but the point we were making was, I never bet at the end, I checked, so there is no such thing as strangulation check only a strangulation bet. If Simon decided to bet at the end, after my check, then he's opened it up for me to raise, which is exactly what happened. Anyway, there started to be more bad feeling in the poker games, because I used to start playing and I couldn't do anything wrong. Dad used to have his dinner; I used to start the games. Many times Dad used to let me stay there all night, but they started getting peeved because there was me at 21 years old playing with the best poker players in the world and I was making money!

Out of all the players, the one that didn't mind me playing in those big games was Italian Paulo, the guy that used to pop down to Inverness Terrace. Now Paulo is one of the most unique characters in gambling and there are many stories to come about Paulo, as he nearly won a lot, a lot of money off my Dad, but I'll tell you that later on. I think Paulo never minded me playing, because he too started at about 20 years old and was playing in very big games. He actually found it quite amusing that I was sitting and playing poker against the best in the world. I remember him saying, "Good call, Stevie! Good call, Stevie! Well played Stevie!" and I used to say to my dad on the way home, "Paulo seems quite chuffed that I'm doing well." He even used to say to my dad, "Maxi, I don't mind playing against you, I don't mind playing against Stevie, it's all fun to me!" and that's Paulo's attitude in general, we still laugh about the old days, when we meet for coffee. After about four or five weeks of me winning, there was definitely a bad feeling with me playing on the table. Dad used to mess about on the roulette wheel and a few of the poker players, used to say, "Max, when are you coming back into the games?" After a while Dad decided to start playing poker again, after a four or five week break. When Dad started playing it seemed that his luck had definitely changed. He couldn't do anything wrong and when my dad plays poker, as I told you, the games were getting bigger and bigger and it seemed that my dad's luck was definitely in. My mum still always says, "A change is as good as a rest." Well my dad had had the rest and it certainly worked. In fact, one night, it was Dad who absolutely wiped the table clean. He skinned everybody. I remember that night, because Paulo wasn't playing, I remember French Alan, Peter G, Jollyenos and a few others, Dad skinned them all. He skinned them so badly that one by one they all dropped out of the game. There were three players left: my dad, Jollyenos and Peter G. Jollyenos had about £8–10,000. in front of him and Peter G had about £6–7000. I was sitting behind my dad. My Dad looked up and he said, "Boys! it's three o'clock in the morning, I'm going to play roulette." "What!" they said. Dad said. "You heard, I've won enough, I've skinned six players tonight and I'm going to go and play roulette, I can't win a lot more from you two." They said, "We want you to play!" So Dad said. "I'll tell you what I'm going to do. I'll leave £10,000 here for Stevie and he'll play you." Now meanwhile, they were both losing, so they didn't decline the offer because, they thought, well they've got a chance with me. Don't forget three-handed is a different game, it can get very aggressive! Dad trotted off into the other room, with my brother, to play a little bit of roulette for the last hour. The infamous last hour. I started playing poker with Peter G and Jollyenos. Now, I'll tell you what was going through my mind, believe it or believe it not, there was no fear. Dad had won an absolute fortune that night and if I was to lose £10,000, I don't think it would have really mattered and I mean that. So I was playing very aggressive, but I'm going to tell you what happened in one big pot. Peter G opened with an Ace showing, Jollyenos called with a Queen showing. I had a Queen showing and I looked at my hole card, and it was also a Queen, so I raised £400. Peter G called straight away the £400 and raised £1200. Jollyenos called the £1600. Now, what was going through my mind was, I don't think Jollyenos has got Queens backed up, because I had Queens backed up, so I put him on an Ace. I thought Peter G might have the Aces backed up, but I put him on a King in the hole but now there was value in this pot and I decided to call the £1200. The second card came out. 7 to Jollyenos, Queen, 7 showing. 7 to me, Queen, 7 showing and an 8 to Peter G. I thought great! I've got it, I've got this pot! Peter G checked. Jollyenos checked. So straight away, I'll tell you now what was going through my mind. Peter G had a King in the hole and Jollyenos had an Ace in the hole. OK! Well I bet the pot nearly £4000. Straight away, Peter G called the £4000 and raised all in, I thought, My God! he's got the Aces. I'm 99% sure he had the Aces. Jollyenos thought and thought. I thought to myself, "My God he's thinking, he must have the Queens." Jollyenos called the rest of his money, another £6000. Now there was about £19,000 in the middle. I only had about £4000 left and I'll tell you exactly, what was going through my mind again. Peter G's, got the Aces, Jollyenos must have the Queens. I don't think I can win this pot. I can't hit a Queen; maybe I can hit a 7. I called the bet and I think it was a bad call, but I called for £3800 all in, putting about £22,000. in the pot (a bit of value now) As everybody was 'all in', we all showed our cards. Peter G showed he had the Aces, I showed I had the Queens and Jollyenos showed he had the Queens. There was very little way that I could win this pot because the next card came out, the one before the last was a 9 to Jollyenos, a 7 to me, giving me Queens and 7s but wait for it, an 8 to Peter. Now Peter had showing Ace, 8, 8. He had Aces and 8s (by the way this is called the 'dead man's hand'). It was now very hard for him to lose this pot. Well this time, the last card came out and it's not one of those bad beat stories, because it's one of those stories, that I actually won the pot! How did I win the pot? I hit a 7 on the last card, the very last 7 to make a Full House of three 7s and 2 Queens. Peter G's face was an absolute picture, in fact, this pot is still remembered today by the dealer who is now one of the top Pit Bosses in a leading London casino. He saw me very recently and he said to me. "Do you remember me?," I said, "I remember your face." He then said, "I was the dealer that gave you the Full House over Peter G" and it was him that made me remember this story. However, the story gets an even better ending because as I scooped the £23,000 I looked at both of them and said to them, "Any more boys?" They both said, "We're through, we've lost all our money to your Dad and now you." As I got up from the table, my brother ran in the room and he said, "Steve, quickly, Dad has just hit a repetition on the roulette wheel, he has hit number 11 to the maximum, 11 again to the maximum, and the ball is spinning for the next spin. As I ran in the room, the ball had just landed back into number 11 for the third time! So Dad hit 11! 11! 11! Three times on the trot, while I was skinning the other two poker players. What a night. Now that is a story you can certainly tell your kids!

At Aspinalls, Dad was cleaning them up. Week after week, Dad was playing with a lot of confidence and the whole tide had turned. One night when Dad was winning on the poker table, he said to me as I was sitting behind him "Steve pop to the roulette wheel next door, [as the roulette tables were next door to the poker room at Aspinalls] and go and tell me what number is on the roulette wheel at the moment." So off I went and I came running back into the poker room and I said, "Dad the ball is in number 35 and the Croupier is just about to spin the next spin." Dad said to me, "Quickly put this £100 chip straight on number 29." I rushed back in and the ball was already spinning, I put the £100 straight up on 29. Bang! 29 it was. I picked up the £3500 winnings and took them into the other room to my dad. I said, "Dad, look, 29 has just come up, we've won!" Paulo who was sitting next to my dad and playing poker with him at the time said, "Maxi you are very, very lucky, but I'll tell you what I'll do with you, if you want to have a bet on the roulette wheel, don't send Stevie into the next room, have a bet with me and I'll lay you 40/1." Now the odds on the roulette are 35/1, so here's Paulo willing to lay 40-1! Dad said to Paulo, "OK Paulo, Stevie go and check the number that is on the roulette wheel and come back quickly." I ran off again into the other room and I saw that the ball was in number 27 and the Croupier was just about to spin. I came back into the poker room and I told this to Dad. My dad then said to Paulo, "Paulo £100 on number 30 at 40-1." Paulo said, "You're on Maxi." I then rushed back into the other room, yet again, to see the ball spin. When the ball landed, I couldn't believe my eyes; it went straight into number 30! Again I ran back into the poker room and said, "Dad, Paulo, its gone into number 30!" Paulo looked at me and said, "Stevie are you sure?" I said, "Paulo, I promise you, the ball landed straight into number 30! Go and have a look for yourself." Paulo said, "Stevie, I don't even have to look, you wouldn't cheat me, because I love you and I love your Dad, Maxi here are your winnings." He paid dad £4000 across the poker table. This is just to show you the trust and respect that we all had for each other and that many, many poker players have for one another. Paulo had lost four grand without even getting up and checking!

A big pot that I do remember Dad playing very fearlessly was against a ship owner called Nickos. Dad had a queen in the hole and was showing Queen, 9, 8 with one card to come. Nickos had showing 7, 9 and he hit a King. Nickos bet the pot £8000, Dad called the £8000, and raised all in £24,000 to which Nickos called straight away. I thought, Oh! Oh! We've done our money, but Dad played it perfectly because Nickos had a pair of 7s and Dad had a pair of Queens. That was the kind of form that Dad was now hitting at Aspinalls and Dad was going from strength to strength but there was one more little twist to the tale, slowly the games started to die off.

Around this time, Dad used to go to Wembley dogs with his very close friend Mr Nick on a Friday night (the guy that packed up playing roulette after I span 29 at the office for him). I'll tell you a story about Mr Nick.

Mr Nick had a small restaurant in the City. It was in the basement and he used to do business lunches. It was mostly Greek food. Many times he used to have the bank managers from next door come down for lunch. He was quite a modest guy. Mr Nick used to look after them, serve them lunch and one day he sat down and had a drink with them. They asked him how much he wanted for his restaurant. He was laughing and said, "My restaurant is not for sale, and I'm very happy where I am." They said, "Think about it, if you want to sell." He said, "I don't wanna sell." A couple of months later, they came down for lunch. Same story, "Do you want to sell your restaurant?" He said, "It's not for sale." Now I'll tell you something, the reason they were interested in his restaurant is because next door, as I said, was a bank. Now, in the basement of that bank, were the vaults, where they kept all the money. Now apparently, this bank seriously wanted to buy Mr Nick's Restaurant, so that they could extend the vaults, this Mr Nick did not know. A couple of more months went by. They came down for lunch and they said, "We're very serious; we want to buy your restaurant." Mr Nick said, in his Greek accent, "You'll have to give me £1 million." Now you're talking mid to late 70s. Well I'll tell you this; they walked in the next day and offered him £850,000. Mr Nick sold! He then put the money in shipping and earned a lot of money. He then bought a piece of land in the very early 80s in The Docklands and he turned it into £8 million. That piece of land now is worth over £400 million. That's what you call a 'Rags to Riches' story. Mr Nick died in the mid-80s, but he was an absolute gentleman and sadly missed.

For my 21st birthday in 1982, we all went to Maxim's casino, about 25 of us. I went with a couple of very close friends, one nicknamed 'Chinny' and the other named Luke. After dinner, we went downstairs to the casino. Now, downstairs in Maxim's casino, which was quite small, they used to have four roulettes in one room. Each roulette wheel was placed in a square. There was one big punter that I saw, which was possibly the biggest roulette player that I've ever seen. He used to lay out £20,000 on one spin and as the ball was spinning, he used to move to the next roulette wheel and lay out £20,000 again. And again, as that ball was spinning he used to walk around and lay out £20,000 on the next roulette wheel and as that roulette wheel was spinning he used to then lay out £20,000 on the fourth one. Once he'd laid his money out on the fourth, he used to then go back to the first and ask them if he had any return or did he win any money? He used to do this for eight hours a night. This was one of the biggest roulette outlays I've ever seen. I won't mention his name, as he is well known, but this man was laying out £80,000, every time he walked around the table and that was within 3 or 4 minutes!

1982 was a great year. It was the year that Italy won the World Cup and I'll tell you about that because when Italy were in the quarter finals, they went into a group with Argentina and Brazil and I do believe that after the World Cup Finals of 1978, with all the controversy that went on with Argentina, they decided to do the second round on a further group basis. Once Italy went into the group with Argentina and Brazil, the Bookmakers quoted Italy at 16/1 to win the group and 25/1 to win the Cup. Well, my dad said, and I'll never forget it because I was in the office, "That's tremendous value." My dad was always a gambler for value. He backed them at 16/1 to win the group. He then backed them to win at 25/1 to win the World Cup. He said to me, my brother Mick and Ali, who used to work in the office. "If Italy win the World Cup, I'll give you £1000 each and £500 for Ali." Well there probably came the greatest game of football that we've ever seen. Not because we were going to win a lot of money, but it was the Brazil–Italy Match. Brazil only needed one point or a draw to go through to the next round and Italy needed to win. Italy won 3-2 and for all those football fans reading this, they will remember that game! In the final, one of the Italians was the first man ever to miss a penalty in a World Cup Final with the score standing at 0-0. Italy then took the game by the scruff of the neck and went on to win the Cup 3-1. This was a very profitable World Cup. My dad won a huge amount of money at the time. We were all very happy and we were jumping up and down for joy.

One day my brother and I were in the office with Ali, Dad phoned in and said that he would be in towards the end of racing. It was a big meeting and there was quite a lot of action that day. The biggest race of the day was the 3:45. at Epsom. There was a horse called Jellerby, two furlongs out, it was ten lengths clear of the field. We were watching the race on the TV and all of a sudden my brother shouted, "Oh my God! Oh my God! I've laid a Yankee [a Yankee is four horses with doubles, trebles and an accumulator. It's 11 bets]. I've just noticed that the first three horses have won and the last horse, is this horse Jellerby and this bet comes to £14,500!" In 1982 it was a lot of money, it's still a lot of money now! Well a furlong out Jellerby drew clear of the field and it was about 15 lengths clear. Inside the final furlong, Jellerby went further clear of the field. Twenty-five yards, just before the line, the front legs of the horse buckled, the jockey fell off the horse and the horse was on the ground. We couldn't believe it. The punter that had the Yankee rang us up after the race and he could not believe what he had seen. This horse must have been a million to one 'on' coming inside the final furlong and it lost! The punter that had the bet still talked about that bet for the next 15 years, every time we saw him until the day he died.

In the summer holidays of 1983, I went off to Cyprus with a very close friend of my dad's, Andrew from Plymouth. We had a friend named Mario, who I did mention earlier who came to my 16th birthday, he had a Card Club up in the mountains. So Andrew and I decided one night to go up to the Card Club and play poker. The problem was when they played Five Card Stud in Cyprus you weren't allowed to think, literally! When you made your bets, you've got to make them very quick or it's not a bet. Well Andrew and me played for about 20 minutes but we didn't like the way that the Cypriots played and we said we would continue playing if they played English Rules, we could take our time and relax. They also used to play 'Resta', which meant that you could bet all your money at any time. This we also didn't like and we changed it to Pot Limit. So talk about us going there and changing all the rules, I don't think we were too popular! Anyway, we played for three or four hours and we had a good game and we both won a couple of grand. On the way out from the Card Room, there were these three or four old Greek ladies and they were talking in Greek. They looked at me and they said in Greek, "Does your Dad know you play poker?" I said, "Why?" They said, "A young man like you, how old are you? I said, "Twenty-two." They said, "It's absolutely disgusting that you play poker, and your father should know!" I said, "He does." "He does?" they said. "How long have you been playing poker?" they said to me. I said, "I've been playing poker, since I was ten." They were flabbergasted. Then Mario came out. They said to Mario, "Does his Dad know he plays poker? He's playing with all you professionals in there, aren't you disgusted with yourself that you are allowing him to play poker with you?

Poor young man! Poor young man!" This was all going on in Greek. They were shouting and screaming and Mario couldn't get a word in edgeways. He then shouted in Greek, "Shut up! Shut up! This young man has just taken all our money we're losing thousands of pounds and you're going on like we've taken his! Well, he's taken ours! And he's taking it back to England." You should have seen their faces; they were a picture. Andrew and I were laughing so hard on the way back down from the mountains that night. In fact Mario lent us his Jaguar to get up there, what we didn't know on the way down is that the Jaguar's gears were not working and we nearly ended up going over the other side of the mountain! We managed to brake quite severely but we had to do a three-point turn and turn ourselves around on the mountain and we nearly ended up over the cliffs, I can tell you. We still laugh about that today, but it wasn't funny at the time.

Around the same year, back in London, I met up with Mr Nick and Dad, as I was on my way to Plymouth for the week. Mr Nick had never been down to Plymouth and he decided to come with me for a couple of days. Well, he went into Dad's friends casino down there, he was playing blackjack and winning £7000. He then realised that he was in Dad's friend's casino and I tell you what kind of gentleman Mr Nick was. He said, "Oh! My God, I'm winning £7000 here in your Dad's best friend's casino and we're staying in their hotel. I feel so bad." Mr Nick then lost all the money back! Obviously, he had to lose it legitimately, but he made sure that he never won a penny from my dad's friends. Andrew who owned the casino at the time said, "Mr Nick, don't be silly, don't worry! Cash it in!" Mr Nick said, "No! No! I can't do that, Max sent me down here, you're looking after me, I'm staying in your hotel, I can't do that." In fact, I tell you the kind of guy Mr Nick was. We used to go down to Gregory's Taverna. Gregory, who I mentioned earlier on in the book, had a lovely Taverna with great food, and Gregory would never ever give us the bill. So Mr Nick said, "I'm going to make sure that you give me a bill!" and Gregory said, "Mr Nick! You can come here every day of the week and you'll never have a bill." Mr Nick said, "OK! If you don't want to give me a bill, on Friday night I'm going to book a table." So Gregory said, "No problem! Book a table." Mr Nick said, "I'm booking a table for 80 people." Gregory said, "We only hold 60 in the restaurant, Mr Nick." Mr Nick said, "I'm booking the restaurant for 80 people and I want a bottle of champagne on each table. Now Gregory, I'm having a party for everybody in Plymouth, who I've met, because everybody has treated me and Stevie so fantastically and I'm going to make sure that it's the best party you've had down here and you're going to give me the bill!" Gregory's face, what could he say. I saw Gregory and I said, "Gregory, this is the way Mr Nick is. He doesn't want to take liberties, he just wants to give away or give back money." We had a party down Gregory's that Friday night and I think the party lasted until about six o'clock in the morning.

One night my mum and dad had been out to the theatre and after they popped to a casino for some breakfast. Breakfast usually is served in casinos from about 11 pm. Dad tells me it was about midnight and who was in the casino at the time? Mr Nick. Dad said to Mr Nick, "We're not staying long, we're having some breakfast and shooting off home." Mr Nick replied, "Max aren't you going to stay, are we going to play any roulette tonight?" Dad said, "Not tonight Nick." My dad had his breakfast, he went to say goodbye to Mr Nick, who was playing punto banco at the time, Mr Nick said to my dad, "Let's put £1000 each, you go home and I'll play punto Banco and we're partners" Dad said, "No problem Nick." Dad went home and at nine o'clock the next morning the phone rang. Dad answered it and it was Mr Nick. He said, "Good morning kombare." Now kombare means best man in Greek. He used to say this many times to my dad, as they were very close friends. He continued to say. "I'm going to make you two offers. The first offer is do you want your £1000 back as we might have lost our £2000 in our partnership? Or you've got a chance to leave the partnership as it was from last night?" Now Mr Nick was a 100% straight guy, so he was joking with my dad, but believe you me, if he would have lost the money, knowing Mr Nick he would still make this offer of the £1000 back to my dad. So dad laughed and said, "Nicko we're partners, now tell me, have we lost the £1000? Mr Nick said, "Pop down and see me." (Mr Nick used to live one minutes' walk away). Dad got there and said to him, "Well how did we do Nick?" Mr Nick gave my dad a cheque for £25,000! He said to my dad, as soon as he had left with my mum after breakfast, he couldn't do anything wrong on the punto banco and he turned the £2000 into £60,000 but he lost some back and then decided to cash in. I think that was probably the most money my dad has ever won after he's gone to bed!

Around the same year in 1983, Stringfellows was definitely the place to go. One night I was there, it was a Saturday night. One of the bouncers came down to the dance floor and said, "Steve you're wanted on the telephone" I said, "John, What's the matter?" He said, "I don't know who it is, they told me to call you and you're wanted immediately." I went upstairs to the entrance and got to the telephone and I said, "Hello, who is it?" The voice on the other end said, "It's Agi! Agi Alison." Now we called him Agi Alison because he lived in Alison Road in Haringey. He continued to say, "Steve, get out of Stringfellows and get yourself down to the Empress because there is the biggest poker game you've ever seen." Now I've seen big poker games, so I thought how big can it be? I said, "Agi, I haven't got a lot of money on me!" He said, "Never mind about money, you don't need money! Just get down here." I was with my friend Jimmy Manchester. We're on the way down, and as I got into the club, Agi pulled me outside the poker room, he said, "Now whatever happens I've got you down here tonight, I want 30% of your action. I said, "Not a problem." Jimmy said, "Stevie, I want 30% of your action. I said, "Not a problem guys you've got 30% each and I've got 40%. Then all of a sudden a little guy appeared we've known a long time, his name was Laggis. Laggis said, "Can I have the other 10%, please can I have the other 10%?" We all laughed and I said, "Yeah! You can have the other 10%. So there's Jimmy, Agi, Laggis and I and we're all partners. I decided to sit down and play. The host that night said I was able to play Call or Pass on credit with chips. Just before I was going to get the first hand of the night, Jimmy said, "Goodnight boys." We looked up and said, "Jim, where are you going?" Jimmy said, "Look I've left my money in safe hands, it's 2:45 in the morning, I'm going to sleep." I said, "Jim you're partners, come on stick around a little bit." Jimmy said, "Steve you're a safe partner, I'm going to bed." Well I'm going to cut this story very short, but that night I hit form and I won a tremendous amount of money. I couldn't do anything wrong. The game was getting bigger and bigger and I was on form. The next morning I called Jimmy when we'd finished playing at about 11.30 am and I said, "Jim what are you doing?" He said, "I've just woken up." I said, "Jim do you wanna know how I've done last night?" He said, "Of course, tell me." I said, "We can go out and buy a Jaguar Jim." (I knew Jimmy had always wanted to buy his favourite car, which was a Jaguar.) He said, "Very funny Steve." I said, "Jim I'm not joking." He said, "Steve, OK you're not joking, well if I go out and get a Jag, I ain't going to share it with you, Laggis and Aggie. Now thank you very much for winning the money, but I'm not going to share a Jag with you!" I said, "Jim you didn't hear what I said, you can go and get yourself your own Jaguar with your share with the money that I've won!" Jim was speechless. You can now estimate what we had all won. We still talk about that night to this day.

Around this time in the West End, I met a guy named Reggie. Now that was not his real name by the way, but we used to call him Reggie because he used to drive around a guy named Lennie Bloom. Lennie Bloom owned a lot of nightclubs in the West End and we used to call him Reggie. In fact, his real name was Mark, but to this day, I still call him Reggie! Now, I thought I'd better mention him now because he plays a major part in certain stories that have got to come. One of the greatest characters that you'd ever meet! He later owned a restaurant in New Burlington Street and called it Rocky's. Reggie used to run poker games once a week and he used to have buffet nights and free food for any poker players, but I'm going to tell you about Reggie later on, but it was this year, 1983, that I met Reggie.

In 1984, there were no longer any more games in Aspinalls. We used to pop there a couple of times a week, but the players had moved on. One night Dad walked into the roulette room and he said to the Croupier, "Spin the ball." Now the floor manager's name was Angelo. Dad said, "Angelo, I'm going to make a bet here and if this is not number 27, I will never play roulette again" (that's the kind of confidence that my dad now had in the last year). The Croupier spun the ball and the ball went straight into number 27. That's a true story, but it just shows you the form my dad had hit. Angelo looked like he'd been shot between the eyes and he turned around and said, "Thank God Max that it was number 27, we would hate to lose you as a customer." Then Angelo walked out of the room. I later heard that Angelo said, "Max is unbelievable, he said, "if this is not number 27, he would stop playing roulette. First spin of the night and the ball went straight into number 27, how does the man do it? We can't beat him!" The system we used that never used to fail was my dad would bet on the roulette and usually only back one number. That's the way he used to play. My brother and me used to stand right on top of the wheel, then my brother used to concentrate on the number on the wheel and I used to concentrate on the ball as both were spinning. That's right, sounds crazy doesn't it, but it's true, but I know for a fact that in one year we never ever lost!

There was another night Dad was losing, he cashed up some more and said to me, "Stevie, play for me for a while." Dad left the room and went to the toilet. I then put £100 on number 5. That's all, one chip, one number, one bet. The Croupier span the wheel and it landed straight into number 5. They paid me £3500. For my second spin, I took my winnings and placed them on and all around number 5. Hundred pounds (which was the maximum) on the number, 200 splits, 400 corners. I laid out the whole lot back on number 5!

The Croupier picked the ball up and he pushed the wheel and span the ball so fast I could not see the numbers. Dad came back in the room as the ball was spinning around. I said to Dad straight away, "I hit number 5 and I've put it all back on number 5 and look how the croupier is spinning!" Well the ball landed straight into number 5 again! My Dad looked at me and said, "It doesn't matter how he spins, the roulette wheel has got a mind of its own." We had recovered our losses that night and won a lot of money.

A lot of people ask me, "In your betting shops, what bet sticks out in your mind?" and I always say the same thing, "In 1982 someone had a 10 p Super Yankee (five horses and five winners). He laid out £2.60 and he won back £23,000. Apparently, this customer used to go into the betting shop, every single day and lay out £2.60. After Dad gave him the cheque, it was in *The Sporting Life*. The next day, the customer walked in and he laid out a 20 p Super Yankee and laid out £5.20, so he'd increased his stake by £2.60. I don't think we ever got that money back from that customer!

Around 1985, after work in the office, I wasn't playing much snooker and I used to go to Wood Green Shopping Centre. There used to be a place called, The Italian Touch Coffee Shop and I bumped into an old friend of mine called Billy the Boxer. We used to sit there and have coffee and we would talk about boxing in general, as Billy had about nine or ten fights and was an unbeaten professional Featherweight. I said to him that, I would like to box. He said, "Why don't we, on Tuesdays, get together and do some sparring." We started sparring every Tuesday. I really got into boxing and Bill was such a nice guy to spar with, as he would never ever take liberties being a professional boxer against me being a novice. But I really enjoyed it. I then went to a newsagent and started ordering the *Boxing News*, which used to come out on a weekly basis and I started reading about all the fighters. There was this fighter who used to fight every other week and he was only 18 or 19 years old at the time, and his name was Mike Tyson. I was reading that he was knocking out boxers on a weekly basis and he was trained by a guy name Cus D'Amato. Now Cus D'Amato was responsible for making Floyd Patterson, the youngest Heavyweight Champion in the world. I started reading more about Cus D'Amato and more about the way he was training Mike. Billy and I used to talk about Mike Tyson and I said to Billy, "One day, I'm telling you, he's going to be the youngest Heavyweight Champion in the world." Billy said, "What makes you think that?" I said, "I've been reading small reports about him in the *Boxing News* and I think they're gearing him up to be the new Heavyweight Champion."

I was in Stringfellows on a Monday night and I bumped into a guy named Rod and we were talking about boxing and I said to Rod, "What odds do you lay me, if I can give you a name of a fighter, that you've never heard of and he will be Heavyweight Champion of the World by the end of 1986?" Rod looked at me and said, "I'll give you 16/1." To which I replied, "I'll have £100 at 16-1. We shook hands and he went on his way. I carried on sparring with Billy and I heard that Mike Tyson was winning fight after fight and they then started to match him with higher-class boxers, but again he was knocking them out. Well I'll tell you what happened to my bet later on because I never saw Rod for the rest of the year until after Tyson's title fight.

Meanwhile in 1985, I was running my own games. Private games down at the Empress Club and a lot of my friends used to come down and play Five Card Stud. Well I tell you this because there was a young Greek Cypriot boy and his name was Johnny K. John used to come down and he'd never ever gambled before and I'll tell you why I'm telling you this. We got him to play poker one night and he lost £250 on the poker table, that's all he lost, £250, which was a very small amount of money to lose. Johnny got up from the table, was a perfect gentleman, and said "Gentleman, I bid you goodnight. This has been a very, very, very expensive lesson for me, I will never, ever, ever gamble again." He called me the next day and said to me, "Stevie! I'm so upset that I've lost that money." I replied, "Johnny, it wasn't a lot of money for you to lose, the game was quite big." He said, "I'm going to be honest with you. I was so upset about losing that money, I got in the car and I smashed my fist against the windscreen and I said to myself, good, I hope my hand hurts, because I've been an absolute fool. Let that be a punishment to me, because I never want to gamble ever, ever again." Now that was an interesting statement from Johnny K, as you will read later on!

One night while I was running one of the games down at the Empress Club and towards the end of the game, the last couple of hours, early in the morning I had smelt something 'fishy', something wasn't quite right. Even in today's games I can go into a Five Card Stud Game and after half an hour or 45 minutes, I can smell if there is something wrong. That doesn't mean to say that the cards are marked, it could mean players could be colluding or there is some 'monkey business' going on. I don't know sometimes exactly what it is but all I know is sometimes things aren't quite right. Well this happened one night at my games and I only got that feeling towards the last one and half hours of the game. I started to look at one or two particular players and

I could see that one of them was marking the cards. It was being very cleverly done. Slowly, slowly he started to mark them all. Now this has been done at poker before, but obviously when you sit down and play poker, you always expect a nice clean game but sometimes this does not happen. Anyway after 45–50 minutes of me sussing out what was going on, I said, "Gents! The game is finishing at 6 am." (A couple of my guests who were playing that night were losing money and slowly, slowly the guy that was marking the cards was winning the money, so I thought I'd better stop this game as soon as possible.) They asked me, "Why Steve? It's 10 to 6, we want to play on." I said "No! The game is finishing at six o'clock dead on the dot." Six o'clock came, I cashed in everybody's chips. The guy that was marking the cards, I said to him, "I will cash your chips in at the end." I don't know if he smelt that I knew what was going on. I cashed in everybody one by one. I then went to cash in his chips and as I counted them out, he had about £2400. I got all of his chips in front of me and I went to the door and locked the door. I came back to the table and he looked slightly worried. I said, "Now! I know you've been marking the cards." "No! I haven't," he said. I said, "I know you have." He says, "I haven't, I promise you, I haven't been marking the cards." I said to him, "If you do not tell me the truth, I'm not cashing you in." He said, "I haven't been marking the cards." I said, "You didn't hear what I said, if you do not tell me the truth I'm not going to cash you in." He said, "OK! I was marking the cards, but I was only marking them for the last hour." Now I knew he was telling me the truth because as I said to you, I smelt that the game had gone a bit funny in the last hour and a half. The funny thing is with him marking the cards, he hadn't won much money. I estimated he had a couple of thousand pounds in front of him and he'd won an extra £400–500. I said to him, "Ok! I'll cash you in but never come to my games again." You might be asking yourself why did I cash in all of his money if I knew he was cheating? Well, if I never cashed him in, he could go round saying that I refused to pay him and I then could go round and say I'd refused to pay him because he was cheating, it's his word against mine. I know I was telling the truth, but I thought to myself, look I know he's only been marking the cards for the last hour, he's only managed to win £400–500 in that time. What's the use of 'making waves'? Cash him in, ban him from the games and he cannot go round saying anything. Needless to say, slowly in the next couple of years, he was banned from all the games in London. I haven't mentioned his name on purpose because he is still around today.

Around the same year in 1985, I used to pop into the West End sometimes in the morning to collect some money for my dad. He used to say, "Pop down to the West End, collect this money for me and make sure you are in the office before the start of racing." Now summertime the racing always starts at 2 pm, so I had plenty of time. Now the fact of the matter is that I could get back for the first race, but when I used to go to the West End, I always used to go for coffee in South Molton Street and I always used to be late. Well this time, I was going round and round looking for a parking meter, I found one eventually and it was in front of the William Hill Betting Shop. When I went to put some money in the meter, I realised I had no change, so naturally I popped into the betting shop and I said to the guy behind the till. "Excuse me governor, I know it's a liberty, but I've parked my car outside on a meter, have you change of a tenner?" He said, "I can't give change, I can't open the till." So I grabbed a betting slip and wrote out a bet for a 50 p accumulator, the first two favourites at Uttoxeter and the first two favourites at Yarmouth. My bet was a 50 p accumulator, four favourites. I gave him the slip and he laughed because now he had to open the till and give me the change from the 'tenner'. He gave me my £9.50 and I quickly went outside, put the money in the meter and collected the money that had to be collected and got back to the office. Well I forgot all about the betting slip that I had left in the car. Dad came in towards the end of racing, I said, "Dad, I collected that money for you." He said, "Were you here for the first race?" I said, "Yes! I was." He said, "Are you sure?" I said, "Yes! I definitely was because I found a meter outside … and then I stopped. He said, "What's the matter?" I said, "I just realised Dad, I needed some change today and I had this 50 p accumulator." Dad said, "You don't bet!" I said, "I know I don't bet but I needed change." I then started to tell him the story. I've looked up at the results screens. The first two favourites at Uttoxeter had won. The first one had gone in at 9/2 favourite. The second one had gone in at 7/2 favourite. I then looked to the other side at Yarmouth. I've then seen the first one at Yarmouth has gone in at 5/1 favourite, I've then seen the second one at Yarmouth has gone in at 11/2 favourite. I've jumped up and down for joy. Ali said, "What's the matter Junior?" (He used to always call me Junior.) I said, "Ali, This bet comes to money!" We started to work it out and we couldn't believe it. The bet from 50p had come to £500! Ali then said to me, "Only you Junior, only you can go and get change for a parking meter and have a bet and have a 50 p accumulator for it to come to £500!" Well the next day I went back and I collected my winnings from the guy that wouldn't open the till to give me change. I said to him, "I've just parked my car outside and need change for the meter!" He looked at me and said, "I can't open the till!" I said, "I know, here's my winning betting slip from yesterday, you had better open it!!"

1986 came round quite quick and the Tyson fight was approaching. In the summer Frank Bruno fought Tim Witherspoon for the Title of the WBA Championship of the World. Everybody thought that Frank Bruno was going to win that belt. We all went to Wembley to watch the fight, as it was one of the biggest heavyweight boxing contests that England has ever seen. We all backed Bruno and as everybody knows Tim Witherspoon beat him up in the 10. What we heard was that Tim Witherspoon came over to London and was shopping in the West End and wasn't even training, but he managed to beat our Big Frank quite convincingly. We all lost our money that night betting on Frank Bruno, as Frank was the favourite to win with the bookies over here. What we didn't know was that Frank was a big outsider in Las Vegas. I found this out later on. This was going to be a clue as to how I could make some money from the boxing game. I still hadn't seen Rod. He had disappeared.

It was around 1986 that Hold'em, first started taking place in London casinos, but I wasn't interested. I was still getting regular games of Five Card Stud. In the November of that year, Tyson was to fight Trevor Birbeck for the WBC Heavyweight Championship of the World. At the time Dad was quite friendly with a guy named Maurice. Maurice was an Iranian guy and one of the loveliest guys you would ever meet. He was 100% gentleman and when he used to gamble on the poker table or the blackjack, you could not tell whether he was winning or if he was losing as he always had the same temperament and he would always say the same thing. "I'm losing Stevie!" in his Iranian–American accent. So I said, "A lot Maurice?" "A lot of money but it's no problem!" Everything to Maurice was "No problem." Maurice said to me, "If you go to Vegas for the big fight, I'm coming and we've got to stay at Caesars Palace, I know the casino host there and they will look after us." I said, "Maurice, let's go, I'm going to win money on this fight because Tyson is going to be the youngest Heavyweight Champ, let's go to Vegas!" The day before we were due to set off, Maurice phoned me at home and he said, "Stevie! I'm going to meet you in Vegas." I said, "Maurice, I'll see you there." He said, "Go to Caesars Palace, I've got your room booked and I'll meet you there for the fight." Well I flew to Vegas and I went into Caesars Palace, a fabulous hotel. I went up to the desk, to check in and they said to me, "Sir, you have your reservation, but I'm afraid to say your room isn't ready, but it will be ready in half an hour, we'll page you, where will you be?" As I looked up, I saw about 20 crap tables, which is dice tables, but the Americans say craps, in front of me. So I said, "I'm going to go over there, I'm going to go and play craps." I walked over to one of the tables and I took out $100 and I got some $5 chips and I put $5 on the win line and I said to the Croupier, who was holding the stick on the dice table at the time. "What's the point?" He said to me, "The point is 6." He then said to me, "Hey buddy, where are you from?" I said, "I'm from England." He said, "Yeah! I can tell you're from England, but where are you actually from?" I said, "London." He then said to me, "I learnt this game in London, I learnt to become a croupier in London." So I said, "Really, where?" He said, "Phew! You wouldn't know it, it was in North London and it was back in the 60s, before you were born." I said, "Well try me, whereabouts in London?" He said to me, "I learnt to deal in a place called Wembley." My eyes widened up, I didn't say anything. I looked at him and I said, "Yeah! What was the casino called?" He said, "The casino was called the Wembley Spinner Club." I said, "Really, the Wembley Spinner Club, where did you go after the Wembley Spinner Club?" He said, "Hey! This guy who owned the Wembley Spinner Club also had another joint, not far from there and it was by Haringey Dog Stadium." I said, "This guy by chance, his name wouldn't be Max would it?" Well as soon as I mentioned Max, his jaw hit the floor. He said, "My God, do you know Max?." I said to him, "Max is my dad and he owned the Wembley Spinner Club and the Club in Haringey!" He then came round the table. He hugged me, he picked me up. He then said to his pit boss, I'm taking a break and I'm taking this man around the casino to introduce him to all the staff, I mean I had only been in Vegas five minutes! He then took me to the staff room of Caesars Palace, there must have been about 600 croupiers taking breaks and he got everyone to be quiet and said, "You see this man, I used to work for his father, in London, in the early 60s." We sat down and had a coffee and he started to tell me all the stories of how Dad used to train the Croupiers in the old days. Dad used to take them to Charlie Chester's after they closed for the night at the Wembley Spinner Club, as Charlie Chester's was 24 hours, and Dad used to give his entire apprentice Croupiers £5 each to play the dice and they had to learn how to deal. That's how Dad taught them. He said to me, "Your Dad was one of the greatest gamblers and greatest characters I've ever seen. How is he?" I said, "Glen, he might be coming over in six or seven months to Vegas." He said, “I would love to see him.” After a while I went back to the casino floor and they paged my name to go to my hotel room. The hotel room they gave me was a beautiful suite with a four-poster bed. Twenty minutes of me being in the room, the phone rang. I answered the phone, the voice on the other end said, “It’s Maurice.” I said, “Hi! Maurice, where are you?” He said, “Stevie! I don’t think I can come to Vegas, but I spoke to the casino host, who I know very well and I told her to look after you. Anything you want, anywhere you wanna go, boxing tickets on me, you name it, you got it buddy, it’s no problem!” I said, “Maurice, thank you very much, it’s a shame you can’t come over to Vegas, because I’d love to be with you.” Two days later was the fight and as we all know Tyson knocked out Trevor Birbeck in the second round, to become the youngest Heavyweight Champion in the World. What I was told very recently was that, as we know, Tyson was the youngest Heavyweight Champion of the World, but what a lot of people do not know he was also the youngest Heavyweight Champion of the World to lose the title, I didn’t know that. Well anyway the fight against Trevor Birbeck made me happy, I’d won my bet from a year ago. What I found amazing in Las Vegas was, when you walked into a casino, there were so many dice tables. I was used to going into the Vic or Charlie Chester’s and there was only one or two. In Vegas, there used to be 20 to 30, all lined up. Well one night walking back to my hotel room, I heard a loud cheer on one of the dice tables. I looked across the room and I could see a lot of people crowded around. There were 20 other dice tables and they were all empty. This one was packed, so I figured this table must be hot! Now, I never knew about Hot Tables until I got to Vegas, because as I said, there only used to be one or two tables in the casinos in London. So either a table was Hot or it was Cold, but I’m telling you now, if you walk into a casino in Vegas and there are 20 tables, one is going to be Hot! And Hot means that the punter is going to win. Well anyway, I walked over and there must have been 30 to 40 people around this table, I couldn’t even get in. I managed to sneak myself in at the corner and I managed to pull out $10 and put it on the win line. I looked at the guy next to me and he said, “You’ve missed it all buddy, this guy has been shooting for over 20 minutes and he’s made a five timer.” I said, “Well! If I’ve missed it, I’ve missed it, but I’m now in the game.” After half an hour and another seven good numbers he was looking for a 4 and everybody had hundreds and thousands of dollars on the 4 and all this guy had to do was throw a number 4. I had a stack of $5 chips mounted up, about seven inches high, with a stack of $5 chips behind it.

I was winning $2000. from $10, so could you imagine, what the others were winning? The guy threw the dice, one of the dice hit the table edge, hit me in the chest and then landed right on top of my stack of $5 chips. When I saw the number that had landed on top of the chips, it was a number 5, we all then looked to see the other number on the dice, which had landed properly on the table, it was a number 2. 5 and 2 is 7. A punter never wants to see 7 when he's at the dice table. That means everybody loses and the casino wins. So my natural reaction was, when I saw the 5, I blew the dice off my chips. This all happened in a second. The dice rolled off my chips and landed on the table and it landed on a 2. Now since the other number was 2 and this was 2, we had our number 4, a winner! This all happened so quickly and everything went quite because everybody saw that I blew the dice off the top of my chips. There was silence. It seemed like there was silence for eternity, but it must have been for about five to ten seconds. The Pit Boss, whispered something to the croupier, the croupier whispered something to the Pit Boss. The Floor Manager was called over. Now there was tens of thousands of dollars riding on this 4. They obviously were asking what exactly went on. I could see them looking over at me and I could see them explaining that the dice hit the edge of the table, hit my chest, it then went back onto the chips and you know their hands were moving around as they were talking. I mean I didn't know what to do. After about five minutes, they looked up and they said to the Croupiers, "Pay everybody, the winner is 4!" an almighty cheer went up. I got patted on the back and everybody was clapping. I couldn't believe what had just happened. The guy that was throwing the dice, continued to throw the dice for another hour and a half. He made 21 good numbers that night. I think that was a record for any dice table in the world. I cashed in $5000 and I started two hours before with $10. My trip to Las Vegas for the second time had been very successful. Caesar's Palace had looked after me incredibly well. I had limousines to pick me up, limousines to drop me off, fight tickets and complimentary food and rooms. Once I got back to London, it was back to work as normal.

It wasn't until three or four weeks later that year that me and my friends decided to go to Marbella. I'd never been to Marbella before, but I decided to go with Johnny K, he was the guy that doesn't gamble, if you remember rightly. We went over to Spain together and we were just doing the normal things of sunbathing and going out at nights, no gambling. We heard that Reggie was coming over in a couple of days' time, so we went to meet Reggie at the airport. Reggie came off the plane and he looked rather chuffed with himself. He was telling us that he had won £400 off an American guy playing spoof on the way over. Reggie continued to say, "I couldn't lose." I said, "How comes Reggie?" He said, "Well every time the guy was putting the coins in his hands [now spoof is a game where you play with three coins each and you've got to guess the total number of coins in both hands, simple as that] because the American had a few drinks, I could see the amount of coins that he was putting in his hands." So Reggie couldn't lose. Johnny and me were laughing. Johnny now wanted to know how to play spoof. Reggie showed him how to play, and Johnny lost £50. Johnny wasn't happy to lose £50. Johnny was a little bit upset about losing £50 at spoof, but I told him to forget it. All night long we were sitting outside a nightclub drinking. There was a group of us as we had some more friends that came over and Johnny was thinking about a way to get his £50 back. Jay, whose another close friend of ours, was living out there at the time, said, "There's only one way you can get it back, why don't you arm wrestle someone for £50." So Johnny said, "Who can I arm wrestle?" Now Johnny was quite a big and a strong guy, so no one of our group wanted to arm wrestle him. As luck would have it a guy walked out of the discothèque, who I believe Jay knew and said, "Neil, will you arm wrestle my friend for £50" The guy looked up and said, "No problem! I'll arm wrestle him for £100." Well Johnny arm wrestled Neil for £100, Neil put Johnny down in one second! I think we'd picked the wrong guy to arm wrestle! Johnny then had a rematch with the guy. Neil put Johnny down in two seconds. That was it, the guy went off with the £200 and now Johnny was £250 behind. The last couple of days of our holiday, there was a casino in Marbella and Reggie was winning a couple of thousand pounds in the casino, but we did have one poker game that Johnny K, Reggie and myself and another boy called Hugh sat down and played and Reggie lost £2000. Johnny actually broke even and I think now he realised that he could break even at gambling, maybe there's a chance that he could win!

Coming back from Marbella with all the boys, Johnny had done a few quid arm wrestling and it ended up being a bit of a gambling holiday and as I said to you, Johnny K had finished dead even on the poker game. We got to the airport and we checked our luggage in and when all of us had arrived at Heathrow, whilst waiting for our luggage Reggie shouted, "£100 my suitcase comes out first, Stevie! Do you want the bet?" I replied, "Reggie, I'll say £100 my suitcase comes out." Johnny then piped up, "No! I'll say £100 my suitcase comes up first." Then another guy Colin who was on holiday with us shouted,

"£100 my suitcase comes up first!" Then Hugh joined in and said, "£100 my suitcase comes up first." I then said, "I'll tell you what we'll do, let's all put £100 in the pot and whoever's suitcase comes out first is the winner." So we put £500 in the middle on the floor at Heathrow Airport and we waited for the suitcases to come out, we were waiting and waiting. There was £500 to be won on a suitcase! The conveyor belt started to move round. Reggie started rubbing his hands saying, "Let it be Reggie's, let it be Reggie's!" He started getting excited, the suitcases started to come out. It seemed like we were waiting for an eternity. All of a sudden a big scream went out, "There's my suitcase! There's my suitcase!" It was Johnny K's. He'd run over and grabbed the suitcase. Reggie being Reggie said, "Wait a minute! Let me check the name on the suitcase to see if it's yours Johnny." Johnny looked at Reggie and said, "Please! Please! Do you think I would cheat you about this not being my suitcase?" Reggie said, "Let me see the name on the suitcase." Sure enough it was Johnny K's. He had scooped £500 by being the first suitcase out. Reggie then said again, "Stevie! I bet you £100 that my suitcase comes out next?" I said, "Hold on Reggie, Johnny has won the bet." He said, "Forget Johnny, he won the £500, I bet you another £100 that my suitcase comes out first." Colin and Hugh again said the same thing. The 4 of us then put the £400 in the middle again. A big scream went out, it was Hugh's suitcase. Hugh had won £400 with his suitcase coming out first. Reggie said, "Wait a minute, let me check the name tag." Hugh replied, "That is my suitcase! None of you here have got Harrods suitcases!" Now if you knew Hugh, all of his suits were from the top designers and his entire luggage was from Harrods, Reggie didn't even check the label. I said, "Reggie what do we do now?" He said, "Stevie! Me, you and Colin put £100 each and the next suitcase that comes out takes the £300. We did, and Colin won the £300. It was now Reggie and me. We were now £300 each behind waiting for our suitcases! So Reggie said, "I'm losing £300 and your loosing £300. £300 you and me Stevie, next suitcase that comes out! I said, "You're on Reggie!" Well the next suitcase that came out was mine, Reggie couldn't believe it, he had lost £600 and we were laughing. Johnny K was ecstatic because that's the first time that he had won at gambling. I said, "Well Reggie! You want to introduce these silly games at Heathrow Airport, you are going to lose your money." He said, "Boys can I tell you all something, I should have won all of that." I said, "Why? We all had a suitcase, so it was fair odds." Reggie said, "No it wasn't fair odds, I had three suitcases on that flight and none of them have come out yet!"

When I got back to London, it was work as normal. There was no poker in Haringey and there hadn't been for a couple of months. I'd heard that there was another gambling club that had opened 50 to 60 yards from my dad's Club. I didn't know who owned it, until one day someone said to me Vellie owned the Club. So I said, "Vellie who?" They said, "You know Vellie, Vellie who used to play poker with your Dad." Now Vellie was the man who, when I was a kid scared me and told me, "One day, I'm going to skin you like your Dad is skinning me." I've always remembered that. So one night, at about midnight, I drove to Haringey and I drove to Vellie's Club, it was closed. I rang the doorbell, this guy shuffled towards the door. He opened the door. He didn't look that big to me, hair slightly grey. He said, "Can I help you?" I said, "Are you Vellie?" He said, "Yes." I said, "Do you know who I am?" He said, "No?" I said, "I'm Max's son!" He said, "Max's son… Your name?" I said, "My name is Stevie." Then Vellie said, "Come in Stevie, how is Dad, how is everything? Have a coffee." We sat down at a table and had a cup of tea. I said, "Vellie, I'm here, because do you remember what you said to me?" I then told Vellie, the story of when I was 12 or 13 years old, Vellie laughed. He said, "You know, I didn't mean it." I said, "I know that Vellie, but I'm here to play you poker. Heads Up, so I can go back to my dad and say I've played the one and only fearless Vellie." We went into the back, we had an agreement that we would play for only two hours. We would sit down with £1000 each, no one could draw any more money. This was more of a friendly game it's called a Freeze Up. Two hours later, I was winning £300, the time was up, I then said "Vellie, I'm winning £300, but I'm willing to put it into the middle and have a Five Card Draw for the £300, what we call a 'squeezy'." Vellie said, "You've got a bet." We dealt the five cards, Vellie won the squeezy, so we finished dead level. He shook my hand and I said, "Vellie, I've been waiting to play you Heads Up for 12 or 13 years now and I did and I'm happy thank you." I've never seen Vellie since. I've heard he is in Cyprus somewhere, but no one knows.

Jay, our friend from Marbella came over to London one week and he brought a friend, he was a Spanish guy named Jose, he used to be a Roman Wrestler. He was a very, very strong guy, but he didn't look a big guy but Jay explained to me that we could make a lot of money because Jose was an unbelievable arm wrestler. I said, "Well is he good Jay?" He said, "Steve I'm telling you, he is so strong at arm wrestling, he's unbeatable. Well to me he didn't look that strong, he weighed about 13 and half stone, which was about 180 lbs. We started going to all the nightclubs in London and we got Jose to arm wrestle the biggest bouncers in the nightclub. We used to arm wrestle the bouncers for £50 or £100 a time. When they used to see Jose, he didn't look a big guy, but I'm telling you this guy was unbeatable. Or should I say, nearly unbeatable. I'll get to that in a minute. We went to Stringfellows one night and there was a big guy there called Tony and he was about 260 lbs. Jose beat him." The thing with Jose was, it was the way he beat his opponents. He never seemed to struggle. He used to put them down within three seconds. He used a very good technique. We won a lot of money, going around all the nightclubs in London but the bouncers at Stringfellows said, "Steve, you should of told us as you know us so well that Jose was a good arm wrestler. We want a chance to get our money back. Bring Jose down on Saturday night and we want him to arm wrestle a guy that we will bring down." Meanwhile in the next three or four days we'd run out of nightclubs to go to. Just to let you know how strong Jose was, Johnny K could beat me easily in an arm wrestle. Jose used to beat Johnny K very easily. The point I'm trying to make is when Jose arm wrestled me he used to beat me in one second flat. When he arm wrestled Johnny Kay he used to beat Johnny K in one second flat. So I said, "Jose, Johnny can beat me within five seconds, you can beat me in one second and you can beat Johnny in one second, he's obviously stronger than me." Jose looked up and said to me in a Spanish accent, "I don't know, I feel nothing. I arm wrestle you, I feel nothing, I arm wrestle Johnny, I feel nothing." This was the strength of the guy. Jimmy Manchester was with us one night. Now Jimmy Manchester was a very strong arm wrestler. He wasn't a big guy but he also had a very good technique and he was unbeaten. We got Jose to arm wrestle Jimmy Manchester. Well he got beat. Just to give you an idea, Jimmy Manchester used to beat Johnny Kay in five seconds. Jose beat Jimmy Manchester in one second flat again. I said, "Jose did you feel anything this time?" He said, "Steve, no I felt nothing." Well this guy was superhuman. We then let Jimmy have a head start and by this I mean Jimmy had Jose two inches from the table and all he had to do was put down Jose's hand another two inches. That's the handicap we gave Jose. Well it took Jose two and half seconds to bring up Jimmy's hand and put Jimmy down. Jimmy looked at Jose and said, "This is unbelievable." I said, "Jose how about now, did you feel anything?" Jose looked at me and said, "Yes, I felt something, I felt something." This was to show you the strength of the guy. One night at Rocky's (Reggie's restaurant) Jose arm wrestled a guy named Big Bad John and when I say big this guy was humongous, he was around 29 stone about 400 lbs but Jose beat him, which was an unbelievable victory. Anyway, Saturday approached, we all went down to Stringfellows and we were all down stairs at the time and the bouncer came and got me and he said, "Bring Jose upstairs, we've got our man to arm wrestle Jose, but before you see him give us a chance to get all our money back from the other night." I said, "No problem boy's, you're on, whoever it is." Jose came upstairs and we met the guy that he was going to arm wrestle. The guy's name was Selwyn. This guy was 6 feet 2 inches and 280 lbs (20 stone) and he was rock solid. Well not only was he rock solid, he'd done a lot of arm wrestling championships. Now first of all in an arm wrestling championship, Jose wouldn't be matched against Selwyn. Well they arm wrestled and Selwyn beat Jose. He didn't beat him easily, but it took him about realistically four or five seconds to put Jose down. Once you've got the technique at arm wrestling you can become three or four times stronger. Selwyn had the power and the strength and the technique. He was a professional bodybuilder, this guy could bench 550 lbs for 8 reps. He was a very strong guy. We conceded, we'd lost our money and like gentlemen we paid.

Around this time 86–87, friends of Reggie used to have a barbecue and at the end of the evening they played poker. Well I went to two of these barbecues and I realised that when they used to play poker, they were signalling to each other what they had, they were cheating. I played twice in these barbecue games. I lost my money twice, not big amounts, but I realised there was cheating going on. In fact, one night I was losing a couple of hundred pounds and I got up and said I was going home. I was woken the next morning by the guy that hosted the barbecue and he said, "Was everything alright last night Steve, we just wondered why you stopped playing?" I said, "I stopped playing because I knew I was out of form and I was going to lose my money." That's all I said. This guy that used to have the barbecues, a couple of years later, started working for Dad in the betting shop. I did tell Dad, that this guy could not be trusted. A couple of years later he was fired from our betting shop for thieving money.

There was some other poker games that year. My Dad's friend, whose name was Jimmy 'Moutas'. Now Moutas in Greek means, the nose. He's known as Jimmy the Nose. Why? Because he's got a big nose! Anyway, Jimmy and I decided to get some games going. He had a restaurant in Ilford, called the Sombrero, fantastic steak there. On a Saturday night, we used to all pop up there for something to eat. I used to take two or three customers that wanted to play poker, he used to have two or three. We used to eat and at midnight, play poker. We used to finish on a Sunday afternoon, after the football, at about five o'clock. Sunday matches in those days were the Old First Division and ITV showed the Sunday match live. The games in Ilford lasted about five months. I never, never, ever, ever lost in those games at Ilford, except one night towards the end, I was doing a nice 'few quid', about £4500. And as everybody went to go and cash in their chips, we decided to do 'squeezys' and as I've told you before 'squeezys' are Five Cards down, the highest hand wins. It's Pot Luck, you never know who is going to win. In the first 'squeezy' six of us put £300 each in, so for me, it didn't make a difference because I knew I was going to lose on the night. We had three 'squeezys' that night. The first one I won, the second I won and the third one I won, I recovered all my money on three pots of squeezys! Now the dealer at the time was Ali (the Ali that used to work in the office for us) and he said in his very rough grumpy voice. "Junior only you could get out of trouble tonight, only you. You've hit some tremendous form and some fantastic cards recently."

One night when we were running the games in Ilford, after winning week after week, Jimmy Moutas or Jimmy the Nose said to all the players, "We can't beat this Stevie, Stevie! We can't beat you, what's your favourite drink?" I said, "Jim there's only one drink that I love, I love Dom Perignon." He said to the waiter, "Bring out a bottle of Dom Perignon and open it up." While we were playing poker, we all started to have a couple of glasses of champagne and I noticed the waiter kept on filling up my glass. Now I'm actually a non-drinker, I'm a very social drinker but I don't drink when I'm playing cards, but my glass kept on getting filled up with Dom Perignon. Now that was an offer I couldn't refuse! I must have had five or six glasses; in fact we'd gone through three bottles. What I realised was it was only my glass that was being filled up. After a couple of hours I felt worse for wear. I said, "Gents I'm just popping to the loo, I'll be back in a minute." I've gone to the loo downstairs and my head was spinning and as I got back into the room, I knew that Jimmy and the boys had given me enough DP to get me drunk and for me to lose my money. Well I realised something in poker that I'd never realised before, I was playing so 'karabina' or tight, I wasn't even calling! I was just passing my cards straight away. Sometimes it was for me to open the bet but I used to pass! When it was me to call a bet, I used to pass them again. I used to look at the hole card, but if it wasn't strong enough, I used to pass. Well I can honestly say that the drink had an opposite effect on me. Unlike many poker players when they get drunk or have had a few drinks, they play very aggressive, very carefree and they throw their money, the Dom Perignon had the complete opposite effect! I was playing the tightest game that I'd ever played. Jimmy the Nose could not believe it. He even said to me, after the game, "Do you know I was giving you DP to see if you could lose a few quid to us?" I said, "Jim! I know, but I don't know what happened, I used to look at my hole card and it was a bit blurry and if I couldn't see the hole card did not match the showing card, I used to just pass." Jimmy was laughing. Anyway the games soon faded out, as I've told you before there was only one winner. I took all my winnings and I brought a brand-new Mercedes Sports Car. It was a 280SL Mercedes Sports. Jimmy Moutas still laughs until this day, because he always turns round to everybody and says. "Uh! You know that Mercedes Sports that Stevie's got? I bought the wheels, I did a lot of money in those games."

After one of the poker games at the Sombrero in Ilford, as I was leaving the restaurant Jimmy Moutas said, "Stevie, your dad has ordered a big fresh salmon fish, when will you see him?" I said, "Jim, I will probably see him tonight at home." He said, "Do me a favour can you give it to him, because he hasn't been up to the restaurant for a while and he wants it." I said, "Not a problem!" I took the fish and I didn't think any more of it, literally! Well I'll tell you what happened. About three weeks later, I was at home. The phone rang and it was my dad on the phone, he says, "We're at the Sombrero Steak House and we've just finished dinner, did Jimmy give you a fish to give to us?" Then all of a sudden, I remembered. "Uh! Uh!" I stuttered, "Yeah! He did Dad." He said, "Well this fish that Jimmy gave to you, where is it? Because Jimmy has just asked me, did you enjoy the fish, Max." And I said to him, "What fish?" and he said, "The fish I gave to Stevie three weeks ago! So where is the fish?" I said, "Dad! I forgot to give it to you." He said, "Yes! I know that, but where's the fish?" I said, "Um! Um! The fish Dad, I think it's where I left it." So Dad said, "OK! Where did you leave it?" I said, "Dad I left it in the boot of my car." He said, "What?" I said, "As soon as Jimmy gave it to me, I put it in the boot of the car and I've left it in the boot of the car." Dad wasn't too happy. I put the phone down and I went straight to my car in a bit of a panic. I'm going to be honest with you, when I was driving the car around during the last week or two of this happening, I knew there was some kind of fishy smell in the car, but I thought it was the rain that made the carpet smell! I didn't know what it was. I never knew I was riding around with a dead fish in the boot of the car! I got to the car and opened the boot up and woof! It hit me. There laying in the boot was a massive great big salmon fish that was three weeks old and I can tell you it stunk! Out of pure panic, I then done the most stupid thing I've ever done in my life. I took the fish and quickly put it into my family's fridge, as if it was going to become edible once again! I really don't know what came over me by doing this or why I did it, I just panicked. Mum and Dad arrived home and by now the whole house was smelling of fish and it only made the situation worse. Mum had to clean out the whole fridge! Even today, Dad sometimes gives me things to deliver, presents etc., etc., and still looks at me and says, "Don't forget it in the boot Stevie!" and this is 20 years later!

I managed to pop back down to Stringfellows one night and who did I bump into? Rod! Rod was the guy that I had the bet with for Mike Tyson to become the youngest Heavyweight Champion of the world. I said, "Rod where have you been?" He said, "I've been out of town." I said, "Shall I give you a call during the week?" He looked at me a little bit puzzled and said, "Yeah, do that." I said, "I'll call you Wednesday." Wednesday came round and I called him. I said "Nice to see you again Rod." He said, "Nice to see you." I said, "When shall we meet up?" He said, "Well we met up the other night!" I said, "Yeah, when shall we meet up and sort out our money?" He said to me "What money?" I said, "Rod! The bet that I had with you that Tyson would be Heavyweight Champion by the end of 1986." He said, "Are you serious?" I said, "Yes!" He said, "I thought you were kidding me." I said, "I wasn't kidding I had £100 at 16-1 and shook your hand." He said, "Come on Steve, you know that was a joke bet." I said, "Rod! Are you being serious?" He said, "Yeah! Because you're joking!" I said, "Rod, Dad always tells me it takes two to make a bet and there were the two of us there and we had a bet and you know it." He said, "I thought you were joking, anyway, how's things?" I said, "Rod! Are you paying me my money or not?" Then Rod started laughing and said, "Come On! You were joking." I said, "Rod! When it comes to gambling, I never joke." I then put the phone down. I never ever got that money for Mike Tyson being the Heavyweight Champion of the World. Well as they always say gambling bets are a debt of honour and it just goes to show, you've got to be careful who you bet with.

1987 came around quite quickly. The games were now at the Barracuda casino. They were getting quite big and quite regular and there were some very good action games. Now it's in the 80s, it was £10,000 minimum to sit down at a table. The games were on again. Earlier in the year obviously Tyson in the boxing world was causing quite a stir and one night on the poker table in the Barracuda casino, I mentioned that Tyson was fighting James Bonecrusher Smith in March, in Vegas. Out of the blue Dad said, "Why don't we all go to the fight?" Maurice, who was there, said at the time, "Let's all go and I'll tell you what we'll do, we'll play poker on the plane on the way over." Everybody was up for it. Once you mention poker on the plane, that kills the ten-hour flight straight away, everybody wanted to go to Vegas. In fact, every poker game on Wednesdays and Fridays at the Barracuda, everybody was actually getting excited to go. Well March '87 came around and we all decided to meet at Heathrow Airport. When we all got there, Paulo, Mickey Fitz, Dad, Brian from Southampton there was about five or six of us. Where was Maurice? Maurice phoned and said, he couldn't make it. This was funny because as Paulo said, it was Maurice who got us all to go to Vegas and like before when I went in 1986, he now wasn't going to show. Maurice said to everybody, "Have a good time and I'll join you, no problem!" We all knew Maurice wasn't coming! Anyway, we had Paulo and as I told you before, Paulo was a character. Now! What I never told you is that Paulo used to call himself the 'Italian Prince'. Italian Prince because he was handsome and he was good looking, as he used to say. He turned up at the airport and when he saw us all, he shouted out, "Liberace! Liberace! I am here." We really didn't know what he was going on about, but he kept on saying "Liberace! Liberace!" Anyway, Paulo was such a character. We got on the plane and we'd booked on a TWA, the Ambassador Class. In the old days, the Ambassador Class was about 16 or 18 seats upstairs. Well we'd booked the whole lot, because Maurice, I forgot to tell you, told us that we could change the configuration of the seats. I remember him saying distinctly at the Barracuda on the poker table, "Guys you will be able to play poker upstairs on the TWA plane, because you can change the configuration." I remember thinking what's configuration? He said, "The seats swivel round, you can put a table and you can play poker." Maurice talked us into it. When we got upstairs, the seats never moved an inch! We couldn't move the damn things, so we were all stuck in our seats, ready for take-off, thinking how were we going to play poker. Just before take-off, I told you before that Paulo nearly won a lot, a lot of money off my dad. Well I'm now going to tell you how.

About ten minutes before take-off we were all in our seats. Paulo, being the joker he is, decided to press the stewardesses button. The young lady came round and she knew us all by our names and she said, "Yes Mr Paulo, what can I do for you?" He said, "Miss," in his strange Italian accent, "Miss, I want to go to New York." She said, "Excuse me?" He said, "I want to go to New York!" She said, "I'm sorry Mr Paulo, this plane goes to Los Angeles." He said, "I don't care, please go and see the captain and tell him there is an Italian Prince on board and he wants to go to New York." Meanwhile, we were all laughing. We were all jovial because we were off to Vegas. We knew the plane went to Los Angeles and then we had to catch another plane to go to Vegas, so we're laughing, she started laughing too. She came back and said to Paulo. "Paulo I've got some bad news for you, this plane is going to Los Angeles." I'll never forget this, Paulo said to my dad, "Maxi! You're a bookmaker; I would like to have a bet, I say this plane goes to New York!" Now you've got to imagine this. This plane is going to LA. We're all sitting there and we are laughing. My Dad said to Paulo, "Paulo! Why are you messing around like this? We want to start the poker as soon as we take off." Paulo replied, "I'm not messing about, please lay me odds to go to New York." Now meanwhile he's laughing, we're all laughing. Dad said, "Paulo, you can have a million to one." Paulo pulled out £20 from his pocket. Now imagine the scene, we're still all laughing, we've had a couple of drinks at the airport and he went to hand over to my dad the £20 note and he said to my dad, "What odds is it again we go to New York?" My Dad said, "One million to one Paulo." Paulo goes to give my dad the £20 and as my dad takes the £20 he snatches it back and Paulo says "Ha! Ha! Do you think Maxi, I'm mad? I know you call me 'Mad Paulo' but do you honestly think I'm mad? I wouldn't give you £20."

Now remember Paulo is a multimillionaire. He then continued to say, "I wouldn't waste £20, let's wait for take-off and let's get the poker started." As soon as the plane took off after 20 minutes everybody wanted to play poker. I had the chips, I had the cards. The problem was, everybody had to turn round in such a fashion that some were getting backaches and some were getting neck aches but they were so desperate to play on the plane to kill the journey time. The stewardess gave us a hard plastic board that we could put across the two seats and I had to sit at the back and I was sitting in the cloak cupboard and dealing the cards! Just imagine it, me the dealer, sitting in the cloak cupboard dealing. It was small and it was cramped and I really couldn't shuffle well. About 20 minutes into the game, Paulo turned round and said, "Look! We've got a dealer and we must look after the dealer, so I suggest let's all put some money each and we will tip the dealer now and every time we play, we will give him a certain amount." So I'm thinking great! I can earn a couple of hundred pounds. Paulo said, "Let's all give the dealer £200." Now as there were five players, that was £1000 for me. Can you believe that? £1000 for dealing the cards for three or four hours! Anyway, they all gave me the £200 and I started dealing. Four hours into the flight the captain came on the loud speaker. He said, "This is your captain speaking, we have a problem! But do not be alarmed, Ladies and Gentlemen, one of our engines has blown, I repeat do not be alarmed as we have three others, owing to engine failure, we will be landing in New York!" Paulo's jaw hit the floor. He looked at my dad; my dad looked at him both speechless and he turned round and said, "I cannot believe it Maxi! I nearly gave you the £20 note and I snatched it back and you were going to lay me £1 million to one that the plane lands in New York, I would have won £20 million off you!" Now I know what you are thinking, what would have happened? If my dad took that bet, Paulo would have won £20 million. Well I shudder to think. The bet, if it were struck had to be paid. It was almost like the sweetshop man again back in the 60s, if he had of cashed in! But this time it was megabucks. Paulo couldn't believe it. Everybody couldn't believe it and then we all started to think, what are the odds for a plane to take-off from Heathrow on its way to LA, but not reach LA and end up going to New York? Well as any flight attendant or any Captain will tell you, it's not a one million to one. It's probably 1000-1, but definitely not a million! The lesson here is before you make the odds, you've got to think about the bet!

We landed in New York and were asked by the crew if we wanted to stay for four hours in New York and wait for the engine to be repaired, or we could jump back on plane. Some of us wanted to wait, some wanted to take another plane that went to Vegas from New York via Phoenix Arizona. Me and my dad and one other guy, called Eddie decided to go on the plane to Vegas via Phoenix. (Eddie was one of those fearless poker players and a couple of years later he beat me in a monster pot at the Barracuda while my dad was in Cyprus, but I'll tell you about that later on.) Well the whole trip to get to Vegas took us about 20 hours! We were absolutely worse for wear. We had to stop in Phoenix and eventually we got to Vegas. We got off the plane in Vegas and as we were walking through the airport going to get our luggage, we hooked up with the other poker crew that had got in at the same time, just by coincidence, so it made no difference if we waited in New York to get the plane direct or we went to Vegas via Phoenix, we all ended up in Vegas airport at the same time. Everybody looked shattered. Everyone was a little bit down because it had been a terrible, terrible flight, but what was about to happen next was to cheer everybody up. As we were walking through the airport, by one of the exit doors waiting for an incoming flight was a guy in a tracksuit and a baseball cap. He didn't look a big guy. He was black and he looked quite athletic. We all walked past him and I took a 'double take' at him, I then stopped. I then looked back at him. I then called out "Dad! Dad! Stop a minute, we've just walked past Mike Tyson." Dad stopped and looked back at the guy who was sitting down with his baseball cap on over his eyes and Dad said, "Don't be silly, Mike Tyson is a big guy." I then looked again, I said, "Dad! Dad! It is, it's Mike Tyson." Dad said to me, "I'm telling you that's not Mike Tyson, I've seen him on TV, he's a big guy." I then walked up to the guy and I tapped him on the shoulder, I'll never forget it, I said, "Mike? Mike?" He looked up at me and said, "Yes?" I said, "Mike Tyson?" He said, "Yes!" I said, "What, what are you doing here?" He said, "I'm waiting for my friends to come off the plane who are coming to see me fight and they've been delayed, so I'm sitting here waiting for them." I mean can you believe this, Mike Tyson sitting at the Vegas airport, by himself, this was unbelievable. I said, "Mike, we've come all the way from London to watch you fight, I've followed your career since you were 17 or 18 years old with Cus D'Amato, I came over to watch you beat Trevor Birbeck for the WBC Title and I told everybody that you were so fantastic, I've bought everybody from London to see you fight." He said, "No?" I then called everybody back but before they got back to us Mike jumped up and he walked over to everybody and I said, "Mike these are all my dad's friends from London." He shook everybody's hand and hugged everybody and said, "Thank you, thank you very much for coming." Now Brian from Southampton got out the camera and he started taking photographs. Now Mike's got his arms around Paulo, Paulo's got his arms around Mike. Dad's hugging Mike Tyson. I'm in the middle. You should have seen all our faces. This was one of the best treats we've ever had. Mike spent a good ten minutes with us shaking everybody's hand and hugging and he kissed everybody. He then said, "I must go," and he left. Everybody was so happy that we met Mike Tyson at the airport and really after the 20-hour journey, it made up for everything. As we got our luggage, there was a limousine waiting for us to take us to Caesars Palace, as that is where we were going to stay. We jumped in the limo and everybody was on a buzz. All of a sudden, Brian from Southampton looked a little bit concerned. He said, "Boys! I want to tell you something, boys! Listen to me, I want to tell you something." So everyone said, "What's the matter, Brian, what's the matter with you?" "Boys! I've got some bad news for you." What Brian was going to tell us next, was to ruin, not all of the vacation but it certainly made him very, very, very unpopular for the next six nights. Brian continued to say that he had forgotten to put the film in the camera! Everybody was so upset, so upset. Brian from Southampton was now out of favour for the rest of the holiday. Paulo was calling him all the names under the sun. I was so devastated that we'd had 20 pictures taken with Mike Tyson and we hadn't got one! We got to Caesar's Palace, but one thing Brian done right is that everybody had a beautiful suite in Caesars for the rest of the week. Brian's suite was huge; I think it was about 5000 square feet. Dad and I had a beautiful three bedroom suite and Paulo's suite was also magnificent. While we were in Vegas for some unknown reason Italian Paulo kept on saying all week "Liberace! Liberace! Liberace!" I don't know what had got into Paulo. He kept on talking about Liberace and the £20 million that he had nearly won!

The poker games were to take place in Brian's suite and every time the poker players used to give me a £1000, I was in my element. I was in Vegas, I was earning money but I'll tell you about one night that I dealt, I must have been one of the highest paid people on the planet at the time.

I dealt the first two hands and then Paulo and Dad said, "Let's look after the dealer!" So they all gave me their £200 each and I'm sitting there with a £1000. On the very third hand, Dad made a flush to Paulo and Paulo lost about £14,000 in one pot, a flush at poker is five cards, all the same suit and I remember it distinctly, they were all Clubs. I had only been dealing for about two minutes. He then said, "Stevie! If you don't mind, I think we would like to deal ourselves today, just to break the rhythm of the cards." Now I can certainly understand this because after 45 minutes usually the dealer has a break, but what with me the only dealer there, he had a point. Well I worked it out; I earned £1000 for three minutes work. That works out at about £5.50 a second. £333 a minute! After the three minutes, I didn't watch the poker game. I went with my friend, who came over from Los Angeles to watch the fight as we had a spare ticket, and we went downstairs in Caesars Restaurant and had a lovely dinner. His name is Jay, that's the guy who was living in Marbella and now lives in LA and we still keep in contact today. He couldn't believe that I got a £1000 for three minutes work. The Dom Perignon was flowing and so were the games.

One day my friend Jay and I got back to the hotel suite after going to the gym and decided to get changed for dinner. It was about 4.30 pm. In the other room, my dad was taking a rest, reading the newspaper. We said to him, "We are getting changed and we were going to the bar to get something to drink" and asked him what he was doing. He said, "I'm going to read the paper and I'm going to take a nap." I said, "Did you gamble today Dad?" He said, "Yeah! I've done a 'few bob' (as that was my dad's favourite expression)… on the dice but I'm going to read the paper, take a nap and I'm going to wake up and go to the gym and have a workout, have a massage and take a sauna and a steam and I'm going to come back to my room and get dressed and go downstairs onto the dice table and get my money back." That's exactly what my dad said to Jay and me. Jay said to my dad, "Uncle Max! (Jay used to call my dad 'Uncle' out of respect), I like your style and confidence." Dad looked at Jay and said, "That's gambling Jay, I always try and do what I say." Jay was laughing. We all met up at about 7.30 pm and Dad was on the dice table and he had quite a lot of money in front of him. It was about $8–9000. He said to Jay, "That's it I'm going to cash in now, because we are going to go for dinner." I said, "How did you do Dad?" He said, "I've recovered my few bob and I've won a few bob on top." Jay said, "Seriously though Uncle Max how did you do?" Dad said, "Exactly what I said Jay, I recovered my money from the afternoon and I've won a few bob." Jay said, "I can't believe that, when you were in bed this afternoon at 4.30 pm, you said, you were going to read the paper, have a nap, go and work out, go for a sauna, go for a steam, go for a massage, come back, get changed, go to the dice table and get your money back and I can't believe that you've done exactly what you said you were going to do." Dad looked at Jay like there was nothing really unusual about what he had done but Jay not knowing Dad that well, thought this was an incredible thing to do and still talks about it today.

The night of the fight, when Tyson was to fight Bonecrusher Smith, we'd seen in the sports room, the sports book in Vegas were laying even money for the fight to go over four rounds. Now, me thinking I knew something about boxing, I told everybody in our crowd that this fight, Tyson vs. Bonecrusher, even though I loved Tyson, Bonecrusher was able to hold Mike Tyson to a minimum of six or seven rounds. We all put a small fortune that this fight would go over four rounds. If you've ever watched this fight on tape, when the end of the fourth-round bell sounds, you will hear an almighty cheer go up, I will never ever forget it. Mike never really put Bonecrusher in trouble, but in the 4th round he looked like that he could possibly take Bone Crusher out but didn't and as soon as that bell went we all jumped on our chairs and we were screaming. If you've got the fight on video, check out the end of the round for the 4th, there's an almighty cheer. I think the bookmakers lost a lot of money that day, as we know the fight went the distance and Mike won by unanimous decision. May I hasten to add that Bonecrusher rocked him with a big right, right towards the end of the 12th. Then there was one time, I think in the 11th that Tyson swung such a massive right hook that it missed Bonecrusher by inches and Mike span around, because of the force of the punch, he ended up on the floor. This was the first time that Mike Tyson had ever been on the floor, even though he wasn't hit! It wasn't a good fight, but Mike was able to win the WBA Heavyweight Title Belt off Bonecrusher. He now had two belts, the WBC and the WBA. The last belt the IBF, Michael Spinks was holding at the time.

I was waiting for Micky Fitz down at the bar, five, ten, fifteen minutes went past and I wondered where he was. Eventually, about half an hour later he showed up. I said, "Mike where have you been?" He said, "I've been listening to the English football." I said, "What are you talking about listening to the football?" He said, "I've been on the phone listening to the football." I said, "Sorry Mike, you've lost me here, we're in Las Vegas and you're telling me you are listening to the football?" He said, "Yes! I've been listening to the football on the telephone." I said, "Can you tell me how you've done that?" He said, "Well the football kicks off in England at 3 pm in the afternoon and on Radio 2 (and this is a fact in those days Radio 2 used to always have live commentary for the second half. Only nowadays, commentaries are usually one and half-hours, they go round all the grounds, you know all the scores but in those days it was only 45 minutes of the second half.) Mike continued to say, "Well I rang home and spoke to the wife and said do you know any football results darling? She said, I know a few, some of the half times, she started to get them all confused so I said, I'll tell you what you can do for me, put the radio on Radio 2 and put the telephone by the radio and I'll listen to the commentary." That's right Micky Fitz listened to the whole second half commentary of the football on a Saturday afternoon from England to Las Vegas on his phone from the hotel room! I couldn't believe it, he had backed a team to win a lot of money that day but he lost, because they drew 0-0! Talk about boring, a man listening to a football match and it finishes 0-0 and he is on the phone from Vegas!

Micky Fitz once said to me and his words stayed clearly in my mind, "Stevie look after the money that you earn when you are in your 20s, 30s &

40s." I said, "Why's that Mike?" He said, "Trust me when you reach your 50s, you won't have the earning power and the energy to earn as much." That was something that always stayed in my mind and if you just think about that for a second. In life as we get older, if we haven't looked after our money or put some money away for a rainy day as we say and you hit your 50s, you start to think of all the money that you've squandered, wasted or gambled in your life. So all Mike was trying to say to me was enjoy your life, make money at poker or whatever you do but save some, because one day you won't have the energy to go out and play poker all night.

One evening we all decided to have a walk down the strip and I told everybody that we had to go and see the Hotel and casino named Circus Circus. It was quite an old hotel and has been on the strip for many years, but it is still a great sight to see as they have a circus going on above your head at the same time downstairs when you are playing roulette or blackjack. We entered the hotel and as we were about to enter into the main part of the casino, on the right-hand side was a poker room. There was a poker table that was situated very close to the entrance of the card room and there was one seat that was free. So Italian Paulo said, "Wait there boys, I'll be back in a minute." So my dad said, "Paulo, you're not going to play poker now?" Paulo replied, "Maxi, give me one minute." He went up to the table and we heard him say to the dealer, "What game are you playing here?" The dealer said, "This is Texas Hold'em." So Paulo said in his Italian English accent, "I'm an Italian Prince and I do not know how to play this game." So as we're watching from outside the poker room, Paulo pulls out a $1000 in cash. He's still standing behind the empty seat. He said to the dealer, "Deal me in." Now the game they were playing was a '10 to 20 Limit Texas Hold'em', that means you can bet a $10 minimum and a $20 maximum. They dealt Paulo two cards, which obviously from where we were standing we couldn't see. All I know is that we kept on hearing Paulo saying, "Raise, raise." That's all we could hear. Apparently, before the 'flop' had come (the flop is the communal cards in the middle that you get at Hold'em), the betting had been capped. Now capped means when you are playing a 'limit game' you can't bet no more. Paulo raised, someone re-raised, Paulo re-raised and then the flop came. We couldn't see what cards had come in the middle, all we knew that Paulo had bet $20, one guy raised and another guy re-raised, Paulo re-raised, the betting was capped again. Paulo is still standing behind the empty chair! The turn came, which means the fourth card at Hold'em, Paulo bet, someone raised, another guy re-raised, Paulo re-raised, the betting was capped yet again. This pot was getting very big. The 'river card' came, which is the last at Hold'em. Paulo again bet, one guy raised, another guy re-raised, Paulo re-raised. The same thing happened all over again! Well Paulo's $1000 went in on the very first hand. All Paulo kept on saying throughout this hand was "I've never played this game before, someone help me, Liberace Liberace, help me!" We're all looking at him and wondering what he is doing and the next thing we know was that it was a 'showdown'. One guy showed two Kings, the other guy showed two Queens and then we couldn't believe it, Paulo showed two Aces and no one had improved on the 'flop', 'the turn' or 'the river'. Paulo scooped the pot that must have been over $3000 and as he scooped all the chips into his hands, he was putting them into his pockets as he was still standing behind the empty chair,he hadn't even sat down! He said to everyone, "Thank you very much for the lesson, I never knew how to play this game, now I know, I will be back later on." He left the poker table and he had shown a profit of $2000 within a few minutes! We couldn't believe our eyes. He then joined us and said, "Maxi, Stevie, you see Texas Hold'em is an easy game, I don't need to buy a book, Paulo, the Italian Prince knows how to play!

Towards the last couple of days, we were in Vegas, no one wanted to play poker because Dad had skinned everybody. He was the only winner, he'd relaxed, there was no time limit of 4 am, like there was in the casino. Now everybody wanted to play some dice. Now Maurice who wasn't with us, told us we must go down to Stupaks. A guy named Bob Stupak owned Stupaks casino. It was the most incredible casino ever. We were told that if you walked into Stupaks you could have any bet you liked to any limit but the small catch was your minimum bet could also be your maximum bet, so I'll give you an example. If you walked in and put $5000 on a number on the roulette wheel, the next spin you could have a $1 bet, but you were able to go up to $5000. We thought we had better go and see this casino. There was a terrible storm in Vegas that night and all the lights had gone out but we managed to get to Stupaks where there was some emergency lighting on so the lights of the casino were not all lit and it looked like that the whole casino was half in darkness and half lit by generators. We got down there and everybody wanted to play Dice. The other thing with the dice table at Stupaks casino was that the dice table had Crapless Craps. Now I won't go into this too much, so I wont confuse you, but it worked out that at Stupaks casino, whatever number you threw you couldn't lose on your first throw! This was unique to Vegas, everybody played Crapless Craps. Stupack was an unbelievable character and he made up his own games. He even had a game of blackjack, where the dealer used to show both his cards so you knew what you had to beat. Any of you blackjack players out there, you must think that this is quite incredible. Well that's right the dealers used to show both their cards! If the dealer was showing 17, you knew you had to beat 17. As any blackjack player knows, the dealer only shows one card but at Stupaks both were open. The small catch though, he used to only pay evens for blackjack instead of 6/4 and if it was a 'tie' with the dealer, you would lose. You still had a bit of an advantage but with 'ties' you lose and with the evens blackjack, Bob Stupak still made his percentage. We also found out on the dice table you were able to go ten times the odds. Again not going into too much mechanics of the game, ten times the odds was ten times better than you get in any London casino. Dice in Vegas is a very fair game to play. Overall the trip was very successful for my dad and I. We had such a good time, we stopped in Los Angeles on the way back for three nights and we went to Disneyland and Universal Studios.

We eventually got back to London and the games in the Barracuda casino were still continuing Wednesdays and Fridays. They were very big games and there was always a lot of action. We talked for maybe the next year about that trip in Vegas. We still never forgave Brian for not having a film in the camera. I thought Italian Paulo was going to kill him but eventually we got over it. One night, in walked Brian from Southampton, he sat down and he said to Micky Fitz, "Have you got $50 on you?" So Micky Fitz said, "What?" He said, "Have you got $50 on you? It works out to be about £32." Now here's all the poker players all sitting down and there must have been about fifty grand on the table and Brian from Southampton sits down with about £5000 and he wants £32 from Micky Fitz! Micky Fitz looks and him and said, "Brian what are you on about, what do you need £32 for?" He said, "You owe the hotel in Las Vegas £32." Micky Fitz said, "What for?" So Brian said, "As you know, everything is comp except for your hotel telephone and apparently you had a 45 or 50 minute conversation with someone in London and it came to about $50 and I paid it for you, so could you please give me my $50 or my £32 please!" Micky Fitz said, "Are you serious?" So Brian said, "100% serious, can I have my money please?" "Yes!" Micky Fitz said, "I will give you your money after the poker game, not a problem" Apparently as I said to you, Micky Fitz had listened to the football for the 45 minutes and he didn't think of paying his telephone bill. The telephone bills in Vegas are never Comp!

So Brian had to pay, but as soon as Brian got back to London, he wanted his bloody £32 back!

I'm now going to tell you the biggest poker game that ever took place on a coach, that's right, a coach and it was going down to Ascot Races one day. We got to the Barracuda casino in the morning and they had laid on a luxury coach to take us to Ascot Races. Dad was with a few of his friends and they started playing poker on the way down to Ascot. Well by the time they got to Ascot within just under two hours, Dad was losing eight and a half grand on the coach! Once they got to Ascot, guess what? No one wanted to get off the coach and watch the racing! They wanted to stay and carry on playing, well they did. They stayed on the coach playing poker and after racing the coach took them all the way back to the Barracuda casino and my dad just about managed to claw his money back and finish levels on the game!

About a couple of months later, I was asleep one night and the phone rang. It was about two o'clock in the morning. On the other end of the line was Johnny K. Now if you remember Johnny K, he was the non-gambler. Johnny said to me, "Stevie! I'm in Jacqueline's Nightclub, you'd better come down!" So I said straight away, "Why, is there poker?" He said, "No! Mike Tyson is on the dance floor and is dancing by himself." I said, "What are you talking about?" He repeated, "Mike Tyson is on the dance floor and he's dancing on the dance floor by himself!" I said, "Johnny, I hope you're not winding me up." He said, "Stevie, I wouldn't do that to you." I got dressed and I rushed down to Jacqueline's Nightclub, which was in Wardour Street in the West End and sure enough Mike Tyson was still on the dance floor dancing! He then sat down with Jacqueline, who was the owner of the nightclub and opened some champagne. Now as Johnny and I knew Jacqueline, we joined them and in walked Reggie. The four of us sat down and had a glass of champagne and I said to him "Mike you won't remember me but I came to Vegas to watch you fight Bonecrusher Smith and we were the English crowd at the airport." He then stopped me and said, "You were the British crowd who saw me at the airport and took some photos." I said, "That's correct Mike, but the man who took the photographs never put a film in the camera." Mike said to me, "Well I'm in town for the next three nights because I'm here making a video on the greatest ever heavyweights at the Grosvenor Hotel with Harry Carpenter, you can get a photograph of me tomorrow night, because I'm going to come to Jacqueline's every night." The next night he did go to Jacqueline's. He walked in completely by himself, a lot of people had cameras and we took a load of photographs with Mike Tyson. Reggie became very friendly with Mike, Reggie and myself took Mike out for two nights and we took him to Stringfellows Nightclub and Fidenzies all night drinking bar and we had a terrific time. One night Reggie never had a car to take Mike out and they borrowed my Mercedes Sports. I went with them and sat in the back. Mike was in the passenger seat and Reggie was driving the car. When Reggie went to put petrol in and I was talking to Mike about boxing, he accidentally broke my telephone that was in the car at the time. It wasn't really broken completely it was just bent. I tell you that because when Mike went to prison, Reggie went to visit him and Mike said to him, "How's all your friends from London?" and Reggie said, "Who?" Mike said, "The guy that I broke his telephone at the petrol station!" (something Reggie didn't know). Reggie said, "We're all doing fine Mike." He said to Reggie, "London was the only place that I really enjoyed, because no one took anything off me and you all treated me well." That always stuck in his mind. Mike Tyson, I feel, was one of the nicest, kindest people you could ever meet. The events that happened to Mike in his life, I always believe, are circumstantial with Cus D'Amato, his father figure and Jim Jacobs both dying quite close to each other, I believe that it threw Mike off track and as Kevin Rooney once said, "Mike Tyson could have been the greatest heavyweight that ever lived, and the only person that can beat Mike Tyson is Mike Tyson!"

I'm now going to tell you about one of the quickest poker games I've ever been in. We went down to Jacqueline's Nightclub one night. Reggie and I were there and in walked a guy named Dave. We called him 'Dave School Dinners' because he had the school dinner's restaurant that was on Baker Street. We started talking about poker and Dave said, "I'll play any man poker, any time." Now this was a challenge that no one could refuse. I said, "Dave, I'll play you now." Reggie also said, "I'll play you too Dave." So Dave said, "Let me see the colour of your money." So we said, "Let's see the colour of yours." Dave took out a wad of £20 notes; there must have been £2000. I took out all of my money, which must have been between £600–700. Reggie took out about £300. We then went to the office of Jacqueline's Nightclub. We got the cards. Now I never forget this. Reggie shuffled and I cut. Dave never touched the cards. Dave was dealt a 7, I was dealt a King and Reggie was dealt a Queen. I was to open and I opened for £10. Reggie called the £10 with a Queen showing and Dave called the £10 and raised £40 with a 7. I looked at my hole card and I had Kings back to back. I called the £40 and raised £120. Reggie thought for a second. He called the £160 and re-raised the pot. Dave then re-raised and I re raised. All of the money that we had in our pockets went in on the very, very first hand of the night. We all turned over our cards. I had Kings, Reggie had Queens and Dave had 7s. Don't forget there were still three cards to come! Well you'll never guess what happened? Dave hit a 7 on the last card and made 3 7s! This poker game was now over! Reggie and I wanted to continue but Dave wanted to see the money, we had no more money on us. Dave had skinned us up within one hand of poker, which lasted 30 seconds. Probably the most money I've ever lost per minute.

In 1987 Dad and I took a trip to Malta. We went there for a poker competition and there was a lot of Five Card Stud action. The very first night we got to Malta, the night before the tournament started, Dad played a little roulette and Dad won some money. The guy that was running the tournament for the casino looked absolutely choked that Dad had won a couple of thousand pounds on the roulette. We later found out that he had a share in the casino on that week! The Five Card Stud was quite good and there were some quite strong players there. There was a new breed of players coming through. One of the guys was named Mansour. He managed to win the 1991 World Poker Series. Now he was quite a Five Card Stud player, a good and strong one. There was another guy called Derrick, he also now lives in Vegas, he was a very tight but also very strong poker player. Every night there were games.

In the tournament Mansour and my dad had a £5000 'match' bet on who would last longest, which meant whoever got knocked out first would have to pay the other one £5000. Well guess what? They ended up on the same table towards the end of the competition, they then got involved in a 'three-way pot' where one guy raised, Mansour re-raised and Dad went all in! Both called and the third person won the pot, knocking out both my dad and Mansour at the same time! It was only 15 minutes later when they were talking to each other after, they remembered and realised it would have been more profitable and better value if either one of them would have passed!

This was the first of two trips to Malta and they were quite profitable for us. I'm glad there was poker in Malta, because there is not a lot else you can do! I bumped into some friends there. They were from Kent, Margate, and they told me that they had arranged a private game in a flat with a Maltese guy. So we went off from the casino to play in this flat, while Dad was playing poker at the casino. The guy's name from Margate was Linton. Not a bad little poker player but he, I had heard, had run out of money. So he decided to pawn his Gucci watch, which he ended up getting about 120 Maltese pounds. He then went off to play these Maltese boys at poker. Well that night Linton couldn't do anything wrong. He was winning so much money on the poker table, he decided to stay in Malta and play this guy Heads Up poker for the next week! There were four of us playing that night and he skinned everybody except for me. I finished dead even! I was very happy because I could see Linton was on a 'run.' He could do no wrong and I was saying to him while we were playing, "Linton, I'm keeping out of your way tonight!" I think sometimes this is a capability of a good poker player to see when another poker player is on 'fire' and when you see someone is on great form stay out of their way.

The beginning of 1988 saw me with a very close friend of mine, his name was Luke, go round the world. In fact, it was Luke who suggested that he wanted to go to Australia. I went to a travel agent and they said, "Where do you want to stop over?" So I said, "I don't really, I just want to go straight to Australia." They said, "Well you're better off stopping a couple of nights, you can stop anywhere you like, we've got a new ticket out, it's £800 and you can stop off anywhere you like for 6 months," so I arranged the trip, London/Los Angeles/Hawaii/Fiji/Australia/Sydney/Melbourne/Adelaide and back the other side Hong Kong/Bombay and home. It was an around the world trip, one-way ticket. Australia is an absolutely fantastic place. We got to Adelaide. Luke, my friend had some relations there. I had some relations in Sydney but what we heard was that in Adelaide they had a very big casino, in fact it was the biggest in Australia at the time. We heard they had a card room. I said to Luke, "I wonder if they play poker?" I trotted up to the card room and it was quite busy. I went up to the floor manager and I said to him. "Any poker?" He said, "Yes, this is a poker room." I said, "Yeah! But any Five Card Stud?" He said, "Yeah! Those two tables over there." I said, "OK, but any Five Card Stud Strip Deck?" He said, "Yes, those two tables over there." I said to him, "Any Five Card Stud Strip Deck Pot Limit." He looked at me rather annoyed and said, "Yes! Over there." As I walked off, I said "Any spare seats?" He said, "Well go and have a look." I got to the table and it looked like a good action game. It was a full table of eight players. I said, "Any spare seats?" Everybody ignored me. I said, "Excuse me, any spare seats please?" They said, "The table is full." I said, "That's a shame, I'm a first time poker player from London, England and I've got about $5000, I just fancied playing Five Card Stud." Well their faces were a picture. One winked at the other and said, "You can have my seat. The other one said, "No you can have my seat." All of a sudden there were two available seats. I sat down and it turned out to be a very good game indeed. Now there were two Greek Cypriots on the table and what I noticed is that they were talking to each other sometimes in Greek. What they didn't know was that I could understand and after 25 minutes of me playing I heard one say to the other, "This boy can play, he's played before what's he messing us about for?" So I looked up at him and replied in Greek, "I was born playing, Five Card Stud is the game I know." Luke was downstairs and he was playing roulette and dice and when he came upstairs, I was winning a couple of thousand dollars. We didn't intend to stay too late. I got up and I said, "Gents! Thank you very much for the lesson, I'll be back." Luke and I left and we took a cab home. In the morning, we woke up for breakfast and Luke was a bit peeved off because he had lost his sunglasses and he was trying to think where he had left them. Well he tracked back that he must have left them in the minicab on the way to the casino. So I said, "Not a problem lets go down town and buy some more. We passed a couple of sunglasses shops but then all of a sudden there was this sunglass stall with a guy standing there shouting out, "Anybody for sunglasses! Anybody for sunglasses?" So we stopped and he said, "Yes chaps, can I sell you some sunglasses?" in an English accent. We said, "Where are you from?" He said, "London." I said, "London, what are you doing over here?" He said, "My Dad came over here about ten years ago to retire and I came over and followed him." So anyway, chitchat, we buy some sunglasses. He said to us as we were leaving where are you from?" I said, "Well obviously London, North London." He said, "Whereabouts?" I said, "Well all over North, Haringey, born in Muswell Hill." He said, "What do you do?" I said, "Well I work with the old man, he's a bookmaker." He said, "That's funny, my dad's a bookmaker, right up until ten years ago." I said, "Yeah! What's your Dad's name?" He said, "Charlie Baker." I was dumbfounded. Charlie Baker had known my dad for 35 years. I said, "Charlie Baker? Well he knows my dad very well." He said, "Who's your Dad?" I said, "Max the Bookie." Anyway, he said, "I'll tell you what, we won't tell him but we're all going into the casino tonight, meet us at the bar at eight o'clock." Sure enough Luke and me walked up to the bar and Charlie was sitting there. We had a drink, a great dinner that night and we reminisced over the old times. There's another one that could have written a book!

We left Australia and on the way back we decided to stop in Hong Kong. Now if any of you have been to Hong Kong it is one crazy place. I think the only way I can possibly explain it is if you get to China Town in any city, you're probably the nearest you can get to Hong Kong. I mean we're walking down a street, there's about 40 Chinese people, all in a circle, all talking Chinese, looking up this building, looking down at the pavement, we didn't know what was going on. I got close to the crowd and I said, "What's happened?" They said, "Man, man, jumped from building, jump from building," in a Chinese accent. Well I tell you what, that was only one of the incidents that happened over there. A little bit crazy in Hong Kong, I can tell you. We heard that there were five or six casinos off Hong Kong Island, on the Island of Macau. The only way we could get there was to take a ferry from Hong Kong to Macau. We took the ferry one night, it was about eight o'clock in the evening. It was about a 40-minute journey. We had to take our passports with us. Passports had to be stamped because we were leaving Hong Kong and when we got to Macau I said to Luke, "Let's make it our mission, that we go to every single casino tonight." We went to all five of them. We had a lovely Chinese meal. We ordered a whole duck. The duck came out and when they put it on the table, Luke and I looked at each other, because it didn't look like the whole duck. We ate it and didn't say anything. I called the waiter back and said, "I'm going to be very honest with you, I thought we ordered a whole duck and it didn't look like the whole duck there." He turned round and said, "No! Over here we serve the fat off the duck first and then we serve the meat." So Luke and I had just eaten the whole fat off the duck! We looked at each other and it looked like we were going to be sick, then they served the meat! Well I don't think we had any appetite after all of the fat!

Well anyway, I want to tell you about this game that we gambled on when we went to Macau; it was in one of the casinos. I think it was the most exciting game I've ever, ever gambled on. It was a roulette wheel, maybe two and half times bigger than a standard roulette wheel. There were 24 numbers on this roulette wheel and every number was in a shallow groove and the grooves were about 3 inches by 3 inches. The roulette ball that the Croupier span round was the size of a tennis ball and it was made out of solid ivory. Now when the ball went round, it went round a lot slower than a normal ball and when it landed in number, it didn't land in one number particularly, it used to hover over all the numbers, go in all of the numbers and then eventually after you had a heart attack, it would stop and settle in one number. Each spin probably took about a minute. I said to Luke, "This is one of the most exciting games, I've ever seen." The odds were 22/1 and there were 24 numbers on the roulette wheel plus a zero. I think they told me the game was called Boule, but I'm not too sure. Well Luke and I changed a couple of hundred dollars each, it was $14 Hong Kong to a pound. I said to Luke, "Let's put $50 on number 24." The first spin they span, the ball went round and it landed and it started going all over these shallow grooves, going over each number in turn. You're swaying one way, then swaying another because it goes over your number two or three times before it starts to settle. Anyway, as luck would have it, it landed straight in number 24. But I'll tell you, you could have a heart attack playing that game! Luke and I lived like kings in Hong Kong. We were giving $50 tips, which is about £3, to the Bell Captain every time we wanted a taxi. They thought we were the most generous people in town. We must have given out about $500 in tips every single day, which was £35. Well I tell you they knew us well at the Lee Gardens Hotel and I think they thought we were a couple of rich kids from London.

When me and Luke decided to get ready and come back to London we had to pack our bags, but the problem we had was that we bought so many clothes and presents on our trip around the world, our bags were getting heavier and heavier. I ran into Luke's room and said to him, "Luke we're going to have a problem, we haven't time to buy new suitcases, I can't close my suitcase." He then said to me, "Well I'm in the same boat, have a look at my suitcase over there." I then looked over and I saw Luke's suitcase filled to the top. Luke came to my room and we tried and tried to close my suitcase, after about 25 minutes we eventually got it closed and we got it locked up. The only thing was, it was so heavy, it was really difficult to lift. I then went to Luke's room and we did the same again. Luke said to me, "Steve there is no way they are going to check us in at the airport with the weight of these two suitcases." I said, "Luke, lets worry about that when we get to the airport." We got the bellboy from the Lee Gardens Hotel and he just about managed to put them onto his trolley cart and he even said, "Suitcases very heavy, suitcases very heavy." We eventually got the suitcases into the taxi to take us to the airport. I think the limit was 30 kilos or 65 lbs but I'm telling you something these must have weighed 80 kilos each! Luke said to me in the taxi, "Steve, I bet you £50 they will not take these suitcases at the check-in desk." I said, "Luke, I will bet you £50, but I won't bet on your suitcase, I'll bet that my suitcase is checked in." He said, "Why? Your suitcase is probably heavier than mine." I said, "I'm telling you they will take my suitcase at the check-in desk, but they won't take yours. I'll tell you what we'll do, I'll bet you £50 they don't take yours and you can bet me £50 that they don't take mine and if they don't take both we're even but if they take mine and they don't take yours you owe me £100." He said, "Let me get this straight, you're saying that they will take your suitcase, but they won't take mine? So if they don't take yours Steve but they take mine you owe me £100." I said, "Correct." We got to the airport and we went up to the check-in desk. The only mistake that I made on this bet was I went up first. Now I had to lift my suitcase onto the weighing machine without any difficulty, if she saw I couldn't lift it I knew I had problems. I thought the worst way is she is not going to take my suitcase, she isn't going to take Luke's and we were going to be even, I had a plan to try and chat to the young lady behind the desk to try to distract her so I was rambling on about our trip and where we had been. I lugged my suitcase onto the weighing machine and the weight started to settle and I could see it weighed a huge amount over ! I took a little bit of the suitcase off the edge of the weighing machine but it was no use, it didn't go down much. I then proceeded with Plan C. I stuck my foot under the edge of the suitcase that was protruding out from the edge of the weighing machine and I started to lift the suitcase up with my foot, by which time Luke couldn't keep a straight face. Now this worked well as it brought my suitcase down, so I was only 3 or 4 kilos over the weight limit. The problem I faced was keeping my leg supporting that kind of weight and the digital scale of the machine started fluctuating I couldn't keep still! I tried to keep the young lady talking and she said to me, "You're in seat C row 34, but you are little bit overweight." I said, "Well you know, I thought you do allow a couple of kilos extra to go through." She said, "No problem." Boom! The suitcase went off onto the conveyor belt and I was through. Luke's face was a picture. It's £50 I had just won. I looked at him and said "Over to you Luke." So Luke walked up to the young lady & put on all his charm. With huge smile on his face Luke lugged his suitcase onto the weighing machine, he had seen what I'd done and he did exactly the same. He put three quarters of the case on and he kept his left leg under the suitcase to take the weight off, all the while he was leaning on the desk smiling waiting for the young lady to check him in, but Luke was going redder and redder and he was trying to keep a straight face because the weight of his suitcase was killing his legs. He'd brought his suitcase down though. She then said to him, you're suitcase is overweight, oh! No you're not, oh! Yes you are," (because of the movement of the scales she could not see that Luke had his foot also under his suitcase.) He explained to her that we'd been around the world and we'd done some shopping. He said, "I'm only 5 or 6 kilos overweight, please don't let me pay any extra or buy a new suitcase to put some clothes in." She then pressed the conveyor belt and Luke's case was passed and checked in. Luke looked at me and said, "Yes!" I said, "Luke I made a big mistake, I should have let you go first and me go second and then you would have owed me £100." Luke said to me, "I let you go on purpose Steve because I know that when you have a bet, 99% of the time you always win and I wanted to see how you were going to get away with this." Luke and I turned around from the desk and we limped off. Our legs were killing us!

I've always said to everybody, the best education is travelling around the world. Luke and I came back after eight weeks and we certainly had an unbelievable time with some eye-opening experiences. Travelling is the best education and the university of the streets.

Once we got back to London it was back to work. The games were going quite strong at the Barracuda casino. One night at about 10 to 4, the game was so big at the Barracuda that Italian Paulo said, "Let's all go back to my place." We all went back to Paulo's place and the game continued to seven-thirty or eight o'clock in the morning. What Dad and I didn't remember was that we had to be in court in Margate by 9.30 am (80 miles away) as one of our Betting Shops was applying for a Licence. Well, I drove down and I can honestly say it was the most tiring journey I've ever had. In fact, Dad and I kept falling asleep once we got to Margate. We had to ring my brother-in-law Paul and he had to come down by train to Margate and drive us back!

Around 1989, Reggie, whom I've mentioned before, had an all-night restaurant, it was called Rocky's. Now it was a little bit quiet at first but Reggie was always thinking of ideas of how to get people in. Well, the idea he had next, no one would have ever thought up. Reggie bought a Double Decker bus! That's right, a Double Decker bus for £600! He spent £800 spraying it pink, that's right pink! He then painted 'Rocky's Restaurant' on it. He then drove it all around London, stopping at bus stops and he told everybody that if they got on board, it would be half price dinner and drinks at Rocky's Restaurant. One night he set off with me, Johnny K and three or four of our friends. We were on this Double Decker bus going around London and stopping at bus stops! Eventually, we got back to Rocky's Restaurant and about 75 tourists got off the Double Decker bus, and a lot of them did not understand what was going on, but we managed to get about 30 of them into the restaurant! Well Rocky's was really kicking that night. Reggie used to run poker games in Rocky's and we used to play maybe once a week on a Saturday night. There was a guy named 'Gary Bananas', Simon, CJ, me, Reggie, and a couple of others, and every Saturday night we used to have a good game. Many times, I ended up 'Heads Up' with Gary, now Gary was a fearless gambler, a true gentleman. Well, I can only say that CJ to this day will never ever play poker with me. Gary won't and Reggie, I've still got a few stories to tell about Reggie later on when we played 'Heads Up'! The games lasted about four months, again there was only one winner. Reggie had that bus for about three months. He was parking it everywhere in the West End, on double yellow lines and they couldn't tow it away! They couldn't clamp it and they couldn't do anything! Well anyway, New Burlington Police Station used to be down the road from Reggie and I think he was getting a bit of grief from the 'Old Bill' and Reggie got rid of it. So what did he do? Reggie got rid of his Double Decker Bus and went and brought a fire engine! Yes! A red fire engine. He picked up Johnny K, all the boys and me and there we were going down Kings Road in a Fire Engine. Every 20 minutes he's sounding the horn all the way down Kings Road! We hit a traffic jam, Reggie put the siren on, all the traffic cleared for us. Well the fire engine lasted three weeks. I think he got into a bit of trouble over that, so he sold the fire engine and he brought an ambulance! That's right he brought an ambulance and he was driving the ambulance around for two weeks. Well what I didn't know was that legally you could buy a Double Decker bus and drive it. You can buy a fire engine as long as it doesn't say 'fire engine' on it or the company it comes from and you can also buy an ambulance as long as it doesn't say 'ambulance' on it. Well that just goes to show you what kind of character Reggie is!

Reggie and I decided to go on one of those disco cruises on the Thames. It was a pal of ours that was running it. We thought we'd go along, have a good time, get back and we'll go back to Reggie's for a bit of breakfast as he was still running Rocky's in New Burlington Street. We got on the boat, which took off from the Thames at about 7 pm. As we were cruising, we found out that it didn't arrive back until about 5 am in the morning. We suddenly remembered Mike Tyson was fighting Tony Tubbs in Japan at about 2 am. I said, "Reggie! I didn't know that this boat doesn't get back until five o'clock in the morning." He said, "No! Nor did I." I said, "What are we going to do, we are going to miss the fight?" We went to the Captain, who was driving the boat, Reggie said to the Captain, "Can I get off?" He looked at us in amazement. He said, "Excuse me?" Reggie said, "We've got to get off! I've got a very important meeting at about one o'clock in the morning. We didn't realise that you didn't get back until five o'clock, I wanna get off!" The Captain said, "I can't get you off." Reggie said, "You can." Reggie pulls out a £50 note and gives it to the Captain of the boat. The Captain grabbed the £50, put it in his pocket and pulled over somewhere in the Docklands! We didn't even know where we were. The cruise boat had stopped to let Reggie and I off in this derelict place, somewhere down in the Docks! Reggie and I jumped off the boat and we ran to the nearest minicab office that must have been about a mile away, jumped in a minicab and went straight back to Rocky's Restaurant, arriving just in time for the fight that night.

That year, I went to Cyprus for Easter, a friend of mine had a bar out there, which was called the Tycoon Bar and every night they used to play backgammon for money. I wasn't a great backgammon player but I picked up the dice one night. There were three or four guys there, I shook them and I said to the guys who were playing backgammon. "I bet you £5 I throw a 1 or a 2." They said, "What?" I said, "I bet you £5, I throw a 1 or a 2." They said, "Go on then." The dice landed 6-5. I paid them £5. I said, "I bet you £5 again that I throw a 1 or a 2." They said, "Your mad! A 1 or a 2?" I said, "That's right." I threw the dice 5-4. They said, "We'll take that bet all night long." I was throwing the dice for four and half hours, betting them £5 and £10 that I would throw a 1 or a 2. Well I can only tell you that every single person lost their money in the bar to me, because the true odds of throwing a 1 or a 2 or any 2 numbers on 2 dice at the same time is 4/5. That's right it's 4/5 favourite to throw it.

Also that year was the start of me and a guy nicknamed 'Horse'. We used to have a £1000 bet every season and we still do to this day. He picks Chelsea, to finish higher in the division, as he is a Chelsea supporter and I pick Spurs. Well after two or three seasons, I lost my money to him because Spurs used to finish lower than Chelsea and I said to him, "I don't want to bet anymore Horse, because Chelsea will always finish higher than Spurs." He allowed me to change my team and for the last nine years, I changed it to Manchester United! Two years ago I changed it to Arsenal, and last year I changed it to Liverpool. So Horse, all in all, has won three years and I have won about ten. Horse is a good sport and we always have our football bet, every single year without fail.

Around 1989, I was 'working out' in a Health Club called Winners, in Southgate. After training one night, I went up to the bar and in walked a guy named Andy. Andy was a guy I knew from 1977–78, who is actually Tank's second cousin. I said, "Andy, what are you doing here? I thought you lived in Cyprus?" He said, "I've come over here for a holiday and I've come to relax, let's meet up tomorrow." I said, "Andy, tomorrow I'm going to Plymouth." His words were, "Where's Plymouth?" I said, "Plymouth is down by Torquay, Cornwall way." He said, "Never heard of it, never been there." So I said, "Look, I'm going for four days, why don't you come with me?" Andy said, "Great, but I haven't got a lot of money." I replied, "Andy you're with me, you're my guest you don't need any money."

We drove down to Plymouth and we decided to eat in Platters Restaurant. (It was and still is owned by one of Dad's very good friends Rocky.) He's got a lovely fish shop. Now a young lady served us and Andy started talking to her and he had arranged to meet her that night at a Wine Bar. Well he met her and they got on really well. The next couple of nights he was seeing her, but I was playing poker. One night I learnt a very expensive lesson. I'd got up to the casino and there was a good game of poker on, but the problem was, it was eight handed, there was no seat for me. I looked around and no one wanted to give up their seat. The action was that good. I said, "Does anyone want to let me sit down." Everybody declined. I said, "In a loud voice, if anybody lets me sit down, I'll give them £20 for their chair?" A guy looked up and he said, "I'll tell you what Steve, you give me £50 for this chair and you can have it, because it's been useless all night, I'm doing my money and I wanna go to the roulette and have a gamble" I said, "You're on." I gave him £50 to sit down for the last hour and a half, until four o'clock in the morning. I lost £700 that night and that taught me a lesson. Never buy a chair at the poker table, especially from someone who was sitting in it who was doing his money all night long, and what's more important never be eager to gamble! There were some tremendous games in Plymouth around that time and Andy was 50–50 with me. Well after the four nights, we came back with £7000-8000 each and Andy was so happy. He was also so happy that he had met this girl. As we drove back into London, he said, "Stevie! Take me to Paddington Station." I said, "What are you talking about Andy?" He said, "Look we've gone to Plymouth, I never knew where Plymouth was, we went into a restaurant, and I met a girl, we won money on poker, take me to Paddington Station!" Well, I took him to Paddington Station and he went straight back to Plymouth and has never come back! He married that girl he was seeing and they've had three children, (twin girls and another girl). I'm not too sure, whether it was happily ever after though. That's the only thing. The money he won with me at the poker, he invested it in a small share in a restaurant. After a year he brought his partners out. He then opened his own nightclub, and is doing extremely well. It was he who reminded me that it was the poker money that I won that started him off.

1989 also saw my dad getting a pitch at Ramsgate Dogs and having it for about two or three years. Well to cut that long story short, Dad every year used to have a big Derby night and in the three years that we were at Ramsgate, I think we lost enough money to buy the track! There wasn't a lot of money at Ramsgate and obviously when Dad used to go down, being the fearless gambler he was, he used to stand up and take all bets because they knew Max was in town, anybody could get any bet on they wanted. Well, I'll tell you this because this will make you laugh. All bookmakers, no matter who they are when they stand up to make a book, whether it be a dog or a horse race meeting, what do they usually have in their hand? Well, I'll tell you, they always have a piece of chalk. They always have a piece of chalk to change the prices on the board, no not my dad! He had no chalk in his hand. The guy that used to stand up for us on any other night was Keith, our manager. Keith is running around looking for a piece of chalk! He said to me, "I've got to get your Dad some chalk because he doesn't change the prices! He's laying anything they want, we're going to do 'our brains' [a lot of money] tonight. We've got to change the prices!" There's Keith running around looking for a piece of chalk, which eventually he found, he went up to my dad and said, "Here Max, have this chalk." Dad looked at him inquisitively and said.... "Keith what do I need chalk for? We're here to lay them, let's lay them!" Well we didn't finish in front on Ramsgate dogs so that just goes back to what I was saying at the beginning of the book, dogs are not lucky for my dad because we opened a pitch at Oxford and Canterbury dogs and Dad has never made any money from greyhound racing, ever!

We were down Margate for the bank holiday Monday and I went down on Saturday with all the family. There was a game of poker that night in Ramsgate casino and we'd got a phone call in the casino that Johnny K was with a friend and his name was John Michael, they were on the Motorway and were coming down to Margate, of all places. They were going to spend a couple of nights there. Well, they came down to Margate and they played poker. They only caught the last half an hour of the game, so we all arranged to meet the next day at Andy Florides Fish Shop to continue the game. We had our breakfast there at about 11 am and at about 2 pm, we started to play. Andy Florides brought a couple of people that owned some coffee shops in Ramsgate and it was a five-handed game. Everybody lost that night, except for me and Andy Florides. I didn't win a lot, a couple of grand but Andy Florides that night skint the table and just to let you know how much he won, the next day, he went out and brought an XJS. It seems like whenever anybody wins at poker they end up going to buy a Jaguar!

I want to tell you this little story. I woke up on a Saturday morning and I rang my brother straight away in the office and I said, "Mick! I've had a dream." He said, "Oh yeah?" I said, "Yeah! Listen to this. I've dreamt that Manchester City won 2-0, Arsenal drew 1-1, Everton won 2-0, Aston Villa won 3-1 and Norwich won 4-1." He said, "Well, I tell you what Steve, it's not much of a dream because Arsenal's match was postponed this morning and Norwich's match, Steve, is tomorrow on Sunday." I said, "Oh! I don't know Mick, why don't you just do a Super Yankee and put it just as I dreamt it." He said, "OK, I'll have a Correct Score Super Yankee, I'll run to William Hill, next door." When I got in the office at about 4.45 pm as the results came through, sure enough Manchester City had won 2-0, Everton had won 2-0 and Aston Villa had won 3-1 but Arsenal was a non-runner. Now this bet looked like it was going to break the limit. We had Norwich now to beat Spurs 4-1 on the next day. Spurs were at White Hart Lane. If Norwich beat Spurs 4-1, my brother gets a quarter of a million and I get a quarter of a million pounds. The bet already had come to about £8000-10,000 each. Well to cut a long story short, to get you out of your misery, Spurs won 4-1 that day, can you believe it? We had Norwich to win 4-1, but Spurs won 4- 1! The bet still came to money but it could have been massive. Mick and I still talk about that dream to this day.

I used to go very regularly to a nightclub in the West End, it was a very popular club at the time and it was the leading London disco. It used to close about 3.30 am. One night when I was leaving the club, as I was walking past the restaurant upstairs, the famous nightclub owner was sitting at the table by himself. I went up to him and said to him, "Peter I hear you play poker?" Now him knowing me only from the nightclub didn't know that I play. He said, "Yeah! I play poker, why do you want to play with me?" I said, "Yeah! I'll give you a little game." He looked at me and said, "Little game, I'll sit down here and I'll put £10000 down and you've got to match it." I said, "Well I haven't got £10000 in cash with me." He said, "Well you'd better go and get it then and be back in 20 minutes." I said, "OK! Give me half an hour." I was with a close friend at the time and I didn't have my car, his name was Kikis and he said to me, "Do you want a lift home Steve?" I said, "No! I want to go the casino, I want to draw £10,000, I'm going back to play." He said, "Your kidding aren't you?" I said, "I'm not kidding." I wasn't back at the nightclub in half an hour; I was back in the nightclub in 25 minutes. I walked straight into the nightclub and there was the owner still sitting at the round table. As I walked in he got up and shook my hand. He said, "I'm going to be honest with you, I didn't think you were going to come back." So I said, "Well I'm back and here's my £10,000 let's play poker!" We started playing at about 4.30 am in the morning and I'll be very honest with you he was a tough cookie to crack. He was such a gambler, it was going one way, then the other. He was winning a couple of grand; I was winning a couple of grand. At about 6.30 am, I might have been about £1000 up. Peter was a tremendous gambler. We called a time limit of 7.30 am. At about 7.15 am, I was winning about £1200. And then came the 'big pot'. Now the thing is about poker and I'll tell you this, as my dad said, "It's all about one pot." My Dad can lose 60 pots in an evening, but it's about winning that 'one' pot. In a way I'm very similar, I might not lose 60 pots in one evening, I'm quite careful what I enter in to, but I'm usually looking for that one or two big pots. Anyone will tell you that who plays with me. Well, this pot came at 7.20 in the morning. I opened for £100 with an Ace showing. I hadn't looked at my hole card because I had to open. The nightclub owner had a 7 showing and he called straight away, which was like him. The cards came out, King to me, Ace, King showing, 9 to him 7, 9 showing. I immediately bet the pot £200, he called. The next card came out, Queen to me, Ace, King, Queen and 8 to the club owner showing 7, 9, 8. I bet the full pot without hesitation £600. He thought for a second and decided to call the £600. It was a little bit difficult to put him on a hand, knowing Peter he could have absolutely anything! Don't forget now that I hadn't looked at my hole card. This is what you call 'power play' at Heads Up poker, it often works. The top cards usually speak so they come out betting heavy to try and bully out the little cards. Well, I was trying to bully the wrong person that night! The last card came out, 10 to me. Now I had showing Ace, King, Queen, 10 and a 7 to Peter, showing 7, 9, 8, 7, he had a pair of 7s showing. It was him to bet and there was £1800 in the middle. He thought for a second, he picked up all his money, he looked at me to see if there was a reaction, but there was no reaction because I didn't even know what I had and that's the truth, (but he didn't know this) I could have had anything! He thought for about 30 seconds and he said, "I'm going to check to you Steve, because you've got a possible straight there." I then decided to look at my hole card, which obviously was a wise thing to do. I looked at my hole card and it was… Ah! Ah! Well, I'm not going to tell you just yet because the pot gets interesting. I now have seen my hole card and I'm going to keep you guessing. I said to the dealer who was the nightclub bouncer who had stayed behind, "How much is in the pot?" He said "£1800." I said, "I bet £300." Peter the nightclub owner looked at me and said, "You've got the Aces, You've got the Aces! I call the £300 and raise £2400, the full pot." I looked at him and paused for one second, I said, "I call the £2400 and I raise £7200, the rest of my money." He looked at me and said, "You little bugger, you've got a straight… or have you got the Aces? Have you got a straight or have you got the Aces?" He kept on repeating the same thing. Now at Heads Up poker, I suppose anything really goes. What I do is that I always keep my eyes firmly fixed on the pot and I don't move. I now knew what I had. He started to count his money. He said to the dealer, "I call the £6800 I've got left and I've got 3 7s!" I turned over my hole card and there it was… a Jack! I had hit the straight. By betting the full pot all the way along, I had hit the straight. The game was over in one pot. It was a £2000 pot! He stood up and said to me, "Well played, you played that pot very well, by you betting £300 at the end, I thought you had a pair and silly me when I had 3 7s, I decided to raise." That was the end of the game that night and I suppose the moral of the story is, as I said, "It all hinged on one pot." If I didn't hit the straight and he checks, I would have checked along with him. So, I would have lost the minimum. If he would have bet the full pot and I had a pair, I would have called him because he was an out and out gambler! Many times at poker and this is a very important lesson you are not playing the cards, you're playing the player and as any Hold'em or Omaha player, or at any poker game, all poker players know, they are playing the player and not the cards. The difficulty comes in is sometimes when you sit down in a new school and you don't know the players, then you've got to play your cards, not theirs, until you get the feel of how everybody is playing and as any top poker player will tell you, within an hour, you get to know who does what and when. This is the fine art of being a winner and an excellent player, or being an average one.

Around this time, 1989 Johnny Kay the non-gambler decided to rent the Empress Club off my dad in Haringey and decided to put a couple of pool tables in there. He asked me if I wanted to do poker a couple of times a week, to which I replied, "Great John, I'll do the poker." He said, "Stevie! You can do the poker, I'm going to watch." All credit to him, we did start the games and he decided not to play poker with us as he realised it wasn't his game. I think he found some other games and you'll hear about them later in the book.

The games were going full flow at the Barracuda casino. You really needed about £10,000 to sit down. I mean it was £100 openers! Well, do you know when they say, "I want to go and spend a penny?" Do you know what that means? That's right, it means; you want to go to the toilet. Everyone says that phrase, "I'm just going to spend a penny." Well my dad went to go and spend a penny while playing poker one night at the Barracuda casino. I'm sitting behind him as usual and it's a very big game. Italian Paulo was there, Micky F, Eric Dee and a few others. Dad was winning about £20,000–£25,000 that night. After a couple of hours he looked round at me and said, "I'm just popping to the toilet, play my cards!" I said, "No problem Dad." As he got up, the dealer was shuffling and he started to deal the cards and I sat down in Dad's seat to play one or two hands while Dad popped to the toilet. Eric Dee was a £100 blind. This is exactly what happened that night. Micky F called with the Queen. Italian Paulo, the Italian Prince, called with a King. I had an Ace showing, I looked at my hole card, Aces back-to-back! So I called the £100. The blind card was a Jack. Eric Dee looked at the Croupier and said, "No raise," so the second card was coming out. Micky F hit a 7 to make him showing Queen, 7. Italian Paulo hit a Queen to make him showing King, Queen and I hit a King to make me showing Ace, King. Then Eric Dee hit a 9 to give him Jack, 9 showing. So I came out betting the pot, £500. Eric Dee called the £500 with Jack, 9 showing. Micky F called the £500 with the Queen, 7 showing and Paulo called the £500 with King, Queen showing. This was going to be a big pot! I've now put Micky F on Queens; I've now put Italian Paulo on possibly Kings, though a player of Paulo's class would probably have raised the pot there and then. So maybe Paulo had a Jack in the hole, I wasn't too sure, Eric Dee was the blind man, I wasn't too sure again. All I know was that I had the Aces and Dad was in the toilet! The third card came out, the one before the last. King to Micky F, Queen, 7, King showing. Jack to Paulo, King, Queen, Jack showing. A 7 to me, Ace, King 7 showing and an 8 to Eric Dee, Jack, 9, 8 showing. The cards couldn't have come any better for me. This was going to be a big pot and I had it in the bag! I decided to get the maximum. I felt

Paulo to my right, would now come out betting at this pot but it was me to bet first. So I decided to check with the Ace, King, 7. Eric Dee, the blind man, comes out betting £3000! Micky F decides to pass. Paulo, thought for some time and also decided to pass, which was very strange because I thought Paulo had quite a big hand. Now there's Eric and I. I decided to call the £3000 and raise £9000. Without hesitation, I will never forget it; Eric calls the £9000 and re-raises 'All In', another £4000-£5000. I looked up at Eric and I said to him, "Eric, I can't pass, I've got the Aces!" He said nothing. So now there was just under £40,000 in the pot, this pot was mine! They gave me the last card and I hit an 8, I showed my cards straight away and I said "Aces Eric!" Now as I said Eric had showing Jack, 9, 8. They gave him the last card and when they gave him the last card, I breathed a sigh of relief. They gave him a 7. As I went to go and take the pot he said, "Steve! What are you doing? I said, "Aces Eric, you must have Jacks." He laughed and said, "No I haven't, and I've got the 10 in the hole." I couldn't believe it, he had a straight, he'd played all the way and hit a 7 on the last card that made him a straight! I was speechless. He scooped the pot, which was as I said, about £40,000 and I had lost about £20,000 of my dad's money while he was in the toilet! Dad walked round the corner to the poker table and as he walked round, I looked at Dad and I put my arms up, as if to say, "Look what's happened!" Dad saw that all of his pile of chips, about £20,000 worth, had gone down. He looked at me and he looked as if to say, "What happened?" I said, in a loud voice, "Dad, you wouldn't believe it!" Then Eric piped up and said, "Maxi, I've done your son! I've done him up like a kipper!" Dad looked at him and said, "Eric! If you've done Stevie, you must have made a big outdraw and you must have been a big underdog to beat him." He said, "I was, Max, I was about 4/1 underdog to win that pot! But I've done him!" As Dad walked round the table emotionless. I said, "Dad! Do you want to hear about that pot?" Dad said, "Don't worry about it son, all I know is, you must have been unlucky!" Dad went on to win that night and on the way back in the car, I had to tell my dad the pot and the 'coup' that happened with Eric and I explained it to him. All he said was "That's poker son, what can you do? You stuck your money when you were in front but you finished behind." I said, "Dad! That has got to be the most expensive wee you've ever had in history!" He laughed and said, "That's right it was!" Dad knows that when I play poker, I stick my money all in when I'm in front and you've got to come from behind to beat me. Well I say one thing about Eric, he is a fantastic man, a terrific gambler and a lovely, lovely gentleman and even when I walked down into Stagg's casino 6 months ago, he was playing poker there. I walked in the card room; he said to everyone, "There's the young man, I was telling you about." I said, "What's up Eric?" He said, "I've just told them the time when your Dad went to the toilet and I took £20000 off you." They all said, "No! We didn't believe it." I said, "Yes! It's a very true story." They said, "I bet your Dad was upset?" and I said, "Not in the slightest." Eric replied, "Obviously, you guys don't know Max! Max is one of the greatest gamblers." I said, "I know that Eric, but it was a very expensive wee that night wasn't it!" We all laughed.

Another time at the Barracuda, there was going to be a big game on a Wednesday night, they used to always play on Wednesdays and Fridays, but I remember it was a Wednesday and I remember it well. Dad was in Cyprus. Dad rang me from Cyprus and said to me, "Stevie! Go and draw £10,000 and go and play poker at the Barracuda tonight." I said, "No problem Dad, I'll have 25% share with you." He said, "You know how to play them." I said, "Yeah! Dad not a problem." I went down to the Barracuda. The game had just started and on the third hand of the night, I opened with an Ace, £100. There were a couple of callers in front of me and this guy called Eddie, (he was in Vegas with us) called the £100 and raised £300. He had a King showing. I looked at my hole card and it was up to me to call the £300, I had Aces back-to-back. I decided to call the £300, but not re-raise the pot, I was looking to win a very big pot now. Everybody else passed, except for Eddie and me. He had a King showing and I had an Ace. The cards came out, 10 to Eddie, King, 10 showing. King to me, Ace, King showing. I bet the pot £900. Eddie called the £900, putting £2700. in the middle. The next card came out. An 8 to Eddie, King, 10, 8 showing and 10 to me showing, Ace, King, Ten. This was perfect for me. I bet the full pot, £2700. I did that, as I didn't want to 'trap-check' Eddie; because once he'd hit the 8, I felt that I'd won the pot there and then. Eddie thought for a second and I was thinking to myself, "God! He must have the Kings and he's thinking." He said to the Croupier, "I call the £2700 and I move 'all in' another £7000." Well this was perfect for me. It couldn't have worked out better. I called the £7000 and I said, "Eddie! I've got Aces. You must have Kings." Well he turned over his hole card and he was shaking his head as he was turning it over. I said, "What's the matter Eddie?" He said, "I don't think I can win this pot, I tried to bluff you, I didn't think you had Aces." I said, "Why what have you got?" He turned over his hole card and he had an Ace in the hole. So before the last card all he had was Ace, King, 10, 8 with one card to come. I'm thinking to myself very quickly, "Well he can't win the pot." The cards came over: Ace! To Eddie, he had hit the Aces and boom! A 7 to me and I had hit a 7. Now can you believe this pot, Eddie has now ended up with Aces, King 10, 8 and I've ended up with Aces, which I'd already had, King, 10, 7. He had won it by a 'pip'. Before the last card for him to win this pot, he had to hit an Ace, but also even if he hit an Ace, there was only one card that I could hit to lose the pot and that was a 7. The odds for Eddie to win this pot before the last card were probably over 50-1 and that's if an Ace hadn't already passed, which then he wouldn't even have been able to win the pot any way! I had done all of my money on the third hand of the night. I rang Dad the next day in Cyprus and I said, "Dad, it's a bad beat story." Dad said to me, "I'm a bit busy at the moment, tell me about it when I come back." Dad wasn't upset, when he got back, I tried to tell Dad what had happened, but I think up until this day, he never really sat down and listened to that pot between Eddie and me besides reading this. I will never forget Eddie beating me in that pot because in Five Card Stud Strip Deck, this is what you call a bad, bad beat and an unbelievable outdraw.

Early 1990, I was training in a gym in Covent Garden in London and afterwards I was having a coffee after working out. There were a couple of ladies that sat close to me and they started chatting about being psychic. I looked at them and said, "Is one of you two ladies a psychic?" One said, "Yes, I am and I read Tarot Cards for all the top businessmen in London, a lot of Japanese businessmen come to me for readings, have you ever been to a psychic?" I said, "No." She said, "How do you feel about going to one?" I said, "I'd never thought about going, though I feel the need for me to go is not necessary." She said, "What do you do for a living?" I said, "I'm a bookie, buy property and I play poker." She said, "So you're in the gambling business? Do you win at poker or do you lose at poker?" I said to her, "If I ever lost at gambling or at anything in my life for more than five times, I wouldn't do that particular thing that I'd lost at or I'd make sure that I'd got the right odds from the start." She said to me, which was very interesting, "You're a very highly intuitive person." I said, "I think so." She continued, saying, "When you're on your way to a poker game, how do you feel?" I said, "To tell you the truth, many times I feel really good." She said, "The times that you feel good, do you win?" I said, "To be honest with you, I win most of the time!" She then said, "Then that's going back to what you've just said, you usually feel good, have you ever been on the way to a poker game and you don't feel so good?" I said, "Yeah sometimes but rarely I do." She said, "Why were you going?" I said,

"Well you can ask any poker player, who might not feel 100%, but they still go don't they? I mean it's like a snooker player or a football player, they are not going to feel 100% all of the time, you've still got to go and do your job, you've got to try and win the money." She then said to me, "Is there any way that when you are going to a poker game and you don't feel 100%, could you not go, or do you have to go?" The conversation was deepening now, so I said, "Well I'll be honest with you, there's no hard fast rule on whether I have to go or not, but if I said to someone that I'm coming at 10 pm, I usually go." She said, "I want you to try something, two hours before you are going to a poker game, sit down for a couple of minutes and think about the game you're going to play that night, try and get the feeling of how you will feel at the table." I said, "Right and?" She said, "If you feel good, go to that poker game and if you feel bad, don't go." I said, "I'll be honest with you, us poker players have got to take the good with the bad, we couldn't live our lives like that." She said, "Try it." I said, "It would be quite difficult not to go knowing there is a massive game that night then all of a sudden I don't feel too good, I've still got to go." She repeated to me, "Try it." I then asked her, "So what happens if I feel good about going to the poker game and I get there and I lose my money?" She quickly replied, "Well at least you've gone to the poker game in a positive frame of mind, there's nothing worse when you're driving to a business meeting or in your case a poker game and you're not in a positive frame of mind, at least be positive." I was driving home that night and her words started to haunt me. Would it be possible for me to try and think how I would feel, two hours later at the poker table? The next time there is a poker game, I'm going to try this exercise. With all this in my mind, I decided to give it a try and if you've read a few stories about me going to poker games in this book, usually I've always felt good, but on one or two occasions back in the past, I didn't feel that good when I'd lost a couple of times. Thinking back on it, as I've said to you, I've always sat at the table and I've always felt whether I'm going to win or lose that night. That I could do, but could I try and transfer that feeling 2 hours before the game. Well I will honestly say to you, I tried it the next seven or eight times and it worked wonders. Even 14 years later, I still practice this idea and I would say that I've pushed my winning percentage up from 85% to 98%. It works for me and as I've said to you, very early on in the book, every poker player and gambler out there has got a sixth sense. I know in the past I've seen my dad walk up to the roulette wheel and have £50 on 29 and £50 on 28, first bet of the evening, two numbers, £50 each, the ball has spun and went into number 7. (Number 7 is right in between 28 and 29!) and I've looked up at my dad and said, "Dad, is that a sign we are going to lose our money tonight?" I would say if that's ever happened in the past and it has happened on a few occasions, we have lost on that particular night. Same thing on the poker, a big outdraw or bad beat early on in the evening, you can then smell or feel how the evening is going to go. I always say go by your intuition, go by your feelings in life. The human body, I have read, has survival instincts, that's the way we all have evolved. So if we could transfer our survival instincts into our everyday life, it would be very interesting wouldn't it?

In July 1990, Maurice said to me he was going to Monte Carlo, as he always did for the backgammon tournament. It's the World Backgammon Championships. I said to him, "Well Maurice, I'd love to come but I won't be able to play the backgammon, as I'm not that good." He said, "Stevie, Don't worry if you're a weak backgammon player they have three competitions in Monte Carlo. There's one for the Professionals, one for the Amateurs and one for the Novices. I said, "Well, I'll come along and enter the Novices. I went to Monte Carlo that year and yes! Maurice was there. In fact, that was the one time that Maurice actually got where he said he was going to go. We stayed at Lowes Hotel they wanted something like £300 a night. When I arrived and told Maurice this, he went straight up to the desk and said, "I come every year to the backgammon tournament, my name is Maurice." They said, "Yes, Mr Maurice, we know you well." He said, "Please don't charge Stevie £300 a night, as he is with me in the backgammon tournament." They said, "No problem Maurice." They then brought my room rate down from £300 a night to £40 a night! So that was another favour Maurice had done me. He saved me about £2000-£3000. Well needless to say some young 20-year-old girl, who was absolutely different class to what I was, knocked me out of the Novice Tournament in Monte Carlo. The standard in Monte Carlo is very high. That week was a tremendous week and if you've ever been to Monte Carlo on Backgammon Week, you'll know what I'm talking about. During the week they have a show that is outdoors. It was probably the first time that I went to an outdoor theatre and also an outdoor cinema as well. Maurice and I had a tremendous time and Maurice was not only in the tournament with the Professionals, he was also playing backgammon for very big cash money as well. The final is televised on local television.

I got back and after a couple of weeks, Dad and I went out. We were at the casino in the West End, Dad was playing roulette with a colour value of £25 per chip. Well, Dad changed some more money and as he changed the money he said to the Croupier, "Change this money and put my colour at £5." The Croupier gave Dad the chips but forgot to mark up £25 to £5, so that means every £100 Dad was giving her, she was giving Dad 20 chips of £5, but just behind the roulette wheel is where they mark the value of the chip. She'd left the £25 chip against that colour, which meant that every time she passed 20 chips to my dad in a stack, they weren't valued at £100, but they were valued at £500! She had forgot to change the value! So Dad laid out the £100 and if he'd had hit any number he would have got paid five times the amount. But the first spin, Dad didn't hit a number. He changed another £100. Second spin, Dad didn't hit a number. I remember Dad saying to me, "We're going to hit a number in a minute." Third £100, Dad didn't hit a number. Fourth £100, again Dad didn't hit a number. After eight spins, Dad had lost £800 without hitting a number! Any number he would have hit would have returned him for a £5 chip (which was the real value) £875, instead of the correct £175, but we could not hit a number to save our lives! I mean, we weren't cheating it was the Croupier's fault. On the ninth hundred that Dad changed, she had realised the mistake she had made and she said, "Oh! You're playing in £5 chips now, aren't you?" Dad said, "Yes!" We still never hit a number and that just goes to show that when you're out of form, there's nothing anyone can do, even if they are paying you five times the proper odds. I mean the odds to hit a number on the roulette wheel is 35/1. The true odds are 36/1. We were getting 175/1 to hit a number and we still couldn't hit it!

I remember Frank Bruno fighting Mike Tyson for the first time. No one gave Frank a chance. Just before the fight, everybody arranged to go round to a poker player named Jack's house in St. John's Wood. Just before the fight, everybody put £100 and we all had to pick a round. Like a lottery, a lucky dip and I had picked my ticket for round number 4. As the fight goes, Tyson stopped Bruno in the 5th, but he very nearly stopped him in the 4th- I was probably about ten seconds out from winning £1200! That night at Jack's house, there was a massive poker game. It went on all through the night. I left quite early. Dad told me that night, he was out of form and couldn't hit any cards at all, I don't think Dad lost any money. He said, he was 'even' and I think at about 7 or 8 in the morning, he wanted to pack up and stop playing, which was unlike Dad, but I think he realised he was out of form. The game went down to four-handed and he left a guy named Derek W, who was a very strong Five Card Stud poker player and very tight or Karabena as we say. The next day, we found out that

Derek W skint the remaining two players up and had won about £90,000. Dad spoke to the two remaining players the next day and he said, "I could see Derek was hitting some tremendous cards, I was getting tired and I decided to call it a day." That's why I said earlier on, if a lot of gamblers follow their gut feeling, that sixth sense, the little voice that speaks to you, you'd be a big winner, trust me and I think that night Dad escaped from losing a lot of money.

One night at the Barracuda, a Friday night, it was 3.45 am (Saturday morning), the Croupier, dealing the poker, called the last three hands and on the very last hand Italian Paulo hit a possible flush and Dad had 3 9s. Dad checked to Paulo's possible flush (a flush is any five cards with the same suit and getting a flush at Five Card Stud is very difficult), and Paulo went "all in" for £24000. I remember Dad thought for about ten seconds and decided to pass. Then Paulo said in a loud voice, "Maxi!" and as he was saying that, he turned over his hole card and it was the Ace of Diamonds. I'll never forget that. He said, "Maxi! I bluffed you the last hand." Dad looked at him emotionless and said, "Paulo! It's late, well played, see you Wednesday" and Dad got up. Paulo timed that bluff perfectly well, he knows a lot of people will not put that kind of money in on the last hand of the evening. I'll tell you something that Dad used to do at the Barracuda many, many times. Dad used to get up and stop playing poker at 3.45 am. We all remember this very vividly because whether he was winning or losing he used to jump up from the poker table at 3.45 am. and go to the roulette wheel. I can tell you now for two years he used to play roulette for the last 10 or 15 minutes. He might lose a couple of hundred on a Friday, he might lose a couple of hundred on a Wednesday and then boom! He'd win £10,000! They weren't thrilled to see my dad come off the poker table, in fact I'll tell you what, when he used to walk onto the roulette wheel, they used to think, Oh No! Max is only going to play for four or five spins. I've always said that to any roulette player, you want to make money at roulette, only play for a certain number of spins. People say to me, "That's impossible Steve! When you get to the roulette wheel, you've got to play more than five spins." I said, "OK! Play ten." They said, "That's impossible too." So I say to them, "Well I tell you what, "Walk into the casino 15 minutes before it closes and if you know how to press, you'll win."

1990 was the year that my old Mercedes Sports was stolen. I did mention earlier on it still sits on my drive today. Well I'll just tell you, how, when and why.

I popped to Golders Green to a Health Shop and silly me, I left it double parked with the engine running as I popped in to get some vitamins. As

I walked out of the shop, two guys had jumped in my car and drove my car off. I thought it was a couple of friends messing about and I phoned my mobile from a telephone box and they answered the phone, can you believe it! They said, "We're on the M1 and we've got your car!" Well to cut a long story short I was very upset. I reported it to the police and I spoke to Reggie in the evening who came around to my flat and said to me "Stevie! If as they said, they are on the M1, I'm telling you they are not on the M1, they're in London and they've got your car. They've gone for a joy ride and they've parked it up somewhere and it's around the area that you lost it in." I said, "Reggie! I wish you were right, but that car is long gone." Reggie said, "I'll come round and pick you up, let's go out for a drive and I'll bet you £100 we find the car." I said, "Yeah, you reckon?" I jumped in Reggie's car and we were going round and round North London for three and a half hours looking for my Mercedes. As we were turning each corner, Reggie was saying, "I've got a feeling, it's round the corner! I've got a feeling its round the next corner!" Well the car was found three weeks later in Bradford! The only reason it was found is because it was parked outside some old lady's house. Now when the police told me this, they said, this car stuck out like a sore thumb in this street. I got my car back!

That Mercedes Sports is a 1985 280SL. I have sold it three times. Twice to dealers, once to my close friend Andy Twins (the guy I took to Plymouth) and three times I bought it back. The first two times, I bought it back from a dealer for £1000 more. Yep! That's right, even Andy Plymouth (Dad's friend) said, "I can't believe you've bought that car back for £1000 more." Well, I did. The third time, Andy Twins from Plymouth (we call him Andy Twins because he's got twins), brought that car for cash and he changed his mind a month later and I said, "No problem Andy! You can have your money back, because I want my car!"

There was a couple of very big poker games at the Nayland Rock Hotel, in Margate, this year. I didn't go down and play but Dad did. The Nayland Rock was owned by our friend Tony Stavrou and he invited a couple of players and one of the players was Karl from Margate, my dad and a couple of others. On the first occasion, Dad lost a few quid, Karl won quite a lot of money and he went out the next day and guess what? He brought a car! It seems like everybody that wins money at poker goes out the next day and buys a car. I don't know what he brought; I should have asked him, "Was it a Jaguar?" Well on the third game that they played, apparently the game got very big and it ended up Dad skinning the table and everyone had run out of money, but there was one player left and it was Tony. Now Tony as I said to you was a fearless gambler. He would always put his money where his mouth was, but there came one big pot that was to decide the evening. Tony ended up with a possible straight and Dad called him £6000 with a pair of 7s. Dad won the pot, it was an out and out bluff by Tony but may I hasten to add a very, very brave man to try and bluff my dad.

Another time Dad ended up Heads Up with Karl. Now Karl wasn't such a crazy gambler as Tony was but Karl was quite a sensible poker player and this time Karl beat my dad out of a big pot on the very last hand of the evening. It was Karl that ended up showing King, Ten, Jack, 9 and my dad had showing King, Queen, 8, 7 and it was my dad to bet. My dad bet the pot £3500, Right into Karl's possible straight and Karl immediately called the £3500 and went 'all in' for another £800, and my dad passed. Karl turned over his hole card and he turned over an Ace, so all Karl had was Ace, King high. He had bluffed my dad out of that big pot. My Dad said to Karl, he'd passed the Kings but what Karl might or might not know, maybe my dad didn't have the Kings and he bet into Karl to try and bluff him, but it was a double bluff and it backfired on my dad and Karl won the pot.

I got a call from my brother-in-law one day and he said to me, "Steve do you fancy playing 7-a-side football down at the JVC Centre in Highbury?" Now this was a 7-a-side pitch that was just next to the Arsenal Ground, down in North London. I said, "Yeah Paul, great I'll play, who are we playing?" He said, "Well you know Colin and Paul, the two brothers who have got the bakery, every year they both get a team out and they play against each other and it's quite a big challenge match." Now I was a fairly good goalkeeper when I was young, but I was especially good at 5-a-side or even 7-a-side when the goals were quite low and wide. I played in goal most of my life in school and I was offered to play some low amateur league football but to tell you the truth, it used to be an early kick off on Sunday morning, so I thought I'd give it a miss! But just to let you know my abilities as a goalkeeper, in later years I played in a charity match at QPR's ground, Loftus Road and I played with the ex-QPR players, actually by mistake. I was meant to be on the side of the celebrities as a very close friend of mine is Rhino the Gladiator, who called me up and said they were short of a goalkeeper, to which I volunteered. When I got down there they already had their goalkeeper but the ex-QPR Professionals didn't have one, so I played in goal for them! After the game in the changing room, there was Ray Wilkins, Stan Bowles, Mick McCarthy and a couple of others and it was Ray Wilkins who came up to me after the match and said, "Not a bad goalkeeper for a little fella are you?" I thought that was a great compliment coming from a legend like Ray Wilkins. Anyway we turned up at the JVC Centre. My brother-in-law was there, Colin, me and four others that were going to play. Well that night we got beat 3-2, so there was quite a lot of banter in the changing room afterwards. Paul (Colin's brother) turned around and said, "Colin we are too good for you, you could never beat us." So Colin replied to Paul, "Well maybe, we'll beat you next week if we have a rematch." Paul said, "It doesn't matter who you bring along, you won't beat us." Anyway I rang Colin during the week and I said, "Colin if you want to beat your brother Paul who has got quite a good team out there, let me arrange the team, do you mind if you don't play?! Not that you are a bad player, but I can go to one of the Greek Leagues and get a few good players and I know we will definitely stuff them." He said, "No problem." I rang up a friend of mine named Peter Lucroft, I always call him Lukie. I said, "Lukie can you get me 6 players for next week, we've got to beat this guy who has got a bakery? He said, "Stevie no problem, I'll play for you in defence, I'll get Orville, Bash, this one and that one." I said, "Lukie, I'll leave it to you but we have got to win." He said, "We'll win." I rang up Paul and I said to him, "Are you on for next week?" He said, "Yeah next week is fine." I said, "Do you want any added interest on it?" He said, "What do you mean?" I said, "Well let's just say, the loser has to pay the fees for the pitch, which comes to about £60." Paul said, "No problem, the loser pays for the pitch." Well that night when we played, we beat them 3-1. It was a very good game. Afterwards, Paul looked at me and said, "Are you on for next week Steve?" I looked at my boys and said, "Are you on for next week, are you up for it, boys?" They all said, "Yeah!" Paul said, "Same again Steve, loser pays for the pitch but this time we'll have a bit of dinner on it at the same time, so whoever loses has got to pay for the pitch and dinner." I said, "No problem, you're on Paul." A week later we played again. Well, he brought a few new faces and they beat us 4-1, so it cost me money! I said to Lukie, "Lukie what are we going to do?" He said, "Relax Steve, next week I'll find a better team!" A week later we turned up with three new faces. Paul turned up with the same team. Now the faces that Lukie brought down were the top players from the Greek League in London who had won the Championship and they were pretty tasty. I'll never forget it, he brought a guy down called Lee Hendlesby who was up front and this guy was mustard, he had trials for a few professional teams. We stuffed them 9-2! We ran circles around them, they couldn't believe it and their faces were a picture in the dressing room. Paul had to pay the pitch and he had to take us out for dinner. He looked at me and said "Are you on for next week?" I said, "Paul this is getting to be a regular thing isn't it?" "Are you on or are you off?" he said. I looked at my boys and said, "Are you on?" They said, "We're all on, come back next week and we'll beat you again." The following week Paul brought down five new faces. I've never seen these boys before, but could they play football, it was unbelievable. They thrashed us 7-1! These guys were incredible. They were moving and passing the ball around tremendously. I got into the changing room and I said, "Paul, credit to you but who are these boys?" He said, "Steve if I tell you, it mustn't go any further. These boys play for Crystal Palace." A London team in the Premiership! That's right he brought down four players that were currently playing in the Premiership. Can you believe it, that's how badly Paul wanted to win. This was a secret because we used to play on a Thursday or Friday and they shouldn't have been playing. In fact a couple of scouts who watched our matches straight away could see that four or five of these boys had unbelievable talent. I'm not too sure how they didn't recognise them! Well I definitely lost my pitch money that night and the dinner! Lukie rang me up during the week and said, "Steve I'll get a team that will beat any team that Paul is bringing down." I said, "Lukie, how are we going to get a team to beat Paul's team? They are too good, four of them play in the Premiership!" He said, "Leave it to me." The next week we've turned up with a guy named John Sitton, he was about 37 or 38, player/manager at Leyton Orient at the time, another guy named George that used to play down in Fulham FC and is now playing in the Conference League. He also bought along three others and two professionals from Cyprus who were here for a month on vacation. This was the strongest team we could put out. I said, "Lukie, will it make a difference? I mean we've got a semi-professional team out and they've got half a professional team out." He said, "Steve at 7-a-side, it will make a difference trust me. Well that night was one of the most exciting games of football that I've ever been involved in and it finished in a 3-3 draw. When we got back into the dressing room, me and Paul were really laughing. I said, "Look at how much we both want to win, this started out as a one-off match between you and your brother and look what's happened now!" He said, "It's good isn't it, what a great game football is?" We did play a couple of more times, but I think that the players that were playing with us could have got into some serious trouble, so soon the games faded out.

Towards the end of 1990, Johnny K had a holiday and he'd just come back from Santa Monica. He rang me up and he said to me, "Stevie! Santa Monica, Los Angeles, is the place to go, you will love it there!" I said, "Why's that John?" He said, "You can train every day, the beach is there, the food is cheap, the weather is great and the way of life suits you perfectly." I said, "Is there any poker?" He said, "I'll be honest with you, I heard that they've opened up a few card clubs in Los Angeles." I said, "Is there any Five Card Stud?" He said, "That Stevie, I don't know." So I thought to myself, I'm going to go for two or three weeks. I was going to go in the very early part of 1991, but then the Gulf War happened. I know it really didn't involve being in America and it wouldn't have affected me if I would have gone, but my mum was saying, "Wait until after the Gulf War, things are unsettled at the moment, I'll be more happy, if you wait until after the Gulf War." I said, "OK!" I wasn't in a rush to go anyway.

In that time early 1991, I used to go to a Health Club, called the Winners Health Club up in Southgate. The Winners Health Club had a gym downstairs and upstairs were a couple of pool tables bar and snooker tables. Now I'd heard that on a Friday night they were playing poker, they were playing Five Card Stud. One Friday night after I'd finished training and the guys that owned it said, "Stevie, we know you play poker, but really we've heard that you're too good for us upstairs." So I said, "Well look, why don't you let me sit down for an hour as I enjoy a game." Well I did and the first night I lost several hundred pounds. I was always welcomed back. Every Friday night was poker at the Winners Health Club in Southgate. We used to start at around 10 pm on a Friday night and many times we used to finish off at about 10 am on a Saturday morning and the games were tremendous. I mean it wasn't that they were that big, maybe £5–£10 openers, but they were good action games including a couple of the characters that we had there as well. We had a guy that we named 'Camouflage', because he used to wear an army jacket and army jeans. I tell you what, even if I bump into him today, I would say, "What's happening Camouflage?" I still don't know his real name! Then a couple of times 'Cos the Jeweller' used to come up. What a character he was. He was quite a loud person on the poker table, but he didn't really mean it. When he used to bet the pot or make a bet, he used to shout, "I bet the pot! Raise the pot!" He used to shout it out loud. Then we used to have guy named Jack, we called him 'Deaf Jack', why, because he couldn't hear! I tell you what was strange about Jack; Jack out of all of them had an idea about poker. The rest, they were all out and out gamblers. With Jack at the very end of the pot, we'd say to him, "I bet the pot, or I bet £300 or I bet £400," whatever the bet was. Jack would say, "Uh! Sorry, I can't hear you." I said, "I bet £400 Jack." "Uh! Uh! I can't hear you, speak up!" "I bet £400!" I used to say in a loud voice. He'd say, "Uh! I pass." But I tell you something with Jack, when he used to have you beat and he'd bet the pot, when you used to pass, he'd say, "Uh! I wanted you to call." Sometimes he never had a hearing problem and sometimes he did, if you know what im getting at. He was deaf when it suited him! Who appeared one night on the games? Johnny K. Johnny K sat down one night and decided to play. Johnny K doesn't gamble, except on the odd occasion, if you remember rightly. Well one night there was a good pot between Johnny K and myself. I'll never forget it, I was bluffing. I said, "Bet the pot John, £1400." He said, "Stevie! I call." I remember saying, "Sorry?" He said, "Stevie, I call." I said, "What do you mean?" He said, "I call the bet £1400." Just like that within a second! I said, "That's £1400 you've won, because I was bluffing!" The games at the Winners Health Club lasted exactly 16 weeks. The first week I lost, but the next 15 weeks I skint the table. Yes! I skint the table every week! Now as I said to you, they weren't massive, but you could nick a couple of grand a week, no problem. We used to have guys coming up there that couldn't even play the game, can you believe it? We had a guy called John Michael; he'd only played poker once or twice and once was in Margate with us, a while ago. Now the reason I'm mentioning this to you is because John Michael or Mike as we call him turned out to be, not a bad poker player. He can hold his own and win money in certain poker schools, but with Mike he knows his limitations. If you put him in front of four or five professionals, they will definitely swallow him up, but he wouldn't sit down because he's not that stupid. Anyway Mike couldn't play poker and he sat down at the Winners and let's just say it cost him a lot of money to learn. There was another guy called Chris P, a fearless gambler. There was one interesting pot at the Winners Health Club and I'll tell it to you. It was between me and a guy named 'Spiz'. Spiz had showing 7, Ace, I had showing King, Queen and I had a Jack in the hole (there were two cards to come). Spiz bet the pot £80. Everybody else passed and I called. The next card came out, a 7 to Spiz, he now had showing 7, Ace, 7 and a 10 to me, I'm now showing King, Queen, 10. (Don't forget I've got a Jack in the hole.) My hand is looking really good. Spiz bet the full pot £240. I knew I was going to call him but I didn't want to call him too quickly. I'll be honest with you, I was pretty sure Spiz was winning at this stage, but I had an 'up and down' straight, no 9s out and I could only see one Ace out and that was Spiz's. Maybe he had another one in the hole, I wasn't too sure, but I really fancied Spiz for maybe two pairs or possibly 3 7s. I decided to call the £240 because I knew if I hit my card I was going to get paid. The last card came out bang!... a 9 to me, I've now got showing King, Queen, 10, 9 and I've got the Jack in the hole! I've got the straight and then an Ace to Spiz, he is now showing 7, Ace, 7, Ace. It was Spiz to bet. Well what do you think he did? Well I'll tell you. He bet £720 right into my straight! I thought for about three minutes and then I looked up at him and I said, "Spiz you win, you win because I think you've got a Full House." He said, "Steve you've waited three minutes to tell me that? Why are you wasting time? Obviously you haven't got the straight." I replied to Spiz, "What makes you think that Spiz?" He said, "Well if you had the straight you would call me." Again I said, "I pass my cards, you win Spiz." I never show my hole card at Five Card Stud, which was a rule I learnt since I was a kid from my dad. I've always made sure that my hole card was kept down. Then someone said to me at the table, "Steve, really you were wasting time, if you haven't got a straight" I looked up and said, "Who said, I didn't have a straight?" They said, "Come on, if you'd had a straight you would have called him." I then stood up and I turned over my hole card and I showed the table the Jack in the hole. Spiz shouted, "You passed a straight!" I said, "Yes Spiz, because I genuinely feel you have a Full House." I never asked to see his hole card and he said to me. "Do you know what I've got?" I looked up and said, "Spiz, I don't want to know what you have, because I never paid to see. After the game, Spiz came up to me and said, "I can't believe you passed that straight." I replied, "Spiz, I passed the straight because I fancied you with a Full House." He said, "I'm going to tell you something Steve, I had the Full House." I said to him, "I thought so." Spiz still talks about that pot, right up until today! The games at the Winners were fantastic value. You'll never see poker games nowadays like that with everyone dying to gamble and dying to lose their money. Anyway as soon as the games dried up, I booked my ticket to go to Los Angeles.

When I got to Los Angeles, I decided to stay on Venice Beach at the Marina Pacific Hotel. When I left the airport and the taxi driver was taking me to the hotel, he took me through Marina Del Rey and it looked like a great place, then we turned the corner and everything changed, we had entered Venice. Venice back in 1991 was definitely a down and out place, although it's somewhat improved now. I thought to myself "Oh my God! Where am I staying?" I've got to the hotel and as I've checked in, there's this big guy that's walked in. He must have weighed about 20 stone, 280 lbs, and a big bodybuilder. His eyes were black, his lip was bleeding and there's me trying to check in. The receptionist said to him, "Are you OK buddy?" He said, "No! I'm not OK, I've just been beaten up by two guys on the beach," in his American accent. "Call the ambulance, call the police!" I thought to myself, "Oh! My word, where the hell am I staying? This must be one dangerous place." Anyway, I checked in, came down in the morning and I said to the guy that was working on the reception, "There was a guy here last night, he was beaten up black and blue." He said to me, "Whatever you do, never walk along Venice Beach at night, you might just not get to the other end." I said, "Are you serious?" He said, "You want me to be serious, I'll be serious, if you walked along the beach at night the odds of you getting from A to B are pretty good, but I'll tell you what, if something happens to you while you're walking from A to B, it will be fatal, the guy last night that got beaten up was very, very lucky. Usually, you'll get stabbed or shot and you're left for dead, so just to take a beating he did good." I said, "I won't be walking down the beach at night, but I do want to go to a poker Club" So he got out his books and showed me where the nearest poker Club was and that wasn't any better because it was in 'Commerce'. Commerce was similar to Venice, it was about a 40-minute drive and it was a little bit down and out but they had a lovely poker Club there, maybe 300–400 poker tables and in a separate section they had Five Card Stud, it was called "Asian Stud." They had games that were $100 to sit down, or $500 sit down. It was no limit game. Now remember I'd never played No Limit, I'd always played Pot Limit, so I decided to sit down on the $100 table and play No Limit. Everybody else sat there with $1000 or $2000, there possibly was about $10,000 on the table. I sat down with $500 and Boom! Lost the $500. Pulled out another $500 and Bosh! Lost the $500 again. I drove home that night, didn't chase my money and thought, "I must be playing wrong somewhere." I was thinking about my play that night. Well I tell you what it was; I don't play No Limit. I play Pot Limit! So how can I now restructure my game to get into No Limit and make it pay? Well the solution is especially with Strip Deck, you've got to play a lot tighter, a lot more Karabena, I tell you. You can't build pots the way you build them at Pot Limit. You can't do it; you can't play Jack showing 10 in the hole, you can't play Queen showing Jack in the hole and build a pot from the beginning, you can't do it, I'm telling you, I tried it. Next night I went back and I finished even but I can tell you now, I didn't play as tight as I should have played.

The next night, I didn't go back because I was a little tired. I was training twice a day. I used to work out at the Gold's Gym in Venice. Now if anybody trains and loves the gym, Gold's Venice is the governor. There is no better gym on this planet then Gold's Gym Venice. It's got four rooms, maybe 30,000 square feet and the atmosphere in there is fantastic. I decided that I was going to play poker only three days a week in LA while I was there. Otherwise going there, playing poker five or six nights a week, getting up early to train twice a day was going to get too much for me. People still say to me, "What did you do out there Stevie?" I said, "On Monday I used to train and play poker, on Tuesdays I used to train and go and see a movie, on Wednesdays I used to train and play poker. On Thursdays I used to train and go out for dinner, on Fridays I used to go and play poker and train but on Saturdays and Sundays, I used to rest." They used to laugh, but it is actually true. Saturdays and Sundays I never used to train and I never used to play poker. I used to relax, maybe go up to Hollywood. I had a couple of friends in Los Angeles and I also had a cousin that I used to go and see but I slowly made more friends in LA who I still keep in contact with today. One of them is probably the 'flakiest' guy you'll ever meet. I'm telling you he is 'flaky' and 'flaky' in LA means he never turns up for anything. I'm coming down from my hotel room one day and there are a couple of guys in reception, bodybuilders that I knew from the gym, and they said "Steve! Where are you going? I said, "I'm just going to grab a coffee." They said, "Why don't you come with us, we're going for a non-fat yoghurt." I said, "Let's go" They said, "No we're waiting for our friend George to pick us up." George never showed. In fact four days later George turned up and he took us out for yoghurt! George and I have stayed friends all these years, having said that, it's me who always calls him and me who always stays in contact with him, but George is still a good friend and he is a very funny guy.

Back at the poker club, playing three times a week, I started to make money. Realistically, it took me a couple of weeks, but then all of a sudden I started to make maybe $300–$400 a night. Not a lot of money, but I wasn't there to win a lot of money. If I could cover my rent, food and my expenses I was happy. I got it down to a knack in LA. It wasn't that I was going there to win $300 and stopping. Obviously, if the game was good, I was continuing, but the point is with No Limit Five Card Stud you have to play very tight. All your money is at risk at any time. Do you know I probably saw two straights in the three years that I was there; maybe three and they were 'all-in coups'. So the name of the game was to play exceptionally tight, have patience and if you lost, walk out. If you won, win what you felt you should win and walk out. A lot of discipline was involved. I actually put myself on a time limit. I used to want to get up and train early in the morning. I was up at 8.30 am every single morning so I never used to play late. The games were early in the Commerce Club. They used to kick off at about 8 pm. It was great, I used to arrive at 9 pm and maybe leave about midnight or one o'clock in the morning.

One night the game got very big! Very big, and I was there until six o'clock in the morning. This was an expensive lesson for me because I sat down with my usual $500. I turned it into $9000 and I lost it all in one pot. I tell you the pot, because I played it correctly, but I lost it! I had Kings back-to-back. Kings showing, King in the hole. A guy had a Queen showing and I didn't know his hole card. I opened for the usual $20 and he raised $100, I made it $300. Now, I could have raised all-in but he would have passed. So obviously, me with the winning hand, I'm looking to extract as much money from him as possible. He hit a 7 and I hit a Jack. I had showing King, Jack and he had showing Queen, 7. I bet $1500. I bet over the pot. He called the $1500. I now put him on Queens. He then hit an Ace, Queen, 7, Ace and I hit an 8, King,. Jack 8. He bet 'all in' $6000 and I called him straight away before the last card. The last cards came out, nothing to him and nothing to me. He hit the Aces, it taught me a lesson. Even though I played the pot 100% correctly, at No limit Five Card Stud you can go skint in one pot! That I didn't want to do, so every time I got infront by a good amount, I used to stop.

While I was in LA that year I'd met up with a couple of friends whose names were Gordon and Jay. Jay was the guy that came to Vegas with us a couple of years before and they told me that they were going to watch the big fight that was taking place that night. I asked them who was fighting and they told me the unbeaten Champion Chavez. Apparently, Chavez was unbeaten in so many fights and that he was probably one of the best fighters pound for pound that's ever lived. So I said, "Where are you going to watch the fight?" They said, "Well meet us on Sunset Boulevard and we're going up to our friend's in Beverley Hills as it is a Pay Per View (Sky box office) fight and he's going to order it." I said, "Sounds great to me, what time shall we meet?" They said, "About 7.30 pm. I said, "Great!" We met outside a restaurant in Sunset Boulevard and I was dead on time. Jay and Gordon turned up and we all jumped in my car. There's a reason behind why I'm going to tell you this story because, well I'll continue shall I? On the way up to Beverley Hills, we were talking about Chavez, about boxing and fighting and then Jay was telling me about how lovely his friend is. So I said to Jay and Gordon, it's a good idea if we stop off at a supermarket and we buy something for their friend as he was having us over to watch the fight. We stopped off and spent about \$60–\$70 in chocolates, fruit, food, crisps etc. You name it we brought it. So anyway we got to the apartment. We rang the bell and went upstairs. He was there in his beautiful penthouse suite. It was a five bedroom, 4000 square foot flat in Beverly Hills. He had one of those big massive projection TV's and some of the undercard fights were already on. He then took us downstairs to the garage and showed us his three Ferraris and two Porches. Obviously, this guy had done well for himself. We then went back upstairs. We opened some wine that we brought in, we had some chocolates, and I mean there must have been two or three carrier bags full of stuff. We started to watch some of the fights, but just before the big fight, as Chavez was walking to the ring, Jay and Gordon's friend gets up and comes over to me and says, "Can I have \$10 please?" I said, "Excuse me?" He said, "Can I have \$10 please?" I said, "I'm sorry, what do you need?" He said, "Well I've ordered the fight tonight and its cost me \$40. So if you put \$10, Jay and Gordon put \$10 and I'll put \$10, that's \$40 as I've paid for the fight. I was taken aback, as many times I've been thrown into funny situations, I know how to handle them, but this was one of the best ones, wasn't it? I looked up at him and said, "Go and see Jay, I'm his guest he will give you the \$10." Meanwhile Jay was over in the kitchen getting some wine and crisps so he didn't know what was going on. As Jay's walking into the lounge, this guy goes up to Jay and said, "Jay can I have \$20 please?" Jay said, "Excuse me?" The guy said, "Can I have \$20 please? \$10 from you, \$10 from Gordon, \$10 from me and \$10 from Stevie, which adds up to \$40, I ordered the fight!" Jay said, "You can't be serious!" He said, "I am!" Jay said, "I ain't paying!" I mean Gordon's face was a picture. I mean for the rest of the night, you could have cut the atmosphere with a knife. After the fight that Chavez won, I was very polite, I said, "Thank you" and we left. We were talking about it all on the way home. Jay said to me, "Steve, I feel so bad, that he came up to you." I said, "Jay, forget about it, that's the way people are." He said, "I can't believe this guy, this guy's a multimillionaire and he's asking us for \$30." I said, "Jay, in life it takes all sorts and this guy was definitely an all sort."

STEAK & CHICKEN HOUSE

to
ROCKY'S
All Buses go to
ROCKY'S
842
DYE

MAZE

MAZE

ST 5885

Frozen
Bananas!

After about three months, I thought I'd made enough money; I'd bought myself a convertible Mustang. I was staying at the Marina Pacific Hotel Apartments and I had a lovely studio apartment. I was going to treat myself and I was going to go to Hawaii, Yep! Hawaii, it was only a five-hour flight from LA. I thought I'd go for two nights. I jumped onto the plane and flew to Honolulu. I didn't stay two nights, I stayed two weeks! This time I was on holiday. I flew back to LA and out of the blue, I found out that my mum, sister, nephew and niece were coming over to go to go to Disneyland. To tell you the truth, I probably would have been coming home about that time because I started to get homesick, but what with them coming over, I decided to spend another couple of weeks. After they went, I thought to myself, I'm going to go to Vegas, I haven't been to Vegas for five years, and I'm going to go. I flew to Las Vegas and I decided to stay downtown in the Golden Nugget. There had been a lot of money spent on the Nugget in 1991 and it was now a great hotel to stay in. The buffet, I'm telling you is one of the best in town. Across the road is Binions. Binions is where they hold the World Poker Series every year. I actually went to Vegas, not really to gamble. I went to go and see the town and spend my 30th birthday. I wanted to be in Vegas by midnight. There was a delay but I managed to get on the Dice Table at 5 to midnight, just before my birthday began. Dead on twelve o'clock and I mean exactly twelve o'clock the dice came round to me. As I picked up the dice, before I threw them I said to everybody, "What is the time?" So a few people shouted out "Midnight!" I said, "It's twelve o'clock exactly, I've picked up the dice, it is now my birthday and I'm 30 years old today." Everyone sang happy birthday to me on the dice table. It sort of brought back memories of my 16th birthday, when we won all that money. So everybody said, "Well buddy, let's just hope your birthday starts off real good, throw the dice." Well no I didn't throw a 13 timer like when I was 16, but I threw six good numbers and as any dice player knows, six good numbers is not a bad result. I cashed up winning $300–$400 and I thought what a way to start my birthday. Binions were offering 12 times the odds at that time. That means if you put a $1 on the front line you could have $12 behind, which to a Crap player will tell you is fantastic value. I won about $1000 on the trip. I spent a lot more in the shops because there is an Outlet Mall, just outside Vegas, about twelve miles out, that does all sports gear and equipment really cheap. I flew back to LA and I knew it was time for me to come home, I wanted to come back to London.

Just before I decided to come back, I'd left a substantial amount of money in the 'cage' at the Commerce Club, the poker club that I'd been playing at. So I had to draw it all out and they gave me everything in $100 bills. Two armed security guards had to walk me to my car from the Card Club. I thought to myself when I got back to the hotel, "I don't really want to take all these dollars back to London with me." I went back downstairs to the hotel reception to see the Manager and I said, "Look, I'm going back to London, I've got this money, but I don't really want to take it all back. Can you do me a special rate when I come back to Los Angeles later on in the year or maybe the same time next year?" They said to me, yes they would, so I left them all the money and I worked out that I had paid one year's rent in advance, so I was paid up for the next year to stay at the Marina Pacific Hotel. I knew I'd never stay the whole year but I would definitely stay three months at a time, so in other words I'd had the next four years paid for from my poker winnings. I'd managed to stay in Los Angeles for about four and a half months and had the time of my life. Training, shopping, eating out every night and generally having a great time. Going to Vegas, winning money and paying for the next 12 months of accommodation. Who said poker doesn't pay!

I was having breakfast one day in the Fire House Café, which is close to Gold's in Venice. I heard a couple of people speaking about Seattle. They told me Seattle was a beautiful town and you know what I said, "I'm going to go there! I'm going to change my ticket from LA to London to go LA, Seattle to London. So I flew to Seattle. Seattle is a beautiful city. It might rain all the time, but it's beautiful. I spent three nights in Seattle and then by chance I heard that Canada was only 260 miles away. Yep! Vancouver was 260 miles away. So I changed my ticket again, this time from, Vancouver to London and I'll tell you how I got to Vancouver, I decided to drive. One night I left Seattle at about midnight and I drove all the way. I got to Vancouver at about six o'clock in the morning as the sun was rising. Now if anyone has been to Vancouver, it is a very pretty city to see. I stayed in down town Vancouver. I wanted to find a couple of casinos to see if they had any cards! Well they had casinos in Vancouver at that time, but I don't think they were allowed poker for some reason. They also weren't allowed Craps but they used to play this crazy dice game with six dice instead of two and it was a little bit more like a 'roulette shoot' than a 'crap shoot'. I played a little, I won a few quid, but I never really gambled. I just went there to see the action. I spoke to one of the Pit Bosses and I told him that I was from London and he told me that he used to work in London at the Olympic casino in the 70s and he knew a guy called Adonis. Adonis used to manage the Olympic casino right up until it closed. Four nights I spent in Vancouver and then it was time for me to come home. I got to London and it was now summertime.

It was very weird being back in London after spending so long away in LA. Everything seemed so much more expensive. Once I got back, I got into the swing of things. Reggie had taken over for the second or third time, the restaurant called Rocky's. Rocky's was the all-night restaurant that used to do breakfasts up until seven o'clock in the morning. Well Reggie was the governor there. Reggie used to start having poker games every Saturday. They weren't big games but they always ended up with Reggie and I playing Heads Up poker and me skinning Reggie. After I'd skinned Reggie a few times, he always used to borrow a few quid off me. I used to give it to him saying, "Reggie! You owe me this couple of hundred I'm lending you." He'd say, "No problem Stevie." Well, I'm telling you that for a reason, because every time we played and he lost, I used to give him a couple of hundred pounds, not give it to him as I said, but lend it to him. Every time we used to play the next time he'd say, "I can't play because I owe you a couple of hundred pounds." We then used to auction what he'd owed me. Now that sounds a little bit confusing, but I'll explain it to you. I'd say to him, "You can't play tonight Reggie because you owe me a couple of hundred from the last game." He'd say, "Stevie, what do you want now cash, settlement?" So I would say, "Well give me £150." He would then say, "£150? I'll offer you £10." I then used to say, "£10! You owe me £200! Give me £150." He said "Alright! I'll offer you £15." I'd say, "Alright give me £120." He used to reply, "I'll give you £20 maximum." Anyway this used to go on every week and usually we used to end up settling for £25, me buying breakfast and me buying the cigarettes for Reggie! So in other words, I used to let him off the £200 but it didn't matter, the games were good and I was winning.

After about 10 or 12 games, everybody stopped playing poker at Rocky's. They said that I'd won too much money! Reggie said to me, "Stevie! That's it, I'm never playing poker with you again!" I said, "Why not Reggie?" He said, "I'm better off going on the roulette table, I can win at that can't I? But I can't beat you at poker!" I said, "Alright Reggie, No problem I'll still come in here on Saturdays and we won't play poker." We decided not to play anymore. The games finished at Rocky's, but we used to still always go there on Saturdays for breakfast.

Also that year I won a substantial amount of money on a boxing match, but this time I gave all the money back to a charity. It was when Michael Watson was fighting Chris Eubank and that was the fateful night that Michael Watson sustained his terrible injury. This fight left Michael in a very bad way as we all know. After I heard that his life was in serious danger, I felt deep down it was not correct to win any gambling money on this fight, so I donated it to the "Michael Watson Benefit Fund" that was being run by the Ex Heavyweight British Champion, Gary Mason.

That Christmas of 1991 we all decided to play poker after lunch. I rang Reggie to come. Reggie said, "Stevie! I'm not playing you." I said, "Reggie, you can still come because my dad is playing, you've got more value with my dad." He said, "How comes?" I said, "Well at Christmas time, we don't allow my dad to play unlimited money, we put a restriction on what he can sit down with so he can't bully us." He said, "Sounds good to me." Reggie came over and Reggie could do no wrong. He skint me, he skint my brother, he skint my uncle and he was winning about £1400. It wasn't a big game. He then said to my dad, "Max! I'm on form tonight and no one can touch Reggie! Reggie! Reggie!" and the truth of the matter is when Reggie is on form, Reggie is on form. He said Max, "I'll play you Heads Up poker." Dad said, "Bring it on Reggie, and let's play." I left about midnight, from my mums, and I went home. The next day I got the call, "Stevie! Stevie! Stevie!" the voice said. "Reggie! Reggie! Reggie!" I replied. "Whose poker's number one?" he said, "Whose poker's number one?" he repeats. I said, "I don't know Reggie, I'm half asleep here." He replied, "I've beat Max for £5000 last night." I said "No!" He said, "Max was bluffing, Reggie was calling, Reggie had Max, Max was calling. I steam rolled over your Dad, he didn't have a chance, £5000 to Reggie." Reggie was buzzing. He had beaten my dad at Heads Up poker and he's never forgotten it to this day!

At the end of 1991, we decided to take a vacation to the Grand Floridian Hotel in Florida. If anyone has ever been there, it's one of the nicest hotels; I've ever stayed in, probably outside Las Vegas, that is.

January of 1992 I flew from Florida to Los Angeles. This time I stayed in Marina Del Rey, in the Oakwood Apartments. (I still had my credit at the Marina Pacific Hotel). I think Venice was getting a little bit too rough for me to tell you the truth! The funny thing is after I used to work out at the gym at Gold's in Venice every day, I used to end up going to the Marina Pacific Hotel for my breakfast. I used to spend more time at the Marina Pacific, than

I used to do in Marina Del Rey and the same old routine set in. Three or four nights a week, I used to go to the Commerce Club to play Five Card Stud. The games weren't as good as they were the year before, but there were still two or three tables. A couple of times when the tables were full, I used to play on the limit Five Card Stud, where you could bet $10 the first card, $20 the second, $40 on the third and fourth but that structure is absolutely useless. You cannot play Five Card Stud on a limit basis the way they play Hold'em in Vegas. Impossible, no one can make it pay. I didn't mind playing No Limit, as I've adjusted my game now to suit the No Limit style and as I said before, it had to be very tight. On the weekends they used to arrange a $500 or even a $1000 sit down. What I used to always do was sit down with the minimum, maybe $500 and play very careful for the first hour or two. As you now know you are putting all your cash at stake at any one pot, so you had to be very careful. The games were going well at the Commerce and I was always nicking between $300-$500 per session. What with my training and spending my time by the beach, it used to cover my expenses perfectly. The funny thing is, sometimes I used to phone home and speak to my mum and then dad for a while and I always used to tell him some kind of pot that I was 'outdrawn' in. He knowing me now, knew that I was watching every move they used to make, but the games were good and the games were straight. After three or four weeks in Los Angeles, I decided to take a trip to Vegas. Again I stayed down at the Nugget, as it felt familiar to me. Binions Casino still had 12 times the odds on craps and I'd figured a way to beat the game. The idea was to go to a crap table where you thought that the table was 'hot'. Sometimes you'll walk in and I'd walk around for about 20 minutes, that's right 20 minutes, until I heard a cheer go up on one of the 20 dice tables. When I heard that cheer that means that, that table was 'hot'. I used to go and change $100. Put a dollar on the win line and $12 behind. You always had to take the full odds and press when winning and if the table went cold, I used to go home but usually that table was warm for about an hour. So when I went to Vegas that time, I nicked about $1000. I know, not a lot of money but it was more for fun.

I got back to Los Angeles and I received a phone call. I answered the phone, the other voice said, "Stevie, its Johnny!" "Where are you? I said." Johnny K said, "I'm in Los Angeles, I'm at the Oakwood Apartments and I'm here for two weeks." I said, "No!" He said, "Stevie! I want to go to Vegas." I said, "Johnny I've just come back from Vegas." He said, "I've come over for two weeks, I want to go to Vegas!" I put the phone down and we met straight away. Johnny had opened a jewellery shop a year previous to that, but he got robbed and decided to close it down. He then decided to take a vacation and he'd come to meet me in Los Angeles as we were good friends. He said, "I've come over because I've never been to Vegas in my life." I said, "Johnny! You're talking to the right fella because I know Vegas like the back of my hand and I'll take you!" I got on the phone and I spoke to the casino host at Caesar's. I said, "Can you get me two rooms for this weekend?" They said to me, "Any weekend but this weekend, we've got a very big convention in town." I said, "Please! I've got a good punter here, he likes to have a little gamble, maybe $2000–$3000," because at this stage now, Johnny used to have a 'little punt' now and again. They said to me, "Look, we are genuinely booked up, but we'll see what we can do, we'll call you back." About half an hour later, they'd managed to find us two rooms. Now I know they were genuinely busy because when we went to go and "check in" at the hotel, there were people in front of us that were rather upset that certain rooms had been double booked. Apparently, there was a massive convention in town and Vegas gets very busy some weekends. We got to the Reception Desk and they said, "No problem Mr K, we've got your rooms." Johnny and I had quite good rooms, not the best, but good rooms. He put his luggage down and he said to me, "I'm in Vegas! I've got to have a bet, I've got to have a bet!" This is someone who doesn't gamble remember! He seemed to have got the flavour. We went downstairs on the Punto Banco, or the Baccarat, as its known in the States and Johnny straight away lost $2000. He put $3000 down and lost $3000! He then put $3000 down and again, lost the $3000. He'd done about $8000 in about four minutes, quite incredible eh?! He looked at me and said, "Bloody Vegas! What kind of place is this?" I said, "Johnny! Johnny! You've only been in town for five minutes!" He said, "Let me go on the blackjack." As we left the baccarat table, the Pit Boss came up to us and said, "Guys! How long have you been in town?" We said, "Half an hour." He said, "Look we've got a law in Vegas that you can only change $10,000 on each game, unless we take the details on your passport." Johnny said, "No problem! I'm from London and I'm here to gamble." Apparently in Vegas, you can only change $10,000 in cash on one game at a time and I think Johnny had already done that. So he went onto the blackjack table and he put $2000 on one box. He then doubled and he won $4000. He left the $4000 again and he got blackjack. He'd got his $10,000 back in 2 hands, yes! He looked at me and said, "Stevie, I've lost

$8000, I've won back $10,000 all within ten minutes, what a place this Vegas is! I love it!" He was happy. We went to the shops in Caesars and he brought me some Cartier aftershave. He then said, "That's a present from me." We then went to the ticket desk in Vegas and booked two ringside tickets for the Kickboxing Championship the next night. It's a shame because the fight lasted about 20 seconds and we had paid about $500 for these tickets but Johnny didn't care, he was happy. I said, "Johnny! Take it easy, let's go out, let's go for dinner, let's go and see shows, and relax, what's the matter with you? He said, "You're right, no more gambling, no more gambling! I'm winning a couple of grand so, no more gambling." Well the next day Johnny started playing blackjack again and he'd won about $5000–$6000. The day after, he played blackjack again and he won about $4000–$5000. Now all in all we were there for about four nights. And Johnny was winning about $28,000. We were going to the best restaurants in Caesars. We were signing everything to the room. He was ordering $500 bottles of red wine and we were really having a good time, we were living it up. I said, "Johnny, you're winning $28,000 relax!"

One night I got downtown with Johnny K and he was losing a couple of thousand on the blackjack and I told him, "Let's go to Binions and we'll recover our money on the dice!" He said, "How can you be so certain?" I said, "Leave it to me John. We will walk around for an hour, study all the dice tables and we wait for the hot dice table." I then explained to him about hot tables. Well anyway sure enough, there was a hot table that night in Binions. There was a cowboy who was throwing the dice and apparently he'd made a four or five timer that night. We got ourselves into the table. Johnny put $100 on the win line, which I quickly took off and exchanged it for $20. He said, "Why did you do that?" I said, "John in Binions you are allowed to take 12 times the odds. So don't put $100 on the win line, put $20 on the win line and then you can put $240 behind." I tried to explain it all to him. I said, "Just leave it to me, I'll do your staking, you do the betting!" Anyway this cowboy who was throwing, he had the hat, shirt, jeans, and I don't know where cowboys come from but he definitely looked like the real deal! Meanwhile we were looking for a ten. Johnny had $300 on the hard ten. We had about $50 on the front line and $500 on the behind line. We needed this ten badly and every time this cowboy picked up the dice, he was looking at us and saying, "I'm going to throw a ten for you English guys down there." So Johnny said to him, "I'm not English, I'm Cypriot and I'm proud to be Cypriot and we want you to throw a 'Theka so the cowboy said, "What's Theka?" So Johnny said to him, "It's number ten in Greek." Theka means ten. So when the cowboy was throwing, Johnny was shouting "Theka Re!" Now 'Re' means mate. There's Johnny shouting Theka Re! Theka Re! So you gotta picture this, the cowboy is throwing the dice. We're all shouting Theka, the whole table; even the cowboy is shouting Theka! Theka! The cowboy threw many numbers and then all of a sudden he threw a ten. All of the people on the table shouted Theka! Theka! Theka! Even to this day, if I phone Johnny K, I've only got to say two words to him and he knows it's me and those two words are "Theka Re!"

One day Johnny and I were walking up to the Excalibur Hotel, which was newly built at the time, and opposite it there was a completely open space with one crane in the middle of it. We walked into the Excalibur, there was a model building of the hotel that was going to be built opposite and we asked someone there, "What's this hotel?" They said, "That's going to be the new MGM Grand Hotel, it's going to be the biggest hotel and casino in the world." So Johnny said to them, "So when do you believe that it will be finished?" They said, "It will be finished in 1994." Johnny said, "Wait a minute, it's now February 1992, are you saying you are going to build the biggest hotel and casino in the world by 1994?" They replied to him, "Our logo will be, 'We'll roar in 1994!'" So Johnny said, "You've got 18 months to build that hotel before it hits 1994." Well the MGM Grand opened its doors, I do believe for the Christmas and the New Year of 1993. Vegas had built the biggest hotel and casino in the world at the time, within 18 months. This was quite astonishing! Johnny and I walked down the strip of Vegas and Johnny used to stand and look at some of the hotel signs that were up in lights and he used to say, "I've never seen lights and signs advertising their casinos better in the world." He said, "Stevie! I'm going to be very honest with you; I'm not doing badly in life, I used to wipe my bottom with grass as a kid in Cyprus!" I was laughing as he was telling me, "now look at me, I'm in Las Vegas, we've had limousines everywhere, we've gone to shows, we've eaten in the best restaurants, and we've been looked after. I've come a long way from Cyprus." And he had.

We still hadn't met the casino host in Caesars, and it was now Tuesday afternoon at about 3 pm, Johnny stopped playing on Monday night and as I said, he was winning just under $30,000. Our flight is on Tuesday night at 7 pm. Tuesday morning we had our breakfast in one of the coffee shops in Caesar's Palace. I got a phone call from my mum to see how we were doing.

Johnny spoke to my mum and my mum said to him on the phone "Johnny! You're winning a few quid, Stevie told me, relax and enjoy Vegas, you're leaving tonight!" Johnny said, "No problem, there's no more gambling, I don't like gambling anyway but I'm happy, we've had a good time." At about 5 pm, we had to pop and see the casino host. We went into her office and she was going to comp our rooms and our beverage. She had a look at the computer and she could see that we had run up quite a lot of room service, restaurants, etc. We'd signed everything to the room. I think it came to about $6000. The casino host said to us, "Look! Guys I can see that you're winning, that's not a problem, but you've only played for about four hours." Johnny said, "Is that a problem?" The casino host said, "It's not a problem, we don't mind if you win, but we look for action, we look for turnover." That's the way it works in Vegas. They don't mind if you win a million dollars, but they are looking for action. So he said, "What are you trying to say?" The casino host said, "Look, I'll comp the room but I think you're going to have to pay the beverage, which was the food and drink." So I said straight away, "Not a problem." Johnny and I jumped back in the lift, Johnny looked at me and said, "Stevie, we've signed a lot to our room." I said, "We did Johnny but it's not a problem, it might come to about $6000. The casino host said that they would take care of the room so we've got the beverage, it's not a terrible thing. We'll pay $3000 each, which is about £1800 each, but what a time we've had Johnny, what a time!" He looked at me, put his hand on his chin and started to think and said, "We've got to play bigger?" I said, "What are you talking about? Your winning $28,000." He said, "They want action, I'll give them action." I said, "Johnny! What are you going on about? No more gambling. We'll pay the beverage, forget about it." I looked at him and I looked at him very sternly. I managed to get him to the coffee shop and I tried to talk some sense into him. After 15 minutes he said, "You're right, no more gambling, forget about it." I said, "Johnny, I'm going up to the gym, you wanna come and join me?" He replied, "Stevie! I'm going to get myself a massage and I might take a walk after to get some fresh air." I said, "Johnny?" He said to me, "Before you say anything, No More Gambling," I said. "OK!" I took myself up to the gym, which is on the top floor at Caesar's and I started to train. I'll never forget it because as I was training and I pumping some weights, I'd just finished an exercise, I looked up and Johnny walked into the gym. Now when he walked into the gym he looked white and the colour had gone from his face. I walked to the entrance of the gym, I said, "Johnny, what have you done?" I knew something was wrong. His words were to me, "Have you got any money?" I said, "What?!" He said, "Have you got any money?" I said, "What are you talking about?" He said, "I've just lost the $28,000." I said, "Are you kidding me?" He said, "No! I've just lost the $28,000 but listen to this, once I lost the $28,000 I rang and asked to be put through to the casino host straight away, this is Johnny K here, I said, I've just lost $28,000 on the blackjack, you must comp me the beverage. The casino host said to me, let me just check that Sir! She came back within 2 minutes and said, everything is complementary, your room, your beverage. Stevie, we've got everything complementary." I said, "Yeah! We have, but you've just done $28,000!" He said, "Never mind I wanted it comp and I got it comp, have you got any money?" I said, "Johnny! The time is 5.30, we've got the flight at seven o'clock! We've got to check in at six o'clock so we've got to be at the airport in 25 minutes." He said, "What have you got in cash?" I said, "$2000." He said, "Give it to me!" We ran downstairs; all I've got on is my vest and my training gear. We got to the safety deposit box and I gave him the $2000. He's run over to the blackjack table and put $2000 on the box, straight away, no hesitation. He won! He's then put the $4000 straight on the same box. He won again; he's now got $8000. He puts $3000 on the box and then doubles. Bosh! He makes 21. He wins another $6000. He plays a couple of more hands and he wins about $17,000 all within four hands. He runs to the cash desk and cashes in. We then run to the bell desk, who already had our cases and Johnny K said, "Can I have two limousines to the airport please?" The Bell Captain looked at him and replied, "Excuse me?" Johnny said, "You heard, could I have two limousines to the airport please?" The Bell Captain looked at Johnny, who was dressed in jeans and a tee shirt, looked at me dressed in a vest and my training gear on and he said, "How are you going to pay for this?" Johnny says, "I'm not!" The Bell Captain says, "Oh! Yeah? And what's your name?" Johnny replied, "My name is Johnny K." The Bell Captain picks up the phone. He makes a phone call, he whispers something, puts the phone down and says, "Um! You've got your two limousines sir waiting outside and its complementary of Caesars Palace, is there anything else I can do for you sir?" This Bell Captain all of a sudden was running after us, left right and centre. Johnny took one limousine and I took the other. We had two limousines to take us to the airport! When we got out of the two limos Johnny looked at me, and said, "You see Stevie, we got two limousines to the airport and we got our hotel complementary, we had a good time didn't we? And we won money" I said, "Johnny you're going to give me a heart attack!" We got back to Los Angeles and over dinner that night Johnny said, "I've done some thinking." I said, "Oh! Yeah? And what was that?" He said, "Stevie this gambling is no good, I'm telling you it's no good and I'm stopping." I said, "Johnny, do you mean that?" He said, "I do indeed, I'm not gambling anymore." I said, "Thank you Johnny, good for you because you're not doing my heart any good!"

Around Grand National time of 1992, I used to be quite friendly with Billy F. Billy F was the guy that played down Inverness Terrace and had the three Kings against my dad. Believe it or not, Billy F gave me the Grand National Winner seven out of eight times. He used to say to me, "Son give me a call around Grand National time and I'll give you the winner!" Well I can tell you one thing, he gave me seven winners before he died. I asked him after a couple of years, "Bill how do you get all the winners?" He said, "Son, I'm going to tell you now, I follow the horses a lot, as you know, there's only two, three or four horses that can win the National and usually I always give you one that's good value. So I'm going to be honest with you, you have been lucky, I always pick two or three out that can win it and I'll give you the value one." I've got to tell you one thing about Bill, he was one of the greatest punters at picking winners at Hunter Chases. Hunter Chases is when the horses jump over the big fences. And Bill was the governor. Well as I've told you, I've backed seven out of eight National winners on the trot. Ben Nevis 14/1, Little Polvier 28/1 and five others.

Around the summer of that year in 1992, we were invited down for a party in Plymouth. As I said, Dad's got close friends down there and it was one of his friends 60th birthday party. I didn't know if I was going to go or not but I thought to myself, yeah it will be a nice drive down, it will be a nice break. On the way down, I spoke to Johnny a couple of times, as we both now had mobiles and we decided to back Germany to beat Russia in one of the matches of the European Championships of 1992. I said, "The only thing is Johnny, are you going to watch the match? Because I'm driving down to Plymouth." He said, "What are you going to Plymouth for?" I said, "Oh, I've got to go to a party there." He said, "Well when you get to Plymouth, why don't you watch it there." I said, "Look, by the time I get to Plymouth, the match will be over." As I was driving on the motorway, I thought, I know, I'll stop in Bristol and because the party is tomorrow night, I'll stay in Bristol for the night. I'll watch the match in the hotel room, I'll go and workout in the gym, I'll pop to the casino in the evening and I'll go to Plymouth tomorrow, no rush.

I checked myself into the Swallow Hotel in the City Centre. The Swallow in 1992 was recently renovated and it was done to a very high standard, very impressive. I got into my room, put the TV on and boom! The match was just about to start. Germany won the match 1-0 from a free kick in about the 72nd minute. I thought great, Johnny and I have won some money, I'm going to go and train. I went downstairs to the gym and I said to the young lady, "Your equipment here is not heavy enough, where do you feel that I could go and work out." She said, "Are you walking or have you a car?" I said, "Since it's a nice day, I'll walk." They said, "Well there is a gym that's close by and it's 20 minutes from here." I walked to the gym and as I went in, I met a young lady that afternoon, who was later to be my wife. That's right, all these events that had taken place during the last 24 hours. The Germany bet, The Swallow Hotel, going down to Plymouth, staying overnight, walking to the gym and by not working out at the hotel gym, I met the person I was going to marry. I didn't know that then, but that's the way things worked out.

A lot of things in life, I feel are sometimes meant to be and all these events that have taken place, and all these stories maybe they were all meant to happen for a reason. The next day I travelled down to Plymouth. Had the party and came back to London.

Meanwhile, in London, friends of ours had arranged a Five Card Stud poker Game in Cockfosters, it was around their house. There was going to be six players. The game was on a Friday night. I wasn't too happy about it. The problem was, I had to go to King's Cross afterwards as someone else had arranged a poker game on the same night and I promised faithfully that I would get there, not knowing that there was going to be a game at Cockfosters. I asked the fellow who'd invited me down to King's Cross, "What time would the game finish?" He said, "We'll be going on until Saturday morning/Saturday afternoon at least." So I thought to myself, "Right! Great! Go and nick a few bob in Cockfosters, run down to King's Cross, play for three or four hours there, nick a few bob there, no problem! That's easy." Well, I got to Cockfosters and the game got big. I was quite even at the time and there came this big pot. Mr G was £50 blind. Everybody had passed and I had an Ace showing, when I looked at my hole card, it was an Ace, I had Aces backed up. I called the £50. The blind card was a Jack, which I thought at the time was quite handy because two Jacks had already passed. Mr G said, "No raise." The cards came out Jack to Mr G, two Jacks on the show and a 10 to me, Ace, 10 showing. Don't forget I've got the Aces, I can't lose this pot, two

Jacks had already passed. Mr G bet £100. Immediately, I called the £100 and raised £300. He thought for a second and he turned round and said, "Uh! Knowing you Stevie, You must have the Aces, but I'm going to gamble." He called the £300 putting £900 in the middle. The cards came out, 10 to Mr G, Jack, Jack 10 and 10 to me, now I've got showing Ace, Ten, 10 and I've got the Aces, don't forget. There's £900 in the middle and Mr G decides to bet £100. Well I know he can't have three Jacks because as I've said two Jacks have passed and even if he's got Jacks and Tens I've got Aces and Tens, so he can't win. Straight away, I call the £100 and raise £1000 without hesitation obviously. He thinks for about 10 or 15 seconds and puts £1000 in that puts £3000 in the middle. The last card now comes out. Ace to Mr G and he's now got showing Jack, Jack, Ten, Ace and a 7 to me. I end up showing Ace, Ten, Ten, 7. Two Jacks to bet, Mr G picks up all his money and bets the pot £3000! I thought, "What is he doing? He can't have three Jacks, if he's got Jacks and Tens he has lost the pot. The only way I can lose this pot is if he had hit an Ace on the last card and made Aces to match his hole card, but I had the Aces! Without hesitation I called him and I said, "Mr G, I call your £3000 and the only way you can win this pot is if you've got Aces and Jacks because I've got Aces and Tens." He said, "Your right and I've won it! I've got Aces and Jacks." Mr G had paid £1000 to hit an Ace and the odds of him winning this pot were possibly 33/1 and he had won it! That was one of those nights and I couldn't win any money. I ended up doing about £4700. That was my biggest loss at poker, up to date. I had won many, many times that kind of money but not lost that amount. To tell you the truth I took it on the chin and just to prove to you that I did, after the game at about 4 am, you know where I had to go don't you? King's Cross because I'd promised my friend that I was going down there. Now just think about it, I had to get from Cockfosters to King's Cross, I'm doing £4700, do I really want to go? But I gave my word that I would go and visit his game and give him a spin. When I walked in the game wasn't big, it was only about £5 openers, there must have been about £2000 on the table. I thought, "Oh! My God! What am I doing here.?" I can only lose my money and I'm already doing £4700. I said to the guy who was hosting the game, "Look I'm a little bit tired, but I'm prepared to play for two or three hours." Now I'll tell you a little bit about the temperament that I've got on the poker table. I sat down with a £1000 and I looked at it that this was a fresh day, fresh night, and fresh cards. No it's not what you're thinking, I didn't manage to claw back the £4700 but I managed to claw back £1500 and to tell you the truth, when I sat down at the game in King's Cross, you know what I said to myself? "I will be very, very happy if I win a monkey tonight," which is £500 by the way. It was like a test to me, to hold your record loss and then go to another game and sit down like it had never happened is a tough thing to do. I don't care what you say, any poker player out there will tell you it's down to one thing, temperament. I managed to nick £1500 and as I was driving home I was actually quite chuffed. Not that I was upset coming from Cockfosters anyway because they wanted to play again the next week, but the next time we played there, I skint them all. I'd got back the £4700 plus a couple of grand on top. They then wanted to play again, and I skint them again. A similar thing happened between Mr G and I, like the pot before, but this time he didn't hit the Aces and I skint him. We played four more times and then guess what? The games fizzled out because no one wanted to play anymore. They actually thought that they were going to beat me but they were wrong.

I think I always managed to get games because people thought that they could beat me at Five Card Stud and sometimes within the first game or two, I might lose. They might say to their friends, "Uh! Steve's not all that he's cracked up to be, they told us he was unbeatable." But like any percentage game, if you go to the casino tonight you will see many gamblers there, over the course of the period, they will never win, but they are still there aren't they? They are looking to win that night, or the night after, they are looking to win one night only and then they deal with tomorrow when it comes. I think me on poker, a lot of people look to beat me or see if they can beat me. This rarely happens, and never ever in the long run.

I was invited to a poker game one night down in the West End. While I was playing, after about an hour, there was this American guy, 90% of the time, when the last card came out he used to shout out "Ooh! Arrh! Ooh! Arrh!" Every time you got your last card. It didn't make sense. I couldn't see at the time if there was anything wrong with the game, but what I realised after two hours, he had marked the cards and every time the last card came out, if you would have hit the winning hand on the last card, e.g. you hit the straight, flush, Full House etc., or your hole card, he would cringe and blurt his Ooh's and Arrh's, so he was giving the game away!

Around August time of 1992, I took another trip down to Plymouth and I very conveniently stopped in Bristol as I was now seeing this young lady and again, I stayed overnight at the Swallow Hotel. This time I stayed a couple of nights in Plymouth just to see Dad's friends Andrew, Rocky, Gregory and a few others. One afternoon I was playing a little bit of roulette. I'd cashed up £10, that's right just a 'Tenner', and I got 40 chips, each valued at 25 p each. It was about four o'clock in the afternoon. I took one chip valued at 25 p and I put it on number 27. The Croupier span the ball and the ball landed straight in number 27 and then Ginger, who was on his way to the toilet from playing Kalooki in the Card Room, said to me, "Stevie! you've hit at a number." I said, "That's right Ging!" (Now remember Ginger, he was in the casino in Torquay, back in the 60s when the shooting happened.) He said, "What's the value of that chip £25?" I said, "£25 Ginger? 25p!" He said to me, "Don't be silly, are you telling me that one solitary chip on that number is worth 25p? I don't believe you. It must be a £10 chip, it must be a £5 chip." I said, "Ginger! It's worth 25p and he's just about to pay me £8.75. He looked at me and said, "You should be embarrassed! Max's son, you a great poker player, a big gambler, your Dad also." I said, "Ginger! Didn't anyone ever tell you, first of all, I don't play roulette but second of all and most important of all is that you do not need big money to win a lot at roulette." He said, "Obviously, you're not going to win any money by putting 25p on a number!" I said, "Ginger! It's the next spin that counts, not this spin." The Croupier paid me £8.75 and I told the Croupier to spin the ball again and I said to Ginger, "Watch!" I then put all my winnings, the £8.75 back on 27… and would you believe it repetition! Ginger's face was a picture. I'd now won £300 from 25 p. I said, "You see Ginger!" I then asked the Croupier, "What's your limit here?" He replied, "It's £25, Sir!" I said, "Ginger, watch this!" I put £25 on number 27 and £10 split. The splits mean that I can get a little bit more money on the 27, as the limit didn't allow me to. The Croupier span again and the ball landed… "No! not in 27 but it landed in 24. I had a £10 split on it and the Croupier paid me £170. I said, "Thank you very much," and I cashed in. As I cashed in Ginger asked, "How much have you won?" I said, "Ginger I've won just over £480 from 25p." I wouldn't lose more than a tenner at roulette; it's a mug's game!

When I got back to London that summer, I'd heard that the Victoria Sporting Club, the Vic in London as we all know it was having Hold'em Competitions, £25 entry fee and sometimes the prizemoney could be £3000–£4000. I'd heard they were terrific value. The only problem was that I'd never played Hold'em. Sure, I knew how to play it, but I don't think that I could really play it, if you know what I mean. So what did I do? I trotted back off to Foyle's bookshop, in Tottenham Court Road and I found myself a book on Hold'em and I read the whole book within a day! I then entered the competition on Saturday. There were 130 runners and as luck would have it and I believe it was luck, I ended up finishing 6th. I thought to myself, maybe I can be a Hold'em player! Because Hold'em does take a lot of patience. There is a very good player at Hold'em, possibly one of the top players in the world and his name is Ben Roberts. Ben saw me play that night and he said, "Stevie! It seems like you've got the hang of Hold'em." I said, "Ben, this is the first time I've ever played." He said, "Stevie! If you play like that, you won't go far wrong. This was a great compliment coming from someone like Ben who is a top professional. The week after, I went back but I got knocked out early. The week after the same thing happened. I realised with tournaments you have to be lucky. I don't consider myself a good tournament player as in tournaments you have to change gears at the right time. When I'm playing cash poker games, I want to change my own gears. That means I want to feel when I want to press and I want to feel when I want to retreat, but in a tournament you are governed by the 'ante' and the ante goes up possibly every half an hour or every hour. You've got to know how to control your chips.

On a couple of Saturdays I got to the Vic and I was a little bit too late to play the Hold'em Tournament, so me and my girlfriend who now used to come down on the weekends, used to pop to a lovely Greek Restaurant by the name of Rodos. This was by the Centre Point building in Tottenham Court Road. We used to walk from the Vic in Edgware Road, along Oxford Street to the Greek restaurant, have our dinner and walk back. I'm telling you all this for a particular reason. One Saturday night we had our dinner at the Greek restaurant and we walked back to the Vic. It was quarter to one in the morning. When we got back to the Vic, my girlfriend and I had a drink at the bar and I went downstairs to the card room to see if there was any action. I saw Maurice at the back of the card room and it looked like they were playing Kalooki. I went up to say hello. I said, "Hi! Maurice, how are you?" "Fine Stevie! How are you and how's Dad, the family?" and Maurice as I've said is 100% gentleman. I said, "What are you playing Maurice, Kalooki?" He said, "No, we're playing a game called Mythical." Mythical to this day, I still don't know how you play but Maurice apparently was a very good Mythical player and a good gambler. He was playing with four other guys. Maurice said to me, "Where's Dad? How is Dad?" I said, "Dad's fine Maurice, I don't know where he is, he's probably at Oxford dogs," (because at this time, Dad had a pitch at Oxford and on a Saturday night Dad used to pop down there to see what was going on and what the action was like.) Maurice continued to say, "It's a shame you can't get hold of him because the guys that I am playing with at the moment love to play poker." I said, "What do you mean Five Card Stud?" He said, "Yeah! Get hold of Dad and we'll have a little Five Card game. Now a little Five Card Game to Maurice means a big Five Card game! I went to the pay phone at the Vic and I rang Dad on his car phone. Dad answered it, I said, "Dad, I'm down at the Vic, where are you? He said, "We've been to Oxford Dogs, we've had something to eat and I'm heading home with a couple of friends." I said, "Well Dad if you come to the Vic now, they're willing to play poker." He said, "What do you mean?" I said Maurice is here, he's got four friends and they're willing to play Five Card poker." He said, "Are you sure? I'm not going to come all the way down there and there's no poker! I said, "Dad, there will be poker." Dad said, "I'm on my way!" We never used to take our mobiles into the casino in those days and I'll tell you why, they were too big! They were like bricks, if you remember rightly. About an hour went by and I rang Dad back on his car phone and said, "Dad! Where are you?" He said, "I'm just heading into the West End now." I said, "It's a quarter to three in the morning! They've asked me where you are?" He said, "I'll be there in five minutes." Sure enough within five minutes Dad walked through the door. Came up to the Card Room, said hello to Maurice and his friends and they went onto the poker table. The game was a £10,000 sit down, Dad and four others. The game lasted 30 minutes and I'll tell you exactly what happened.

Around 20 to 4 one of Maurice's friends outdrew Dad and made three Jacks. Boom! Just like that. Dad had done the 10 grand. Maurice's friend said, "Come on Max! Come on Max! Get some more money." I'll never forget it. Dad looked at his watch and said, "Not tonight, we'll play tomorrow night." They said, "We want to play tonight, we might not be here tomorrow night." Dad said, "Look! You've beat me tonight, I'll be here tomorrow night." They said, "OK! What time?" Dad said, "Early, so we can play for six or seven hours." The game was on for eight o'clock the next day. Well the next night was a Sunday night, the game started at eight o'clock. It was a very good game and at the end of the night, Dad broke even. They'd managed to attract another one or two big players and it looked like the games were really going to take off at the Vic. The next night, Monday night, the game was on again eight o'clock start. I was sitting behind Dad, I had a share with my dad and I can tell you now that if you ever have a share with my dad at playing poker and you're sitting behind him, I advise you not to look at his hole card. (I will tell you of an instance a couple of years later when I get to it, about someone who did sit behind my dad and did look at his hole card.) All I can say is he can certainly scare you, even if you have a share with him. So what I did was not to look at his hole card and that way I didn't know what Dad had got. The games got very, very big at the Vic. After a couple of weeks, I said to Dad, "That guy who won that money off you the first night looks very familiar." Dad said, "I don't recognise him." I said, "I'm telling you Dad, I've got a feeling that guy is the same guy, the same little guy that used to sit down at Aspinalls, ten years ago by the name of Taleef." Dad said, "I don't think it's him." I said, "I think it's him." Well it turned out to be the same guy, ten years later Dad was sitting back at the table with him.

The games at the Vic got so big, there was a £25 running ante each of the eight players. The opening bet was £100 or £200. So with two or three callers there was always a £1000 in the middle on the first card. They were and this is a fact, the biggest Five Card Stud games that I'd ever seen. They also were the very last Five Card Stud games for that size in England. Five Card Stud never really was played again on that kind of limit. The end result after six weeks was that Dad skint the lot of them. I had a 5% with Dad and I won a hell of a lot of money. Just so that you can estimate, it was a 10 grand table and every player had to sit down with a minimum of 10 grand every night. Some players would sit down with 15, some with 20, Dad always used to sit there with 25 and Dad never lost for five and a half weeks, he skint them all every night. I'll leave it for you to estimate the winnings of those games at the Vic. Having said that and Dad will say this himself, he hit some terrific cards and he was hitting form, but the difference is as I've always said, when you're hitting cards and you know how to maximise your winnings, this is what determines winning poker players from losing ones. Dad maximised every single night's winnings and as I told you, when he sits at the table and he hits form, God help you! If I would have hit those cards that Dad hit at the Vic for those five weeks, sure I would have won, but I'd never have won the amount of money he had done. I was very happy with my 5% share, the only thing I was worried about was that my now girlfriend who had just moved to London didn't see me for 5 and a half weeks! I was coming home at five in the morning and getting up about midday. She says now after eleven years of marriage, "I couldn't believe it, I moved in and it was like you moved out playing poker every night." I always say the same thing to her, "Those games in 1992 were the best, they will never come back those games of 1992."

Someone said to me very recently, "Steve do you know you get those guys who play poker once a week for 20 years? They all get round someone's house and play poker and the games always last, do you know why the games never last with you?" I said, "Yeah! because I always get the money" He said, "That's right, have you ever thought that these games that last 20 years once a week, the reason they last are because the money goes round?" Now the point he was trying to make here is that the money goes round and round, so at the end of 20 years, there are not really many winners and not really many losers so the game can continue. "But you Steve," he continued to say, "You end up winning all the money and after three or four months the games are finished. Take it easy a little bit, give some back!" Well this as you know is easier said than done. The games at the Vic fizzled out after six weeks because as I said Dad absolutely got the lot. You can't help but maximise the wins on the poker table, no matter what you say, poker has an element of luck. All I say is how you maximise the winnings and how you minimise the losses is what counts.

In November 1992 I took my girlfriend to Vegas and we stayed at the Excalibur Hotel. Now if any of you know the Excalibur is at the top of the strip. One morning my girlfriend and I woke up at about nine o'clock, got some breakfast and we started to walk slowly down the strip. We stopped in every casino that took our fancy. She played a little 'slots', even though she was 19 at the time, I played a little poker for maybe 20 minutes. Well we set off from the Excalibur at 10 am, we got down to the Golden Nugget by foot at 7.30 pm that night. We had walked for nine and half hours, obviously stopping in most of the casinos and having a coffee and playing a little, but by the time we got down to the Nugget we were absolutely starving and we ate in the Nugget, which I still believe is one of the greatest buffets in Vegas. I looked at her and said, "Well one thing's for sure, we can't walk back, can we?" and we laughed. We took a cab and as we jumped into the cab, we told him that we'd walked from the Excalibur and at first he didn't believe us. I said, "We did, could you tell us how many miles it is?" He said, "I can tell you now, it's about seven and a half miles but did you know that there is a really bad part of town that you had to walk through before you got Downtown? After the strip finishes and before Downtown begins, there are a couple of blocks of really 'no go' areas in Vegas." My girlfriend and I looked at each other and said, "Wow! We must have been lucky."

By the end of 1992 some very close friends of mine, Bambos, Leffey, Roula, and Johnny K all decided to go skiing. I'd only been skiing once before and

I wasn't a good skier. My girlfriend hadn't been skiing but I booked her about seven or eight dry slope skiing lessons so at least she could 'snow plough' and keep up with the rest of us. When we got to Heathrow Airport our flight was delayed. They said there would be about a two- and half-hour delay. The girls were all together having a coffee and the boys didn't know what to do for two hours. Actually, it was Johnny K that suggested that we play poker at the airport. We ran to the shop and brought a pack of cards and we started playing. The game got bigger and bigger and as people were walking past where we were playing, their eyes lit up at the amount of money that was on the table. There must have been about two grand in cash on the table. There was someone who knew me from Plymouth who was on his way to Cyprus, he came over and said, "Stevie! Only you can get a game of poker at the airport." He then continued to say to the other boys, "Don't you know who he is, he is going to skin you, he is going to end up winning his holiday money." They all laughed. We did play a couple of times when we got to the ski resort, but it wasn't really the right time or place. Anybody that's been skiing knows that you get up really early in the morning, so poker was not on the agenda. We were having dinner one night and as my girlfriend finished her meal she undone the top button of her trousers and said, "Cor! I've over eaten tonight." Johnny K looked at her and said, "Cor! You must have eaten a lot your tummy is coming out a bit, to which I immediately replied jokingly, "That's right John, she's expecting." Everybody laughed even my girlfriend and me, except Johnny. Johnny K turned round and said, "Stevie! My gut feeling is that she is pregnant." I said, "Don't be silly John." He said, "I'm telling you and he put his hand on his chin and when Johnny puts his hand on his chin, he's usually thinking and he repeated, "I'm telling you she's pregnant." I then said, "If she's pregnant, we're going to Las Vegas, all of us and we're getting married, on one condition that everybody on this table comes to my wedding. Bambos then looked up and said, "And if she is pregnant, I'm the godfather." I said, "Deal!" The next day everything was forgotten. We got back to London and yes my girlfriend was pregnant, so it was time to go to Vegas. This time not for gambling, but for a wedding and what a wedding it was going to turn out to be!

The beginning of 1993 was very hectic with the arrangements for our wedding in Las Vegas. When we were last there we noticed that the Excalibur Hotel had a lovely chapel on the top floor. So I said to my girlfriend that's where we are going to get married! I said to my friends, everybody that was at skiing, we're going to set the date for March. Everyone was looking forward to going to Las Vegas together. It looked like it was going to be about 15 or 20 of us, but there was a lot of arranging to be done, flights, accommodation etc.

There wasn't too much happening on the poker scene during the first couple of months of 1993. One night I popped to the Vic to see if there was any action and who did I bump into? Reggie was playing roulette. I said, "What's happening Reggie where have you been hiding?" He said, "Stevie, I've decided to knock poker on the head with you and I'm playing a little bit of roulette." I said, "How are you doing?" He said, "To be honest with you, I'm losing about £1000." As time went on, it was now 10 to 4 in the morning. Reggie was about £800-£900 behind and the Croupier called last three spins. The third spin from last, Reggie didn't hit a number. He then put £100 on number 5, the second spin from last. The Croupier span the ball and it went in to number 5. Reggie had won £3500. He said, "Reggie, Reggie, Reggie! Only Reggie can hit £100 straight up on a number." So I said, "You must be winning now Reg, yeah?" He said, "I'm winning about £2500 Steve." I said, "Good, one more spin to go and it's a winning night for you." The Croupier span the ball, Reggie put another £100 on number 5 and he covered all the neighbours and as luck would have it, boom! Straight into number 5 repetition. Reggie scooped £7000. He was now winning just over £9000 on the night! He was over the moon. He said, "I told you Stevie roulette is my game." He cashed in and as we were walking down the stairs to leave the Vic, he said, "What are you doing now?" I said, "Reg it's 10 past 4 in the morning, I'm going home." He said, "I'll play you poker, Heads Up." I said, "Reggie please you said to me, you're never play me poker again." "I'll play you poker," he said. I said, "Reg, this time I'm going to say to you, no." You know what he said to me? "I'm telling you why you've said no, because you know Reggie's on form, Reggie, Reggie, Reggie, when Reggie's on form, you know he is going to skin you." I said, "If we play poker and I win, you're going to get the hump." He said, "I've never got the hump, good luck to you, I'll tell you what I'll do, make me a promise, I'll come back to your place and I want to sit there with only £3000. If I lose more than £3000 you can't take it off me, do not let me lose another penny." I said, "There you go, don't let me lose, you said. You're already thinking you are going to lose." Reggie said, "You wanna play me or not?" I said, "I can't believe you, alright follow me." We went back to my flat and we set up the table. We each put £3000 in front of us and I'm going to tell you exactly what happened because I'll never forget it. Within

25 minutes Reggie was losing £2980 and all he had left in front of him was a £20 note. He wasn't upset. He was still winning over £6000 on the night but he said, "I knew I shouldn't play you at poker. I've always said, Stevie's too good." I said, "Reggie don't blame me, because I told you." He said, "I'll tell you what I want to do, I want a squeezy." This is what happened. He put his last £20 in the middle; Reggie won the squeezy for £20. He then left the £40 in for another squeezy. All I had to do was win this squeezy and Reggie was out of the game and I could go to bed within half an hour of starting. Reggie won the second squeezy. He now had £80 in front of him. He said, "I'll do another squeezy. I said, "Go on Reg stick it in." He stuck the £80 in and he'd won the third squeezy. Now he had £160 in front of him. He looked at me and said, "Lovely, let's play poker." Now the game was back on. Don't forget I had just under £6000 and Reggie had £160. Well in the next two and half hours Reggie started to claw his money back and I've always said, when he hits some form, Reggie can be dangerous. By eight o'clock in the morning, Reggie and me were still playing and I said to him, "Reggie, it's late I wanna count up?" He said, "What do you mean, are you stopping?" I said, "I'll tell you what if we're levels [because meanwhile, Reggie had been winning pot after pot], I'm stopping." He said, "Steve you got a deal." I said, "Reggie, even if you're winning, I'm going to stop." I'll tell you why, I could see the tide going Reggie's way and I'll tell you what, he would have skint me that night and I was getting tired. I mean after 25 minutes you're winning £2980 from the guy and the next thing you know, three and half hours later you're losing, or your even levels, I wanted to call it a day. We had a count up and I had in front of me £3020. Reggie had a count up and he had £2980. He was losing £20, I was winning £20. We laughed. I said, "Reggie, I'm taking that £20 because that's my bus fare for tonight." He was laughing. He said to me, "I'll tell you what I'll do Steve, I'll squeeze you for the £20, so I can finish dead levels on the night, when I win the squeezy." The first squeezy Reggie lost. He then put in £40, the second squeezy Reggie lost again. He then put £80, the third squeezy Reggie lost. He looked at me and said, "Put £160!" I said, "No Reggie, let's play poker!" We started again. My girlfriend got up at about ten o'clock in the morning and made us tea and breakfast, as we were playing. Well it took me till 1:30 in the afternoon to take every single penny off Reggie. He wasn't upset and I looked at him and I meant this when I said this to him. I said, "Reg why didn't you stop when you were levels?" He said, "I weren't levels I was losing £20!" I said, "You know what, you should have

said to me, 'give me the £20,' I probably would have given it to you." He looked at me and said, "Steve, you won fair and square." I said, "Yeah! But what a battle it was." He said, "Can you do me a favour?" as he was leaving. I said, "What's that Reg." He said, "Lend me a couple of hundred quid until the next time." I said, "No problem Reggie, I'll speak to you during the week." Reggie left.

I'm going to now tell you the most money I've ever seen won in a casino from a £10 note. That's right just a tenner. We were walking out one night from the Park Towers casino with my dad and it was around 10 to 4 in the morning, there used to be a roulette wheel, which was close to the exit door. There was no one on this roulette table and just as we were walking past the table the young lady Croupier called, "Last three spins." Dad pulled out a tenner and he put the £10 note on number 29. The ball landed in 29 and she paid him £350. Dad took the £350 and put £200 back on 28 and the £150 on number 29. This was going to be the second spin from last. She span the ball and the ball went into number 28. She paid my dad £7000. She then called the last spin. In those days the limit was £200 on a number. Dad put £200 splits around 28, £200 on 29 and £200 splits again. The last spin of the night went into number 29! So let me just recap. The ball for the last three spins went 29, 28, 29! Dad had won just under £30,000 with a tenner. That's right just a tenner and we were on our way out of the casino at the time! Very few gamblers are able to win this amount of money from such a small amount.

March came round and it was time to go to Vegas for the wedding. We all met up at Heathrow Airport. Eventually, 30 friends and family were all going to fly to Vegas. I told my friends and relations in Los Angeles and they were also going to meet us there. We flew Virgin Atlantic and once the crew knew that we were all going over for a wedding party, the Virgin crew looked after us really well. Now I know that there were quite a few of my friends who couldn't make it genuinely because of work commitments but I want to tell you about a couple of friends that I've got that are barristers. Leffy was married to my best man and friend to this day, a guy named 'Chinnie', that's his nickname. She had a court case on Monday morning in London and she was defending a person. My wedding in Vegas was on a Saturday and we were flying on the Thursday. Leffy said, "Steve, we are not missing your wedding." They flew with us on the Thursday, I got married on the Saturday and they left on a Sunday morning from Vegas and arrived back on Monday morning and Leffy went straight to court to defend someone. So sometimes when people say they cannot make it because of business commitments, we all understand and sometimes it cannot be helped, but sometimes if you really want to go somewhere you'll get there.

Anyway I want to tell you a little bit about our stag night. All the boys got together and we all met at Caesars because Johnny K was staying there. He now had a good relationship with Caesars Palace and they looked after him. He had limos everywhere. We're all staying at the Excalibur, nice hotel, maybe not in the class of Caesars but still quite a good hotel. We all met at about eight o'clock, about 15 guys and I said, "Let me plan the stag party boys, first of all we're all putting $200 each and we are going to give it to my dad." No one asked any questions. I said, "Right dad, now you've got $3000 and we're going down town and we're going to play craps, 12 times the odds at Binions." We went down town and we'd lost $1000 in about 45 minutes. No one was too unhappy; after all we'd all put our money together. I said, "Look guys, let's go up to Stutbacks, where you can have any limit, crapless craps." Then everybody started saying, "What's crapless craps Steve?" I said, "Don't worry let's get up there and I'll tell you." We went straight on the crapless craps at Stutbacks and dad done another $1000 within 20 minutes. Then everyone was saying to me, "Steve, this crapless craps is crap," and they were all laughing at me. I said, "Look guys I can only tell you that when I come to Vegas a couple of times a year, I always make money." We only had $1000 left. Dad went onto the roulette and when Dad went to place his first bet, Bambos said to my dad, "Max I fancy number 30." As the ball spun, Dad never heard Bambos, the ball went into number 30. He said, "There you go Max, I fancied that and you didn't listen to me." Dad said, "Bambos, I didn't hear you, you should have shouted it to me, what do you fancy now Bambos?" Bambos said, "I fancy number 26." That time dad put our money on 26 and what do you think the ball went in to? Straight back into number 30, 'repetition'! We looked at each other and couldn't believe it. If we'd had the first 30, we would have had the second 30 for a lot more, I'm telling you. The third spin and only my dad can do this, trust me, he then puts the rest of our money back on number 30. So we all looked at dad and said, "Dad, we've missed the boat! We missed 30 the first time and we missed 30 the second time, we've missed it." Dad looked at us emotionless and said nothing. The ball went into number 30 for the third time! Dad looked at us and said, "You see." The big shame is we never got number 30 the first time, otherwise we would have won a lot of money that night. We recovered all our money and we were winning a couple of thousand dollars, everybody was happy and they said, "Let's go back on this crapless craps, the game that Stevie says we can't lose at." Well I'm going to cut a long story short, we done the whole $3000 plus the extra $1500 we were winning, all on the crapless craps! Everyone looked at me as we walked out of Stutbacks and said, "Steve, that was a load of crap!" We all went for dinner at Caesars, where the statues moved in the shopping mall. We were all laughing because after all we only lost $200 each. I can tell you now, that was the first time and the only time I've ever lost in Vegas and that was for $200 on my stag night. I still say this to my wife today, the only time I ever lost in Vegas was on my wedding trip!

The next day on the Saturday, was the wedding. All in all there were about 45 people. A couple of the guests made me laugh. They drove all the way from LA. His name was Scottish Steve and he lived in LA at the time. He walked in with his girlfriend and his two friends, who I didn't know but they were very welcome. As he walked in, he said to me, "I'm sorry we're all not dressed but we've just come straight from the gym in LA as I realised that your wedding was at 3 pm and I said, to my friends we've got no time to wash, shower, change nothing, let's get to Vegas. You know Steve, the speed limit over here is 55 mph, I was doing 75–80 mph to get here on time and I've just got here." I said, "Steve it doesn't matter how you dress, you're welcome, you're here." The guy made the effort; he drove five hours to get to my wedding. They were all in their workout gear, the vests, bodybuilding pants, everything, it was so funny. The Excalibur Hotel really looked after us. They gave my wife and me a lovely Jacuzzi suite when they knew we were getting married. The next afternoon on the Sunday, I had to make sure I was up early because Leffy and Chinnie were going back to London. Dad had left early in the morning for Caesar's Palace with Mario from Plymouth, Chris his brother and Bambos. They put $100 each and they decided to play roulette. With the first $100 bill, dad hit a repetition 32 and won $12,000, which obviously had to be divided up four ways, but the boys came back to the hotel and they were absolutely ecstatic that within four or five spins dad had won this money with the first $100. I looked at them all and I said, "Uh! Because I got up early to see my friends to the airport, you guys went to Caesars and you won 12 grand." They all looked at me and said, "Steve, you want to be in it, we'll put you in, and you can have a share of the winnings." I said, "Guys, you know me well enough, if I wasn't there and I didn't put my $100 in, I'm not in, good luck to you all, but remember only Max can win this kind of money from a $100 bill." I still believe until this day, that Vegas is the most incredible place there is on the planet and if you've never been there, whether you gamble or not you've got to go and witness the hotels, the shows and the food.

One night 10 or 12 of us got together and we decided to pop down town as we'd seen that the Golden Nugget was advertising $1.99 breakfast, steak and eggs, all you can eat. "Wait a minute," we all said, "$1.99 steak and eggs, all you can eat? We want to see this." We then went up to the restaurant at the Nugget. They said, "Sir our breakfast starts at about midnight, you pay $1.99, and you're allowed to eat as many eggs and as much as you like that's on the buffet but you're only allowed one steak." So my dad said to the guy and I'll never forget it, "Can we see the steak that you're going to give us?" He said, "By all means." We went into the restaurant and this steak was like a 10–12oz Sirloin Steak, it looked unbelievable. We all paid $1.99, which included unlimited soft drinks, and the steak was incredible. I've heard recently that they've stopped doing this in the last five or six years. Obviously, they couldn't have been making any money, but I'll never forget those $1.99 breakfasts. Dad asked the guy for another steak and the guy said, "You can have another steak sir, but it's another $1.99. Dad said, "No problem, I'll pay you the extra $1.99!" To this day you could never beat that for value.

After a week in Vegas, my wife and I went to Los Angeles to see a few friends who didn't come over for the wedding and we decided to go out one night. There was George that I still keep in contact with. (You know the guy who never turns up for anything) and also I made arrangements to see Jay. That was the guy I knew from Marbella and Vegas, he had got married to a young lady called Kim. He told me a story and I thought I'd share it with you. He too got married in Vegas, at the Mirage Hotel. One day, Kim his wife went swimming and when she got out of the pool she realised she had lost the diamond in her ring. She was really upset as it was the engagement ring that Jay had given her a year or two previously. They notified the swimming attendants and they said, "When we clean out the pool, we will definitely let you know as we know this means a lot to you." A couple of days went past and they'd found nothing. Just before they were leaving the Mirage Hotel after a five-night stay, on the last day, Jay was swimming and as he dived in, he was swimming under water and from the corner of his eye about 20 yards away he could see something glisten or sparkle. He swam over to it and could you believe it, it was the actual diamond stone to his wife's ring! He's picked up the stone and as he's come up from the water he shouted to his wife, "I've got it! I've got it, I've found it!" He had found the diamond stone that lay at the bottom of the Mirage Swimming Pool after five days of it being lost, quite incredible. I wonder if Jay had said to me, "Steve what are the odds that we find the diamond after five days of it being missing?" Well it could have been another million to one chance.

After Los Angeles we took a couple of weeks in Honolulu and we stayed at one of the nicest hotel resorts in the world. It was the Hilton Hawaii Village, a superb hotel with over 3000 bedrooms, set in its own location with its own restaurants and own beach, right at the top of Waikiki Beach. After the two weeks went by, it was time to get back to London.

Everything seemed a little quiet back 'on the western front' as we say. There seemed to be no poker. A couple of months went past and there were still no games. It seemed to be getting very quiet on the poker scene. I met up with Reggie a couple of times and we had a coffee in Hampstead, not far from the station. He came with another friend of ours named Mark. We were sitting there having a chat and after lunch, it was Reggie that suggested that we play Spoof and the loser pays for the bill. Of course Reggie won and me and Mark split the bill. Mark and Reggie started playing spoof and within no time at all Reggie had taken about £100 off Mark. Mark said, "You're too good at spoof, I'll play you heads or tails." Meanwhile we're sitting outside this restaurant at the top of the hill in Hampstead High Street and Reggie and Mark decided to flip a coin for £20. Reggie flicked it quite high in the air and he couldn't catch it, the coin bounced on the floor and started rolling down the hill. Mark and Reggie immediately left the table and they started chasing this coin down Hampstead High Street to see what it had landed on. They'd run about 20 yards and all of a sudden I heard, "Reggie, Reggie, Reggie's won again, it's heads!" Mark said, "I can't believe this." I decided to go and join them and as they were standing outside the tube station, Reggie said to me, "Steve, I bet you £20 the next person that comes out of the tube station is a female." I said, "Reggie, what are you on about?" He said, "I bet you £20 that the next person to come out of Hampstead tube station is a female." I said, "OK you've got a bet, I say it's a male." Now at Hampstead Tube, they have to come up by the elevator, so we're waiting by the front doors and we couldn't see who was coming out. All of a sudden the elevator doors open and about eight to ten people get out, men and women. I'm cheering for a man to come out first and Reggie's cheering for a woman. Reggie won the first £20. Ten minutes go by, Reggie said to me, "Stevie again, £20 I say a woman comes out of the tube station but this time, if she's wearing glasses you've got to pay me double but if a man comes out wearing glasses I've got to pay you double." "You're on," I said. As we're standing again outside the tube station, the elevator doors open. One woman walks out of the elevator and she's got glasses on, can you believe it! I paid him £40. He then said, "Steve, if you want to get your money back we will wait for the next train and I say the next person that comes out is a woman and if she's wearing glasses, you've got to pay me double and if she comes out with a child you've got to pay me treble." I said, "Wait a minute Reggie, I haven't got a chance because a man is not going to come out of the tube station with a child! He might be wearing glasses but the odds are he won't have a child with him. To level it off a little bit, you can have your bet if the woman comes out with glasses and a child, I'll pay you treble, but if a man comes out with glasses and a briefcase you've got to pay me treble." (Me thinking I've now got an edge.) So the bet was on, Reggie is rubbing his hands. We're waiting and waiting, the doors opened. It was full of people; there must have been about ten businessmen with briefcases. Now I'm looking for the one with glasses to get paid the maximum! Just towards the back of the elevator, I could not believe what I saw. The men in the elevator helped a lady out, she had a pram with her, she started to walk towards the exit and she had glasses on! Well sure enough, she came out first. Reggie took out a fiver and put it straight into her hand and said, "Thank you very much, you've just won me £60, because I've just had a bet that a woman will come out with glasses and a child." She said to him, "You should have got paid more because I've got twins in there!" Reggie looked at me and said, "Stevie that's £80 you owe me." Sure enough I paid Reggie £80 for that bet! All in all Reggie nicked off us about £300 that day and I said to him later on in the evening, "Reggie good luck to you, you've done me and Mark up like a kipper. Him on the spoof and the heads and tails, and me at the tube station, guessing whose going to come out first, but can you tell me something Reggie, why were you picking women all the time?" He said, "Stevie, don't you know why?" I said, "No, tell me." He said, "You're meant to be a shrewd boy." I said, "Obviously, I'm not that shrewd because last time we had a bet at the airport, you had about four suitcases on the bloody flight and I didn't think about that, how have you won this?" He said, "What time were we having the bets at?" I said, "I don't know Reggie four or five o'clock, I don't know." He said, "No, we were having the bets at about 3:35 pm, no later than 4:15." I said, "So?" He said, "I had the odds in my favour." So I said, "How comes?" He said, "Come on Stevie think for a second, the kids finish school at 3 30, 3.45, maybe 4 o'clock. The mothers pick them up, what man usually finishes work at 3:30 or 4:00pm." I looked at Reggie and I said to him, "Your right Reggie, this time you done us!"

Another time I was in Hampstead having a coffee with Reggie and Johnny K, it was Bank Holiday Monday. Usually on bank holidays they have a fun fair up on Hampstead Heath. We decided to walk along and have a look at the fair. Johnny was getting very hungry and we stopped off at a hot dog stall in the middle of the fair and Johnny had a couple of hot dogs, one after the other. Reggie said to Johnny, "Cor John you must have been hungry, you've eaten two hot dogs within a minute?" Johnny looked up and replied, "Reggie I'm so hungry, I could eat another five." Reggie looked at Johnny and said, "Johnny, I bet you £20, that you can't eat another five and I'll buy the hot dogs for you, but if you lose you've got to give me £20 and the hot dog money." Johnny said, "Reggie, order them!" Reggie ordered five hot dogs and Johnny ate one after the other, Johnny won £20! Reggie then said, "I can't believe that, you must have been hungry Johnny give me a chance to get my money back, I bet you double or nothing, you can't eat one more hot dog." Johnny shouts, "You're on!" Reggie said, "Wait a minute, I'm not finished, you've got to eat this one more hot dog [as Reggie was saying this, he was pointing up towards the sky] from up there!" Johnny said, "Up where?" Reggie said, "Up there, do you see those two rockets that are going up and down at the bottom of the fair?" Johnny said, "Yeah?" Reggie said, "You've got to take the hot dog, go down there, get on the ride and you've got to eat the hot dog when the rocket reaches the top!" Now this ride Reggie was talking about, there were two rockets, they went up maybe 100 feet up in the air and when the rocket came down the other rocket went up 100 feet up in the air and they both span round revolving, at the same time! It was like a circular motion, one rocket up and one rocket down, spinning continuously. Johnny looked at Reggie and said, "You're still on!" Johnny ordered the extra hot dog but just before we left the hot dog stand, Reggie grabbed the tomato sauce and said to Johnny, "Give me that hot dog for a second." Reggie then plastered it with tomato ketchup! Johnny said, "You're having a laugh Reg aren't you?" Reggie replied, "That's the bet, you've got to eat the hot dog only when the rocket reaches the top." Anyway we got down to the ride, Johnny jumps into the rocket at ground level with the hot dog in his hand. Reggie said to Johnny, "Don't forget, only when you're at the top, stick your head out and eat the hot dog, if you don't eat all that hot dog, you've lost your money." Well the ride set off, it was building higher and higher because it didn't go to the top straight away. All of a sudden the rocket gets up to the top, Johnny is spinning around in the rocket, Johnny's head comes out of the rocket and bang! In goes the hot dog. Tomato ketchup all over his face! The rocket starts to come down. Johnny shouts out to Reggie, "Reggie I've eaten half of it." Reggie said, "You've got to eat all of it Johnny!" The rocket then goes back up and Johnny sticks his head out when he's at the top again.... Bang! Again he puts the hot dog into his mouth and tomato sauce again goes all over his face! He came down, Reggie said, "Looks like I've lost?" Johnny said, "Not yet, there's a little bit left!" Then the rocket goes up for the third time and is spinning 360 degrees, it gets to the top and Johnny sticks out his head yet again, he then sticks the last bit of the hot dog into his mouth. Well Johnny came down looking worse for wear. He has got tomato sauce all over his face, all over his clothes, he gets out and said, "Reggie give me my £40 now!" Reggie said, "Wait a minute." Johnny said, "Why?" Reggie said, "Let me inspect the rocket." Reggie jumped into the rocket and was looking for pieces of bread or a bit of sausage, which could be left from the hot dog! Reggie got out and looked very disappointed. Reggie said, "You've won John, I can't believe you've eaten that hot dog!"

Towards the middle of 1993, I heard that there were some very good poker games in Haringey at a Club called the Casanova Club. I'd never been in this club, but I heard the games were good. One Saturday night at about two o'clock in the morning, I popped down and the game was in full flow. Walking into the Casanova Club reminded me of walking back into the Empress Club as a kid. It had the same décor; it looked like it hadn't been decorated for 30 years! I sat down at the table and I started to play. The next thing I knew, after about ten minutes, the player on my right tapped me under the table on my shin. I looked at him, but he didn't look at me. About five minutes later, he tapped me on my shin again. I looked at him to see what he wanted, again he didn't look at me. This guy who tapped me on my shin, I've known him all my life, he was playing poker when I was in my nappies. I thought to myself, why is he tapping me? I started to look around at the table, to see if I could see if there was anything going on. I couldn't see anything, but every five minutes he was tapping me. All of a sudden there was quite a big pot between two players on the table and the attention of the table went to this pot. He looked at me and said under his breath, "This game is not for you." I looked at him and again he said, "Did you hear me? This game is not for you." I said, "Why not? It's a good game" He then tapped me under the table again. Another 20 minutes later, now I've been there almost 45 minutes, he said to me again, "The game is not for you," whispering it under his breath. Now I think, I knew there was something not right, maybe this guy was trying to protect me. I haven't mentioned his name on purpose. I still see him to this day. I announced to the table that I would be leaving in half an hour. No one said anything. I got up and the guy that was hosting the games asked me, "Was everything alright Steve?" I finished dead levels and all I said was "Fine." I wished everybody goodnight and I left. I know what the guy meant, (the one that was tapping me under the table). The game wasn't straight. This is the problem, right up until today about Five Card Stud. As I said before, Five Card Stud is the best gambling game there is at poker but the problem is, with one hole card it is exposed to cheats and crooks. That's why and any of you reading this will know that Five Card Stud can only be played with people you know and people you trust.

There wasn't a lot else happening in 1993; it was one of those quiet years. I mean there were a few poker games with me and Reggie etc, and a few gambling activities but not really a lot to report on. Come 1994, it was a very exciting year indeed and I'll tell you why. A friend of mine had a restaurant, a kebab place in the West End, close to the Post Office Tower and upstairs he decided to put a poker table. Every Thursday night he decided to run poker games. I got a call, his name was 'Young George', a very nice guy. He said to me, "Steve, pop up and play poker, we have a good game every Thursday and you're welcome to come." A couple of Thursday's went by and I decided to give him a visit. When I got there, it wasn't a big game, but there were a few old faces. There were no mugs by all means at this table. I mean, there was Ali Karabina and there were one or two others that could play the game. It didn't look like a lot of value. In seat number 7 was Stavros. Stavros is a good Five Card Stud poker player and as I've said before he played many times with my dad. I decided to sit down in seat number 2, you really needed to sit down with about £1000. I sat down with £2000 and the game was flowing. I want to tell you about this pot because when I think about those games, this pot always comes to mind. There was a round blind, which means that every player had to go blind in turn, Ali Karabina was £5 blind. I was £10 over blind and Stavros was £20 super blind. I got dealt showing an 8. I called the extra £10 blind bet. Everybody else passed except for Ali Karabina, he called the £15, and he had showing a 10. As I said, Stavros was the big blind, the blind card came out and the blind card was a 9. So now there are three of us in this pot. Stavros is showing a 9, I'm showing an 8 and Ali Karabina is showing a 10. "No raise," says Stavros. The cards came out. 8 to me, two 8s on the show, 10 to Ali, two 10s on the show and 9 to Stavros, two 9s on the show. I'm going to let you know what I had. I had three 8s, the first three cards. It was Ali to bet with the two 10s. Now Ali Karabina and as I said, Karabina means tight, didn't even come out betting, he decided to check. Stavros came out betting £60. At this point, I'm going to be honest with you; I thought Stavros was trying to nick the pot. I immediately called the £60 and raised £180, I've got the three 8s remember. Ali with the two 10s on the show, immediately passed. Stavros thought for a split second and he called my £180, putting £540 in the middle. This pot was going to get interestingly big. There were two cards to come. Anyway the cards came out and you wouldn't believe what I hit. I hit an 8, so I now had showing an 8, 8, 8 and an 8 in the hole! I've got four 8s and Stavros hit a king. He's now got showing 9, 9, King. I'll never forget it, I'm now looking to extract the absolute maximum and skin Stavros in one pot. I said to the Croupier, "How much in the pot?" He said, "There's £540 Steve." I said, "I'll bet £300." Now I'll tell you the reason, I bet under the pot, I thought to myself, I don't fancy Stavros three 9s and I want to see where I stand. If he raises me, I'm going to re-raise him and skin him in one pot. Stavros thought for ten seconds and then flat called the £300, now to be honest with you, it put me into two minds what Stavros had. I thought now, if he had the three 9s, he never re-raised my £180 raise on the last card, has he got Kings and 9s and he's calling the £300, because of the value of the pot? In a way, I think I outplayed myself, but it didn't worry me when he called the £300, because I knew this pot was mine. It was just a matter of how much can I get from it. Anyway, listen to this, the last card comes out, 9 to me, I've now got showing, 8, 8, 8, 9. Still got the four 8s and King to Stavros, 9, 9, King, King showing. So in my mind, I know I've won this pot, but I had to get the maximum. Very quickly, I'll tell you exactly what I thought. I've hit a 9; I definitely don't fancy Stavros with three 9s. I wasn't too sure now what he had, but I felt deep down, he couldn't beat my three 8s. If this was the case this was exactly what I had to do. I asked the Croupier how much was in the pot and he told me £1140. I looked up and said, "Check Stavros" (I'm now looking to "trap check" him and induce him to bet). He looked at me and thought for 20 seconds and I'll never forget his words. "I check as well Steve, four 8s you win." I said,

"What?" He said, "You heard, if you've got four 8s, you win." I said, "I've got four 8s Stavros." He said, "You win then." I said, "Show cards, check, check you must show your hole card (a rule in Five Card Stud)." He turned over a 9 in the hole! He had the three 9s and very, very cleverly, Stavros lost the absolute minimum. I remember talking to my dad about this pot, this is one pot I played wrong and won. I think Stavros played it slightly wrong with two cards to come, when he had me with the three 9s against the three 8s, but then once I hit the three 8s on the show to give me four 8s, I played it wrong. Dad said, I should have bet the £540, Stavros would have called and then I should have come out and bet the pot again - £1620 and I think Stavros would have called. Well anyway just to put myself out of my misery, I saw Stavros five or six months later and when we had a chance to talk about the games, he remembered the pot and Stavros doesn't lie. I asked him, "Stavros if I came out and bet the £540, with one card to come what would you do?" He said, "Steve I'd call you." I said, "Then the last card comes out, 9 to me and King to you and I come out and bet the full pot £1620, what would you do then?" He said to me, "Steve it's 60/40 I would pass." I said, "Stavros, you've hit a Full House, wouldn't you call me?" He said, "Not necessarily, if you think and go through the whole pot, how it took place, with Ali being blind and how you've raised me from two cards out and two cards to come, I would genuinely say to you, I would probably pass the last bet." So I said, "Well in that case, how was I to extract the maximum?" He said, "The only way you could have played that properly was exactly what your Dad said, bet the £540 and then bet the £1620 at the end and hope for me to call." Stavros was being 100% honest with me because it was exactly what Dad had said, but sometimes you don't always play the pot correctly and this was one of the times. The games lasted about four months in George's Kebab place upstairs and overall I showed a profit up there. Not a big profit but I was a winner. The games soon faded out as a lot a people started going to the Vic to play Hold'em and slowly, slowly they weren't playing much Five Card, so they soon dwindled and stopped.

During 1994, we had a tip for a horse and it's not often that we get tips that I would decide to put money on. When I was given this tip, it was from a very good source indeed and the guy said to me, "Steve, this is my horse and this horse will win today, if not it will not be out of the frame." The only reservation I had was that it was at quite a big meeting and it was quite a strong field. If the horse finishes second, third or even fourth we would win on the bet because the horse was 14/1. As soon as I heard the name of the horse, I rushed round to a betting shop but I didn't have a lot of money on me, only a couple of hundred. I then rang Johnny K and I said, "John where are you?" He said, "I'm in King's Cross coming back from Hatton Garden." I said, "Have you got any money on you?" He said, "Yes." I said, "How much?" "He said, "I've got about £700–£800 on me." I said, "Where abouts in King's Cross are you John, are you near a betting shop?" He replied, "I'm just walking past a Ladbrokes now." The Ladbrokes is still there today. I said, "Johnny, run in very quickly and put me all your money you've got on this horse." He said, "Well if it's a tip, I want to back it myself." I said, "Alright John, you put down whatever you've got in your pocket and I'll take half of it. So you can have £400 on this horse and I'll have £400." He said, "How good a tip is it?" I said, "Well, I'll tell you how good it is, you can put all your money on for me. This horse will not lose today, this is what I've been told." The only thing that I thought of afterwards is that Johnny put all his money to win. The bet I had was "each way," so I would have been covered plus winning a certain amount of money if the horse had finished second, third or fourth but Johnny K would have lost his money, but we were in such a hurry, I've really not gone into great detail with Johnny. Anyway the race was off and the horse won at 14-/1. I've only received maybe three or four tips as I've said and they were very good tips indeed. I probably haven't had a tip for the last eight years. There was a reason I've told you this little story about the horse and the tip, it's because when the horse won, Johnny came to see me at the office in Haringey and he brought all our winnings. He was really happy and as we were having a coffee he said to me, "Do you know what Stevie, I wish I was in Vegas because I would go for a gamble now." I looked at him and I said, "Johnny let's have a look at the Teletext, to see if we can get a flight." We saw a Virgin Atlantic flight from Heathrow to Los Angeles for £170 return, we couldn't believe our eyes. I said, "John look at that, we can go to Los Angeles tomorrow for £170." He said, "How will we get to Vegas?" I said, "Never mind, how we're going to get to Vegas, let's get to LA for £170, it's cheaper than taking some trains anywhere in England." He said, "Book it." I'd got on the telephone and yes we managed to get two flights, Heathrow to Los Angeles, Virgin Atlantic economy, £170 each. A few stories you are now going to hear is because we backed this horse and it won.

One day later me and Johnny went to Heathrow Airport and we checked in. Now I'll tell you what kind of a funny guy Johnny was. As we checked in, he's asked to be upgraded. He's said to the young lady behind the desk,

"I wonder if you could upgrade me please?" She said to him, "Mr K the flight is quite full but you are best to ask just before you board the plane, and if they are able to upgrade you they will." He said, "Lovely, thank you." After we checked in our suitcase I said, "Johnny, listen for £170 each you want to be upgraded?" He said, "Stevie, they will upgrade you if you ask nicely, leave it to me." Now, as we were going to the gate, he's let everybody go in first and sit down. He then went up to the gate and as we were giving in our boarding passes, he said to the young lady, listen to this, "I'm a boxer from London and we've booked first class, but because there was no vacancies on first class, we've ended up in economy, I'm not very happy. I always fly Virgin Atlantic. I've got a very big fight in Las Vegas, I'm the current Greek Cypriot Middle Weight Boxing Champion and I need leg room." I've looked at Johnny and I tell you what, I know I play poker, but I've nearly cracked up laughing. She's looked at John and she said, "I'm very sorry sir, but I'm unable to upgrade you, you're best to go and sit in your seats and after take-off, ask the flight attendant if there is any room and they might upgrade you." We get on the flight. The flight takes off and we press the flight attendant button. The young lady comes over to us, Johnny said to her, "Excuse me Ma'am, is there a possibility that we could be upgraded to first class?" Now Johnny wants to go from economy to first class! She looked at him, she then looked at me and said, "Johnny, Stevie! Don't you recognise me?" Me and Johnny then realised that it was a young lady that we've known for many years from Stringfellows discothèque. Johnny said to her, "Sarah, what are you doing here?" She said, "I work for Virgin Atlantic." He said, "Sarah could you do me a favour? You couldn't upgrade us to first class could you?" She said, "Johnny, it's impossible to upgrade you from economy to first class, but let me go and speak to my supervisor to see if I can get you any kind of upgrade at all." She came back in five minutes and said, "I've got you two seats upstairs." I think they used to call it Ambassador Class in the old days, now known as Premium or Business Class. Me and Johnny moved upstairs on the Virgin Atlantic flight and they looked after us like we were kings. The seats were fantastic, the food was great, the movies were tremendous and we couldn't believe it, we were getting there for £170 return! These tickets she told us were £800 seats! It looked like it was going to be a great trip. When we got off the flight, we thanked our friend Sarah for upgrading us and she mentioned that she was staying at the Double Tree Hotel in Marina Del Rey and if we weren't doing anything to pop down there any afternoon and have a drink. Well the next afternoon we went along and sat by the pool. Johnny and I were chatting to Sarah and we asked her when did she start working for Virgin Atlantic etc. Out of the blue walking towards us was Sir Richard Branson. Richard said hello to Sarah and Sarah said, "Hi Richard, let me introduce you to a couple of very good friends of mine who I've known a very long time." Richard said, "Nice to meet you guys, where are you from?" and we started to make some chit chat. I said, to Richard Branson, "I've heard you've got some new Coca Cola coming out." He said, "Yeah, would you like to try some? It's not out yet, I've got some in my room." I said, "I'd love to." Richard Branson got up from where we were sitting by the pool, went back to his room and came back with a couple of cans of Virgin Coke! We opened it and we drank it. He then invited us that night for dinner up in Beverly Hills. This was very nice of him, as he didn't know us well. On many of his flights, he takes out every single crewmember on the flight he travelled over with and all the crew members that are coming back the next day. Sometimes having a table of possibly 18 to 25 people. We found him a very, very nice genuine down to earth guy. He spent possibly 40 minutes with us, talking about many subjects. I thanked him for his invitation and we said, "We'll probably join you later on for a drink." He said, "Well you are very welcome to join us for dinner." That night me and Johnny did go up to Beverly Hills to the restaurant and we did join Richard Branson and his friends for a drink. All his crew say that he is one of the loveliest guys to work for and is very generous to his staff. As I've always maintained in life, a business is only as good as its staff and if you treat your staff well and they like the boss, obviously you are going to get better results in the business. I do believe that Richard Branson knows how to treat his staff and people in general, because he came across as a really great guy.

We were going to be in Los Angeles for three nights and then Vegas for five. We did the usual things in LA, we went to go and see my close friend George. The George that never turns up for anything but we did manage to meet up with him and go shopping, and those of you who've been to Los Angeles, know you can get some great deals on clothes. All we had to do was get to Vegas, not a problem, or so we thought. We couldn't get any flights at all. Sure there is usually millions of flights to go to Vegas but the time we picked, it was Thanksgiving and a couple of big conventions going on. George said to us, "Hey guys, there is only one way you can go to Vegas, you'll have to drive." I said, "George that's not a bad idea, we'll get going nice and early in the morning and we'll hit Vegas in the afternoon!"

One night Johnny and me were having waffles at Eddie's Diner, it was about midnight, the night before we were going to go to Vegas. I said, "John, I've got a great idea, why don't we go back to the hotel now, get changed, get packed and head off to Vegas." He said, "Are you kidding me?" I said, "No, wouldn't it be great to drive throughout the night. Let's have our breakfast, chill out, have a couple of coffees each and go and get packed." We got back to the hotel, it was about 3.45am. I remember the guy at the reception, thought we were mad. He said, "You guys, you're going to head off now, 3.45am in the morning? You're going to get to Vegas by 9am." I said, "Perfect, we get an extra morning in Vegas, we don't want to waste any time." He said to us, "The more time you spend in Vegas, the more time you can gamble." Johnny turned around and said to him, "No, I've changed my mind! This time we are going to Vegas and I'm not gambling." I looked at Johnny and Johnny looked at me and said, "What's the matter Steve?" I said, "Sorry John, what did you say?" He said, "You heard, I'm not gambling." I said, "Good for you, but the reason we booked this trip in the beginning was because you fancied a gamble in Vegas!"

Those of you that have ever driven from Los Angeles to Vegas, it's about a five hour drive as the speed limit in America is 55 mph, but it really is a lovely drive with great scenery on the way. Me and Johnny were getting quite tired at about seven o'clock in the morning, the sun was just coming up and we were getting hungry too. There was a diner about 80 miles outside of Las Vegas, in the middle of the desert, in the middle of nowhere. We went in and me and Johnny must have had one of the biggest breakfasts we've ever eaten. A young lady served us and every time we were ordering something, she was saying to us, "You betcha, I'll get you some toast." Then Johnny ordered some more tea. "You betcha," she used to say. I said, "Can I have some more scrambled eggs?" "You betcha!" Everything with this waitress was "You betcha!" It was funny because, I don't really think she knew what she was saying. We were on our way to Vegas and she kept on saying "You betcha! You betcha!" Me and Johnny came out of the restaurant and we were laughing our heads off. We said, we're going to Vegas, we're not going to gamble, but this waitress keeps on saying, "You betcha! You betcha!" He looked at me and said, "Steve, I think I'm getting tempted." I said, "Johnny you said, no gambling."

At one point when you are about ten miles outside Vegas, you can see the Luxor and the MGM in the distance and it really is an exciting feeling. Me and Johnny were joking because we thought it's great to drive to Vegas, but how are we going to get back? I didn't really fancy driving back to Los Angeles. Johnny said, "Let's not worry about that at the moment, let's worry about where we are going to stay." Believe it or believe it not, we hadn't booked anywhere to stay! Well I had a brainstorm. I said, "John, I was in one of the casinos about six months ago in London and I met a very nice chap who was the top casino host in Bally's." He said, "Steve, let's go straight to Caesars." I said, "Johnny are you going to gamble?" He said, "No, I'm not going to gamble this time." I said, "Well let's go to Bally's, let's go and see the casino host who I met, and let's tell him the truth that we want to pay for the room as you're not going to gamble."

We pulled up at Bally's Hotel, we walked in and we were able to meet the casino host who remembered me from one of the London casinos. He said, "Hi Steve, how are you doing, how's dad, how's everything?" I said, "Rick, everybody's fine can you do me a favour?" We need a couple of standard rooms, but I'm going to be very honest with you, Johnny is not going to gamble, so we would like to pay our room rate, whatever it is, we just want to pay our way." His words were to us, "Steve, you've got it buddy, I'll give you two lovely rooms, but do me a favour, if you or Johnny decide to gamble, I really want to look after you." Johnny looked at Rick and said, "Rick, thank you very much but I'm not gambling on this holiday." Rick replied, "No problem, let me know." We got into our two rooms, which were fine. Me and Johnny got outside of Bally's Hotel and we took a walk along the Strip. Johnny stopped and looked at me and said, "Steve I've been in Vegas for one hour and I haven't had a gamble." I said, "Good for you Johnny, can you keep it up for the next five nights?" He looked at me and he put his hands on his chin and as I've told you before when Johnny puts his hands on his chin, usually he's thinking. I said, "Johnny…? No gambling." He said, "You're right, let's go and get something to eat." The first night we ate in a lovely Steak House at Rio's Hotel and then we went to go and see a show at Bally's. We had a drink at the bar and we had an early night, as we were tired from the drive that morning. Johnny hadn't had a bet all day or night. The second day we got up early and went to work out at the Gold's Gym in Vegas. We then grabbed some lunch down town and went to go see a few of the sites and hotels that had recently been built. We walked up to the new MGM and I'll tell you, this was a hotel that you had to see with your own eyes. It was at the time the biggest hotel and casino in the world. In the evening we decided to go for some dinner, see another show and have an early night, Johnny still hadn't gambled. We'd been there two days and two nights. On the third night we had a drink at one of the bars in Bally's, I had a Long Island Iced Tea, which went straight to my head and I said to Johnny, "John, I'm going to have an early night, what are you doing?" He said, "Steve I'm going to hang around the bar for a while, take a walk and go and get some fresh air." I said, "Ok, I'll see you in the morning for breakfast, be up about nine o'clock" and I went to bed.

At 7 am in the morning, I was woken by a telephone call. It was Rick, the casino host. "Hi Steve, what are you doing?" I said, "I'm asleep Rick, it's seven o'clock in the morning!" He said, I'm moving you." I said, "Sorry?" He said, "I'm moving you, you and Mr Johnny K are moving rooms." I said, "Rick I don't know if I'm dreaming here, but our rooms are fine." He said, "I know, but I told you that if you decided to gamble I was going to move you and look after you guys." I said, "Rick, unless I've missed something here, I've been in bed all night, I haven't gambled and Johnny hasn't gambled either." He said to me, "Johnny has decided to gamble." I said, "When? I've been with him all the time." Then it dawned on me. I left Johnny at the bar, the night before. I said, "Rick can you do me a favour?" He said, "Anything you want buddy." I said, "A really big favour?" He said, "Yeah! You name it." I said, "Move Johnny, leave me where I am!" He said, "I can't do that Steve, I've met you; I've met your family. I'm going to look after you, I'm moving you both." I said, "Rick, where are you?" He said, "I'm in the gym downstairs." I said, "I'm coming down to see you." I quickly got washed and dressed and as I've gone to open the door, there was a little note that had been slid under the door. I took the note and it read, "Stevie, very, very late night last night, please don't wake me until I wake up myself. NO GOOD. From Johnny." Well now it started to all make sense, I'd left Johnny at the bar the night before. He must have started to gamble. I went down stairs to the gym and Rick was on the treadmill. I said, "Rick, look I appreciate you're trying to look after us, but I've unpacked, I'm settled, move Johnny, don't move me." He said, "Steve, please buddy, I want to do my best for you guys, I want to put you in a lovely room." I said, "Rick, put Johnny in a lovely room, I don't want to move" and it's a fact, to tell you the truth, when I get to a hotel and unpack all my gear, you unpack your suits, your jackets, shoes, no one really feels like packing it all up and changing room do you? Rick said to me and I will never forget it, "Steve, you won't have to lift a finger, we will pack everything for you and we will take it to the new room." I said, "Rick you are quite adamant that you want me to move with Johnny." He said, "Yes, and you won't have to do anything." I said, "OK Rick, if you are happy, I'm happy but Johnny is still in bed." He said, "Not a problem, just page me when you want me, and I'll show you the room that is available for you both." I left Johnny a message under his door saying that I would meet him at about 5 pm in one of the bars in Bally's. Sure enough at about 4:30 pm, I bumped into Johnny as he was walking to meet me. I said, "Johnny, what's going on?" He said, "Steve, you went to bed last night and I decided to play blackjack and I lost $7000." I said, "John, you said you weren't going to gamble on this trip." He said, "I know, what can I do? If I've lost, I've lost, nothing I can do." I said, "Haven't you heard the latest?" He said, "No?" I said, "You never got a message from Rick?" Johnny said, "Well my light was flashing on my telephone in the room." I said, "Johnny, he must have left you a voicemail on the answer machine in your room." He said, "Why?" I said, "He wants to move us." Johnny said, "Let's move!" I said, "I'll be honest with you John, I'm not that keen on moving." He said, "Why not?" I said, "Well I've unpacked everything." He said, "Stevie, if Rick wants to move us we move, but I want to see the room they want to put us in." We paged Rick and we were told to meet a young lady by the reception, who was going to show us our new room. I explained to her that we had two standard rooms, so if she was going to show us one room, how was there going to be enough room for both of us, when we wanted our own rooms? She said, "Leave it to me Sir." She took us to the top floor of Bally's. She opened the door and we walked into this lounge area that must have been about 40ft x 25ft. Towards the entrance of the door was a kitchen that must have been about 12ft x 8ft. As you walked through the lounge, it opened up into a bedroom that was about 30ft x 20ft. On the right of the bedroom was an open plan Jacuzzi bathroom with a dressing room area, this looked an incredible penthouse suite. I looked at Johnny but Johnny didn't say anything. I said to the young lady, "Well there's only one bedroom here." "Oh!" She said, "I'm sorry sir, come back out into the lounge." I now had visions she was going to put me in a sofa bed in the lounge! I thought Johnny is going to have the big double bed and Jacuzzi and I'm going to have the sofa bed! As we walked back into the lounge, I hadn't noticed that there was a spiral staircase going up from the lounge to the next level. We walked up the staircase and I couldn't believe what I saw. There was a bigger lounge upstairs, a bigger bedroom, bigger bathroom and a bigger kitchen. This had got to be one of the nicest hotel suites I've ever seen and don't forget a few years ago we stayed in Caesars. We came back downstairs and I was very, very impressed. I didn't say anything to the young lady. She said "Leave it to us sir, we've been told to look after you, we will get all your clothes packed from your rooms and we will bring it upstairs, are you happy?" Johnny looked at her and said, "Is this the nicest suite you've got?" She said, "Yes it is." He said, "Is it the best suite you've got in the hotel?" She looked at him and said, "Yes, it's one of the best." He said, "Would there be a possibility of us looking at the other one?" I looked at Johnny and said, in Greek, "Johnny, come on this is unbelievable." He replied to me in Greek, "Wait a minute Steve, let her answer the question!" She said, "There is one other suite that's slightly bigger than this one I've shown you but it's unavailable at the moment." Johnny said to her, "When will it be available?" "Not until next week," she said. Johnny looked at me and then looked at the young lady, I thought for about ten seconds and then said to her, "We'll take it, it's very nice, thank you very much." She walked out of the room and I said, "Johnny are you kidding me, look at this place, there must be 5000 square feet here." He said, "It is quite nice, isn't it but I did try and get the bigger and better one!"

We arranged to meet Rick that night for a drink. He said to us, "Guys I will look after you, anything you need, any restaurants you go to, it's not a problem." Johnny said to him, "Look Rick, the only thing is, I lost most of my cash last night, Stevie's prepared to lend me some money, is there a possibility that we can get a line of credit here?" Rick replied, "If you've got credit in any London casino, we will make sure that we can give you some credit here." So, I had some credit in one of the casinos in London and I managed to get Johnny about $5000 so he could gamble and try and get his money back. We were eating in the best restaurants in Bally's. We were having Dom Perignon for breakfast, lunch and dinner! We didn't want for nothing. It was probably one of the greatest trips that I had in Las Vegas. On the last morning me and Johnny K were having breakfast and sitting next to us were two elderly ladies and we couldn't help but over hear their conversation, one was saying to the other, "Well thank God I've recovered all my money on the trip, I was losing $8500 and I've just finished even. The other one replied, "Well, so you had a good trip." Me and Johnny couldn't help over hearing this, so I said, "I'm sorry to interrupt, what were you playing, roulette, blackjack?" She replied. "No, I come to Vegas and I only play slots." I said, "Slots! How can you be losing $8500 at slots and recover your money?" She said, "I always play the $5 or $10 slots in Vegas. They are so fair that you can be losing a hell of a lot of money and then recover if I hit a jackpot, which I did. In fact, I nearly won another $5000!" Me and Johnny looked at each other and Johnny then said, "Stevie, maybe slots is the game to play?"

The only small problem was that Johnny did lose his money on the trip. We also had to find flights to get back to Los Angeles to make our connecting flight back to Heathrow, which we managed to do. On the flight home, Johnny said to me, "I'm not unhappy that I lost my money in Las Vegas. I've won there the last couple of times, but they really looked after us didn't they?" I said, "They did John." He said, "Next time I go to Vegas, I know what to do." I said, "What's that John?" He replied, "I'm just going to go for the food and the shows and not gamble." I looked at him and said, "Johnny, isn't that what you always say?" He said, "Yeah, but when I say it, usually I really do mean it you know!"

When we got back to London, I hadn't seen Johnny for maybe six or seven days. I spoke to him a few times on the telephone, but many times during the day there was no answer and sometimes also at night. I'd managed to get hold of him a week later. I said "Johnny where have you been?" He said, "Stevie, "Do I have to tell you?" I said, "No you don't have to tell me, but I'd like to know where you've been for the last week because I haven't seen you." He said to me, "I've found a system." I said, "What?" He said, "I've found a system." I said, "A system on what?" He said, "I've found a system on the roulette." So I said, "Go on?" He continued to say, "I've been going to the casino at 2 pm in the afternoon and leaving at 4 am and I've been winning, I've found this system." I said, "John you'd better explain this system to me because I've been going to casinos all my life and there isn't any system, I'm telling you now in the long run you'll lose your money." He said, "Well I'm winning." I said, "You're winning in the short term." He said, "Well do you want to hear this system or not?" I said, "Go on then." He then told me the name of the casino he was going to and he told me that he used to sit in the restaurant. By the entrance of the restaurant was electronic boards with the numbers showing up after every spin on the six roulettes on the gaming floor. He told me he used to wait for seven reds or seven blacks to come up one after the other. If he saw this, he would then leave the restaurant and go over to that particular roulette and put £100 on the opposite colour. For example, if seven reds had come up on table number one, he would walk up and put £100 black on that table. If it lost and it came up red for the 8th time, he would then put £200 on black. If it lost he would then put £400, doubling up etc., etc. The limit at this casino was £10,000 on red or black and Johnny said to me that he had been doing this for six days and nights, and he hadn't had a losing day! I said, "Johnny you won't have a losing day for maybe four weeks, but then on the 4th week you're going to lose!" He said, "Well I've taken that into consideration and if I lose my ten grand, I would have only lost the winnings that I had and I would be levels." I said, "Yeah, but you don't actually lose £10 grand." He said, "What do you mean?" I said, "Well you'll lose ten grand plus the five grand from the spin before, £2500 before that, £1250 the spin before that etc., etc. I said, you'd probably end up doing £17,000–£18,000. He said, "Steve, this is a system I can't lose." I said, "I've heard of many systems in my life but this is one of the most dangerous systems." Anyway a couple of weeks later Johnny was still going to this casino and he was still winning every single night, sticking religiously to his system.

One night I decided to go down and see him, it was about one o'clock in the morning. I said, "John how are you doing?" He said, "I'm winning today, but there hasn't been many seven consecutive red or blacks for me to have bets . . . But I am winning." I said, "Johnny, you look very tired." He said, "Steve, I'll tell you what this is harder than working! I'm here at 2 pm in the afternoon and I'm leaving at four o'clock in the morning." After about a month Johnny was still winning. I still know in the long run you should lose your money, but the guy was winning. One evening Johnny and I were having dinner at the casino and as per usual he is waiting for his seven consecutive colour to come up so that he could back the opposite, and on table 3 he had seen that seven blacks had come up on the trot. He said, "Stevie can you do me a favour, can you run over to that roulette and put me a £100 on red." Johnny gave me £100 chip and I run up to the roulette wheel but when I looked, the ball was in number 5 red. I said to the Croupier, "Have you spun already? On the board in the restaurant it says the ball had gone into number 24 black." She said, "No, it's number 5." I then looked on the electronic board, which was close to the roulette wheel, and it also said 24 black. So I looked at the Pit Boss and I said to him, "Your electronic boards are wrong." He said, "Sometimes they do throw up a wrong number, very rarely but it can happen maybe three or four times a day. The electronic boards are put by the roulette, only to give you a guide." I rushed back to the restaurant and said, "John I never had the bet and then I explained to him why. He said, "Well that's not good enough, aren't the electronic boards meant to be correct?" I then explained to him what the Pit Boss had told me, that the electronic boards can sometimes throw up wrong numbers two or three times a day. Maybe not every day but it's a possibility. Well Johnny wasn't happy, he went to go and see the casino manager and explained to him that he needed to see the correct numbers. The casino manager said, "99% of the time they are, but obviously sometimes there is a mistake." Well this threw Johnny out of sync. We went home that night and he said, "Steve thinking about it now after five weeks of me winning every single day, maybe it was just pure luck." I said, "What do you mean John?" He said, "Well if I was waiting for seven consecutive colours to come up by watching all the electronic boards and I was backing the opposite, who's to say that within those seven consecutive colours throughout the last five weeks, there hasn't been a wrong number registered on the electronic board?" I said, "Johnny there possibly was as we now understand it." He said, "Stevie, I'm not going to play that system any more. I don't think it's reliable." I said, "Johnny, no system at the roulette is reliable, you've just been lucky." Johnny ended up winning quite a lot of money in the six weeks that he played. After that night he never played that system again.

1994 at the Vic was possible the best year they had for Texas Hold'em cash games. Dad used to go down regularly and it was a £2500 table, a £25 running ante for each player and £50–£100 Blind Pot Limit Hold'em. This is a very big game, possibly the biggest game of Hold'em that was in London at the time. Well I'll tell you about this pot because I want to show you the class of a player named Ben Roberts. My Dad is sitting in seat 10 and Ben Roberts is sitting in seat 9. Ben Roberts has got the dealer button. My Dad was £50 blind and the player to his left was £100 (the big blind). There were a couple of passes in front of the big blind, then one player called the £100 blind and raised the pot about £500. Everybody else passed and when it came to Ben who had the dealer button, he called the £500 and re-raised £1500. Dad passed in the small blind and the big blind also passed. The guy who originally made the raise of £500 called the £1500 and re-raised £4,500. It then came back to Ben, he was thinking and thinking. Now Ben as I've said to you before, is one of the top poker players in the world. He must of thought for about a minute and a half. He then pulled up his cards towards him, he showed them to my dad and as I was sitting behind my dad, I've seen them. It was Kings back-to-back, or 'wired' as they say in Hold'em. Ben was still thinking. After three minutes Ben said, "Pass." Dad looked at him in astonishment. Dad said, "You passed Ben?" Ben replied, "Yes Max, I've passed." This pot was about knowing a player. I asked Ben after the game, "What made you pass Ben? You could only be losing if the guy had Aces." Ben said to me, "Steve, I know the player, 75–85% sure he had two Aces, he raised the £500 and he knows me, and he knows I would only re-raise the £1500 with a big hand. For him to re-raise my raise which was £4500 knowing that I must have a big hand, he's got to have a bigger hand, I think he has got Aces." I saw that particular player five minutes after I spoke to Ben and I said to the player, "That was a good pot that you played against Ben, but you know something, Ben was 99% sure you had Aces." So the player then said to me, "Why, what did he have?" I said, "I don't know what he had, he didn't tell me (I was fibbing), but Ben passed because he thought you had Aces." He said, "That Ben is one of the greatest, do you know something I did have the Aces, I swear to god I had the Aces and he passed." I looked at him and said, "Since you've told me that, I'm sure Ben won't mind me telling you, he passed Kings!" He said, "He's too good that Ben!" I then saw Ben another five minutes later and I said, "Ben you were right, he had Aces." He said, "I told you so didn't I?" At Texas Hold'em Pot Limit, Ben Roberts has got to be one of the strongest players in the world. I would put my money with him any day.

In the beginning of 1995, Hold'em was quite big around the casinos in London. I suppose looking back at those days, there was plenty of money to be made but I was still getting games of Five Card Stud on a regular basis. Going through my life, 1995 was probably the busiest time I've ever had on Five Card Stud. On Friday nights a few of the boys used to go for a drink in a restaurant called Café Totos, in Muswell Hill, North London. All these boys were Five Card Stud poker players as a couple of them used to play with us at the Winners Health Club four or five years previously. I used to pop up and see them at about 10:30–10:45pm. The bar used to close at 11 pm. There were five or six of them, just finishing off their drinks. At 11:15pm, it was chucking out time. There was Chris P, John Michael, Steve M, a guy called 'Nick the Wardrobes' (that was his profession) myself, maybe a couple of others. I suggested one night, let's all go and play poker, now most of them loved to have a gamble and thought it was a good idea to finish off the night with a game of poker. The only thing was Chris P, the guy's house we were going round to play, said he hadn't got any cards or chips. I said, "Never fear, Stevie's here!" I used to carry my chips and my cards in the boot of my car! That's right, I was like a travelling salesman; I used to have them in the boot ready for a game. We went back to Chris's house and it was a minimum £500 to sit down. The games were regular on Friday nights. One week I went up to Café Totos, I suggested that we all played poker as usual. But this time I went, there seemed to be a colder atmosphere. It wasn't that I felt unwelcome, it was just that I could sense something was not quite right. You know the poker players sixth sense, that gut feeling. Well I definitely ignored it that night because I said to the boys, "Come on boys, let's all go back for a game at Chris's house." Chris said, "Oh! I've got to be up early, also John Michael wasn't that keen and a couple of others either. I repeated, "Come on boy's let's go back to Chris's house we'll play three or four hours and let's have a small game tonight. £250 sit down." Anyway a little bit of persuading and we went back. Guess what? I skint them all again. Now I'll go back to what I said when I walked into Café Totos, about the feeling I had when I walked in. I was told two days later by one of the players, I won't mention his name, that early Friday evening, before I had walked into Café Totos, they'd all taken an oath! That's right, they'd all sworn on the bible that they would never play poker with me again as I was too good. Everybody agreed to that, they all took the oath. So when I turned up, they all weren't prepared to play poker, but guess what, they all played! The games all in all lasted about six months at Chris's house, and there was only one winner, Me! I mean it was like taking candy off babies! They were all 100% gentleman, they all paid their debts and it was quite easy to nick £2000-£3000 a week. I did hit some tremendous cards over the period. One night I was losing a couple of grand and it looked like it was going to be one of those nights until this one pot happened. I was £25 blind, there were two callers, Steve M and Chris P. The blind card was an Ace. The two callers had called with a Jack and the other one showing a Queen. When I saw the Ace, I looked at my hole card, Aces back-to-back, I raised £75. The Jack called, the Queen called - putting £300 in the middle. I hit a Jack, Ace, Jack showing, Steve M hit a 7, Jack, 7 showing and Chris P hit a 7, Queen, 7 showing, perfect for me. I bet £300. The Jack, 7 called, the Queen, 7 called, putting £1200 in the middle. I then hit an 8, showing Ace, Jack, 8. Steve M hit a Queen showing Jack, 7, Queen and Chris P hit a King showing Queen, 7, King. It was absolutely perfect for me. I bet the full pot £1200. The Jack, 7, Queen called. The Queen, 7, King called! There was now just under £5000 in the middle. Barring any bad beat or outdraw, this pot was going to be mine. The last cards came out a 7 to me, Ace, Jack, 8, 7 showing, no help. A King to the Jack, 7, Queen, again perfect for me. An 8 to the Queen 7 King, it was a dream. I bet the full pot £4800. Steve M called for another £1400, all-in, Chris P called for another £1200 all-in and I took the pot! This was the kind of form that I was hitting at Chris's house week after week. Guess who appeared on the games one night out of the blue? Johnny K. Looking back now, I wished he'd never appeared at that game that night. Things were never ever the same between the two of us since. I'd known Johnny for about 12 or 13 years. We'd travelled and been through a lot of things together. (Whenever he has needed me, day or night, I was there for him financially or otherwise.) Vegas, LA and many other nights out, so looking back it's a shame he turned up and I'll tell you exactly what happened. You know when a lot of people say there are always two sides to a story. I've always answered no, there are always three sides and they would say what are you talking about? There are two sides, your side and my side and I'll say no there are three sides! Your side, my side and the truth. Well I'll tell you the three sides. Me and John got involved in a pot together, it wasn't a big pot. It ended up being a couple of thousand pounds and I'd won it. About 10 or 15 minutes later, maybe six or seven pots, Johnny checked his chips and said to the Croupier who was dealing the cards at the time, he was £100 short. Well everybody knows no one would take anybody's chips while we're playing. Johnny continued to say that he had put a £100 chip too much into the pot that I was involved with him, 10 or 15 minutes previously. I said to Johnny, "You've been involved in a couple of pots since." He said, "No I put £100 too much in that pot." So I asked the Croupier did he see it? I asked everybody on the table if they saw it and no one saw what chips exactly went in on that certain pot. I asked him, "What shall we do John?" He said to me, "Well I want my £100 back." I said to him, "Well we don't know exactly what went on, do you want to squeeze me for it?" Maybe I was wrong looking back. Johnny took offence to this and said to me, "Do you think I would cheat you out of £100?" I said, "No John, but maybe you've made a mistake." If I knew what I know now, I would probably have given him the £100, even though legally I was 100% correct on the game. I then asked him if he wanted to split the difference of £50 each but he didn't, nor did he want to squeeze me for it. So I came up with another alternative, which made Johnny upset. I suggested that the £100 he felt he had put too much into the pot, I'll add £100 to it and we send the £200 to the Great Ormond Street Charity. Johnny seemed quite upset about this but I said that I felt that this was a fair suggestion. Then he said (slightly annoyed now) that he would put £1000 to charity and I should also put £1000 if we were to donate any money. (The situation now seemed to be getting a little bit silly!) I replied, "My charity begins at home John, all I'm trying to do is look for a solution here." Looking back, I should have just given him the £100 back and smiled but this was all going down the wrong road now. It wasn't getting nasty but there was getting to be a bad feeling in the course of the conversation. In the end, without Johnny agreeing, I just put £200 on the side, and then Chris P like a gentleman turned around and said, "If you guys are putting £200 to Great Ormond Street, there's my £100 also. Then Steve M said, "Well I'll put £100 to Great Ormond Street." So I said, "Fantastic, we've solved it, let's send the £400 off to Great Ormond Street." I sent the £400 to Great Ormond Street Hospital and I asked them to please send us a letter to each of us, Chris P, Steve M, Johnny K and myself, which we received a letter of thanks addressed to us all. Chris P received the letter, he photocopied it and left us each a copy to pick up. I picked up my letter of thanks, so did Steve M, Johnny to this day has never picked up that letter from Chris P's house and that's a fact. I'll tell you another bigger fact, because of what happened that night, Johnny K has never been friends with me since. We'd been through a lot together, if I knew it was going to cost us our friendship as I said for the sake of £100, I should have smiled and given it back to him. Legally we know who is correct. Any poker players reading this will say no he shouldn't get his money back. All players are responsible for their own money and their own chips. I saw the same incident at the Vic like this a couple of years ago and a guy turned around and said he had put £200 in too much into the pot. I'll tell you exactly what happened. The floor manager was called over and he said, there is nothing he could do, but the 2 players decided to sort it out amongst themselves. The one player gave the other player £100 back, so instead of the £200 back, he gave him a £100 and legally he didn't have to do that. I've always been a good mediator at the poker table and I will tell you this is in the 30 odd years I've been playing poker, no one can turn around and say they have had a discrepancy or an argument with me on the poker table. It will not happen and I will always make sure justice is done in the nicest possible way but in this case, in Johnny K's eyes, he says I was wrong, if I was a friend he said, I shouldn't doubt him, even if we are on the poker table. (As someone said to me recently "It was a nice gesture to give that money to charity, even if Johnny is still upset with you! Don't feel bad about it, Steve.") Nothing I can do, that's life I guess.

The year that I'm writing this book is 2003, I have bumped into Johnny K maybe three or four times only since 1995, but I've always said hello and he's always been polite back, but our friendship for Johnny seems to have hinged on what happened that night. Having said that, there's one thing that I will say about Johnny K. He was a gentleman and always honoured everything he'd ever owed in the casinos or even on the poker table on the times he played with us. I will say with Johnny and I really mean this, I've seen him lose money in the casinos, you could walk in the room and he could be losing a 'nice few quid' and you wouldn't know if he was winning or losing, his temperament was always very good. He was a very good loser, a very happy winner, but his conduct was always very good and it's a shame what happened, but it happened. I have called him several times in the last few years and he has been polite to me, but never has he called me. I won't say anymore on the subject, but it was important that I did mention this, as Johnny K came up in a lot of my stories throughout the book but there are no more stories with Johnny in them because of this incident, as we no longer see much of each other.

As for losing my cool on the poker table, it has only happened once and I'll tell you when it was. At the time when Chris P had his games around his house, he had brought one of his uncles to deal and the guy wasn't a good dealer. We thought let him deal as the guy wanted to pass the night away. He had made two or three mistakes and it so happened there was about an hour to go in the game and I was losing about £800. There was one card to come on quite a big pot. Chris P had bet the pot £600. There had been two callers after him and it came around to me and I said to Chris P's Uncle, "Call the £600 and raise the pot," to which immediately he shouted to deal the last card… I shouted, "Raise the pot!" He replied, "I didn't hear you." I said, "You've been making mistakes all night! I said, raise the pot!" He said, "I'm very sorry Steve." I know I lost my cool that night and I apologised to him. It wasn't because I was losing money, I could have been winning but as I've told you before, my poker game relies on two or three big pots in an evening. You might only win one of them. I've always maintained if I win one big pot in an evening, I'll finish levels. If I win two big pots, I'll end up winning. If I win three or four then I'm a big winner. I've said in the past, if my dad wins one big pot, he'll end up a winner. If he wins two or three, he can skin the table. Stavros is the same, that's the style of their play. Well that night was the only night that I've ever lost my cool and I do remember it because it was completely out of character, but there we go. It's happened and I was sorry.

Before I started wearing contact lenses, I used to always wear glasses to play poker and back in the mid-80s on several occasions before the game started, I would always then put my glasses on. Just before the first hand was dealt a couple of the players said, "Steve can you take off your glasses?" I said, "Yeah why?" They said, "We want to put them on." I found this strange, they actually put them on and they started to look at the tops of the cards. I said, "What are you doing?" They said, "We know Steve that you win so regularly at poker, we heard that the glasses you wear enable you to see a special infrared marking on the cards." Well I cracked up laughing. I really couldn't believe that people were talking about me that much at the poker table, thinking that I used to wear glasses to see the cards! As we say in Five Card Stud, many players that I've played with, play with a 'glass' hole card, which means their hole card is 'see through' for me and it's quite easy to determine what they've got.

Once the games stopped at Chris P's house, I said to my wife I was going to take a week off to pop to Los Angeles to see if there was any poker action. I said, "If I do stay longer than a week and the action is good I want you to come over, as we now had a young son, and we'll go to Vegas for a while." I flew to LA and went up to the Commerce Club to see if the action was still any good. Well I'll be honest with you, I think the games at Chris P's house had spoilt me. The action was OK at the Commerce Club but by the end of four or five days, I was a little bit bored. I wasn't losing any money, but the games at the Commerce definitely seemed to have lost their life. I rang the wife up and told her to jump on a plane, we'll take a vacation for a couple of weeks and we'll go to Vegas. Within two days she came over and we flew straight to Las Vegas to stay at the Treasure Island Hotel. I was now on holiday. We went to all the shows, we ate at all the buffets and we were in Vegas for over two weeks. The Treasure Island was quite new at the time and it was a real fun hotel to stay in. There was a poker room, mostly Limit poker. I did manage to play a couple of times for an hour, but it was usually while the wife was getting ready for us to go to a show. I used to pop downstairs, play an hour, Limit Hold'em, and then she used to meet me by the card room, but there was no serious action. There was if I wanted to go next door to the Mirage, but I just didn't want to gamble. I used to go down town late at night when everyone had gone to bed, never gambled, why? I'll tell you why. I've always maintained that if you go to Vegas and you go for a holiday it's the best place on the planet! You can see shows, you can go shopping, you can sunbathe, you can swim, golf, whatever you want to do, you can do in Vegas! You name it, you can do it, but if you gamble and you lose your money, it doesn't seem such a great vacation does it? Altogether we were away for just under a month and it was time to come home.

When I got home and I saw my dad, he said to me, "You should have stayed out there Stevie because next week, we're going to Vegas." I said, "Who's going to Vegas?" He said, "Me, Andy from Plymouth (my dad's best friend), Rocky and Mario." I said, "Mario who Dad?" Dad said, "Mario from Cyprus, whose got the card club, Mario who came to your 16th birthday party, Mario, Mario." I said, "I'm coming with you!" He said, "Come, we're all booked in to go to the Mirage Hotel." I got home that night. I said to the wife, "I've got to go back to Vegas." She said, "What?" I said, "Dad's going with Andy, Mario and Rocky." She said, "We should have stayed there!" I said, "I know, that's exactly what I said to my dad." It's a long journey, I'll tell you what, if any of you are reading this and have done that journey, it's very tiring. It's only in the last year that they've got direct flights from Vegas. Virgin Atlantic runs direct flights Thursdays and Sundays, but in the old days you had to go to LA, change and wait, it was tiring. Anyway, a week later we were going back to Vegas but there was a slight change of plan and I'll let you know it now. Two nights before the flight, my dad called me and said, "I've got some bad news." I said, "What's that Dad?" He said, "I can't go to Vegas." I replied, "What do you mean you can't go to Vegas, Dad you were the one that instigated the trip, now you can't go?" He said, "Something very important has come up and I can't go to Vegas, I've got to go to Cyprus, you go with the boys, I'll take care of everything, flights, hotel everything, I just cannot go." Dad told Mario, Rocky and Andy Plymouth, they were very, very upset. Not annoyed in any way, because they knew that if Dad could get there, he would, but they were really upset because it was going to be Rocky and Mario's first time in Vegas. Andy Plymouth went once before for our wedding. Anyway on the morning of the flight when we got to Heathrow, all Andy kept on saying to me was, "Uh! Where's Max, we need Max?" Rocky said, "Look Max is not coming, let's go and have a good time." I said, "Guys I'm going to tell you something now, I promise you, I know Las Vegas very well and if we do not have a good time in Las Vegas, never speak to me again." Rocky looked at me and said, "Where are you going to take us?" I said, "Leave it to me Rocky." The small piece of good news I had on the morning of us leaving was that Dad said to me, "Steve, I want you to keep this a secret, but you are going to be in Vegas for six nights, there is a possibility and I mean a possibility that I'm going to come for the last two nights and I am going to come over with mum and stay an extra week. But do me a favour don't say anything to anybody, just in case I don't come." I said, "Dad, level with me here do you think you will come?"

Dad said, "Yes, I'll be there for the last two nights, but please don't say anything to Rocky, Mario or Andy, keep it a lovely surprise." I said, "OK, no problem." Anyway on the plane over, Mario and Andy kept on saying, "I can't believe Max is not coming, he was the one that got us all to go to Vegas and he's not coming." In the back of my mind, I thought well Dad is coming but he is going to be here for the last two nights, so it would be a lovely surprise for them. I said, "Look guys, leave it to me, I told you before, in Vegas, I'm going to take you everywhere." We got to Las Vegas and we were staying in the Mirage Hotel, which is still a lovely hotel. Within 20 minutes we lost Mario, he was busy playing baccarat downstairs. Within another 15 minutes we lost Rocky and he was playing in the poker room. Me and Andy were walking around the Mirage together. Anyway we found Mario at about 7:30 pm; he was losing $2/3000 on the baccarat. I said to Mario, "It's time for us to go and eat." He said, "I don't want to eat, I'm losing my money." I said, "Well we've got to eat." "Where shall we eat?" he said." I said, "Well let's go and see the casino host and introduce ourselves and see how they are going to look after us." We went to see the casino host at the Mirage and we told her that there were four of us in the party and that my 'Uncle' Mario was going to be a good punter and as Rocky is a frequent poker player, we would like to go and eat in a restaurant. She said to us, "Look it's your first night here, I will comp you the buffet." I said, "OK, lovely. The buffet is great in the Mirage." She said, "But I'm only going to comp two of you and two have to pay." Now that is not a big deal, it's about $14 each. I said, "Thank you very much, but can you do me a favour, can you get me a 'line pass?'" (A line pass in Las Vegas is so you can jump the line so you can get in quicker.) Now this is great to have, in fact I'd probably have paid double sometimes, just as long as you can jump the queue. Anyway, the first night we ate in the buffet, which everybody really enjoyed. Rocky went back to the poker room and Mario went back into the Baccarat. About two o'clock in the morning, Rocky was still on the poker, Mario was still on the baccarat. I said to Mario how are you doing. He said, "No good, I'm doing $7000. Bloody Vegas, I don't like Vegas." I said, "Mario, we've only been here nine hours, you can't say you don't like it. You've gone from the Baccarat to the buffet, back to the Baccarat, how do you know if you like Vegas?" He said, "I don't like Vegas, it's not for me." I said, "Take a good night's sleep and then we'll start off again tomorrow." The next day, I woke up at about 11 o'clock in the morning. The meeting point was, guess where? The baccarat room! We used to meet Mario at the baccarat, but the problem was the meeting place for Rocky was the poker room. So me and Andy were going to the baccarat to pick up Mario and then to the poker room to pick up Rocky, but Mario would not move from the baccarat because he was losing his money and Rocky would not move from the poker room because he might have been winning! None of them wanted to move so me and Andy were together. Anyway the next evening we decided we wanted to go out for dinner. We went to see the casino host and I said, "My 'Uncle' Mario and my 'Uncle' Rocky have been playing Baccarat and poker since we've got here." She said, "The poker hasn't got anything to do with the casino, but with your 'Uncle' Mario playing baccarat (which meanwhile she had checked up on his rating card, because in Vegas they give you a rating card, she could see that Mario had been playing for a lot of hours). Tonight gentleman, you can go to one of our restaurants and I'm willing to comp the two of you, but two must pay!" I said, "Wait a minute here, last night we went to the buffet and two paid and two were comp, tonight, my 'Uncle' Mario has been playing more and still two comp, two pay?" She said, "Yes, but this is one of our nicer restaurants." I said, "No problem, thank you very much." Mario wasn't too sure what was going on. I said, "Leave it to me Mario, when the bill comes, we will sign it to your room." Anyway we went to one of the restaurants in the Mirage and I must say it was a superb restaurant, we had a lovely meal. Then the same routine set in. Mario went to the baccarat and Rocky went back to the poker. Meanwhile Mario is losing about $17,000–$18,000. In the baccarat room there was a roulette wheel. Mario went over to the roulette and started to play, while me and Andy was watching. Mario put $1000 in front of me and said, "Stevie listen, if your Dad was here, we would have a chance to recover our money, but since he's not I know that you can win money, do me a favour, play up a $1000 for me. I took $100 and I put $25 on number 5 and all around number 5. As the ball span, Mario looked at me rather upset and said, "Well that's not enough you've put on, even if it hits, I'm not going to recover my money." I said, "Mario, please leave it to me. If we hit number 5, I'll make sure I recover your money." Well I'll never forget it, the ball landed in number 5 and the Croupier paid me $2500. I took the $2500 and I put $1000 straight up on number 29. Yes, I promise you, a $1000 on 29. (I pressed a little bit of the 5, but we really wanted 29 to win $35,000!) As the ball was spinning, guess who walked into the roulette room? Rocky. He could see the ball spinning round and I said, "Rocky we really need this number 29 for 35 grand." He then looked and saw that I hadn't covered number 7 or 18, next door on the roulette wheel. He grabbed $500–$600 and placed a couple of hundred dollars on 7, a couple of hundred dollars on number 18 and a couple of other numbers for Mario. As the ball landed it landed it went bang next door to 29, into number 7. They paid us $7000. I said, "Mario, we were half an inch away from winning $35,000!" Mario looked at me and said, "I like this Las Vegas, Las Vegas is good." Rocky looked up and said, "If I didn't walk in the room, you wouldn't have covered the neighbours." Mario took the winnings and sat back down at the Baccarat and he slowly, slowly lost it. The next night, me and Andy, same routine, popped in to pick up Mario from the Baccarat Room and we said we were going out to eat. I'll never forget what Mario said, "It's a bit early to eat isn't it?" I said, "Mario it's seven o'clock." Mario looked at me and said, "Steve, is it seven o'clock in the morning or seven o'clock in the evening?" I said, "Mario are you being serious?" He said, "Yes, I've been playing baccarat for the last 20 hours, I don't know what time it is." I said, "Well have a look at your watch." He said, "But I still don't know if it's morning or night," and he was telling the truth. I said, "Mario it's seven o'clock in the evening, let's go out for dinner, but before we go out for dinner, let's go and see the casino host." We found the casino host and I said, "Now listen, my 'Uncle' Mario has been playing ever since he got into Vegas three nights ago!" She said to me, "I know! you can go to any restaurant you want, the four of you are comp. I'll take care of everything from now on." I said, "Thank you very much." We went to their top-class restaurant in the Mirage called Cocomos, we had a lovely bottle of wine and we had an amazing dinner. Mario wasn't too happy that he was losing about $20,000. He said, "Don't like Vegas, got to gamble, got to gamble all of the time!" I said, "Mario, you don't have to gamble in Vegas, take your time, relax, enjoy Vegas." Mario and Rocky were looking very tired. They had definitely burnt the candle at both ends!

The next night I'd confirmed with my dad that he was coming over to surprise us, they still didn't know this. I told the manager of Cocomos, that we were expecting a surprise and there were going to be six of us, but there will be four of us walking in. So I asked him to give us a nice round table for six, but only put four chairs. Well I say one thing about the Americans, they really listen to what you want, in Vegas especially. Me and Andy picked up Rocky from the poker room, we then walked to the baccarat room to pick up Mario. Now meanwhile, Mum and Dad were in their rooms. They'd arrived at about 5pm and they were keeping a very low profile as they wanted to surprise us in the restaurant. We got to the baccarat room, there was no sign of Mario, I called the room, he answered and I said, "Mario we're going for dinner." Mario said, "Stevie, I'm losing a lot of money, I'm staying in bed tonight." I said, "Mario please come out for dinner." Now everything was racing through my mind, how am I going to get Mario down for dinner? Mum and Dad are going to surprise us at the table. Mario said, "You go ahead and go down for dinner, I'm going to bed." I said, "Mario, please." Before I said any more, he'd put the phone down and I couldn't believe it. We were slowly walking towards Cocomos Restaurant. We sat down the three of us, I then went to the telephone to ring Mum and Dad and said, "We've got a problem, Mario won't come down for dinner." Dad said, "Why?" I said, "Dad, he's losing a lot of money, he's been playing baccarat for the last 72 hours!" Dad said, "Why did you let him play for 72 hours?" I replied, "I can't stop him, what can I do? Dad stay in your room until I give you the OK." I put the phone down. I rang up Mario and said, "How long have you known me?" He said, "Why?" I repeated, "Mario how long have you known me?" He said, "I've known you 20 years." I said, "Mario do you remember you came to my 16th birthday party 18 years ago?" He said, "Yeah?" I continued to say, "I'm asking you for a favour." He said, "Whatever you want Steve." I said, "Anything I want?" "Anything you want," Mario said to me. I said, "Come for dinner tonight please, just come for dinner tonight." He said, "I'll be down in five minutes." Phew! I rang up Mum and Dad and said "Stay in your room until I call you, I've got Mario to come down for dinner, when Mario comes into the restaurant and sits down, I'm going to ring you, but wait for us to be seated." Mario came down, he looked very, very tired and he wasn't too happy. Rocky looked absolutely shattered. He'd been playing poker day and night while me and Andy looked as fresh as daisies. We were sleeping between eight or nine hours a night. Andy and I were seeing shows, walking around and going shopping during the day, working out at the gym, we were living it up in Vegas. The other two were knackered! Anyway, I now called Mum and Dad to come down. I then said, "Mario how do you like Vegas?" "Vegas, not for me," he said. I said, "Mario, Vegas can be a good place." He replied, "No good Vegas." "Rocky do you like Vegas?" I said. Now Rocky, as you know is a bit of a character and said, "I love Vegas, but there is too much poker here." As Rocky was talking to me, I could see in the corner of my eye, coming through to the restaurant was Mum and Dad and they were making their way over. Mario and Rocky couldn't see this, nor could Andy. I quickly looked to Mario and said, "Mario it's a shame my dad isn't here." He looked at me and said to me in Greek, "Where is Max, where is Max when I really need him?" and he meant it. Many times they had been out together and Dad had won money for him on the roulette and poker. You name it, Dad's always bailed him out and has been there for him. He really looked down in the dumps. I said, "Mario! [now picture the scene, my mum and dad were walking closer, they're about 20 yards away from us] do you know the only way you can recover your money in Vegas?" He said, "Yes, I do, but only if Max was here." Meanwhile, mum and dad were only 10 yards away from the table and they were approaching quite quickly. I looked up and said, "Mario, if I could give you Max right here, would you be happy?" He looked up and said, "Happy, it would be the happiest day of my life." Andy looked up and said, "Steve, Mario really needs your Dad, where is Max when we need him?" I said, in a louder voice, "You want Max [and as I was saying this, I stood up and shouted], here is Max!" I shouted it out so loudly everybody looked at me in the restaurant and then Rocky, Andy and Mario looked around as my mum and dad approached the table. Mario jumped up, Rocky jumped up, Andy jumped up and they started hugging and kissing my dad. It was like they had got their money back, by seeing my dad! This went on for five minutes. Anyway we sat down and had dinner. Andy looked at me and said, "You know Stevie, I genuinely thought in the beginning Dad was coming to join us, after two or three nights and we saw your Dad wasn't here, I really thought your Dad wasn't coming and this was a genuine surprise, but I'm surprised you didn't tell me." I said, "Andy, this was a lovely surprise wasn't it?" Dad looked up and said, "What's been happening?" I said, "Dad, what's been happening, what hasn't been happening! We need you." Dad said, "Well I'm here." Mario said, "Max, please after dinner I want you to play roulette for me and win my money back?" Dad said to Mario, "What am I Mario, a Magician, that I can recover your money?" Mario said, "If anybody can recover my money, you can Max." Well they went off to the roulette room at the Mirage and Dad went 50–50 with Mario, because Dad wouldn't just play for Mario, Dad is always looking for action. They changed up $1000 each. Dad put $100 on number 18 and $100 splits. The ball landed in number 15, they paid Dad out $1700. Dad then put $300 on 15. It came repetition 15. They then paid Dad $10,000! Now I'm going to tell you exactly what happened, Dad went for another big number and "all in all" within 12 spins, Dad had won about $22,000, Dad then went to the cash desk to cash in and Mario said, "Max, where are you going?" Dad said, "I'm cashing in Mario, we've won $22,000." Mario said, "Max, you can't cash in." Dad said, "Why not?" Mario said, "I'm losing $30,000." Dad said, "Wait a minute here, I've just got to Vegas, we've won $22,000, we've got $11,000 each, Mario I'm cashing in!" Mario said, "Please play on." Dad said, "Mario, listen to me, I'm cashing in." Dad cashed in the $22,000 and Dad sat down and had a coffee with Mario and said, "Mario, we will play with a couple of thousand dollars tomorrow night." The next day and as I've told you, we were having comp dinners anywhere we wanted in the Mirage, show tickets, anything we wanted. Uncle Mario, he was the king. In the afternoon Mario was still playing baccarat and losing his money. The next night my Dad and Mario put $1000 in each, Dad won $8500 and cashed in again. Mario wasn't too happy that Dad kept on winning and cashing in! I think Mario wanted Dad to win $50,000, but Dad was on holiday. My Dad doesn't go to Vegas to gamble, Dad goes to Vegas to enjoy himself. On the last night of our stay at the Mirage we had to go and see the casino host and she would tell us what she was sorting out and comping with the room and beverage. She told us that Rocky, Andy and me would have to pay our room, but Mario had played so much baccarat and so many hours in the last six nights, she actually thought that he probably never needed a room! On the computer, I think Mario played something like 20 hours a day baccarat! He would be comp and all his beverages too. I looked at her and said, "Listen, I bought my Uncle Mario here and I would be bringing my Uncle Mario back, so just a suggestion, if you comp me, I haven't signed anything to my room and the other two will pay their rooms (as we signed everything to Mario's room!)" Rocky and Andy weren't going to pay, Dad was sorting out everything, but you've got to know how to work them in Vegas. I mean it was genuine, Mario was a very good customer, Rocky had played six days and six nights poker but as I've said before the poker is separate from the casino, and Andy was just going along with the flow! Me, I was running around and keeping everybody happy, so I think I had earnt my room and beverage hadn't I? She said, "No problem, I will sort that out for you." We had a lovely lunch, all of us together. Mario, yes he lost money on the trip, even though Dad had recovered him $15,000–$16,000, but he wasn't too unhappy, that's Mario. I think in the end he really enjoyed Vegas. The only regret I had was that Mario and Rocky never really saw Vegas to its full extent. Mum and Dad one night took Rocky to a show, which he didn't really want to go as he wanted to play poker and he fell asleep the whole way through the show! How can anyone fall asleep throughout the whole show but Rocky did! Overall, it was a very enjoyable trip. Mum and Dad stayed there for another 4 or 5 nights, Dad told me he had played some Pot Limit Hold'em on a couple of occasions. Throughout the whole trip, I never gambled one cent and Andy Plymouth only gambled on one afternoon! Rocky and Mario made up for all of us!

When I got back to London it took me realistically about a week to recover! I'd been to Vegas twice in a month and I'd seen enough action in the last two weeks to last me a lifetime. I needed to unwind. I took the week off and then one night I popped down to the West End on my way to get the early papers, as they usually came out quite early the evening before. I bought the paper and was walking through Leicester Square, I heard from a distance, Stevie! Stevie! Stevie! I looked around, I couldn't see anybody. I carried on walking and I heard again, Stevie! Stevie! Stevie! Again, I looked around and I couldn't see anybody. All of a sudden, I saw out of the corner of my eye, it's Reggie. I shouted, "Reggie! Reggie! Reggie! What are you doing here?" He said, "I've come to get a paper." I said, "You've come to get a paper, I've come to get a paper." I said, "What have you been doing?" He said, "I'm back at Rocky's, everything is buzzing and I'm making a nice few bob and things are looking on the up." I said, "Good for you Reggie." We're walking through the Square and we walked past a casino called the Napoleon Casino. Reggie and I were both dressed in jeans and t-shirts. Reggie looked at me and said, "Are you a member of the Napoleon?" I said, "No, are you?" He said, "No, shall we go down there?" I said, "If you're not a member and I'm not and we are dressed like this, how are we going to get in?" He said, "We're not members, but I know someone who is!" We walked in and Reggie said to the receptionist, "Carlo" something or other and gives an address." They looked on the computer (there were no photographs in those days) and they said, "I'm sorry sir, you're not a member." Reggie said, "Yes I am," and gives the surname again (I can't remember what it was). "I'm a member." He said, "I'm sorry sir, but you're not." We're walking back up the stairs to leave, Reggie said, "I'm sure Carlo is a member, he always comes to the Napoleon. I'll tell you what we will do, let's wait outside, you know who comes here every night? Harry, Harry from the Canton Chinese Restaurant from around the corner." I said, "Reggie, I'll tell you what we'll do, why don't we just go home and I can go to bed." He said, "No, No, No, Stevie it's not a coincidence that we met tonight, we've met for a reason. Let's wait outside here and we're going to get in! We're waiting outside and we're waiting for this Harry from the Canton. Then 15 minutes go past, 20 minutes go past, no Harry from the Canton. Out of the blue, who's walking towards the casino? Harry! Harry from the Canton. Reggie, said "Harry! Harry! Harry! Can you sign us in?" Harry replied, "No problem, I sign you in" (in his Chinese accent.) We go downstairs, Harry goes off to the blackjack. Reggie starts to play roulette. Reggie changes up £20. Reggie goes Bing! Bang! Boom! Reggie's winning £600. Reggie then goes Bing! Bang! Boom! But this time bigger, now Reggie is winning £2000! Meanwhile every time Reggie gets £500 in cash chips, he gives them to me to cash in and says to me "Don't give them back to me." Within 30 minutes, Reggie is winning about 4 grand. Harry comes up and says "Reggie we go now." Reggie says, "We go where Harry?" Harry says, "We go restaurant." Reggie says, "You go restaurant, I stay here and play roulette!" Harry says, "No you not understand. I sign you in, you must leave with me." (As everybody knows in the last eight or nine years that's the new law, when somebody signs you into the casino, you've got to leave together). Reggie says, "Harry, do me a favour, stay here." Harry says, "No, we go now, I have busy restaurant." Reggie takes out £100 and throws it at Harry and says, "Harry, we stay now, you play blackjack, I play roulette!" Harry says OK, "I play blackjack, you play roulette and I'll stay here with you now." Reggie looks at me and says, "Stevie this is my night." Reggie starts to play in £25 chips. Reggie is winning £6000. Then 10 minutes later Harry comes back and says, "Reggie, I go now." Reggie says, "Harry don't start all this again, you stay now!" Harry says, "No, I go now, restaurant need me." Reggie said, "What happened to the £100 I gave you?" Harry said, "I lost it, I must go back to the restaurant." Reggie says, "Don't you start your nonsense Harry, there's another £100! Go back and play blackjack and shut up, I'm winning money here, so leave me alone!" Harry says, "OK, you play roulette, I play blackjack." Reggie's now winning £9000 and I'm holding about £7000 for Reggie. It's Reggie's night and 15 minutes later Harry comes over again. Reggie looks at Harry and says, "Before you say anything Harry, we go now!" Harry said, "Uh! You don't want me to stay?" Reggie says, "Already, I've given you £200 to stay, well I'm winning £12,000, we go now!" We walk out of the casino. Reggie walks out winning 12 grand! We only went to go and get a newspaper at Leicester Square! Reggie looks at me and says, "Stevie, I told you didn't I? Didn't I tell you, let's go to the Napoleon when we were walking past it! It wasn't a coincidence that I met you tonight, I believed I was going to win money tonight." I said, "Reggie, we've had a good night. Do you remember the £500 you owe me from playing poker a while ago." He said, "Stevie! Stevie! Stevie! I don't remember owing you £500, I'll tell you what I'll do, I'll play you poker, we go back to my place and play…" I said, "Reggie before you go into all that again, enough is enough, take your money and go home." "Uh!" He says, "You're scared to play me because Reggie is on form." I said, "No, I'm not scared to play you but last time we were at the Vic together and you hit number 5 and you won a nice few quid you said the same thing. I didn't want to play you, you made me play and you ended up losing your money, do you remember that night?" "Yes" he said. "This time it's different." I said, "No this time it's not different because you owe me £500 from the last time!" He said, "I'll tell you what I'll do, call it clear and I'll play you Heads Up poker, right now on one condition. I can't lose more than £3000 to you. I've won £12,000 on the night. The £12,000 means the world to me but if I lost £3000 to you, I would still be happy winning £9000." I said, "Reggie, you are a glutton for punishment aren't you?" He said, "Yes, but on one condition, I can only lose £3000 to you. If I lose any more, I'm not paying you OK! And you've got to let me off the £500." I looked at Reggie and said, "Come on Reggie, let's go." We went back to Rocky's which had now been taken over by Reggie for about the 6th time and the game lasted about three hours. I think Reggie thought he really was on form as he was really trying to win every single pot in the way he was hitting numbers at the roulette, but it didn't happen and he lost the £3000. In his eyes he said he had only lost £2500 because he was let off the "monkey." Anyway just as I was leaving Rocky's, Reggie was a gentleman and shook my hand and said, "Well done Stevie, well played but I'll tell you something, I'll never ever, ever play you poker again because you're too good, you are too good for me, do me a favour, lend me £500 until next time…" which I did!

Around the mid 90s, Dad wasn't getting a lot of poker in England. So Dad used to arrange a big poker game and go to Cyprus at Mario's Card Club. When Dad first started going he heard that Mario already had good regular games. All the Cypriots in Cyprus used to play 'Resta', which means 'all in' or 'no limit' at any time. Dad went a couple of times and he told me that he had lost. There were a few rules and regulations that they had in Cyprus and it really didn't suit the English style of game, as I've said in the past, so Dad stopped going. Mario used to ring Dad and say, "Max when are you coming to play again?" Dad said, "I'll come again Mario when I can relax and play pot limit, and I can look at my hole card more than once!" (Which you are not allowed to do in Cyprus.) So Mario said, "If you come Max on a regular basis, we will play 'English rules'." Dad said, "That suits me fine Mario, I'll come every month." Well sure enough Dad was getting regular poker games in Cyprus, every four to six weeks and I know for a fact, Dad was a very big winner.

During 1995 Steve M took over a flat in Highgate and we were having poker games every Wednesday night. Many nights, there were only four players. I'll tell you who they were. Steve M, John Michael, Jimmy Manchester (believe it or believe it not), and myself. They weren't very big games, usually £5 or £10 openers but some nights we were joined by other players as they knew that every Wednesday we played poker. Don't forget a lot of these boys were the same boys that I used to play at Chris P's house and they said they would never play poker with me again. Well the games were very regular but I noticed after about 10 or 12 weeks that my profits were getting smaller. I used to sit down and win a couple of grand, no problem for the first 10 weeks. After that I won £300, then I won £200, then I won £100. I was never losing but I could see that the boys were avoiding me in pots. They were only making sure they were getting tangled up with me in a pot when they knew they had me beat, I smelt what was going on. They weren't doing anything illegal, they just felt I was unbeatable. So after about the 14th week, I'm going to let you in to a little secret. I decided to put a slight psychological edge to my action. Now a few of the players don't know this, but I did say this to John Michael a year or two ago, because he brought it to my attention that the players weren't keen on what I was doing and I'll tell you exactly what it was. Before the start of every game, I used to say to the boys as I was rubbing my hands, "Let's go boys, let's go, let's see how much Stevie can win tonight, I'm looking for the school fees tonight and I'm looking to pay the mortgage." I used to do this and I knew that this used to get on their nerves. Now I never, ever used to do this during the game, I always used to do it just before the first card was dealt and that's the truth. Actually, back in the Aspinall days, in the early 80s, there was a guy called French Alan, who I've mentioned before, he was a top-class Five Card Stud poker player. One of the best that ever lived, without an argument and he used to stand up, rub his hands and shout out just before the game, "Get your holiday money here! Get your holiday money here!" and it used to give people the hump. It didn't really worry my Dad, but Alan was trying to put a slight psychological edge to his game. He was a gentleman and a professional on the game once it had started. I think it's a little bit like boxing, before you get in the ring. Boxers do it to each other all the time, until they get in the ring and they then fight fair and square. Before the fight they're saying this, that and the other about the other boxer and that's what I was doing. Well it was working like a treat. All of a sudden I started nicking between £1000-£2000 a game again. It was like the old days and before every game I used to say the same thing. "Gents, I've brought some wardrobes and I've got to pay Nick the wardrobe guy this week, I'll be happy if I win a couple of grand. Only a couple of grand, I don't want to win £5000. I just want to win £2000," and I used to win the £2000!

I'll tell you one pot that happened at the flat in Highgate and in this pot I was quite unlucky. The Ace opened for £5. There were four callers in front of me, all low cards and I raised £25 with a Queen showing. I won't tell you my hole card at the moment. Everybody called. The Ace, the 8, the 9 and the 10. The cards came out a 9 to the Ace, nothing to the other players and a 7 to me. So I now had showing a Queen, 7. The Ace, 9 bet the pot £100. The three others in the pot passed. I called the £100 with Queen, 7 showing, I still won't tell you my hole card. There were now only two people in the pot. The Ace, 9 (the players name was 'Andy Kojak', we called him Andy Kojak because he had a shaved head), and me with the Queen, 7, I still wont tell you my hole card. The cards came out 9 to the Ace, Ace, 9, 9 showing, 7 to me, Queen, 7, 7 showing. It's the Ace, 9, 9 to bet. He bet £300. I called the £300 and raised £900. Any clues of what I've got? What do you think I've got? I've raised £900 with Queen, 7, 7 showing against Ace, 9, 9. No, you're wrong I haven't got Queens and 7s, I've got three 7s! I've played Queen showing 7 in the hole and I've raised the pot from the off and now I've hit the three 7s! Obviously, I'm still scared of the three 9s. Andy Kojak decided to think for a couple of minutes. I was 99% certain that he now hasn't got three 9s. He called the £900. The next card that came out, I couldn't believe it, a 9 to him, three 9s on the show and nothing to me! I'd lost the pot. Yeah! What a pot to lose.

He showed me his hole card and all he had was a King in the hole. He didn't even have Aces and 9s; he had to hit three 9s one after the other to beat me in this pot! Overall, the games were very, very profitable for me but then the boys decided not to stop the games, but to put me on a handicap…. "A handicap?" you might be asking yourselves. How can you put anybody on a handicap at poker? Well I'll tell you how and I'll tell you what they did to me. One Wednesday I got a phone call from Jimmy Manchester, he said, "Steve, they're not willing to play with you anymore, unless when we sit down, we can sit down with unlimited money and you only sit down with £500." I said, "What Jim?" He said, "That's right, you can only to sit down with £500 table stakes, but we can sit down with unlimited money." I said, "Jimmy, I've known you 20 years, trust me this is not a handicap." He replied "Well Steve, they feel that when you play unlimited funds or call or pass, we are limited with our money and you've got an unfair advantage on us." I said, "Listen, in some ways you might be right, but trust me, if an absolute mug sits down and had unlimited funds, he'd lose his money wouldn't he?" Jim said, "Look Steve, it's the only way I can get you back into the games, do you want to come tonight and play table stakes?" I said, "Jim I'll be honest with you and you're a friend, I'll come tonight and I'll play table stakes, but this is not to your advantage." I got to the game that night and the rules were discussed. I was only allowed to sit down with £500. If I lost the £500, I was able to pull up another £500 and play table stakes. If I lost that £500, I was able to pull up £1000, if I lost £1000 on the third time, I had to go home! Listen, I had no choice, they didn't want me winning big money every week, but to tell you the truth this wasn't the way to stop me winning. I just completely changed the way I play poker, that was all. I sat there with £500 and I played Karabina. Oh! A lot of you that are reading this will say, Steve plays Karabina anyway, but no I don't and that's a fact. I play many, many 'funny' cards. What we call funny cards at Five Card Stud are cards that shouldn't be played, but I'm able to do that because I play with money behind me, but when you're playing table stakes, like I did 20–25 years ago, you have to play Karabina. That was the style that suited table stakes and that's how I learnt the game. As I progressed, I progressed with money behind me and opened up and changed my game, but I was always known as a tight player so I always commanded respect on the table.

Anyway the rules were set. The first week, I won £300. I didn't even need the second £500. The second week I won £600, again I didn't need the second £500 but the boys now realised that they had zero value with me. From having little value from me before, they now had absolutely no value! I told Jimmy three or four weeks later, "I told you this was going to happen." I even rang up Steve M and I said to him, "Listen, I know you've instigated me playing tables stakes, it's not a problem, but I'm telling you now, one night I'm going to skin the table badly. I'm due for a big win; I'll never forget that. The big win was to come the very next week. The boys lost 15 grand to me in one night and that was the end of the games in Highgate. I'd turned £500 into 15 grand in one night and they decided to call it a day because they really couldn't stand losing much more! That really was the end of the games, Chris P, Andy Kojak, Jimmy Manchester, John Michael, Steve M and me were still to meet a few years later, but I'll tell you about those games when I get to them. That was the very last time we played at the Highgate flat.

Towards the end of 1995, my second son was born. He was born on Sunday morning at 3:11 AM in a hospital in the West End. Why am I telling you all this? It's because at 4 am, I was in the room where my wife was staying and my mobile rang, which by the way, I shouldn't have had on anyway! It was Reggie. Reggie said, "Where are you Stevie?" I said, "Reggie, I'm at the Portland Hospital." He said, "Well get yourself round here, because Barry is coming." I said, "Barry who?" He said, "Barry the Signs." Now Barry the Signs was a sign maker, he used to make the neon signs for outside shops, so they called him Barry the Signs. I said, "Reggie, my second son has just been born, I can't get round there." He said, "Stevie, get yourself round here, there's poker tonight, me, you and Barry." I said, "What time is he coming?" He said, "When he comes in, I'll call you." I said, "Alright Reggie, I'll be there." Within 25 minutes the phone rings. I'm in the room with the wife. I said, "What's happening Reggie?" He said, "Where are you, we're waiting." I said, "I'll be there in ten minutes." I looked at my wife and I said, "How are you feeling?" She said, "Actually, I feel very well." I said, "Look have a good night's sleep, because I've got to go to 'work'!" She said, "What are you talking about?" I said, "Reggie, is having a poker game round the corner at Rocky's, I'll see you in the morning." On the night my son was born, I went from the hospital to Rocky's Restaurant and played Barry and Reggie poker. I won £1500 that night off Barry and Reggie. Reggie said to me on the way out from Rocky's, "Stevie, I'm telling you now, I'm never ever playing poker with you again, you are too good, too good trust me." I said, "Alright Reggie, we'll see." He said, "No this time, I mean it. Even though you didn't win a lot of money, we can never beat you." At nine o'clock in the morning I went back to the hospital. The wife was just waking up. She looked at me and said, "You look a state and you reek of cigarettes." I said, "What can I do, I was sitting with Barry on my left puffing away and Reggie on my right puffing away and me in the middle!" She said, "Well was it a profitable night?" I said, "It was." Looking back, I don't think Reggie ever has played poker with me again.

After my son was born, one night my wife asked me to pop out and get some milk. I watched a bit of TV and about an hour later, I decided to go to one of the 24-hour stores to get the milk. It was about one o'clock in the morning. As I was driving to the store, I got a phone call on my mobile. It was a friend of mine who said, "Stevie, there is a very big game of poker tonight at Chinese Robbies, down in the West End, you better get down here." I said, "Who's playing?" He said, "Well five or six handed, but it's a lot of value." Well my mind went blank, I went straight down to Chinese Robbies completely forgetting about the milk! About six o'clock in the morning, my mobile phone rang. It was my wife, she said, "Are you OK, where are you?" I replied, "Oh! I've just remembered, you sent me out to get some milk." She said, "That's right, but as long as you are OK, because I got worried." I said, "Yeah I'm OK, I'm playing poker down in the West End, I got a call" and I explained to her the story. The game finished at about 7:30 am in the morning and it was a tremendous game. I finished even that night, but on the way home, I made sure I got the milk!

Around early 1996, we took a trip to Bath to see the in-laws. Many times when we went to the West Country, we always stayed in the Swallow Hotel in Bristol, there were two reasons for that. It was a very nice hotel and the second reason, which is most important of all, was that around the corner from the Swallow there used to be Sergeant York's casino. I'd heard that there were some very good poker tournaments. Well it was Saturday night at about 7 pm and we were in our hotel room, I rang the casino and asked to be put through to the card room. I asked them what time their tournament started and what tournament it was tonight. They told me it was a Texas Hold'em Pot Limit. It was a £10 entry and it started at seven o'clock. I looked at my watch and it was literally three minutes to 7. I said, "If I come along right now, will I have time to enter?" They said, "Well you have to be here literally in two minutes." Well as I said, Sergeant York's was just around the corner, but it was going to be quicker to cut through the back of the hotel and run to the casino. I quickly jumped up from the bed, ran out the room, ran downstairs and got to the casino near enough five past 7. I ran up to the card room, slightly out of breath and the card room manager seemed to be going through the list of poker players. I said, "Where do I put my tenner?" He said, "I'm afraid that the tournament has now closed." I said, "Oh! I just spoke to someone on the phone." He said, "Yeah, you spoke to me, but we've closed the tournament, there's 55 runners tonight and we are completely full up." I said, "Is there any way I can get into the tournament?" He said, "No, everybody has paid and there's no way you can be in it," I was really upset. I know it was only a tenner tournament but I'd heard in Bristol, the prize money could be up to a couple of thousand pounds. Anyway I sat in the bar and ordered a drink. All the players were queuing up to get their seat numbers from the card room manager. As the very last one got his seat number, I still don't know what made me do this, but I walked up to the card room manager and I said to him. "Anybody not turned up, maybe there's a spare seat?" He looked at me and said, "You're a lucky fellow, there is one person that hasn't showed. Give him an extra five minutes when everybody is seated at the table, I'll call you if he hasn't shown." I said, "I'll be in the bar." Sure enough five minutes later, I got the call from the card room manager, this guy hadn't shown up. I paid my £10 and I sat down. Shouldn't really be in this tournament should I? I hit some tremendous cards and before I knew it, at about midnight, I was on the final table. The prize money was £3000. It was £1000 for the winner, a little less for the second going down to the 7th or 8th place. So I've already guaranteed myself £150. The next thing I knew there were only four players left, but my chips were running low. I decided to go all-in on a big pot, I won it and I doubled through. The next thing I knew one person knocks out another one, another person knocks out another and all of a sudden there are only two players left, me and another guy. I never knew one person in this tournament. The blinds were getting bigger and bigger. I went all-in a couple of times, I'd won the pot and I built myself up quite a substantial amount of chips. Next thing I knew I looked at my two hole cards and I saw Ace, Queen suited and I raised. The guy that I was playing re raised, I went all-in and all the chips were in the middle. I had Ace, Queen suited; he had a pair of Jacks. He was slightly favourite. On the flop, the first three cards came Jack, 2, 3. Now it looked like I was going to finish in second place. There was very little way that I could now win this pot. The guy that was in the final with me had three Jacks and all I had was Ace, Queen high. The last two cards came out. The first card was a 10 to give me Ace, Queen, Jack and a 10 and the very last card that came out was a King to give me a straight! I know I was very lucky to win this pot, but as you know at Heads Up, you are going to make a move all-in with Ace, Queen suited and if someone comes over the top of you, you are committed to call. Especially when most of your chips are already in the pot. I scooped the £1000 first prize, but it just goes to show you, I was very lucky from the beginning of the evening! From calling the casino at five to 7, for them to tell me that the tournament starts in a couple of minutes. For a player not to turn up, for me to get a seat and right until the very end when I hit the King on the river, but that's poker!

Towards the summer of 1996, one summer's day I got a call from Reggie. He said to me, "What are you doing?" I said, "Well I'm not busy today, why don't we meet up for coffee?" We met for a coffee in St. John's Wood High Street and Reggie brought a backgammon set with him. He said, "I know you're too good at poker, as I said, I'll never play you ever again, but I'll play you backgammon." I said, "Reggie, you know I don't play backgammon, I'm not a good backgammon player." Now I know for a fact that Reggie isn't a great backgammon player, but he is better than me. He said, "Well we'll start off at £5 a point." A fiver a point, as I've explained before, is when the doubling up cube is in the middle of the backgammon set and the player who feels that he has got the advantage can double up at any time. So if you are playing for a fiver a point, it can double up to £10, £20 or £40 and the game can get quite big. Well anyway, Reggie nicked about £150 off me. He rang me up a week later, we met, we played again and Reggie nicked another couple of hundred quid off me. The third time he rang me up, I said, I would meet him for coffee. We went down to our usual spot; he brought his backgammon set like usual. He set it up and I said to him, "Reggie I'm not playing you backgammon you're too good." He said, "Come on Stevie, we're only playing for £5 a point." I said, "I can't win." He said, "I can't win at poker, but I still play you." I said, "The difference is Reggie, I gamble to win." He said, "So do I." I said, "Well I'm not playing you backgammon, you're too good for me." When I know someone is too good for me at anything and this is a fact, I will never play them more than two or three times. Unless I get the right start, handicap or odds. Reggie said, "I'll tell you what, I'm going to make you an offer." This offer Reggie made me was an offer I couldn't really refuse. He said, "We won't play for £5 a point. We'll play for £25 a point." I said, "Yeah and?" He said, "You can hold the doubling cube." So I said, "Let me get this straight Reggie, we'll play for £25 a point, you can't double at any time, only I can double the game up." He said, "That's right." Well now, those of you that can play backgammon know that the most important thing is the cube. I mean especially, when you get to an average level. I said, "Reggie, that's an offer I can't refuse, give me the cube, it's for £25 a point, but only I can double the game." Well the first game Reggie wins and takes £25 off me. The second game Reggie wins and takes another £25 off me. Well obviously Reggie is going to win more games than me, but he can only win £25. After about nine games, Reggie had won seven of them and I had won two, but on the two games that I'd won, I had won £100 and £100. Wiping out all of Reggie's winnings! Now do you see how important the doubling up cube is! Anyway we didn't have any more time to play but Reggie called me the week after, the same thing happened. Reggie won about seven or eight games. I'd only won about two or three but this time I won £100. I kept my nose in front. On the third week we played, I won eight games and Reggie only won four, Reggie lost £300. The next week, I won six games and Reggie won six, so really we should have finished levels. We didn't because I had the doubling up cube, I ended up winning another couple of hundred pounds. This went on for six or seven weeks consistently. In the end Reggie said, "You can't have the cube." I said, "What do you mean, I can't have the cube?" He said, "You can't have the cube, it's too much of an advantage." Well it was, so I said, "Ok! Well if I can't have the cube, I'll tell you what I'm going to do with you, we'll leave the cube in the middle." He said, "That's fair." I said, "No, if we leave the cube in the middle we go back to the original stakes of £5 a point." He said, "Well we've been playing for £25 a point." I said, "No Reggie, you made the rules, you said I could have the cube, you said £25 a point, I'm going back to the original stakes of £5 a point, cube in the middle." Reggie said, "You're on." Well Reggie lost week after week and I'll tell you why. What happened was after the first two or three throws, Reggie used to give me the cube very early on in the game and I used to 'beaver' it. Now, beaver means that if he gives me the cube to make it £10 a game, I can make it £20. The reason I did this was because Reggie gave me the cube too early, it was too early on in the game and he wasn't really favourite but he was out to gamble. The second reason why I used to beaver it was because I didn't want to hold the cube at £10, I wanted to hold the cube at £20 to try and get maximum advantage.

One night me and Reggie decided to meet up at about 2 am to play backgammon. It was going to be our usual session but because we met out in the street, we had nowhere to play. We decided to set up our backgammon board outside a pub. The problem was, it was one of those wooden backgammon boards and when we threw the dice it made quite a lot of noise. After about 20 minutes of us playing, someone opened the window from the pub upstairs and said, "Will you keep the noise down, we are trying to sleep." We looked up and said, "Sorry Governor, no problem." So me and Reggie were trying to throw the dice really quietly but these dice were making so much noise by bouncing on the wooden board it was very difficult. 10 minutes later, same guy opened the window and shouted out, "If you don't move on, I'm going to call the police!" So Reggie looked up and said, "Well we're not doing anything wrong, we're playing backgammon." The guy looked down and said, "It's three o'clock in the morning, and you're keeping me awake, I own the pub!" Reggie looked up and said, "Alright Governor, no problem." Do you think me or Reggie moved? No, we carried on playing, but these dice kept on making a lot of noise. The next thing we knew the window opened and he threw a bucket of water all over me and Reggie, we were soaked! That was the end of the game. Me and Reggie looked at each and said, "Maybe it's time for us to go home."

Well after three or four months, Reggie lost quite a lot of money and then he said, "I'll play you £25 a point, cube in the middle or we don't play backgammon." Well I'll say this to you, we haven't played backgammon since 1996 and the backgammon board is still in the boot of the car until this day!

I think gamblers in general always talk about coincidences or luck as things turn out fortunately sometimes. For example, like the poker game in Bristol when I won the tournament. Like how the games started at the Vic back in 1992, like most of these stories in this book. Well this is quite a coincidence what I'm going to tell you because this is a funny story and it happened around the middle of 1996. I went to a restaurant in Hampstead Garden Suburb with the wife one night. It was an Italian Restaurant and we had some pasta. The owner of the restaurant started talking to us, he was very friendly and sat down. He asked me what I did for a living and I told him I was a bookie by trade, I do some property but I played a lot of poker. He told me that he had some friends that used to play poker. I said lovely, "Where do they play? He said, "Well they used to get together every week, but I'll ring them up and see if they are willing to play." We swapped numbers. He rang me up and said, "Come down to the restaurant and we'll have a coffee." I went down there and he said to me that they are willing to play next Saturday and as he was renting a flat a couple of doors down above the shops, this is where we could play. So I said, "Whereabouts are you renting the flat? Because I used to live in this block." He replied, "I'm renting 32a." I said, "Wow! I lived in 32a for 10 years," what a coincidence. Anyway Saturday came, we got up to the flat. It was really weird walking into my old flat where I spent ten years of my life. We arranged the poker table. I'd brought the cards, I'd brought the chips and we were ready to go. The problem was no one turned up! The owner of the restaurant apologised. He said, "I'm really sorry Steve that I got you here under false pretences but obviously there is not going to be a game." I replied, "I'll tell you what I'm going to do, since it's such a lovely flat and you've got the poker table here and we've got everything arranged. Can I arrange a game for myself next Saturday and I'll bring a few of my poker friends?" He said, "Yes, by all means, just make sure you leave something for the rent of the flat, I'll make sure I get all of the sandwiches and whatever you need, food and drink. Whatever you need, leave it to me." I started on Monday ringing up everybody and we managed to attract five players for Saturday night. It was some of the old faces that you've read about. Aggi Alison (the guy that got me down to the Empress Club who phoned me in Stringfellows one night), Tony Stavrou (remember me and Tony from nearly 20 years ago now, the big pot he beat me in, he's the one that owns the Nayland Rock in Margate), Cos the jeweller, a guy named Mario (we called him Mario Olympic because he had a pool hall called the Olympic Pool Hall), and one or two others. The first two or three Saturdays the games were not too bad at all and slowly, slowly the word spread that there were some good Five Card Stud poker games in Hampstead, and we attracted another couple of players.

Well I mentioned it to the owner of a restaurant in the West End one night, a Greek guy named Andy. I always call him 'Andy Chicken', not because he was chicken in any way, believe you me, because this guy was a real fearless gambler. It was just that when I first met him, I always ordered chicken in his restaurant and his chicken was so lovely, I used to say to my friends let's go down to Andy Chicken and that's how he got the nickname. One night, on a Saturday while we were in full flow, the front door bell rang. The voice on the other side said, "It's Andy." I said, "Andy who?" He said, "Andy, Andy from the restaurant." Well it was Andy Chicken. He got upstairs and he saw that the game had a lot of action. It was about one o'clock in the morning. I said, "Andy I didn't expect you to come to the game." He said to me, "Look the wife's away, she doesn't like me gambling, but I'm telling you now Steve, I don't mind playing, but I can only play for two hours." I said, "Andy you can play as long as you like." He said, "No only two hours." Andy sat down with £1000. I told the entire table that he was going to sit down for only two hours, everybody agreed. Well within the first hour and a half, Andy skint the table! When I say, skint the table, Tony's ended up doing about 2 or 3 grand, Aggie's done a couple of grand, Mario's done 3 grand. I was losing £1500 and the only one that was winning with Andy was Cos the Jeweller. Remember Cos, the loud guy that always shouts, "Bet the Pot!"? Well I estimated at one stage that Andy was winning about 10 grand and Cos was winning about 5 grand. Now, when Cos plays poker, he doesn't always play for a long time and it was near enough his time to leave. Cos said to me, I'll never forget it. "I'm going to leave Steve after the next hand" and I said to Cos, "No problem Cos, but do me a favour, finish off the round blind and then leave." It's usually customary at Five Card Stud when there is a round blind, for example seat number one is £20 blind, after the hand seat number 2 is £20 blind and then after seat number 3 is £20 blind etc., etc. It goes right round the table that a player leaves after the round blind. So Cos said to me, "No problem." Well there was a pot that Cos was £20 blind and it was going to be his very last hand, because he was in seat number 7. Everybody passed and Andy Chicken called with a King showing, the blind card was an Ace. Cos raised the pot, Andy called. Andy hit a 7, now showing King, 7. Cos hit a 7 to give him showing Ace, 7, Cos bet the pot. Andy called. Andy then hit an 8 to give him showing King, 7, 8 and Cos hit a Jack to give him showing Ace, 7, Jack. Cos again bet the pot. There was about £400 in the pot now. Andy Chicken called the £400 and raised £1200. Cos called the £1200 and re-raised £3600 to which Andy called immediately. It was obvious what both of them had. Andy Chicken had Kings, Cos the Jeweller had Aces. This was going to be a 10 grand pot! The last card came out, nothing to Cos the Jeweller and bang! A King to Andy Chicken, he made 3 Kings! Cos got up and was a 100% gentleman and said, "Gentlemen, that was my last hand of the evening. Thank you very much and I'll see you next week." Cos left and in a way I felt a little bit bad because I told Cos to play the round blind. I know he could have won the pot, but the guy wanted to leave but he was in the middle of the round blind. At Five Card Stud you can leave but it's not really a done thing, but it happened and Cos has never ever mentioned it. Within ten minutes Andy Chicken had to leave. He got up and he was winning about 15 grand. He said, "Gent's I said I would only play for two hours, thank you very much, I'll be back next week." Andy Chicken left us and everybody was losing! There was now going to be an even better game. Sometimes in poker these are the best games. When the winners leave and leave the losers. The game is very open and aggressive. The only problem was that there was definitely going to be a few more heavy losers that night. I recovered my money and so did Mario Olympic and the others shared the losses.

The games were really taking off on a Saturday night. Many, many times we used to start at about 9 pm and it wasn't unusual to finish at around eight o'clock in the morning on a Sunday. One Saturday the doorbell went at about midnight and who was it? Well you could have had 100/1 to guess who it was and I would have laid 100/1. It was my Dad! I let him up. He saw all the boys there and said, "Any seat for me?" I said, "Dad the only seat for you is my seat and I don't really want to give it up." He said, "I only want to play for a couple of hours." I was winning about £700–£800 and you could really win big money on these games, I wasn't keen on giving up my seat. Dad sat on the couch and I could see he was getting tired, I said, "Dad if you want my seat you can have it but if you sit down [and I said this in front of everybody] I've got a 25% share with you." They all looked at me and said, "Steve only 25%?" I said, "Trust me, if my dad sits down, the game is going to get ten times bigger and yes he can win, but he can lose. I only want 25%." The dealer we had on these games was Little Laggis. Little Laggis had reappeared after a few years on the missing list. He was the guy that had the 10% share with me in that very big game in The Empress back in the 80s. Laggis was a very competent dealer. That night Laggis got tired after two or three hours dealing, I dealt for half an hour, just to keep myself alert, otherwise I'd end up falling asleep! Anyway about 7.30 am Aggie Alison had lost a lot of money and he had stopped playing, with all credit to Aggie he said, "I've lost enough tonight, I don't want to play anymore, your Dad has outdrawn me three of four big pots." It was true, Dad was hitting cards left right and centre. At one stage Aggie went all-in with Aces and 9s and my dad made three 10s on the very last card, so Aggie stopped playing that night. At about six o'clock in the morning, the doorbell went, we wondered who it could be. I answered the intercom, it was John Michael. Now, John Michael had just opened up a restaurant in Southgate, he had just finished after a late night and he had heard there was action. John Michael never played in these games, they were too big for him at the time, but he said, "Gents, I've just come up to say hello to you and watch the action." He looked at my dad and said, "Mr Max, I never saw you there." "Good evening Mike," Dad said to John Michael, "how are you?" He replied, "Mr Max, I'm very well, I've never seen you play poker before, but I've heard you are a legend at the game." Dad looked at him and said, "Mike I do my best." He said, "Mr Max, I want to ask you something." Dad said, "Anything." He said, "Would you mind if I sat behind you." Dad said, "Be my guest." "Mr Max," Mike continued to say, "Would you mind if I sat behind you and you showed me your hole card." Dad looked at him and said, "Mike for you, you may." I mentioned earlier on in the book that I never used to look at my dad's hole card, when I had a share with him. It can certainly frighten you, especially when the game gets big, but Mike sitting behind my dad and looking at my dad's hole card wasn't going to make any difference to Mike. He sat directly behind my dad and every time my dad was involved in a pot, my dad showed John Michael his hole card. Mike rubbed his hands the first five or ten minutes and said, "Now I'm going to watch a legend play Five Card Stud and I'll tell you what boys, I'm going to watch every move Mr Max makes because I'm going to learn something tonight." I was watching the game and I could see Mike really concentrating, looking at Dad's hole card, looking at the pot and really trying to learn something. After an hour and a half, Mike got up from behind my dad and I'll never forget to this day what he said, "Mr Max, I've only been playing poker for four or five years, thanks to your son by the way and it's cost me a lot of money to learn. I've sat behind you tonight, to see if I could learn something by looking at your hole card and watching the way you play, because I was told that you were one of the best Five Card Stud poker players there is. Mr Max you have completely bamboozled me!" I burst out laughing and said, "Mike, that's why I never look at my dad's hole card." Mike continued to say, "You play a very, very unorthodox game Mr Max, I have learnt absolutely nothing tonight if anything you've confused me, and you've played starting hands that I would never ever start with. You've bet the pot, when I would never bet the pot, you've passed when I would call and you've called when I would pass, I'm definitely doing something wrong!" I looked at Mike and said, "Mike you ain't a bad poker player but trust me Dad plays a very funny game." Anyway the whole table was in stitches laughing. Mike got up and left and he still talks about it to this day. Dad told me recently, when he heard this story again, he made SURE that he got Mike bamboozled, and he never allowed anybody except me to look at his hole card.

At around nine o'clock in the morning, there were only two winners who were winning a lot of money. One was my dad, he was winning about 10–12 grand and one was another guy and his name was Michael, a Greek guy, late forties and a good gambler. Aggie had stopped playing and there was only about five left, they were going to wrap up and finish playing at about 9:30am. Aggie tapped me on the shoulder and said, "Steve can I see you for a second in the kitchen?" I said, "Sure no problem." We went into the kitchen and Aggie said to me, "Can I ask you for a favour?" I said, "Anything, do you need money?" He said, "No! No! I've lost my money tonight, it's not a problem but Michael the Greek owes me some money, would you mind when you cash in the chips, could you cash him in last. I know he's a gentleman and he will pay me my money but if he cashes in first he might then quickly leave." I said,

"Aggie, it's not a problem." He said, "Thanks, I've been waiting for him to have a win like this, because he owes me a couple of grand and I'm now guaranteed to get it." Well as we walked back into the poker room, there was Michael and my dad in a pot. I'm telling you exactly how it happened because this is how we saw it as me and Aggie entered the room. My Dad had showing Jack, 9, 7, 7 and Michael had showing Ace, King, 8, 8. What I quickly realised was that Michael had checked on the last card and my dad had bet the pot £6000 with Jack, 9, 7, 7 showing. Now Michael was thinking, thinking and thinking. Aggie's looking at me because he doesn't want Michael to call because Aggie wants to get the money, which is owed to him! Aggie whispers to me and says, "What do you reckon your Dad's got?" I said, "I've got no idea, Dad could have anything! I know one thing, Michael hasn't got three 8s." Michael was still thinking. Aggie's whispering under his breath to me, "Pass Michael, pass Michael. Steve I know it's your dad but let Michael pass." Michael shouted out, "I call the £6000, I've got Aces and 8s Max!" Dad slowly turned over his hole card and he had three 7s! Dad had skint the table by the end of the night. It was the last time my dad was ever invited or came to our games. My Dad had sat down and won about 20 grand! A week later there wasn't a game, this was very bad for me. Yeah, great I had the 25% share, but I'd rather that there was going to be a game every week than no games. Three or four weeks later we managed to get another game, but they definitely were not the same size as we'd been having in the past. Within another three weeks the games faded out and died. There were only three winners at the flat in 32a. The biggest winner was me, the second biggest winner was my Dad, (Even though he had only ever played once!) The third winner, but only by a small amount was Andy Chicken because he came back twice more and lost some money but not all of his winnings. Mario Olympic said to me, "Steve, I can see the way your Dad plays, you, you'll win regularly but your Dad, I'm sure if he's out of form he can lose money but when he hits form, not only does he skin the table, he killed the game!" It was Mario Olympic who once said to me, "Whether it's father or son, we may have more value with Max than Steve, but in the long run the result is still the same, Max and Stevie will win!"

In fact Mario rang me up a month or so later to invite me down to his poker games in Tottenham. I went down there maybe six or seven times and I'd won on all occasions then Mario rang me up and said, "Steve you're winning the money every week and I've been told by my customers that they don't want to play with you," which was a fair comment. They'd heard of my reputation and I'd sat down and won a couple of grand every single Saturday for six or seven weeks. They didn't want me back. All credit to Mario he said, if he had it his way I would be welcome back, but he didn't want to lose his customers as they didn't want to play with me. I said, "Mario it's not a problem." Mario and me have remained friends all these years, though if I ever invite him to a poker game he'll always laugh and say, "I'm better off at the casino!"

One Saturday afternoon, the weather was quite good and I decided to have a coffee at the Coffee Cup Restaurant in Hampstead. I was sitting outside and out of the blue along came John Michael, Chris P and Steve M. They stopped off to have a coffee and we were talking about the games we used to have at Highgate the year before and it was Steve M who turned around and said, "I really fancy a game as I haven't played for a while." I said, "Well let's arrange the games again." He said, "No if we arrange the games again, there will only be one winner, it's a shame because I could really fancy a game right now." I said, "Oh! Really?" I got up from the table, walked to my car, went to the boot and got out the chips and cards! I gave everybody £500 in chips each, shuffled up and we started dealing and playing poker, right in Hampstead High Street, outside in the open on the coffee table. We played for an hour with people stopping and watching what was going on, but it was all chips. I ended up winning about £400. John Michael ended up winning about £600. Always in the poker games, I've always got the blame for instigating the game and I would say, yeah, 80–90% of the time it's true. If you ring up everybody to play and you win most of the money, most of the time soon people are going to get fed up. Slowly, slowly they were.

Also that year in 1996, Tyson fought Evander Holyfield for the title. There was a club that was called the Paradise Club and it was run by a guy called Andy G. We all decided to watch the fight there live. When we got there about an hour before the fight, everybody was having bets so we decided that everyone should put in £100 each and you could pick what round Tyson was going to beat Holyfield. Now don't forget this was the first of the meetings between the two. This wasn't the 'ear incident', this was the first fight. The name of the game was we all put our money in and you could pick a round that Tyson was going to win. Well everyone was picking the 2nd/3rd/4th round. Everyone was going to get paid out to the relevant odds. One guy, I never forget it put his £100 in and said, "You guys, you don't know what you're talking about, Holyfield is going to win this fight." Everybody and I mean everybody was laughing. Nobody gave Holyfield a chance that first fight. He said, "You're all laughing at me, I'm telling you, not only is Holyfield going to win the fight, he is going to knock out Tyson." Well in every bodies opinion this guy was nuts. He didn't know what he was talking about, because Holyfield wasn't known as a big hitter, so how is he going to knock out Mike Tyson, especially as Mike had got back on track and he was gunning for all the three belts. Well it's all history now because that guy cleaned up the £3500 pool money because Holyfield knocked out Mike Tyson in the round he said. I think it was the 10th or 11th. I'm not too sure but I know one thing he backed the winner and no one ever gave him a chance!

The beginning of 1997 was probably one of the quietest years on the poker scene for me that I'd ever had. For about two months there were no games. The games had dried up at Chris P's house. The games had dried up at Steve M's flat in Highgate. The games dried up at the flat in Hampstead. After all there was only one winner in all of those games and it was me, so it looked like it was going to be tough to get poker this year. Out of the blue, I got a phone call from Little Laggis. He said, "Steve I've found a property in Stroud Green Road and we're going to start doing poker there, why don't you come down and have a look at it?" Well I got down to Stroud Green Road in North London and he'd done this place up really nice and on Saturday nights he was going to run poker (Five Card Stud). It was going to be owned by the guy named Greek Michael who used to play at the flat in Hampstead (the guy that lost all his money in one pot to my dad at the very end) and it's going to be run by Little Laggis. The first Saturday we got there, there weren't enough players to make a five-handed game. Laggis was sitting there doing nothing so I said, "Laggis, you're not doing anything, why don't you come with me to the West End." He said, "Why, where are you going Steve?" I said, "I know a place in the West End and I think they've got poker tonight, I might go there and have a look and if they have got a poker game, I might stay for a couple of hours." Me and Laggis were driving to the West End and as we were passing the Hippodrome Discothèque in Leicester Square, I heard someone shout out "Stevie! Stevie!" I looked around and it was a guy named Mark G. I'd known Mark G for about six or seven years, he had a club in Golders Green that used to have a couple of pool tables down stairs, four or five pool tables upstairs, couple of fruit machines and a bar. It was just generally a hang out place for the kids. I parked the car over and me and Laggis got out and I said, "Mark what are you doing at the Hippodrome?" He said, "I'm running Saturday nights here and I'm trying to get as many people as I can in." Apparently, he was one of their promoters and he was helping with a guest list or something, I don't know. I introduced him to Laggis and Mark said to Laggis, "What do you do?" Laggis said, "I've just opened a gambling club and we play poker." Mark said, "We play poker down at my club." Laggis replied, "Where is your club?" Mark said, "Golders Green, it's called the 'G Spot'." I said to Mark, "Hold it Mark, I've known you six or seven years, you've never told me you play poker." Mark said to me, "Steve, I've known you six or seven years, I didn't even know that you played poker." I said, "Are you kidding me, I love a game of poker, what do you play?" He said, "Well sometimes we play, Seven Card Stud and sometimes Five Card Stud." I said, "Five Card Stud with the full deck?" He said, "No, we play Five Card Stud with the Strip Deck, but some nights we stick to Seven Card Stud, it all depends what takes our fancy." So Laggis said to Mark, "Why don't you come down to my club?" Mark said, "I can't give you a definite date, but I'll try." They then swapped numbers. I said, "Mark, you've got my phone number, please call me on the night that you are going to play Five Card Stud Strip Deck, that's the game I play." He said, "Sure Steve, we might play Monday." I said, "Well look, I'm not playing Seven Card Stud, I don't like Seven Card Stud." The truth is I can play Seven Card Stud but it's not my strongest game. I want to play a game where I know I'm favourite. Monday evening I got the call. It was just after the football had finished at about 9:45 pm. Mark said, "We're having a game at the club, why don't you pop down?" I said, "I'll be there in about ten or fifteen minutes." I got there about 10:45 in the evening. The game was already taking place. There were four people playing Five Card Stud, but what I was amazed to see was that they were opening for 20p and 50p and most of them only had about £10–£15 in front of them! I went down there thinking it was going to be a decent game. I couldn't believe it when I saw them opening for 20p or 50p. There must have been £50 on the whole table! Anyway I didn't say anything I sat down. I sat down with about £25! I didn't want to rock the boat. I then found out that the four players I was sitting with all played 'call or pass'. Now they didn't know what I meant when I asked them do they play 'table stakes' or do they play 'call or pass'? So I had to explain to them, do you play only with what you've got in front of you or do you play with money in your pocket? So one by one they said that they played 'more money in our pocket'. So I said, "Well how much?" They said, "Any amount." So Marky G, said, "There's no problem Steve with the money, I'll guarantee everybody, but everybody plays whatever they want." So I said, "Let me get this straight, so everybody plays anything they want, so there's no limit here?" They said, "There is a pot limit." I said, "I understand that but if there is a big pot?" He said, "There's not a problem I'll mark them for the money." This was like music to my ears! I didn't care if there were 20p openers, because I knew how to make the game bigger with my experience. Well I'm going to tell you this. The first week I was there that Monday, I lost £400 opening for 50p's! That's right £400! There were 'outdraws' and 'bad beats' like you'd never ever believe. Everybody was calling to the last card. Now it wasn't because of the size of the game that everybody was calling, after all once you don't play 'limit' but you play 'pot limit' you can still blast people out of the pot, but they would not pass. I said, "Are we on for next Monday?" They said, "We sure are." Next Monday I turned up at 10 pm. Well you'd never believe it, this time the game got slightly bigger. It was 50p or sometimes pound openers! I lost £350! Same again, everybody called to the end and I was losing pots that you cannot believe. A week later I lost £280! I'm now about £1000 behind on these games. I wasn't playing wrong but some of the 'bad beats' were quite incredible. In fact I could write a book about the 'bad beats'! I saw my Dad and I said, "I've got myself into these poker games and I'm losing about a grand. They're small games, maybe 50p or £1 openers, but I can't win." He said, "Is the game straight?" I said, "The games are 100% straight." He said, "Do you know the people that you are playing with?" I said, "I know Marky G Spot, he is a 100% gentleman and the boys that are playing all seem to be OK, but there is outdraws after outdraws and the last card seems to count on every time." I couldn't put my finger on it. Dad said, "There were games like that back in the early 50s when I used to work for John Bloom selling washing machines." Something that I didn't mention, Dad was working for John Bloom selling washing machines. The first washing machines in the country, but they used to play poker in the afternoons. He told me that, everybody was the same, they used to always call to the end card. They were only small games, but everyone used to call. I said, "Right the next time I go up there, I'm going to have to change the game slightly." Now when I walked in there for the fourth week everyone automatically wanted to play Five Card Stud. There was no more Seven Card Stud. There were a couple of things that I had to sort out on the games. The first thing I did was that I took all my chips up there. The reason being there was not a problem with the markers or the money but everybody had to sit down with at least £100, they could play any amount of money behind but the minimum was £100. The reason I did this, it's just that I tried to make the games a little bit neater. There were 50p's and £1 coins all over the place! The games were really a mess and there was so much action on the games, I felt that the games had to be more organised for me to settle in. Everyone didn't disagree with the chips. In fact it was so much easier, when they used to say, after losing some money, "Give me another £50, give me another £100." We used to just mark them down and everything used to be settled up within the week, there was not a problem with that. The next thing I did - I tried to make the games a little bit bigger, not a lot but a little bit. I started opening for £1 and £2. I started opening for £3 'no look', 'no touch', I used to say. I had to open anyway. Well on the fourth week, no I didn't win but I didn't lose, I finished levels. It wasn't until the fifth week, that I won £1400. I said to the boys there, "Give me a break, I've lost four times on the trot. I broke levels once, let me win once!" They said, "Good luck to you Steve, see you next week at 10 pm." We started playing earlier. The next week, they started chasing their money. Mark the owner started opening for £4, he started going £10 blind. The games were on. Sometimes before the last card when you used to bet £140–£150, the players now used to think before they bought the last card. It started to swing in my favour. On the fifth week we finished at about 7:30 in the morning with me winning just over £1500 again. They said to me, "You've had a good two weeks Steve." I was now ahead on the games automatically because the amounts I won started to outweigh the losing weeks. There were some tremendous pots at the G Spot and there is one pot that I do remember vividly. Mark G was £10 blind and he called with a Queen showing. The blind card was a King. I hadn't looked at my hole card, he didn't know this and I raised £20, Mark called. He hit a 7 and I hit a 10. It was me to bet. I bet £60. He called the £60. I now put him on a Queen or an Ace in the hole. I couldn't tell you what I had, I hadn't looked yet! I then hit a 9 to give me showing King, 10, 9 and Mark hit an 8 to give him showing Queen, 7, 8. I really felt confident that I was going to bully him out of this pot and I bet £180. I bullied the wrong person because he called me the £180. The last card I hit was a Queen to give me showing King, 10, 9, Queen. He then hit a 7 to give him showing Queen, 7, 8, 7. There was £540 in the pot and he bet £250 right into my straight! I thought for a couple of seconds and I looked at my hole card, it was a Jack! I immediately called the £250 and raised £1000. Mark, I'll never forget his words said, "I'm calling your bet because I had Queens all the way, I've now got Queens and 7s and I think you've got Kings and if you've hit a Queen on the last card, call the £1000." I said, "Mark I've hit the straight." He replied, "Good luck to you."

The games continued at the G Spot for 25 weeks exactly. I told you the first three weeks I lost, the fourth week I finished levels but the other 21 weeks, I was winning between £1200 and £2000 every week, it was like picking up wages. After the games I used to go and pick up bagels, take them home, have breakfast with the kids and then go to sleep. In fact my two boys thought it was fantastic that Dad used to come home at that time and have breakfast with them! I would say that the boys in the G Spot were very genuine, honest and honourable. There was a guy called 'Danny Poker', who was such a lovely guy. He still plays Omaha around someone's house once a week. There was the Manageress who used to sit down and Donna was her name. There was a guy named Chris. It always ended up with about five or six of us. Well as I said at the end of the 25 weeks there was only one winner and that was me! I think the nail in the coffin was the final game when I won about £5000 one night and then no one seemed to want to play anymore. Two weeks later, the club closed. Mark went off to Vegas. Danny Poker started playing Seven Card Stud and Omaha, and a couple of other players dispersed. So it just goes back to what I said earlier on in the book. The games never last. I always said that you need a star at the table, I had five stars in those games!

I used to pop to the Vic from time to time when we didn't have any Five Card Stud games and most of the players always used to say to me, "Steve you should be learning this Texas Hold'em, you're not a bad player, but you could be really good." I said, "I'll be honest with you, I like my Five Card Stud." They said, "Forget Five Card Stud, Five Card Stud is dead and buried, no one plays Five Card Stud." That's what they always used to tell me at the Vic but during the 90s I was still getting some really good and regular games and I never really put my heart and soul into the new poker games coming along because if I could earn money playing a certain style of poker, that's what I wanted to do. For me, at poker, it's about making money, not being a good player.

I did mention before I went into this story about the club in Golders Green that Little Laggis had opened a poker club in North London and they were going to have poker once a week. Well I think I might as well tell you about those games as well because while I was playing in the G Spot on Mondays, I used to go to Laggis on Wednesdays, Thursdays or even a Saturday night. The games were getting good in Stroud Green Road and Laggis was bringing in some very good customers. I was a very regular winner at the games and many times the games used to go to five or six in the morning. After a month, Laggis said to me, "Steve if you come down to the club and I ring you when there's a game going on and you win, you've got to give me 5%." I said, "Laggis 5% of my action, win or lose?" He said, "No, if I ring you on your mobile and I get you down when the games are good, I want 5% of your winnings." I said, "Laggie, no problem." It was a fair deal, if I won a couple of grand, I'd give Laggie £100. The games lasted for about four months in Stroud Green Road. Looking back on it, I probably was one of the biggest winners there. There were a couple of good players that used to creep down there, but there were maybe six or seven very open and aggressive players. Some nights were quite tough to make money. They definitely were not in the class of the G Spot, which was easy money or many other poker games I've been in. I really had to work to win at Stroud Green Road and the funny thing is with poker, what I've learnt over the years is you have to cut your cloth accordingly. By this I mean you cannot walk into a game of five professionals and play the same way as if you walk into a game with 5 'stars'. I used to, but that's why it used to take me three or four visits to adjust to the game. It was very easy to adjust to the professionals because they're playing the correct game, if you know what I mean. It's when you're playing people that throw away their money, sometimes it can be bamboozling. The club closed in Stroud Green Road and very shortly afterwards the owner of the Club, Greek Michael died of a heart attack. He was a gentleman, a lovely guy and sadly missed. Laggis disappeared and that was the end of the games.

I'm now going to tell you which footballer has always cost me money. Back in 1997, I saw Brazil play and there was a free kick just outside the penalty box. Up stepped a player named Roberto Carlos. He hit this free kick so hard that it swerved and bent all the way into the goal. I don't know if any of you remember that free kick, as a lot of people who follow football do, this was one of the most unbelievable free kicks ever seen. After the match they were showing this free kick time and time again and for many years after. Well you're probably asking yourself how did it cost me money? Well I heard that Roberto Carlos always took these free kicks for his club and country and I don't know what possessed me, but every time he played, I always backed Roberto Carlos to score the first goal. He used to be pretty decent odds as well. Maybe 14/1, sometimes 20/1, that's because he was a left wing back and he wasn't a natural goalscorer but I thought as I knew he was going to take all the free kicks, I had an edge! The next game he played, I had £25 Roberto

Carlos to score the first goal. He didn't score. The game after £25 Roberto Carlos to score first goal, he didn't score again. Well I'm going to be honest with you I must have done a couple of grand backing Roberto Carlos, scoring the first goal and he never ever scored a free kick or first goal since! I couldn't believe it. Anyway a couple of years down the line, I stopped backing him. I said enough is enough, this guy is never going to score the first goal! I heard recently that he had never scored a free kick since! Up until the last game of the season, 2003, Real Madrid had to win this game to win the title and Roberto Carlos scored the second goal from a free kick and it was a right thumper, but overall, by me watching that fantastic and unbelievable free kick in 1997 cost me money!

The middle of 1997, I decided to go to Vegas for one week only. There were no games in London. It was very quiet on the scene, so I thought go to Vegas and have a break. On the way over to LA, I flew Virgin Atlantic as I always do, I really enjoy the in flight entertainment on board. There was one thing that I had never done and that was to go and see the pilot's cockpit. I asked the flight attendant, she came back in about 20 minutes and then she took me through. There were two pilots flying the plane and when I walked into that small room, it was totally overwhelming to see all those gadgets and all those controls - hundreds and hundreds of them. The pilots at Virgin Atlantic were very friendly and very helpful to all the questions that I asked them, they answered everything. One of the pilots said to me, "What do you do for a living?" I said, "I'm a bookie by trade and also I play a lot of poker. I'm actually on my way to Vegas now to play poker and a bit of dice." He said, "Tell me about poker, what kind of poker do you play?" I told him. He then started asking me questions about poker. He looked at me and was asking question after question and obviously I was answering him. He said, "I've always wanted to play poker, it fascinates me." He carried on asking me all kinds of questions and his eyes were lit up as though he was absolutely overawed by our conversation. In between three or four questions he was asking me, I used to ask him a question about the plane and he said, "Oh! That button is nothing, that's very easy." So I said, "Well what's this gear stick for?" He said, "Oh! That's nothing either, tell me about poker!" I found it really unbelievable that this pilot was flying a big jumbo jet with hundreds of controls and buttons in front of him and he found playing poker an even bigger fascination than flying the jumbo! You know in life they always say 'horses for courses', well because I've been playing poker all my life and gambling, we don't think anything of it. He's been flying planes all of his life, he probably doesn't think anything of that. He was fascinated about my work and I was fascinated about his.

I got to Vegas and I stayed downtown at Binion's Hotel. If you really want to play poker, if you really want to gamble or you want to be close to the action and you're by yourself, stay Downtown. I didn't really want to stay on the strip. Don't forget Bellagio wasn't built and a few other top hotels and casinos were not there in 1997, so I decided to stay downtown as I heard Binion's was having a hundred times the odds on the craps! Now this was an offer you cannot refuse. I was going to be in Vegas all in all for five nights. On the first night, I decided I wasn't going to go and play poker. I was going to enjoy myself and play a little bit of dice, as I've said before you get tremendous value on the dice in Vegas, better than anywhere else in the world, Vegas is the place to play dice. The first night I've ended up losing $100, not a problem. I thought to myself I'll get it back, not a lot of money to lose but I could see there were no 'hot' tables. Someone told me on the first night I was there to go up to the Stratosphere Hotel and casino, they have got the tallest tower in the world and it stands over 1000 feet. I went up there and at the very top of the tower they have got a 'free fall' fun fair ride. You pay $5 and this ride throws you up 100 feet up in the air and then drops you down. I thought I would definitely try it. I was also told that the food at the Stratosphere Casino right at the top was excellent. So I had dinner there that night, the restaurant revolves around and you are slowly moving 360 degrees within one hour, giving you the sights of all the lights in Vegas and it really was incredible to see. When I left the restaurant I went downstairs and I thought I would change up $50 and play some roulette. There was a guy playing on the table and I decided to have a $5 bet on black, it lost. I then had another $5 bet on black and it lost again. The guy that was playing on the roulette wheel stopped playing and walked off. I said to the dealer, "Can you spin please?" She replied in a very strange and 'funny' accent, "No, no spin." I said, "But I would like to have a bet." She said, "No spin." I said, "You don't understand, I would like to have a bet on the roulette, could you spin please?" She said, "Yes I spin, you bet." I said, "I will bet." She said, "You bet first." I said, "No you spin first!" She said, "No spin." I said, "We are going around in circles, can you spin the ball please?" (This is quite normal whenever you go up to any roulette wheel in England, you ask the Croupier to spin the ball. They will give you a spin and you can then place your bets. If you don't want to bet you will still get what we call a 'free spin' but at this casino they were not giving any free spins!). I continued to say, "I want to have a "$5 bet, can you spin the ball please?" She said, "No I no spin, you no bet, I no spin." OK now I felt she was being very difficult and rude so I started to mimic her and I said, "I no bet." She said, "Well I no spin!" This argument is going on and all of a sudden behind me, the guy who was playing at the roulette before came up to the table and he placed $5 on number 29. She then spun the ball and I then put my $5 on black, it came black. The guy who placed the $5 on 29 left the table again and I said to the Croupier, "Can you spin please?" She said, "No, no spin." I said, "Why no spin?" She said, "You no bet." I said, "Me bet." She said, "You bet first." I said we are going around in circles again! I just had a bet." She said, "No, other fellow has bet, I then spin, you place bet after spin, this OK but must be bet placed and then I spin." I said, "Are you kidding me?" She said, "No I no kid." I said, "I'll tell you what, I no bet." She said, in a louder voice "I no spin!" I shouted, "I no bet!" She looked at me and yelled, "I no spin!" I mean this was a comedy sketch. I'm standing at the table, I'm not betting. She is standing there holding the ball in her hand repeating to me, "I'm no spinning! I'm no spinning!" All of a sudden the same guy appears and changes $20. She spins for him because he placed his bet first, so I then placed my bet. He left the table and the same thing happened all over again, she wouldn't spin for me so I walked off. Just before I left the table I said to her, "This is impossible I can't play with you." She said, "You are impossible I can't play with YOU, goodbye!"

Another thing that I learnt in Vegas, when I went to one of the casinos, they have $1 minimum roulette tables, but they have what they call a $5 spread, so that means you can change up $20 and you get 20 chips but you've got to lay out $5. You might lay out $1 each on five numbers or you might put $5 on one number but as long as you lay out $5 on the spin you can have a bet. It's called a dollar table, $5 spread. Well I changed up $20 one evening not knowing about all of this spread betting and I put $1 on 27, $1 split on number 27, 24. $1 split 26, 27 and $1 split 27, 30. As the dealer was spinning, he said to me, "It's a $5 spread sir." I looked at him and I didn't say anything. He said, "Excuse me sir, it's a $5 spread." I said, "Well that's my bet there." He said, "Well you've only laid out $4." So I said, "So?" He said, "Well it's a $5 spread." The ball was going round and I was taking no notice of what he was saying. He then literally pushed my bet off and said, "It's a $5 spread sir, that's the rules. That's no bet!" What I should have done really was just add another dollar to my bet, but I thought it was so funny at the time.

On the second night I lost $200, not a problem, $200 is not a lot of money to lose. Still again no 'hot' tables! One early afternoon, I was told that there was a pool hall just behind the Sahara casino, about a mile down the block and you might remember I was a bit of a snooker player but I could also play pool. I popped down to this poolroom, there must have been about 50 or 60 pool tables, the American full size tables. I went up to the front desk and I said, "I'll play any man here $5 a game." I knew there were some very good pool players in America but I was looking for a game. He said, "There's a few players here, but they will play you for $50 a game, even $100 a game." I said, "No, I'm from London in England, I want to play pool but I'll only play for $5 a game." (That way I knew that I couldn't lose big money.) He said, "Look if I find anyone, I'll send them over." I was having a few frames by myself and a guy came over and said, "I heard that you want to have a game? [He was in his late fifties]. Rack them, what do you want to play for?" I said, "$5 a game." He said, "$10–20 a game?" I said, "No $5 a game win or lose." He said, "No problem buddy." He broke and cleared the table and I paid him his $5 (within a minute)! They have a rule in Vegas winner breaks. He broke for the second frame and again cleared the table. I paid him another $5! Next game he broke and again he cleared the table! I said to him, "Hey! Wait a minute, are you some kind of champion?" He said, "No, I used to play a lot, I don't play a lot now." I said, "What's your name?" He said, "Gabe, they call me Gabe the Mailman, because I'm a mailman in Vegas." I said, "You shoot some good pool Gabe." We played eight games and I'll tell you straight, I never won one and I can pot a ball, but this guy was mustard. After the eighth game, I said, "Gabe, enough you're too good for me, you've won $40 off me." He said, "Rack-em, I'll play you for nothing." I said, "I can't play for nothing." He said, "No rack-em, save your money." We started chatting. This mailman used to be a dealer and Croupier in one of the casinos in Las Vegas. He started telling me that where he used to work was the casino they based the movie on which Robert De Niro and Joe Pesci starred in which was called *Casino*. He said that he was working in there from the mid 70s right up until the late 80s and the movie was 95% the truth. He said it was an unbelievable experience to be working in the casino at the time. He then took me over and introduced me to three guys who were the top American pool players and there was a game going on at the time which was for $100,000! They were playing 9-ball pool and it was whoever reached a certain number of frames clear of the other person would win the 100 grand. He explained it to me; you had to go 20 frames clear. So for example if you were 3-0 up, 5-0 up, 7-0 up etc. etc., you wouldn't win 100 grand but if you were up 20-0 in frames you would win the money, but if you were 19-0 up and the opponent won the next frame, the guy that was 19-0 up would have to win the next two to make it 21-1. Hence the 20 clear frames. I said to him, well hold it one second, the score could be 15-14, the guy that's 15-14 up is only one frame clear. He said, "I know, games can last for months!" Well I watched a few of the frames and these guys were proper, they could really play pool. It was such an eye-opening experience to be in that environment amongst the top pool players in the world.

The third night came and I lost $200 again! Well, wait a minute this is a first, I'm behind $500 on dice for the first time in Vegas, three nights out of three. I looked at it and I thought I'm here for another two nights, I'm not going to lose more than $1000. That is more than ample to lose on the dice and don't forget I was playing very, very carefully. I wasn't chasing my money, I think you all know me by now, but it just wasn't happening. So I thought to myself on the fourth night, I'll change up $200 and if I lose it, on the fifth night, I'll change up $300, I won't go above $1000. Well, yeah you've guessed it. On the fourth night, again there were no hot tables. I'm running around Binion's, because Binion's was the only place that was laying 100 times the odds. I'm looking all around, no hot tables. At one stage I ended up on the 50 cent table and only having 50 cents on the front line and two or three dollars on the back line! I wasn't even taking the 100 times odds because I could see the dice were cold. On the fifth night, it was more of a question of if I could recover a couple of hundred dollars, I would be happy. I changed up my usual hundred dollars and I started to play very carefully as per usual. Lost it! Walked around played another hundred dollars, again playing very carefully. Remember this is my last night I'm in Vegas. In my heart I said, "Well I've had a good time and I'm going to lose a $1000." I've won many times in Vegas, except once on my stag night and that was only $200, so you can't expect to go to Vegas every time and win. I changed up the third and final $100, someone threw a couple of good numbers and I built my money up to about a couple of hundred dollars and then it all went cold. Slowly, slowly I lost it all. I wasn't upset. Actually, I laughed to myself and said really how could you expect to make the dice pay? Look I know at any game there is a percentage against you, but I've still maintained that on the dice in Binion's when it is a hundred times the odds and you're just playing the pass line and taking the odds to the maximum by walking around and finding a warm table, you've got to have a better chance. The fact of the matter is you're still probably going to lose 0.127% or 0.124% whatever it is, but I felt that with the right structure of your bets, you could make it pay. Well I'd not seemed to make it pay on this visit had I? I'd lost $1000! It was about three o'clock in the morning, I definitely wasn't going to change another $100 because that would be against my principles. I was making my way back to my room to go to bed, and I saw a Croupier leaning against the wall having a cigarette and I said to him, "Are you on a break?" He said, "No I'm actually just going to relieve one of those Croupiers over there on the dice table and I'm just waiting for their shift to finish, I'm on in a couple of minutes, where are you from?" I said, "London." We started to chat. He said, "Do you come to Vegas often?" I said, "Yeah, I come to Vegas quite a lot." He said, "What do you play?" I said, "Craps or poker, but mostly craps because of the value, I think its tremendous value, this 100 times the odds." He said, "I'm telling you, if I was a punter, there's only one game I would play and that is craps in Vegas. You've got tremendous value." I said, "Yeah tremendous value and meanwhile on this trip, for the first time ever, I've lost $1000." He said, "But you've won before?" I said, "I've won all my life in Vegas, but to tell you the truth I'm not grumbling I've only lost $1000." He said, "How do you play?" I replied, "To be honest with you, I start a dollar on the win line and I don't take the full maximum odds straight away." He said, "Well really you should." I said, "I know you should but if you do that, you're risking more money straight away. I might put $25 behind and if it wins I go full odds." I told him exactly the system I play. I told him that I always look for hot tables. He said, "It was a good system." I said, "Great system, meanwhile I've done my money on this trip!" He then said to me, "You see that table over there?" I said, "Yeah?" He said, "I'm going to deal on that table in a minute. Do you see those two players who are playing on that table?" I looked over and this table was empty except for two men playing, they were standing right next to each other. They both had baseball caps on, jeans and shirts hanging out. He said, "Do you know who those two guys are?" I said, "No." He said, "They are probably Vegas's biggest dice players." I said, "Are you kidding me?" He said, "No, go over and have a look at their action." I walked over to the table. I didn't stand too near to these two punters but I had a look at their bets. One of them was playing $200 on the front line and wait for it… $20,000 the back line! He was taking the full odds! The other one was playing $500 the front line and $50,000 the back line!

Meanwhile they were looking for a 4. Boom! They made a 4. Then they were looking for a 6. Bang! They made a 6. The guy that was playing the $200 on the front line increased his bet and doubled it to $400 on the front line and $40,000 on the back line. The other guy that had the $500 on the front line was now having $800 on the front line and 80 grand on the back! This was far the biggest game of dice I had ever seen. They seemed to be friends but what was astonishing, after they had thrown two or three 'good' numbers there was no cheering, there was no excitement. These two players had to be the coolest customers I'd ever seen! Do you know what I did? I broke my cardinal rule of gambling. As I told you I was $1000 behind on the trip. I wasn't going to gamble any more but I broke a rule, I pulled out a $20 bill. That's right $20, I was standing about four foot away from these two guys that were laying out over $100,000 every throw of the dice and I then put my one single dollar chip on the front line and I put $19 behind. They were looking for a 5, they made the 5. I put all my winnings on the behind line, I had to get up to the maximum as quick as I could. They were looking for a 9, they made a 9. They then were looking for a 10, they made a 10, then they were looking for a 6, they made a 6. All of the time, I kept on pressing, pressing and pressing. I think they had now reached the maximum at Binion's, they both had $1000 each on the front line and $100,000 each on the behind line and they couldn't do anything wrong! In fact, the Pit Boss brought over an extra two racks of chips so that they could pay these customers. Each chip valued at $5000 and there were 200 of them. That was a million dollars! They continued to throw. They were looking for a 4, they made a 4. They were looking for a 6, they made a 6. They were looking for an 8 they made an 8. I estimated that they were winning well over $600,000 each! Meanwhile, I'd built my $20 into $2000. The table was very quiet as I said, every time they were throwing a winner, there wasn't even a murmur! I kept quiet, if they ain't murmuring, I ain't saying anything! I was winning absolutely pennies compared to them. They continued to throw. They were looking for a 5, they made a 5. They were looking for a 10, they made a 10. The Pit Boss brought over another 200 chips valued at $5000 a chip. They were winning about a million each, by which time I now had $30 on the front line and $3000 on the behind line because slowly, slowly I had been pressing my bets and taking off some money. I had an investment on the table of just over $3000. I already had $3000 racked up in front of me. I'm now winning $2000 on the trip. The point was 4… If they made this 4 they would have got over another million dollars and

I would have cleared another $9000! Boom! They threw '7 out'. That meant, that 7 had cost us all a lot of money. The dice came round to me and I could hear the two of them say, "Let's count up." They started to place all their chips in front of them while the Croupier started to count them all. I stopped playing and passed the dice, so that was the end of the game. I estimated they had won easily over a million each. On that game I'd won $3000 from $20! If they would have thrown that 4 I would have won another $9000, but I was happy. I think they threw about 14 or 15 good numbers… but that's not the end of the story… They left the dice table and I thought to myself, I'm going to throw these dice. I then moved around to where they were standing, I picked up the dice. I put $1 on the front line and $100 behind, maximum odds straight away as I was now winning $2000 on the trip. I threw two numbers, good numbers and I was winning about $500–$600. I kept on thinking about that number 4, if they would have thrown it. The waitress came over to me and she asked me I wanted anything to drink. There is only one drink I always have when I'm playing dice in Vegas and that's a '7 & 7'. It's a whiskey and lemonade, but it's a special type of whiskey. I continued to throw and then threw a 7 out. I managed to nick an extra $400. The dice then passed round to one young man who was now at the other end of the dice table completely by himself. I grabbed my drink, had a couple of sips and then put it back just under the dice table. If there are any of you that play dice, you know they have a small ledge under the table, where you can put your drinks. It's easy access for the dice players. This young man threw the dice and then I put $1 on the front line and $100 behind. Meanwhile I'm grabbing my drink and putting it back on the ledge just under the table. He threw a couple of numbers and then threw 7 out. So I thought I'm going to throw the dice one more time. I'm standing to the right of the Croupier and on the ledge of the table is where I've put my drink down, about eight inches to the side of that was an ashtray, which was full up with cigarettes left by the two guys who had won the two million dollars. The Croupier noticed this and he quickly called the waitress up to clear the ashtray and as she was coming, he decided to reach under the ledge just exactly where I was standing to give her the ashtray. He then said, "Oh! Oh! What's this?" He's then quickly put the ashtray back on the ledge and grabbed eight chips that were next to my 7 & 7 drink. These chips that he had grabbed obviously belonged to the two guys who were there 15 to 20 minutes ago and each chip was worth $5000! They had left $40,000 under the ledge on the dice table right next to where

I was standing, right next to my drink! He then immediately gave them to the Pit Boss and the Pit Boss put them into the cashier's desk. I couldn't believe it, these guys had left 40 grand behind at the table! I'll never forget that. I told a few people the story and asked. "What would have happened if I'd had found them, what would I have done?" Well I think the best thing I could have done was to take the eight chips and go and see the manager of the casino. I think this would have been the proper thing to do and then ask to see the two customers who had been playing previously and say to them that they had left some chips behind and would they be willing to give me a reward. That way, I think you couldn't get into trouble and that you've done everything correctly legally and morally. I mean they could turn around and say that they are not giving you anything for finding the chips and then so be it, but I think by doing what I said, you would have done the right thing.

The next morning I was leaving Vegas, but I did have a quick roll of the dice and I saw from a distance the same two guys playing again. I walked over and I saw that they were not playing that big. They were having $25 on the front line and $2500 behind and I said to them. "I was on the table with you last night, do you know that you left some chips behind?" They said, "Yeah the casino called us and told us we'd left the money behind and we popped in today and we collected it." I mean this was an incredible story. The very last meal I always have in Vegas, I always go to Rios Hotel as they have one of the biggest steaks in town. That was my last stop before returning home.

When I got back to London every person I saw I was telling them about my Vegas experience. I bumped into Maurice one night at the Barracuda casino and I told him about the unbelievable dice game that I'd seen and about the guys who had won easily over two million dollars. I even told him about the $40,000 worth of chips that were left under the dice table, we were laughing. He told me a good story that I wanted to share with you.

Not too long ago a young Iranian man walked into Binion's casino, he went up to the cash desk with a briefcase and in the briefcase was a million in cash! The young man said to the cashier, "I want to place this million dollar on the 'Don't pass line' on the dice table." Now the 'Don't pass line' means the guy wants to see a 7 out. When you play dice, the customers at the table never want to see the 7 but this guy wanted to put the million dollars that he sees a 7 before a number is made. This is what we call as betting 'out'. The story goes like this, the top guy of the casino came over to see the young man, and the young man explained to him exactly the bet he wanted to have. One bet only, win or lose a million dollars! They took the million and they gave him one red chip and they said to him the value of that chip is worth one million. The young boy proceeded to go over to the nearest dice table. He waited for a 'fresh' thrower to throw the dice. He then said to the dealer, "Put this chip on the 'Don't pass line' please." The dealer held up the game for a couple of seconds and asked the Pit Boss. The Pit Boss said to him, "I'll just check that with the floor manager," within one minute the bet was accepted. The dice table and the dice crew who were working at the time didn't know the value of the chip! The red chip went on the 'Don't pass line'. A guy threw the dice and the point was a 9, so that means if a 9 comes up again this young man loses his single red chip worth a million! If a 7 comes up then he wins a million. The very next throw of the dice was a 7! The guy with the stick (the dealer) called "7 out loser." The young man had won his million. He then went back to the cash desk with a matching red chip and got paid his million. The young man never had another bet at the casino even though he was still in Vegas for another week!

I'm now going to tell you the most money that I have ever won and lost all in a single evening. Someone I know rang me up and asked if I would like to go and play poker at their house as he was having two or three friends over. Then they were going to watch Tyson vs. Evander Holyfield fight No 2 (the ear incident). I said, "What time will the poker start?" He said, "Well if you come at about nine o'clock in the evening we'll play five or six hours of poker, but we won't carry on playing poker after the fight because it's going to be a bit late." I agreed, and got there about nine o'clock. By 9:30 no one had turned up. By ten o'clock still no one had turned up. We were sitting at the table, me and this guy whose house it was and it looked like no one was going to show. By about 10:45, we started messing about head-to-head opening for fivers. By 12:30 in the morning still no one showed. Meanwhile the guy was losing about £1200 to me. At 1:30 in the morning still no one had turned up. He was now losing a couple of grand to me! The game got bigger, bigger and bigger. About 2:30 in the morning he was losing about £4500 and he said to me, "I knew I shouldn't have played you Heads Up poker, you're too good." The fight was due on about 3:30 am. By about 10 past 3, the guy was losing about £8500 to me and the game was still getting bigger. I didn't really want to win this kind of money off someone who'd arranged a poker game and for no one to show. I was calling certain things that I really shouldn't have called, but it was my night and everything was going my way.

Towards the end of the game I was giving the guy a lot of what we call 'loose calls' (or having a gamble), but I want to tell you about this pot, because this is probably the best call I've ever made at poker. It was right towards the end of the game. The guy was £50 blind and I called the £50 with a Jack showing, the blind card was a Jack. He looked at me and said, "Pass." I said, "You can't pass, you can check." He said, "Ok then, I check." The cards then came out, a 10 to me, Jack, 10 showing and a Queen to him. It was him to bet with the Jack, Queen, he then bet £200! It was hard to put him on a hand, but I definitely put him on a low card, because don't forget he wanted to pass when the blind card came out. I called the £200 with a Jack, 10 showing and I'll let you know now, I had a Queen in the hole, so I had a strong hand. The next card came out, it was a 9 to me, I've now got showing Jack, 10, 9 and an 8 to him and he's now got showing Jack, Queen, 8. He's bet £600! Now I'll tell you what I was thinking, I've put him on possibly a pair of 8s. Jacks definitely not, Queens no way, not even a 10 in the hole, I've put him on a pair of 8s. I've called the £600 because I've got an up and down straight. The last card came out, a 7 to me, so I now had showing Jack, 10, 9, 7 with a Queen in the hole, so that means I had absolutely nothing! And a 9 to him, he now had showing, Jack, Queen, 8, 9. He has then bet £1800! Well, I won't go into too much of the mechanics of Five Card Stud but I'm pretty sure he was bluffing. He couldn't bet £1800 unless he had the straight because my hand looked like I had a possible straight. Even if he had a pair of 8s or he had hit a pair of 9s on the last card, he just wouldn't do it. I'll tell you exactly what I've now put him on in the hole, because I've now changed my mind. Since he wanted to pass from the very first card, I believe he has tried to blast his way out of this pot all along and I've put him on a 7 in the hole. I thought, and I thought. I must have been thinking for a couple of minutes and he said to me, "Are you calling or are you passing?" I replied, "I'm entitled to think here" and as I said that I turned over my hole card and said, "I'm not passing, but I'm thinking, I've only got Queen, Jack, 10 high! The only way I can win this pot is if you've got a 7 in the hole so let me think!" I ran through the whole game in my head again. An Ace I knew he couldn't have, or a King or the Queens or the Jacks and he couldn't have a 10. It was either a 7, 8 or a 9 and since he wouldn't bet into my possibly straight with a pair, I put him on a 7. I said, "Call the £1800! I've got Queen, Jack, 10 high." He looked at me and said.... "You win, I've got a 7 in the hole! What made you call that?" I said, "What swayed it for me was the very beginning, when the blind card came out you wanted to pass. Having said that, you were blasting away at the pot and I nearly changed my mind towards the end, but as I was winning a lot of money off you, I thought what the hell."

We both agreed that when the fight started we would stop playing and we wouldn't continue the game. That was the agreement from the off. Well as soon as Tyson and Holyfield were in the ring eyeing each other up, we called for the last three hands and he lost more. Overall on the Heads Up poker, I was winning £14,400 off him. He wasn't too happy. He asked me if I knew the odds for the Tyson vs. Holyfield fight. Now I'll be honest with you, I knew Tyson was 4/7 and Holyfield was 11/10, I said, "I don't know who do you fancy?" He said to me, "Holyfield has beaten Tyson once and he'll do it again." Deep down in my heart, I thought Tyson was going to beat Holyfield in the second fight and I said to him, "I'll tell you what we'll do, I'm winning quite a lot of money off you. If you want a couple of grand on Holyfield, I'll have a couple of grand on Tyson an even money bet." I knew I was nicking the odds, but hey, I'm up for none here, I'm winning on the poker. He said to me, "I'll tell you what we'll do, I owe you £14,400 on the poker, I'll have the £14,400 on Holyfield." I said, "Hey, I've worked all night to win this money and I'm going to lose it all on one fight?" He said to me, "I thought you fancied Tyson?" I said, "I do, but I don't want £14,400 on him!" He said, "Well, are you a gambler or are you not?" Now listen, deep down as I've said, I knew Tyson was 4/7 so the way I looked at it, I'm taking even money, a 4/7 chance, I've got the value and I was winning on the night. I looked at him and said, "You're on, I've got Tyson, you've got Holyfield double or nothing! Well it's all history now because Tyson bit Holyfield and that bite cost me £14,400 because he was disqualified and lost the fight! You might be asking yourself, why have the whole lot on Tyson, well as I've said to you, I was taking even money a 4/7 chance, so I've backed Tyson at evens. I was winning that money from the poker and I knew if Tyson would have won, the money was 100% guaranteed and I decided to take a gamble. On the way home, as I was driving, I wasn't unhappy about the money that I'd lost on the fight and to tell you the truth and I mean this. I was genuinely more unhappy with the way Tyson had started to lead his life and fight in the ring. Don't forget I had spent some time with Mike Tyson years before and it was a shame to see him going downhill so rapidly.

At the beginning of 1998, Chris P, who had played poker with us before wanted to play. He called me and said, "Steve I fancy a game of cards." So I said to him, "Chris I thought you'd stopped playing with me?" He said, "Well I've been away for a while and someone has been giving me some poker lessons and I now feel that I can take your money. Most of all I really fancy a game though. Can we get a game on?" I said, "Chris, I'll ring up a few players and see what I can do, we need a venue because we haven't got anywhere to go at the moment to play." He said, "You can all come around to my house." Two Saturday's time the game was on. Chris had a couple of players and I had three or four players. It was a couple of grand to sit down, £5–£10 openers. We had a couple of new faces come along that we had known for a long time, good boys. One of their names were Little Ozzie, whom I'd known for 25 years and his brother-in-law Angelo, an Italian guy who has got a wine bar. There was Steve M, Chris P, myself and a couple of others.

It was going to be one of those nights, I can smell them, trust me, I can sit down at a poker table and I can smell if I am going to lose my money. Within the first hour I was losing about a 'monkey', but I could see that it was going to be a struggle that night. The cards weren't going my way and as I've said to many, many people in the past, it's not what you do when you're winning at poker, it's what you do when you're losing. There came a big pot with Little Ozzie and me and by the third card, I didn't really want to get involved, I passed. There came another big pot with Chris and me, he outdrew me. Now I knew it was definitely going to be one of those nights! I was losing a couple of grand. At two o'clock in the morning there was a knock at the door, it was John Michael. I said, "Mike [we always call him Mike], where have you been? You knew there was a game tonight." He said, "Steve, I'm sorry I'm late, I'm running a restaurant now as you know [Mike owned a restaurant up in North London] I've just cashed up, just finished and have just come for coffee. If I do fancy a game, I would like to play, but I didn't bring any money with me." So I said, "It's not a problem Mike, you can always take chips, and your credit is good." After half an hour Mike sat down and decided to play. Within an hour and a half he was losing £7000! It wasn't his night either! I'm losing £3000. I think the only person I beat in a pot that night was John Michael, so it looked like we were both out of form. The rest of the table was winning. By about 3:45 am, we set a time limit of 7:30 am and the game would finish. I tell you what was going through my mind, if I could recover half of my losses, I would be very happy. Mike, well I don't know what was going through his mind, but he was certainly getting involved in a lot of pots that he shouldn't. I started to tread more carefully because once you start entering pots that you shouldn't enter, you're asking for problems. At four o'clock in the morning my mobile rang. I thought who could that be at this time of the morning? I answered it, it was my Dad. Dad said, "Where are you?" I said, "Dad I'm up in North London, at Chris P's house and we're having a tremendous game." He said, "Is it a good game?" I said, "Fantastic, it's a great game, I'm doing no good, but it's a great game." Dad said, "Well, I'm with Mario." I said, "Mario who?" He said, "Mario from Cyprus, the Mario that has got the card club in Cyprus who came to your birthday, you know which Mario, he wants to come and play poker." I said, "Dad, send him up." He said, "Well he doesn't know how to get there." I said, "Where are you?" He said, "We're at the Barracuda." I said, "Dad, we'll get a cab for him and we'll give the cab driver the address of the house, tell Mario not to worry about it, we'll get him here for sure." I said to the boys, "We've got a punter coming, he can play Call or Pass, I guarantee him. He is a true gentleman and a fearless gambler." At 4:45am in the morning, Mario turns up, I'm still losing, John Michael is still losing. The rest of the table is winning the money. Mario sits down. It looks like I've got two and a half hours to recover my money. There came an interesting pot between John Michael and myself. John Michael opened with the King. There were a few low callers in front of me and I decided to raise the pot with a Jack showing. John Michael called and the rest of them passed. It was me versus John Michael in this pot. He had a King showing, I had a Jack showing. The cards came out Queen to John Michael, King, Queen showing and 10 to me, Jack, 10 showing. I'm not going to tell you my hole card, it was John Michael to bet. He bet £160. I immediately called. John Michael knows me and I know 90% that he now puts me on Jacks because we've played for the last three or four years together consistently. I'm still not going to tell you my hole card. The cards came out, 7 to John Michael. King, Queen, 7 showing and 7 to me, Jack 10, 7 showing. It was John Michael to bet with the King, Queen, 7. He bet the full pot £480. I thought for about a minute, I then called. I knew I was going to call him, but I didn't want to call him straight away. 99% for sure he has now put me on Jacks. I'm still not going to tell you my hole card. The last card came out Ace to John Michael, King, Queen, 7, Ace showing and 8 to me Jack, 10, 7, 8 showing. John Michael thought for a second, 99.9% he has got Kings, Queens or Aces for sure. I know he has got a big pair and I'm thinking if I'm right, John Michael thinks I've got Jacks and he might bet into my possible straight. He thought for about a minute and it was for him to bet or check,

I didn't say anything. After about a minute he done the sensible thing, not always the best thing, because you CAN bet into straights at Five Card Stud, especially when you know your opponent, and especially when you know how the cards have fell, but he did the safest thing. He checked. I looked at my hole card, I bet £1440 the pot. Now John Michael started to think. He then said, "You raised the pot from the beginning with a Jack showing, you hit a ten, you called, you then hit a 7 you called, now you hit an 8 and I checked to your possible straight and you have now bet £1440? I put you on Jacks, Steve." When Mike said that he had put me on Jacks, that's what I knew he had put me on from the second card. He continued to say, "but if you had Jacks and I checked to your possible straight, you wouldn't bet £1440 with Jacks, you would check with me?" That's where Mike was dead right. Any Five Card Stud poker player will tell you the same thing. If he checked on the last card and I had Jacks I would check along with him. So now he seemed to be mystified why I'd bet the £1440. After three minutes of thinking, he said, "I call the bet of £1440." Immediately, I turned over a 9, I had the straight. He said to me, "You raised the pot on the first card and you ended up paying £480 for a middle pin 8?" I looked up at him and said, "Yes, I did Mike." He said, "That's not like you, Steve." I said, "No Mike, it's not like me, but with you I have to play differently." He said, "Why's that?" I said, "Because you know me, we've been playing together twice a week for a few years now! You know my moves, you're not stupid." It's true if you carry on playing with someone, you get to know how they play. So with Mike I had to go a step beyond and play a different game that he doesn't know and make more manoeuvres. I can also tell you this, if the last card that came to me wasn't an 8 to make my straight and I would have hit a pair on the show, Mike had hit his Ace to give him showing King, Queen, 7, Ace as he had, I would still bet the pot £1440. Then 95% and I only say 95%, Mike wouldn't call me because he would have put me on two pairs. It was a pot I then would have nicked. It was good for me that pot because I recovered a couple of grand, even though I was still losing. It was bad for Mike because he was now losing maybe just under £10,000 and we only had about two hours to go. At seven o'clock in the morning by which time the tide had turned for me, I was winning 5 grand! Mike had clawed some of his money back, but not a lot and then there came a pot between Mario and Mike. Mario meanwhile is already now losing about £10,000! Mike is still losing and the rest of the table is winning. Mario was £25 blind and Mike was £50 over blind. There were two or three callers and Mario had called with the Queen showing. The blind card was also a Queen, Mike immediately raised the pot. Everybody passed. When it came round to Mario he then re-raised the pot and Mike called. This was going to be a big pot. Mike had a Queen showing, Mario had a Queen showing, the two losers looked like they were really going to slug it out. The cards came out, 7 to Mario, Queen, 7 showing and 9 to Mike, Queen, 9 showing. Mike checked. Mario bet the pot, £450 with the Queen, 7 showing. I knew what Mario had, Mario had the Queens, Mike called. Once Mike flat called, I knew he didn't have the Queens. I was watching this pot carefully because they were both chasing their money. The third card came out, 10 to Mike, Queen, 10, 9 showing and 8 to Mario Queen, 7, 8 showing. It was Mike with the Queen, 10, 9 to bet. He checked again. This was weak play. Mario bet the pot £1350. Mario for sure has got the Queens and he's got Mike by the throat. Mike thought for a second, I didn't fancy Mike with a Jack in the hole. I didn't fancy him for a pair. I'll be honest with you, I put him on an Ace or a King in the hole, but either way this was not good play by Mike to check and then flat call. It's not good play at any poker game. Anyway Mike decides to call the £1350 and the last card came out. King to Mike, he's now got showing Queen, 9, 10, King and a Jack to Mario showing Queen, 7, 8, Jack, it was Mike to bet again! Now I'm thinking to myself Mike has got to come out betting the pot, no matter what he has got and he did. He bet £4050. Mario picked up his chips and called immediately to which Mike then turned over Kings. Mario then turned over his hole card… Queens! I looked up at Mike and I said, "I'm not saying you got out jail with that King but Mario was very,very unlucky. Mike didn't reply. He had scooped a pot of about 12 grand!

Mario was losing about £27,000. Everybody on the table is now winning. Mike has now recovered and is winning £3500! There is only one loser, Mario. I'm sitting very comfortably with about £6000. We decided to call the last three hands. On the very last hand of the evening, Mario was blind, I had Queens backed up. Everybody passed because they didn't want to get involved in the last pot of the evening. The blind card was a Queen and Mario raised the pot. I thought, "Oh! No! last pot of the evening." I tell you something, I know poker players out there when they are winning a few quid and the last hand of the evening comes, they would probably pass the winning hand. That's right, I've seen them do it, I just can't. I got Queens backed up. He's raised the pot, he was the blind man and he's got showing a Queen. I've re-raised the pot. Mario flat called. I hit a 10 and Mario hit an 8.

I came out betting the pot £600, Mario called. There's now £1800 in the pot, do I really need to be in this pot at 8 in the morning? No! I hit a 7 and Mario hit a 7. I've now realised that this could get to be a really big pot and I decided to check Queen, 10, 7, I had the winning hand. He had showing Queen, 8, 7. I tell you what was going through my mind, if he bets the £1800, I promise you I would re-raise the pot and I'm going for broke with the winning hand, but when I checked, I was half hoping that he'd check with me, so the pot wouldn't get too big. After all don't forget it was the last pot of the evening and he could still have the Queens with me! He checked. Now that little check gave him a free card. He hit an Ace and I hit a 9. He ended up showing Queen, 8, 7, Ace and I ended showing Queen, 10, 7, 9. Mario bet the pot £1800. I called him straight away. I thought this is the last pot of the evening, if he's hit the Aces good luck to him. I said, "Call Mario, Aces you win, I've got Queens." He looked up and said, Yeah! I've got Aces." That's £3000 I lost in that last pot. Why did I call him? Well trust me, Mario could have had absolutely anything in the hole. Anyway I wasn't too unhappy, I'd still won £3000 on the night, but I could have won a lot more. I did think to myself on the way home that if I would have bet the pot before the last card, what would have happened, but I'll tell you what, Mario would have still called, still hit the Ace and then I was committed and I would have lost more money. Even thinking back now, I feel I did the correct thing bearing in mind that it was the last hand of the evening (and also me feeling it wasn't going to be my night from the start)! That night at Chris P's house was probably one of the greatest games that I've ever played in, even though I didn't end up winning a lot of money. The whole table ended up winning. Mario recovered some money, though he had still done about 20 grand on the night. Mike won, Mario went back to Cyprus and we never played again at Chris P's house.

Around the spring of 1998 I got introduced to a guy that owned a gambling club in Haringey. His name was Tony A and he asked me if I would go down there and play poker once a week. He said to me, "I've heard Steve that you are a very good Five Card Stud player." I said, "Is that what they say Tony?" He said, "I've heard Steve that you are the best, better than your old man." I said, "He's good Tony." He said, "Well I've heard you're better." I said, "Well I wouldn't like to meet the old man over the table." I went down there that Saturday and actually, it was probably the first time that I'd won a bit of money on the first visit to a new school. I think that the players I was playing with showed me too much respect and I think they were a little bit scared about my reputation. There was Angelo from the wine bar, who played at Chris P's house, a young guy called Lefko. Tony A played and a couple of others, we were about six or seven handed. I ended up winning a couple of grand and Tony said to me afterwards, "You are really good aren't you? You're the governor mate!" I said, "Tony, I always play to win and I always play my game, what does that mean, I can't come back?" He said, "You can come back whenever you like. We will have poker here every night of the week." I said, "Every night?" He said, "Every night!" I said, "That's great Tony I won't have to go to work!" He laughed. I did used to pop to the club about two or three times a week and there were some really great games there. That was one place I had a 100% win record and I never lost from the start!

I'll tell you a funny story. I walked into the club that Tony had in Haringey one night and no one turned up to play, just one of those nights. In walked Kenny, we call him Kenny Icky Flicky. I said to you earlier, one of gambling's greatest character and he is. I'll tell you this story because this is a funny one.

As soon as he saw me he said to me, "Where's the poker?" I said, "No one's turned up tonight Ken." He said, "Well I'm holding a few quid, I want to play poker." I replied, "Well there is no one here to play." He said, "Do you want to play me?" I said, "Ken, not really, I don't want to play Heads Up with you." He said, "Why not? The old man would play me Heads Up, your old man will play anyone." I said, "Ken with Heads Up, first of all I don't think I'm a great Heads Up player and you, you're a fearless gambler, you could skin me Heads Up." He said, "That's right, that's why I want to play you!" I said, "I'll tell you what we will do Ken, how much have you got on you?" He said, "I've got about a monkey." I said, "You've only come with a monkey and you want to sit down in the poker games, that's not enough?" He said, "I've come with a monkey, but Tony A was going to lend me a monkey." I said, "Alright, I'll tell you what we'll do, I'll play you £500 freeze up." Freeze up is when you put £500 each and you play to the death. No one can play any more money from their pocket. Anyway an hour and a half went by and I took the £500 off Kenny. So Kenny then said to me can you lend me £100? I said, "No I can't Ken." He said, "The old man would lend me £100." I said, "Well that's the old man, he's not here." He said, "Please lend me £100." I said, "Ken please, you've just done a monkey, now you want £100 back?" He said, "You know I'll give it back to you." I said, "I know you will Ken. I'll tell you what I'll do Ken, I'll make a deal with you. There is a poker game at the moment going on in Edmonton." He said, "Well let's go." I said, "What do you mean let's go? You've got no money." He said, "Well you can lend me £100 and I'll play." I said, "The reason I didn't go there Ken was because it is a small game." He said, "How small?" I said, "£100 table, you only need £100 to be in the game." He said, "Exactly, lend me the £100 and I'll sit in the game, come on, take me down there." We jumped in the car, we're driving from Haringey to Edmonton and I said, "Ken I'll tell you what I'm going to do, I'm not going to lend you this £100," and he said, "Oh! You're out of order!" I said, "Give me a second hear me out!" He said, "Yes I did, you've just said you're not going to lend me the £100!" I said, "No, I'm not going to lend you the £100, I'm going to give you the £100!" Ken said, "You're a star!" I said, "Hold it, you still didn't hear me out." He said, "Go on." I said, "I'm going to give you £100, I'm going to take you in there, you put the £100 in front of you and we are 50–50, whatever you win I'm 50–50 with you. If you lose the £100 you don't owe me anything." He said, "You're on, I love you!" I said, "Alright Ken don't forget we're 50–50 and another thing, I'm going to stay for an hour then I'm going to leave. Call me tomorrow and tell me the score, whether we've won or whether we've lost." He said, "You've got my word of honour." We get down to the club in Edmonton. There was a small game going on, £1 openers, £2 blinds. Ken sits down with the hundred. He builds it up to a couple of hundred pounds but now it's getting late and I want to go home. I signal to Ken that I'm going home. He said, "I'll call you tomorrow."

Next morning I don't hear anything. In the afternoon, I popped into the office, still never got a call from Ken. Dad's in the office and then we receive a phone call from our betting shop in Westgate, Kent. It was the manager and he said, "There is a customer here Max, do we want to lay him £100 each way at 10-1?" Dad said, "No problem lay him Keith." Next race, the manager called again and said, "Same customer Max, he wants £300 at 5/1." "Lay him Keith," Dad replied. The two horses got beat. Next race the same thing, the manager called and said, "Same customer Max he wants £800 the 2/1 favourite." Dad said, "Lay him Keith, but can I ask you, have you ever seen him before?" He said, "No Max, he's a new face, I've never seen him in the shop before." All the horses he backed were losing. Keith rang up the next race and said, "Now he wants £500 each way a 16/1 chance!" Dad said, "Well Keith, lay him £250 each way at 16/1 and £250 each way SP (starting price)," which is commonly done in betting shops when they don't want to lay all the money at a certain price. They'll split it up and it's still a fair bet. If it was a regular and you knew the guy, you would always lay him anything he wanted. So Keith rang back in five seconds and said, "No Max, he's demanding the £500 each way at 16/1." Dad said, "Keith tell the customer he has got £250 each way at 16s and £250 each way at SP." Keith said, "He won't accept it Max because he says he knows you." Dad said, "Who is it?" Keith said, "He wants to speak to you." Keith passes the phone to the customer. Dad said, "Who is it?" I hear my Dad say, "Ken, what are you doing down in Westgate in Kent?" It was Kenny who I was with the night before. He is now in Westgate, 80 miles away and he has found one of our betting shops! He said, "Max it's a long story." Dad said, "Because it is you Ken, I'll tell Keith you can have any bet you want." My Dad speaks to Keith and says, "It's OK we know the customer. I've known him for a long time, he is an out and out gambler, lay him anything he wants." Keith said, "Now you've given me those instructions Max, it's not a problem." I think at the end of the day, Ken backed a couple of winners, but then be backed a few losers. I don't think he lost any big money but he was having some big bets. Before the end of racing, I got Keith on the telephone and said, "Keith, I want to speak to Ken." Ken comes to the telephone and I said, "Ken you're having all these bets in my dad's betting shop, obviously you've won money last night, am I 50–50?" He said, "Steve I lost your £100. I lost all of the winnings when you walked out. I lost the £100 that you gave me." I said, "Right and…?" he continued to say, "I also borrowed £100 off someone who knew me in the café." I said, "OK and…….?" He said, "I also lost that too." I said, "Carry on…?" He replied, "We then started playing 'Greek' dice, but I only started with my last £20." I said, "And…?" He said, "I skint the table! I ended up winning about 8 grand, I was with a pal of mine and we decided to take a drive down the coast." I said, "Are you serious?" He said, "100% serious, we finished gambling at 11 am and it was a lovely morning so we decided to take a drive down to the seaside. We went past a Ladbrokes, we went past William Hill, and we didn't think of having a bet in there and all of a sudden we found one of your Dad's betting shops. I immediately parked up the car and I said to my pal, we could get a good bet with this Max, because I know him personally." I said, "So that's how you ended up in Westgate? Well I took you down to Edmonton and you won good money, are you going to look after me?" He said, "I already did! That's the only reason I went in your betting shop, instead of the others!"

I was with Dad one day and we were driving past our betting shop in Kentish Town. We popped in to see what was going on. There were about three or four punters in there at the time and guess who was one of them?

Well, you won't guess so I will tell you, it was Reggie! As soon as Reggie saw us, he shouted, "Stevie! Stevie! Stevie! Maxie! Maxie! Maxie. Whose pokers number one?" So my dad said, "Yeah Reg, you beat me at Heads Up at Christmas didn't you a few years ago?" Reggie said, "Max, I've told everyone at the Barracuda, I've told everyone at the Vic, Max is number one poker player? No Reggie is number one!" Dad said, "Well anyway Reg what are you doing around here?" He said, "Well I popped in for a bet Max, so I thought I'd come into your betting shop because I always know I can get a fair bet on." Anyway, chit, chat, all of a sudden, there was a dog race. A couple of minutes later Reggie said to my dad, "Max, what price is trap 5?" My Dad said, "The price is on the board Reggie, it's 3/1." He said, "Max, you've got to lay me better than that." Dad said, "Well all right Reggie, seeing it's you I'll lay you 7/2." He said, "Max you can do better than that, the dog opened at 6/1." My Dad said, "I ain't laying you 6/1 Reggie, the dog is 3/1 now." "Maxie, Maxie," Reggie said, "You've got to lay me a fair bet, give me £300 at 6-1?" Dad said, "You can't have it Reg." So Reggie then said, "Well give me 11/2?" Dad said, "You can have 4/1 Reg and that's my final offer." Reggie said, "Lay me 5s." Dad said, "Reg, since it's you, I'll lay you 5/1." Reggie had the £300 at 5/1, trap 5! The race was off and guess what… trap 5 won by a distance! Reggie was shouting the betting shop down. "Reggie! Reggie! Reggie! Reggie always beats Max at anything he does." Dad said, "Good luck to you, you've nicked your £1500, and me and Stevie were just passing by. Don't forget always come back here and have a bet!" Reggie said, "I love you Max, I'll always have a bet with you, you know why, you can always get a fair bet with you."

Towards the beginning of 1999 John Michael opened a phone shop up in Southgate, North London. At the back of the phone shop, he put a poker table and he said, "Every Monday there is going to be a poker game, Steve if you get a couple of punters and I get a couple of punters we could have a six-handed game." Well I started ringing up a few boys that I knew, but they were not that keen on playing. Cos the jeweller came up a couple of times. We had a couple of new faces. Eventually, we got the games off the ground but it was only four or five handed. I'll tell you about this pot at John Michael's shop one night, it was between me and a guy named Marino. Now this Marino guy didn't play poker, but I'll tell you that he was a fearless gambler at anything he played. He came up for a laugh one night, he knew how to play but he wasn't really clued up at all and he'd admit to that. He had two 10s showing and I had showing King, 10. There were two cards to come, one 10 had passed. Marino bet the pot £300 and I called the £300, raised £900. I knew he couldn't of had the third ten. I had the Kings back-to-back by the way. Marino flat called the £900 and the next card that came out was a 7 to Marino, 10, 10, 7 showing and a 7 to me, King, 10, 7 showing, nice cards for both of us to hit. Marino checked, I bet the full pot £2700. Marino without hesitation flat called. Now I knew that he didn't have two pairs and I knew that he couldn't have three 10s, so I started trying to guess his hole card, but it was too difficult knowing Marino. He could have had absolutely anything! The last card came out, King to Marino, 10, 10, 7, King showing and an Ace to me, showing King, 10, 7, Ace. It was the two 10s to bet and Marino said, "I'll go all-in." He went all-in. Another £2000. I immediately called him and said to him, "Kings back-to-back Marino." He then slowly turned over his hole card… Yeah you've guessed it, he hit a King on the last card to make two pairs! I couldn't believe it. It was just under 10 grand that pot and the funny thing is, any card he would have hit on the end, I would have called him. A couple of reasons for that was it was very hard to guess how he plays and the second and most important one, was that when he bet £2000 all-in to a 7 grand pot, it became a value pot. Well that night – it was one of those nights, I lost my money. I ended up losing £4000 that night! One of my biggest losses, (that, and the game in Cockfosters a few years ago) it didn't hurt and I wasn't upset. Word got around that I lost and everyone was keen to play. Well the games lasted for about four months at John Michael's shop. There was only one winner, I lost twice, the rest of the weeks I was nicking between two to three grand. It now seemed people didn't have the appetite to play Five Card Stud anymore. Maybe it's because they knew I was at the games. Many people that I'd mentioned previously in this book who I'd played poker with, no longer wanted to play with me. That was understandable after all I was a regular winner at all the games. They were very dangerous! I mean, someone came up there one night and lost 20 grand just like that. You had to have your wits about you at all times, but as I said, four months down the line, it all dried up.

Around this time at the Vic, there was no Hold'em. I used to pop down there to see if I could get a game but everyone was playing Dealer's Choice or Omaha. Now back in 1999 I never played Omaha, so things went quiet on the poker scene for a while. I heard that on Tuesday nights there were some very good games in Edmonton. Close to where I took Kenny that time. It was in Bounces Road, they'd been playing for about a month but I hadn't been invited obviously. I turned up one night and I wasn't made welcome at all. I'll be honest with you, I asked them if there was a spare seat and if I could sit down and play. It looked a very good game, to which nobody replied! I then said again, "Is there a spare seat and may I play?" I couldn't believe it, no one looked up and no one answered! I knew the guy that was running the games called George. I said, "George, I'm being straight with you man to man, if you don't want me to play, there's not a problem, just say, Steve have a coffee, but don't play, I'll understand." He said, "I don't mind you playing, it's up to the rest." Now there was another guy and his name was 'Harry Satellites'; we called him that because he installed satellite systems. He said, "I'm not keen on Steve playing." So I said, "Why's that Harry?" He said, "Simple reason Steve, you're too good for this school, in fact Steve, you're too good for any school at Five Card Stud!" I said, "Maybe, but I'm going to tell you something Harry, YOU'RE too good for this school here!" Harry is not a bad poker player and he gets himself into some good poker games but he cringes when I turn up on the doorstep. He is a nice fellow and he doesn't mean any harm. I can understand he is there to make a few quid. Anyway eventually they did let me play that night at Bounces Road. I won £3000 the first night and I was told to never go back again! They told me I could go there and eat or drink whatever I wanted but please don't play poker. You might be asking why win that amount of money? You can ask any poker player on the planet, he is never going to sit down and lose money on purpose so he can go back next week, is he? We're not talking about playing a guy a game of snooker and that you're so superior in skill than your opponent. We are talking about poker and when you are sitting down one night, you are not going to give up the chance to win a nice few quid because the next night, you might have a few outdraws or bad beats like I did that night with Marino. So you really have got to maximise your wins as much as you can. People say to me today. "Steve you cannot get into any more poker games because you've skint everybody! Sometimes you should have let everybody win." I said, "That's easier said than done when you are playing a game with an element of luck. In the long term the good players will win, but on the night luck is also involved. The good player will only win over a period of time." Notice I say element of luck. You can play a pot perfectly, but you've still got the bad beat at the end and then you've lost your money. I've always played my game and I've never hustled at poker. You can't afford to, it's as simple as that. The games at Bounces Road apparently went on for a good year and there was only one winner, Harry Satellites. That's why he didn't want me to play!

In 1999 I was invited back ten years after I'd played the famous nightclub owner Peter S, Heads Up poker. He was to have a game at his nightclub starting at 3:30 am. There was no time limit and it was a £10,000 sit down. I went along and there were five players. It turned out to be a very good game and we played till about midday the following day. Well for me there were no bad beat stories and no outdraws. In fact I'll tell you something, this was probably the worst cards I ever, ever hit at the poker table and I mean to say they were bad. I actually won two pots all evening! Just two, but with my ability and my strength at Five Card Stud, I ended up only losing £650. I mean this was a pure miracle, trust me. A friend of mine, who came along to watch said to me, "Steve, I'm telling you now, if anybody, anybody, even your Dad, especially your Dad, would have sat in that chair, they would have done 20 grand." Do you know what I said to him? "Poker is a funny game. I can sit in a chair and within a couple of hours, I know if I am going to lose my money that night and if I know that, I try and lose the minimum. I can't get up and go home. All I try and do is lose the minimum but when I feel good, which is very frequently, then I know how to maximise my winnings." That night it was a disaster. Do you know the funny thing was, I'll never forget what French Alan said to my Dad in Aspinall's 17 years previously when he went through a losing streak, and French Alan was one of the greatest Five Card Stud players that ever lived. He said, "Max sometimes the cards can make you look so bad, I don't know what I am doing wrong." This was one of the greatest players. He went through a losing streak of about two months, it can happen to any poker player. That night I knew it weren't my night and do you know what? When I was driving home after having lost £650, I honestly felt like I'd won £10,000 because that's what I really should have lost. Trust me.

Towards the end of 1999, there wasn't much poker around for me. I was invited to a game at a club in North London, it was to start at about 10 pm but I was out for dinner and I decided to go along at about three o'clock in the morning. Well the time I got there, the game was so big, it was £100 openers, £200 blinds and you really needed £10,000 each to sit down! The problem I had was, I walked into the game at 3:15 am and four players were losing about £30,000. The other couple of players were winning and it was like I had entered a battlefield. I'll be honest with you, I sat down and I was a little bit out of sync as we say. I'll try and explain it to you. If I had sat down at the beginning of the game or an hour into the game, you get into the rhythm and the way the cards are falling, but by walking into the game after five or six hours play, it was like a war! I decided to play, but I played very carefully. I knew I was only going to play until six or seven o'clock in the morning but it was probably the most tight that I'd ever played. At the end of the night, I won a couple of grand but to tell you the truth I did myself no favours at all and there were some complaints about me after I left. They didn't mind that I went in late but they could see that I was playing too carefully. The game had got so out of control that I thought to myself, I'll sit down and I'll play very karabina because the losers wouldn't care how they got their money back. They were willing to call and raise anything! I was way too careful and that was the last time they ever invited me to play!

At the very beginning of the year 2000, I decided to take a trip with the family to Vegas as I knew at Harrah's casino they were having a poker tournament so I thought I would combine poker and a vacation. When we got to Vegas we stayed at the MGM Hotel. The reason we stayed there was because I had the kids with me and I knew it was very child friendly with many things for them to do if I went off to play poker. When we checked into the hotel and got to the room, the bellboy who unloaded our cases was very helpful and told us where we could get something to eat straight away as we'd had a long flight. I gave him his tip and we started chatting. I noticed outside our hotel room window that there were some large buildings and I asked him if they were convention rooms and he said, "No sir, they are our deluxe suites at the MGM, they are 3000 square foot each…" So I said, "Who stays in there?" He said, "The million-dollar customers, if you can gamble a million dollars or more, you can have one of those." He then said to me, "I'll tell you this story, do you know Mr P?" Now I'd rather not mention his name, it is a well-documented fact that this Mr P is one of the biggest gamblers on the planet today. He can walk in and lose three, four or five million dollars in a night. In fact I believe his record loss was eight million. He continued to say, "Mr P used to stay in there." I said, "What do you mean used to, he doesn't stay there anymore?" He said, "No, Mr P doesn't gamble with us anymore." I said, "Why is that?" He said, "Well have you got five minutes, I'll tell you?" I said, "Yeah! I'm interested, maybe one day I'll write a book!" He said, "Well Mr P used to come in and on one of his visits he was playing blackjack at the maximum of $100,000 a box. He was chatting to the dealer and in the conversation Mr P was talking about real estate, where the dealer lived, prices of property etc. The dealer mentioned that she had a mortgage and she owed about $80,000 on it [this was obviously in the course of the conversation]. Mr P won that night $1.6 million on the blackjack table. Just before he left the table he then said to the dealer. "How much was it that you owed on your house? She replied, "$80,000." He then said, "There is $80,000 tip, pay off your mortgage!" She replied that she couldn't do that because all tips in Vegas are split with the dealers who are on the same shift at the time. He then called the Pit Boss and said that he wanted this dealer to have the $80,000. The Pit Boss replied, "Mr P this is not our house policy, she must share it with the other dealers." The story goes like this, Mr P was quite adamant that the dealer was to have all of the $80,000. The Pit Boss in the casino was adamant that it had to be shared. The dealer then quit her job on the night and took the $80,000! Mr P was so upset with the casino that he never went back there to gamble again." This is a story that I'd heard from the bellboy, the fact of the matter is, Mr P hasn't been back to the MGM since.

There was another story about Mr P, quite a funny one. He was gambling one night at the Bellagio Hotel and he wasn't having his usual massive bets, he was having $5000 on one or two boxes instead of $50,000 or $100,000 a box on the blackjack. On the same table as him was a young guy in his mid-thirties having $10,000 or $15,000 a box. This young guy had a few drinks and was being quite loud. Behind him he had five or six young ladies with him, cheering him on, laughing and joking. Mr P, I've heard is a very non-flash billionaire who keeps himself to himself. The story goes like this. After half an hour Mr P was winning about $50,000, pennies for him. This other guy was also winning about $50,000. The young man became louder and louder with his small entourage of five or six young ladies, they were kissing him, hugging him, ordering cocktails, well you can just imagine the scene. The young man looked at Mr P and don't forget Mr P is a multibillionaire, who is probably worth two or three billion, asked him, what he did for a living. Mr P replied, "I'm in real estate, buying and selling, and publishing, I've got my fingers in a few pies." Mr P never asked the young man what he did but the young man turned round and said, "Well I do real estate and I've just done a deal today and earnt myself half a million dollars." Mr P then said to him, "Well congratulations I can see you're enjoying yourself in Vegas." The young man replied, "Well that's why I'm playing so big and I brought all my girlfriends here tonight." Now, you have to picture the scene, the young man now was giving it the 'biggun'. After an hour I was told that Mr P started getting agitated and the young man started to say certain jokes, which were a little bit offensive to Mr P, he also started taking the mickey out of Mr P. Mr P looked up and said to the dealer, "Excuse me can you stop the game for a second?" Mr P then said to the young man, "What do you think you are worth?" The young man replied, "Millions!" Mr P continued to say, "Millions eh?… I'll ask you again, what are you worth?" The young man said, "I'm worth $10 million." Mr P looked up at him and said in front of everybody, "I'll toss you a coin right now for your $10 million." The young man said, "Excuse me?" Mr P said, "You heard, in front of you and your friends who've been making a noise and taking the mickey out of everybody including this young dealer, I will flip a coin, heads or tails for your $10 million. I'll call the money over now and get it in front of me, but you have to as well." Well the table went quiet. The young man said, "You are kidding me, aren't you?" Mr P called over the Pit Boss and asked for $10 million to be brought over. The Pit Boss then turned around and said, "Mr P, if you would like $10 million I can arrange it for you within five minutes sir." The young man looked up and said, "So you are Mr P, are you?" To which Mr P replied, "Yes I am." The young man said, "You're a multibillionaire!" Mr P continued to say, "Yes, I am, but money cannot buy class or style, I don't make as much noise as you, nor do I take the mickey out of people and I am definitely not as flash as you are!"

There's a golden rule I always have when I go to Vegas. I never gamble on anything the first night I get there. It sounds easy doesn't it but you all know when you get to Vegas, you're shattered, you get into your hotel room and all of a sudden you come alive! It's unbelievable, it really is, but I make a golden rule of never gambling on anything the first night. We got to Vegas and the first night I walked down to Harrah's casino, where the poker tournament was taking place. I wasn't going to gamble and I didn't, but there were some tremendous cash games going on. There was a game of Dealer's Choice, there must have been £300,000 on the table! It really was a massive game. I only knew one of the players that were on this table and his name was Ali. I said, hello, as I've known him many years at the Vic and I'll tell you something about Ali, he is a gentleman, you could never tell if he was winning or losing. I said, "How are you doing Ali?" He replied, "I'm losing Stevie, but don't worry I'm going to recover." He had the very same temperament as Maurice but Ali was a funny guy. He could play in a $1000 game, he could also play in $100,000 game, it didn't matter to Ali. He was one of the most fearless gamblers that I'd ever met. I walked around for an hour and there was another table with possibly about $100,000 on. I was amazed to find that in Harrah's they were all playing with $100 bills and chips. In fact there was a big sign saying, "The only cash allowed on the tables is $100 bills." I'm telling you there must have been about three million in cash in this poker room, which had about 200 poker tables, and plenty of armed security! I saw the two-time winner, Johnny Chan. In fact, he played a pot, in a $600–$1200 Omaha limit game. Johnny Chan bet $1200 and the guy raised $1200, Johnny Chan re-raised $1200 and the guy then re raised $1200 and Johnny Chan passed! I thought this was really strange at the time after having invested so much money into the pot, but I'm sure he knows what he is doing. Aftcr all , he has won the World Championship twice but being a limit game, I'm not too sure of the strategy.

I took an early night and woke up the next day thinking I'll go down to Harrahs for about 6 pm. It wasn't too busy, but as I walked through the poker room, Ali was on the poker table and he was playing a guy Heads Up poker. I said, "Hi Ali, how are you doing?" He said, "I'm doing OK." I said, "Do you mind if I sit behind you?" He said, "Pleasure Steve." I said, "I'm actually waiting to play a Pot Limit Hold'em. (They had all kinds of games, Pot Limit Hold'em, No Limit Hold'em. You name it they had it.) That's the great thing about Vegas when there is a tournament going on. Ali told me he hadn't left that table for two days and two nights. I said, "Are you kidding me?" He said, "No, you saw me here last night." I said, "You're right, you're at the same table and in the same chair." I couldn't believe it. Well it was true, Ali was playing this guy Heads Up poker and his name was Sam. Now Sam looked like Al Pacino, I don't know where he was from, but he looked like Al Pacino anyway. I said, "Are you only playing Heads Up Ali?" He said, "No, sometimes players come and join us and after five or six hours they leave. They win, they lose, leaving Sam and I carrying on playing. So Sam said to Ali, "Ali when you leave I leave." Ali said, "I'm not leaving Sam." Sam said, "Well I'm not leaving either!" So I looked up at both of them and said, "Well, you've got to leave by the end of the week because the tournament finishes!" They looked at me and said, "That's when we will leave, but we'll probably end up going to Bellagio or the Mirage to continue." We were laughing. Ali said to Sam, "Sam, my friend here is from London and his name is Stevie, if you want a game of poker, a big game of poker, you want to play with his Dad, Max. He is one of the greatest gamblers of all time." Sam said and he meant it, "Get your dad on the phone, fly him to Vegas." I said, "Sam, he won't come to Vegas, he only plays Five Card Stud." Sam said, "I'll play anything, anything he wants to play, I'll play him." Ali said, "If your Dad comes, I'll even play Five Card Stud." Anyway the game continued between Ali and Sam and there was a lot of chitchat between them, they were playing $400–$800 limit Dealer's Choice. After about 25 minutes Sam said to Ali, "Ali can we raise the stakes?" Ali said, "Sure." Sam replied, "Can we play $600–$1200 limit?" Ali said, "No problem Sam." After about another twenty minutes, Sam said, "Ali I'm losing." Ali said, "I know!" Sam said, "Can we raise the stakes?" Ali Said, "No problem Sam." Sam said, "I want to raise it to 800/1,600." Ali said, "Be my guest." They started playing 800/1,600. After 40 minutes Sam was still losing. Sam again said, "Can we raise the stakes Ali?" Ali replied, "Sam I'll do anything you want me to do." Sam said, "I want to play $1000–$2000 limit." Now this is a big game. Even though it's a limit game, you can get some big pots, it's massive. They were playing it for two minutes and after two hands went by, Sam said to Ali. "You know what, I want to raise it to $2000–$4000 limit." Ali looked at Sam and said, "No problem Sam, $2000–$4000 it is!" Sam said, "Ali I was only joking." Ali said, "I wasn't! Sam you know me, any limit you want to play, I'll play." Sam replied, "I know you Ali and I know you mean it." I watched them play for about an hour and a half, it was quite an incredible game to see. There were pots of $50,000–$60,000 grand, and then all of a sudden over the loudspeaker my name was called out to play. I decided to get myself into a $500 sit down, Pot Limit Hold'em. I sat down with the minimum of $500. Everyone sat down with $1000–$1500 but I felt comfortable sitting with $500. I didn't play Hold'em a lot, though I understood the mechanics of the game. I was playing quite careful and then I was in the big blind. There were three callers. When I looked at my two hole cards, I had King, 7 of Clubs. It was for me to check or raise. Obviously, I checked. The flop came King, 7, 2, 2 Diamonds. It was me to bet and I checked. The guy on my left came out and bet the pot of $80, two people passed. The guy on my right called the $80 and raised $240. I decided to go all-in. The guy on my left passed. The guy on my right that raised the $240 called. The next card that came out was the Jack of Clubs and the very last card was the 3 of Diamonds. The guy had 2 of Diamonds in his hand and with the matching 3 of Diamonds on the board, he had a flush! So I just lost a $1200 pot. I pulled out another $500 and I ended up losing $200 of it. I left that night losing $700, it was a good game.

The next night I walked in, there was a very good game of Pot Limit Hold'em and I decided to sit down. I ended up winning about $1000. You know, people have said to me that I play good Hold'em. I think I do, but

I always explain to them for me it's like if you wear a size 8 shoe and you're very comfortable with that pair you've got, and then you go and buy a very similar pair that's also size 8, they never feel quite the same. That's like me at poker.

Vegas was a very good trip, I didn't win much money, $300 or $400. I started to look around to play dice Downtown, wherever I could get a 100 times the odds. Well this year, there were no 100 times the odds, it had all finished! It was back down to 12 times the odds and I didn't play. So with the family most days we used to go and see shows, go for the buffets and go to the shops. We went outside the Bellagio Hotel to see the fountains and this was one of the best hotels I've ever seen in my life.

From Vegas we decided to go to San Diego and I'd heard in San Diego there were some poker clubs, it was in the Indian Resort, just outside San Diego. I popped there and it really was a big card club. I didn't play that night but they had some very interesting games going on. One game was blackjack, but because it was illegal for there to be a casino in San Diego and only a card club, you were allowed to be the banker at the blackjack. That's right you were allowed to be the banker! If no one on the table wanted to be the banker then the house would be the banker, but the house had to offer the opportunity to the punter to be the banker. Sounds incredible doesn't it? But there was a little catch, not a big catch, just a little one. If you were the banker you had to pay a certain amount of dollars per hand to the house for the privilege of becoming the banker! It might have only been a dollar per hand, but if you're paying six or seven dollars a hand over a shoe it could amount to quite a lot of money, but obviously the casino had to make their money. They were allowed these games in the Card Club as long as the house didn't have a direct percentage, which I found very interesting. Anyway, after the trip to San Diego in Vegas, which was a lovely holiday, I was back in London.

One night I met up with a couple of guys, by chance, who were friends of Mark the G Spot from Golders Green and they told me they played poker. I asked, "What nights do you play?" They said, "Monday nights." I said, "What style of poker do you play?" They replied, "We play High Low, 7 Card, Omaha, Hold'em, Dealer's Choice, 7s Wild, Douses Wild, you name it we play it." I thought to myself, "Do I really want to go to this game?" They told me that they had been playing on Monday nights for the last three years. I decided to go one night and give it a try. They used to play from 8 pm to 11 pm. They were very nice boys. There were six of them and me, seven. I was welcomed into the school. Some of the games they used to play were pure luck. They used to have £100 squeezys, but full deck poker, what I noticed was that come the last hour they used to Strip the Deck, and take the 2s, 3s, 4s, 5s and 6s out and leave a 32-card deck. Now don't forget none of them ever requested to play Five Card Stud when it was there turn to request a game and deal. I did a couple of times when it was a full deck, but as I said to you before, Full Deck Five Card Stud hasn't got much action however when they stripped the deck and the deal came around to me, I requested Five Card Stud. No one had ever played that game before! When it was my turn to deal, I said, "We are going to play Five Card Stud Strip Deck, this is the game I play." One of the players named 'Shooie', turned around and said, "Uh! This is the game they tell me that you are good at." Well one hand of Five Card Stud out of seven, I thought I couldn't lose my money every time it came around to me! Then there used to be a request for Strip Deck Hold'em. That's right they used to play a 32 card deck Hold'em, which is a very dangerous game indeed, I couldn't believe it. I would win the hand and then request Five Card Stud, but I was losing money at my own game! Over 3 or 4 weeks of us playing, I was winning at the lucky games but I was losing at the Five Card Stud! Slowly, slowly they started to request (whoever deal it was) Five Card Stud, which was handy for me so we could play more hands in a night. One night all they wanted to do was play Five Card Stud! That was the night I actually finished levels! I think deep down they didn't think I was a strong player, but I tell you what, they always used to call to the end, so it was really difficult to put them on a hand. It took me about six weeks of Five Card Stud, consistently on a Monday for me to start showing a profit. It was probably one of the toughest schools that I'd been in and they couldn't play the game! Sure they had poker sense and obviously that does help but they had never played the game before. The games were terrific and the guys were really genuine, but it was just difficult to make it pay until the seventh week. It was then one of those weeks I couldn't do anything wrong. It's funny how it panned out, because this is one of the poker schools that I'd been in that actually lasted a whole year! That's right a whole year of Five Card Stud strip deck every single Monday! The guy that used to host the game was called Adam and on two or three occasions I ended up playing him Head's Up, but he never beat me. After a while he went very 'cool' on the games and he didn't want to play anymore. I think reading between the lines I knew a Greek boy that knew Adam and I believe he told him not to play with me and save his money. We then started going around to someone else's house to play. They got the bug and wanted to play Five Card Stud all the time! After 6 months the games stopped and there was only one winner; You already know who that was!

It was now getting difficult for me to get games. I heard the Grosvenor casino in Luton was doing Hold'em on Thursday nights. I used to pop up there because they used to have a good value tournament with about £5000 prize money. I went up a few times with a good friend of mine, Andy Gus. He used to enjoy his Hold'em. He was a Five Card poker player, but he had got into Hold'em. He then told me that there was Hold'em on the internet and got me registered on a couple of poker sites. I started to make some money online. For me this was incredible that you could sit at home, play poker, win money and go to bed without even leave your front door! This is the way that things were going. Within a month, I was winning around $6000 at Limit Hold'em on one of the biggest sites, I only invested $200! I then started to play the 20/40 which was there biggest game at the time, but slowly, slowly within three months I had lost the whole $6000 back plus an extra $200! My account to this day on that site is $400 behind. I don't know I just didn't fancy it after a while. You might say I should have taken the $6000 and ran, but that's easier said than done, now I've lost it back. I did go onto another poker site, which was running Pot Limit Hold'em and within three months I was winning $1800 and then I stopped. It sort of lost its buzz. I don't know sitting at your computer playing poker against no one you can see, you can't get the feel for the cards, you can't get the feel for the players. Overall on the internet, I'm in front and have been winning a lot of money recently, but I'll tell you about that later on.

I heard there were some Five Card games going on very close to Haringey in a Bouzouki place, a Greek Taverna, on a Tuesday night. Someone told me that the games were really good. Well when I went down, there were four or five players playing, but one of the players was Harry Satellites again! Apparently, he had skint everybody at Bounces Road and he was now playing at this Taverna. When I got down there his face dropped. I said, "Any spare seats?" They all said, "Steve, there's no seat for you!" I said, "Harry is it you, that's telling them that I'm too good and that I can't play?" Harry said, "Steve, I will play with you, you are a very good player and I genuinely enjoy playing with you, but your reputation now precedes you." This was now going to be a problem because if my reputation preceded me, how was I ever going to get a game of Five Card Stud? Anyway, I started to watch the game, after about 20 minutes, just before one of the hands, one of the players named Andy L jumped up and said, "I'm busting to go to the loo, deal me in and I'll be back in a second." As they dealt Andy in, I said to Andy, "Andy since no one wants to let me play here, can I take your card and play one hand for you?" Andy replied, "Sure Steve, no problem." My first showing card was an Ace and I opened for £5. (Now don't forget I'm playing for Andy L who is in the loo.) The guy on my left, his name was Bambos the Singer, called the £5, Harry Satellite called the £5 with a Jack showing and the guy on my right with a 9 showing, also called the £5. There was four of us in this pot and there was £20 in the middle. The next card that came out was a Jack to me, I was now showing Ace, Jack, a 9 to Bambos whose showing 7, 9, a pair of Jacks to Harry, he's showing two Jacks and a 7 to the guy on my right, he is now showing 9, 7, it's the two Jacks to bet. Harry came out and bet the pot £20, the guy who was showing 7, 9 on my right called the £20. I've called the £20 and raised the pot, which was £80. Bambos on my left passed, Harry thought for about ten seconds and called the £80, putting £240 in the middle. The guy on my right then passed, so now it's me and Harry in this pot. He's got showing two Jacks and I've got showing Ace, Jack. Now I'll tell you what I had, I had Aces back to back, but at this stage of the game I was still worried about Harry's three Jacks. With the mechanics of Five Card Stud and without going into too much detail, if Harry never had the three Jacks, he's got to be a little bit worried about me because I could have raised with the two Jacks, Ace kicker. Well anyway, I knew there was £240 in the middle and Andy L was still in the toilet! The next card that came out was a 10 to me, I've now got showing Ace, Jack, 10 and a 9 to Harry. Now I knew in my mind that that was a pretty safe card for Harry to hit or should I say a bad card for him, but a safe card for me. Harry checked, now I'll be honest with you here, if it was my money that I was playing with, I would have bet the pot £240. So I started to think and as I was thinking I noticed that Andy L had now come back from the toilet. I said, "Andy I'm playing this hand but do me a favour, I'm going to play it how I would play it with your money and not mine." He looked at me and said, "Steve whatever you do I've got faith in you, do what you want to do." I looked at Harry and said, "I check along with you Harry." Now don't forget there is one card to come. The last card that came out was a 7 to me, I've now got showing Ace, Jack, 10, 7 and a 10 to Harry, he's ending up showing Jack, Jack, 9, 10. Harry thought for a split second and said, "I bet the pot £240." Well this started to make me think. I must have been thinking for 30 seconds then Andy L said to me, "Steve can I have a look at your hole card to see what you've got?" I said, "By all means Andy, it's your money." He looked, and saw that I had Aces. He said, "Steve, I do trust you, but to tell you the truth, if it was me sitting in that seat I would call him straight away." I said, "Andy, please let me play this pot." I carried on thinking, could Harry have the three Jacks or could Harry have hit the 10s at the end! I must of thought for about a minute Andy L then said to me, "Steve call him, don't worry it's my money." I looked up and I said, "Harry, you win I pass my cards." Harry never showed his cards and the next hand was dealt. Andy L then took his seat back and he said to me, "Steve, I would have called him." I said to him, "Andy, you might have called him, but there was a reason I never called Harry." Harry looked up and said, "What's the reason Steve?" I said, "Harry I think you hit the 10s at the end but having said that, I wouldn't put it passed you that you had the three Jacks, but I passed because I made a decision." Harry never said anything. Five minutes later, Andy again said, "Steve, I told you I would have called him, I could have recovered my money on the night." I never said anything. Harry never said anything, Ten minutes later the same thing, Andy said again, "If only you would have called him!" Harry looked up and said, "Andy, that's why we don't play poker with Steve and we play poker with you because you would have called me, Steve wouldn't have called me and Steve didn't call me so I don't want to play poker with Steve, I'd rather play poker with you!" I looked at Andy and said, "Andy, does that answer your question? We lost money in the pot but we lost the absolute minimum." Harry looked up and said, "That's why Stevie is one of the best Five Card Stud poker players there is!

I'm now going to tell you about a poker game which I was involved in where I couldn't win! I was on my way to Margate, it wasn't a crooked game, but I'll tell you exactly what happened. A friend of mine three of four months previously said to me that there were some terrific games in Margate and if I ever went down there he would get me in, but he wanted 50–50 share of my action. He told me who was playing, I said, "sounds good to me, you get the game on and you can have 50–50." Before I left to go to Margate, I got a call on my mobile from another friend of mine, he said, "Where are you going Steve?" I said, "I'm on my way to Margate to play poker." He replied, "Can I have 25% share with you?" I said, "Yeah not a problem." He said, "Give me a call tomorrow, I know my money is in safe hands and let me know how you did." When I got to the poker game in Margate, one of the players pulled me to the side and said to me, "Steve, you are too strong for this school, do me a favour, can I have 25% with you, win or lose?" I said, "Yeah by all means, but you know me, when I'm on the table, I always play my game." That's a fact, my dad always told me, when he used to start the games back in the old days, he might have 25% with one player or another player, so they can get the games rolling, so if someone had only turned up with £300–£400 one night, back in the 70s, he might give them £300–£400 and he'll have 50–50 with them, but once the old man sat down, it didn't matter who was in the pot, he was firing after everybody! So by giving this guy 25% that was on the table, it didn't make any difference to me because he knew that I always played my game dead straight. I'm in the game thinking that I've only given one friend 25% of my action on the way down, and then I've given another 25% of my action when I've got to the game. Three hours into the game, I'm winning £1500. I got a phone call from the original guy (who's obviously found out I'm in Margate) reminding me about his 50% share, I couldn't believe it, I'd forgotten all about him! Now you might be saying to yourself, well he's not entitled to 50%, but I was sitting down with the players who he was going to arrange for me to play. So when my mobile rang and I've answered it and he said, "I've heard you're playing with this one, that one and the other, poker in Margate? I'm in for 50%!" What can I say to the guy? I can't say to him, no you're not in. Well I'll cut a long story short. That night I won £1100. I gave £550 away to the original guy who supposedly got me into the game. I gave £275 to my friend back in London, because he called me when I was on the motorway and I gave £275 to the guy that was playing on the table at the time! What can you do? It's cost me £35 in petrol to get down to Margate, so I actually lost at the end of the night!

In 2001, a friend of mine named Stelli (we call him 'Big Stelli', because he trains every day in the gym and is about 18 ½ stone) called me up and said that he was going to Vegas and if I knew of a few places that he should visit because I know Vegas so well. I told him four or five of the hotels and a couple of the shows he must see. When he came back, he told me a funny story about what had happened to him while he was playing poker one night on the £5–£10 Limit Hold'em at the Ballagio. He said he was sitting down with eight or nine players. He didn't know any of them and obviously no one knew him, but every time Stelli's friend came behind to talk to him, they were talking in Greek. Stelli noticed that there was an Israeli guy on the table at the time and he felt that he understood what he was saying. So as Stelli's friend was talking to him, Stelli could see that the Israeli guy was listening but not saying anything. There came a big pot between the Israeli guy and Stelli and on the very last card 'the river'. Stelli said in Greek to his friend, (who was now sitting behind him watching the game,) "I've got four 2s." The board was showing a 2, King, Queen, 6 and the last card was another 2, so when Stelli told his friend in Greek that he had four 2s, the Israeli guy passed and when the Israeli guy passed, he showed Stelli that he had passed pocket Kings and with a King on the board, that was three Kings! Stelli told me that after the pot, he showed his friend his two hole cards and all Stelli had was three 2's, but Stelli was convinced that the Israeli guy could understand Greek, so he thought that he would have a laugh and tell his friend that he has got four 2s and it worked! Fifteen minutes later, Stelli said to the Israeli guy, "Do you know I had four 2s?" (Now Stelli was lying to him.) So the Israeli guy replied, "Yeah, I knew you had four 2s, because you were silly and you said to your friend that you had four 2s and what you don't know is I understand Greek!" Stelli and his friend were really laughing and he made me laugh when he told me this story.

I'm now going to tell you about possibly one of the greatest bluffs I've ever seen at poker. It was in the 2001 Texas Hold'em Poker Million Tournament. It was on the final table and it was between two very good tournament players. One was Tony Bloom and other one was John Duffy. John Duffy was running low on chips and he was in the big blind. Everybody passed but when it came around to the button man, who was Tony Bloom, he raised about £20,000. The small blind passed and John Duffy flat called. Now I'm going to tell you exactly what they both had because it was on the television and we could see their hole cards as they were playing it. Tony Bloom had King, 2 of Spades and John Duffy had Queen, Jack off-suit. The flop came, Ace, 2, 6, rainbow (rainbow means all off-suit, this was a good raiser's flop). John Duffy checked. Now this was perfect for Tony Bloom because he had King, 2 in his hand and with an Ace, 2 and 6 on board, he had a pair of 2s, but his hand was strong as he was on the button and he was going to bet into the blind man. Tony Bloom bet £50,000. John Duffy thought for about 25 seconds then he called the £50,000 and went all-in, another £80,000! Tony Bloom then passed. I've seen Tony Bloom a few times at the gym and that pot always comes to mind when I see him and I've always said, "That was the most unbelievable raise and bluff I've ever seen at poker." I've seen John Duffy a few times at the Vic and I've said to him, "John that was the most unbelievable bluff I've seen at poker, how did you make that bluff?" He looked at me and said, "I was possessed!" John Duffy possibly played the best poker ever seen that night on a poker table and I think all you poker players would agree to that. He never made one fault or mistake on the final table, each bluff was timed perfectly, each bet was perfect, he played the perfect game!

I decided to go up to Luton because they had a very good tournament going on one week and I decided to play in the £300 Pot Limit Hold'em, which was held on the Saturday afternoon. You were allowed one re-buy, so I thought I'd pop up there and give it a bash. The tournament was to start at 3 pm. By 5.30 pm I was chip leader, I couldn't do anything wrong. I was playing with a lot of confidence and a lot of flair. I honestly thought that I was going to win the tournament. I knew that we were going to stop for a break at about 7 pm. By 10 to 7, I was still the chip leader and I was going from strength to strength. A couple of the guys on our table got knocked out of the competition, so it left our table down to four players and I was still chip leader. I was looking around and no one was even close to me. The card room manager who was running the tournament came over and gave us four cards to pick, so we could go on to our new designated tables for the next ten minutes before we broke for dinner. I picked up my card and it was table 11, seat 3. I'm looking around for my table 11 and I've realised it was in the restaurant section where they had set up additional poker tables for the tournament. As I'm walking towards the table someone looked up and said, "Shall we deal you in this hand, are you coming to this table?" I said, "Yeah, is that seat number 3 there?" They replied, "Take a seat, you're just in time." I entered in the small blind, to the right was the button man. On my left, the big blind. Everybody passed and when it came around to the button, he called and raised the pot. Now I felt as a lot of Hold'em players feel that he was trying to nick this pot from what we call 'position'. I looked at my two hole cards, Kings! Backed up or as they say in Hold'em 'Wired'. I immediately called the raise and re-raised the pot. The big blind passed. The guy on the button called my re-raise and went all in for about another 6500 units, I was committed. The pot was about 50,000 units. I called him and we had to turn them on their backs, as you do in tournaments. I showed him my Kings and he showed me his… Aces! The flop came, 2, 6, 9. The turn came Queen. The river came 5. I was out of the tournament in one hand, by me changing tables! I seemed to have timed it perfectly for me to get caught in this pot and to be knocked out of the tournament.

Many people always ask me, "Steve you're an odds man, you're a calculated gambler, what do you bet on the lottery?" I always answer, to tell you the truth, I wouldn't even bet the lottery and that's the truth, but there is a but. My wife has got six numbers and she feels that if we didn't do our £1 a week on the lottery, these six numbers would definitely come up! Like everybody else in England! So my answer is, I do £1 a week on the lottery, but I'll be honest with you, if it wasn't for the wife, I wouldn't even do £1 a week. I was told by a very good friend of mine, George in LA, the system that he does on the American Lottery, it's quite a calculated system and it's what I would do if we didn't have those six numbers every week. He says he always waits for a roll over or a double roll over and he always has a $5 Lucky Dip. That way you are not set with any numbers and after the roll over or double roll over you are getting near enough the correct odds. I know the money is so much bigger in the US than England, it's not a bad system so that's what I would do, but I don't do it! I do my £1 every single week. Sometimes I lay out an extra £1 Lucky Dip, if it's a double roll over. I still say if you walk into any betting shop, pick up a football coupon, lay out the minimum amount of money and you are able to win a million pounds, that's good value. You've got to get the odds haven't you?!

One afternoon I decided to go up to Costco. Costco is a place where they sell all the wines and food at wholesale prices, you name it they do it and its wholesale! I had to go up to get some wine that day. I walked in at about 3 pm, to my left was a full-size American Pool table and it was on sale. It was about £1700 and it really looked a good solid table. I thought to myself if I had the room, I would have one of those pool tables. I started doing the shopping and as I went to pay for my wines, I saw a small crowd gathering around by this pool table. As I walked towards the crowd, there was a notice saying that Jimmy White would be coming in at about 4 pm to sign his autobiography. I looked at my watch, it was already 4.15 pm, so I asked a member of staff at Costco, "What time will Jimmy be coming in?" They said, "Well he is due in now." I waited around five or ten minutes, no sign of Jimmy White, but I thought I'd give him an extra ten or fifteen minutes. All of a sudden coming in through the entrance of Costco was Jimmy. Now I don't know what possessed me to do this, I walked up to Jimmy and I said to him, "Are you alright Jim? Are you here to sign your book?" He said, "Hi, yes I am." I said, "Well there is a pool table over there, I'll play you the best of three for £50, me and you right now!" Jimmy stopped in his tracks and he looked at me and I'll never forget his words, he said to me, "Who are you, Father Christmas?" I replied to him, "I may be Father Christmas to you, but I want you on the pool table, best of three, £50." He said to me, "I'll play you, rack-em, but first I've got to sign some books!" As Jimmy was signing the books he was very friendly talking to the people, he then said to me, "Have you set them up yet?" I said, "Whenever you're ready Jim, I'm ready." He said, "Let me sign a few more books and I'll play you." Look, the way I looked at it, I was going to give Jimmy White the best of three for £50, I probably knew that I was going to lose 2–0, but at least I can turn around and say that I played Jimmy White at pool. Now trust me, Jimmy would never ever remember, 22 or 23 years previously, I played him when he was about 16 years old down in South London. He's played a million players since but if you've played Jimmy White, you will always remember that. Well I tell you what happened. He said to me, "You can break." I broke the balls and a 'stripe' ball went in, so I was on stripes (we were just playing normal 8 ball). I cleared the whole table and I was on the black he then said to me, "You've played before, haven't you?" Before I took my shot on the black, I said, "Jim you would never remember me, but the last time I ever played you, you broke the balls and I stepped in and made a 54 break." He said, "I don't remember that." I said, "No you wouldn't, a lot's happened in your life." Anyway I went down to pot the black and I've missed it! Jimmy cleared all his 'spots' and then took the black and he was 1–0 up. The next game Jimmy broke and he cleared the table, just like that! I didn't get another shot! So I'd lost 2–0 and lost £50, but Jimmy turned around and said, "I'll give you the third frame for free." Now I was getting value for money wasn't I? Getting three frames instead of two with Jimmy White. After the third frame, Jimmy played a couple of other people that were waiting in line to sign his book, which he didn't have to, but he stayed there playing pool with everybody, signing books and playing pool! Jimmy is one very, very friendly guy and I know for a fact he plays anyone. I pulled out my £50 and said, "Here Jim, here's your £50 and he looked at me and said, "No I don't want your money." I said, "Jim, you won the £50, there's your £50." He said, "No, no I don't want your money." I looked at him and said, "Jim, I'm a gambler, I'm a bookie, I'm a poker player, if I lose, I have got to pay, there's your £50 and you've got to take it, because if you would have lost I would have taken your £50!" I've pushed the £50 in his hand and then we started chatting about poker and gambling - as you already know Jimmy does like to have a game of poker or a bet or two! Overall when I came out of

Costco, I rang my wife, my mum, I rang everyone I knew and said, "I've just played Jimmy White, best of three for £50." I think that £50 was the greatest value and entertainment I had.

I took a trip down to Margate in the summer and I popped in to see Karl from Margate. He now had a pub, it was about 10:45 pm and he was just closing up. He asked me where I was going that evening. I said, "I'm going to pop to the casino have a coffee and see if there is anyone there I know." He said, "Can you do me a favour Steve, if you see Eddie can you give him this £50?" I said, "Eddie who Karl?" He said, "You know Eddie, he plays poker, he's in all the tournaments." I said, "I don't know him." He said, "When you see him, you'll know him." I said, "OK, do you owe him £50 from a bet?" He said, "No, but I really like Eddie and I want you to give him this £50, tell Eddie the £50 is for him and it's a present from Karl, but on one condition. He has got to let you play roulette for him and you must show him how to play the minimum to the maximum', because Eddie will take the £50 and put it on one number and that's the way Eddie is. He is an out and out gambler. Get some 25p chips and try to see if you can build up and win some big money for him." So I got to the casino, I'm looking around for this Eddie, I'm asking if anyone knows Eddie, no one knew Eddie. Out of the blue 20 minutes later, someone came up and said, "Are you looking for me?" I said, "Are you Eddie?" He said, "Yeah, what do you want?" I said, "I've been told to give you something." He said, "What is it?" I said, "Well I've been told to give you this £50 from Karl." He said, "I don't know anything about it." I said, "Well Karl has told me that you've got to come to the roulette wheel with me, I've got to play for you and I've got to show you how to go from the minimum to the maximum and win big money." So we've gone to the nearest roulette and I've changed up £10. He said, "What are you doing?" I said, "Karl told me that I've got to play carefully with this £50 and I've got to build it up for you Eddie." He said, "Don't be silly, just put the £50 on number 29!" I said, "No Eddie, that's not the way to do it, you've got to build it up slowly." He said, "Build it up slowly, you'll build up nothing!" I changed up the tenner and I lost. I said, "There you go Eddie, we've still got £40 to play with, your system we would have had nothing left." I changed up the next tenner. (They were giving me 25p chips, so we were getting 2 stacks.) Again we lost. We changed up the next tenner and we lost it again. Another tenner, lost it. Now we're down to the last £10. All the time Eddie is having a go at me and saying. "You won't win any money by putting two chips on a number, one chip here and one chip there, for God's sake you've only got 25 p on number 27!" (This was as the ball was spinning.) Well lo and behold the ball landed in 27 and they paid me £8.75. I took the £8.75 and I laid it all around 27 and the splits evenly and with the very next spin, the ball went into number 24, so we picked up £34 from a split. So I now said, "Eddie, watch this? I'll show you how to go from the minimum to the maximum." Eddie didn't say anything. I took the £34 and I put £10 on 24, £5 splits and £10 on number 207. The next spin the Croupier bought 27 and paid us £435! I got hold of the £435 and I put £50 on number 24, £50 splits, £25 on 27 and 25 splits. The ball span... Boom! 27 repetition! The Croupier paid us about £2500! I shouted "You see Eddie, minimum to the maximum! This is what Karl told me to do because he knew he could trust me to win you big money." I've then gone for a massive bingo to the maximum 27, and it's lost. I've cashed up £2000 and said, "Eddie there's your £2000." He said, "It's lovely this minimum to the maximum." I replied, "Yes, but thinking about it, I'll tell you what I'm going to do, I'll give it to you tomorrow at the pub, that way at least you can walk out of the casino knowing you've won £2000 tonight." He replied to me, "Steve don't be silly, I wouldn't lose that kind of money, £2000 from £50, in fact £2000 from 25p, I wouldn't lose that." I said, "Eddie, I'll see you tomorrow at Karl's pub, 6 pm, I'll give you the money." As I was walking out of the casino he came up to me and said, "I promise you I won't lose that money, Karl gave you the £50 to give to me, you've played for me, thank you very much and you've won, so that £2000 is mine." I said, "Eddie it's not a problem, I'll give it to you, but are you going to gamble?" He said, "No." I gave him the £2000. The next day, in the pub, I saw Eddie, the first thing he said was, "You know that £2000 you gave me... I lost it within ten minutes, as soon as you walked out of the casino!"

I went to the Vic one night, it was their tournament week. I didn't go there for the tournaments, I went there for the cash games. On these weeks they usually have many tables that play cash games and you can always get a game of Hold'em. Well I'll tell you about this because this was a funny incident. I was sitting in seat number one and there was a guy named Carlo. His nickname is Carlo 'The Diamond' Citrone. I actually don't call him Carlo the Diamond, I actually call him something else, but I'll tell you that after the story. The game was a Pot Limit Hold'em, it was a 5–5 Round Blind. Carlo was 5 blind and so was I, the big blind, it was the person to our left to call, he passed. Everybody else passed, it then came around to the guy on the button, the button guy raised the pot, Carlo called and I then passed. So, there were two people in this pot. The flop came out 4, 2, 4. It was Carlo to bet, Carlo came out and bet the pot. It wasn't a huge amount, about £45. The guy on the button called the £45. The turn came (the fourth card) it was a 9, Carlo then checked, the guy on the button bet £130, the full pot. Carlo thought for a second and then said to the dealer, "I've just noticed, I've only got one hole card!" She said, "Excuse me?" We all looked up and said, "What?" Carlo said, "That's right, I've only got one card!" Well as everybody knows at Hold'em you get two cards faced down, Carlo had only one! He then looked on the floor, he looked around him but couldn't find the other card, he had only been dealt one card! And it's the middle of the pot! The dealer said, "Well what do you want to do?" Carlo said, "I'll play the hand!" He then turned around and said to the guy on the button, are you willing to play it?" He replied, "Yes I am." We are all laughing so they've turned around and said, "Well, we've agreed to play the hand out!" Carlo then calls the £130, with one hole card! Don't forget the other guy has got two! The river card was a 10. When the 10 came out, Carlo laughed. The guy on the button has laughed, everybody is laughing on the table. We're all wondering what's going to happen next. The board read like this, a 4, a 2, a 4, a 9 and a 10, it's Carlo to bet, Carlo is still laughing. The guy on the button is still laughing, we're all laughing. After about 20 seconds, Carlo said to him, "I check!" Now we all burst out laughing. In a louder voice the guy said also laughing, "I check too!" Carlo said, "I've got nothing, I've only got an Ace in the hole, so all I've got is a pair of 4s, Ace, 10, 9. The guy turned over King, Queen and said, "You win!" Well we were all in hysterics that night at the Vic and since that night whenever I seen him, I always called him Carlo 'One Card' Citrone.

I want to tell you this story, I think it's quite an amazing one. Two very close friends went to the casino one night. They were 50–50. They put £1000 each and within an hour they were winning £10,000. One friend said to the other, "I want to cash in, take my half, as I'm happy winning £4000 tonight as we only walked in with £1000. The other friend said, "No problem." So we've got one friend who cashes in and wins £4000, the other friend continues to play. He then turns his £5000, which he has got in front of him into £30,000 and cashes in. They left the casino and then got in the car together. The friend that won the £30,000 said to the other one who had won £4000, "As we are friends, I feel bad that I've won so much money, but you stopped early." So the guy that won the £4000 said to him, "Don't feel bad, I'm happy for you."

The guy that won the £30,000 said, "I'm going to give you £5000, after all we came in as partners, you stopped and I continued, I know I risked my £4000, but I ended up winning another £30,000, so don't argue, there's £5000 for you." The guy that won the £4000 took the £5000 and said, "That's very kind of you, thank you very much." As they were driving through the West End, the guy that had won the £30,000 (which was now £25,000) wanted to go to another casino. The guy that was winning the £4000 (the one that had been given the £5000 gift from his friend), wanted to go home, but he said, "I'll come to the casino, but I'm not playing." They went to another casino in the West End and the guy that had previously won the £25000 lost the whole lot back and he was as sick as a pig! He then went up to his friend and said, "I've lost all that I've won tonight, is it possible that you could lend me £2000 and I will pay you back tomorrow?" The other guy said, "I'm sorry, I never ever lend anybody any money in the casino!" Can you believe it? I had to put this story in, I was told who the two friends are and that's why no names are mentioned, quite incredible hey!

That summer I strongly fancied Brazil to win the World Cup, and there was a very good reason. In 1998, I'd heard that they felt that they had let their whole country down. Brazil was in mourning after being beaten 3–0 by France in that final. They really wanted to get their hands on that World Cup. Six months before the competition they had trouble qualifying. Brazil were 7/1, which still I thought was tremendous value. I backed them, Dad backed them and I got a lot of my friends to back them, so that we could all win a lot of money. No one really strongly fancied them, but I did. I put on all their bets and I got them all the best prices. Entering the semi-final, I rang up all of my friends, who had their bets and told them, "Now Brazil are in the semi-final, they are strong favourites to win the World Cup, I would suggest that we make sure we cover our stake bet" (which means that we wouldn't win as much if Brazil won the Cup, but we wouldn't lose a penny!). This is a sensible thing to do, to be 'up for none'. One person out of the four didn't want to cover at all, the other person listened to me and covered perfectly, the small mistake I made was this, I made the other two cover because that way they wouldn't lose any money at all, wouldn't we all like to have free bets? Well as you know Brazil won the World Cup. Out of the four friends who backed Brazil from the beginning of the tournament not forgetting, I made sure I got them the best price and I then forced them to cover their bets, so they couldn't lose any money, they weren't happy! The reason being, they said, they knew that Brazil was going to win the World Cup! My argument was that it was me that told them in the first place! Well I've always believed that if I can have a bet for nothing, this is the best bet of all. As they say, you cannot keep all the people happy all of the time but you can keep some of the people happy some of the time!

I want to tell you about this gambler that I know. He is mentioned in this book, but I don't want to mention him by name as this is one story that I think you should know. It is to show you sometimes the state of a gamblers mind. This fellow walked into a b etting shop with his mate and he won £1200. When he stepped outside the shop, it was raining. The fellow that had won £1200 kept on stopping every 20 yards and fiddling about with his shoe. His friend said, "What are you doing?" The guy who had won the £1200 said, "I've got to get these shoes mended, there's a hole in the bottom, it's raining and they're leaking." The other guy said, "Well let's get to a shoe shop." So the guy that had won the £1200 with a hole in his shoe, turned around and said, "I haven't got any money!" The other fellow turned around and said, "What do you mean you haven't got any money, you've just won £1200 in the betting shop?" The guy with the hole in the shoe turned around and said, "You silly fool, that's gambling money, that's not money for shoes!" Just makes you think doesn't it?

One night in the casino in Ramsgate there was a good game of poker. By 3:50 am, Karl from Margate was winning £2400. He could see out of the corner of his eye that there were a couple of people hanging around and these people were always known to 'tap' a few quid from the winners (that means they always try and borrow some money). Now if someone is winning £2400 you are going to end up giving someone £50 or £100 when they ask you for it, but what Karl did, was before the game finished at four o'clock he got up from the poker table and went over to the roulette and said to himself, well I know I was going to end up giving someone that was hanging around the poker table £100, but I'm going to spin the £100 up on the roulette. Karl put number 23 and the neighbours by £25, £125 bet. The ball landed in 23. The dealer paid Karl £875. He then went to the maximum 23 and the neighbours by £100, £500 bet. 23 came again! He then left his bet one more time as he couldn't press it as he had already reached the maximum. Number 8 came a neighbour of 23, Karl cashed in another £8000. He only went to the roulette table because he thought someone was going to try and tap him for £100. Well that £100 that he was going to end up giving away, turned into another £8000!

Out of the blue Ken gave me a call one day. You know Ken, the one that was down in the Westgate Betting Shop, the crazy gambler. He said to me, "There might be poker at the snooker hall up in East London." It was a Thursday night. I went down but there wasn't enough players to get a game going but Kenny's cousin at the time was playing a guy snooker for £100 a frame. Now Kenny's cousin wasn't that great of a snooker player, he's playing a guy that was giving him 14 start, a handicap just to make things fair. I was watching the game and neither of them were great players but with £100 a game it was a very cagey game indeed. All of a sudden Kenny's cousin was about 22 in front and there were two reds left on the table. He put down the cue and he said to the guy that he was playing, "I'll give you the cube." So the guy he was playing said, "I accept." I looked at Ken and said, "What's going on?" He said, "The game is now for £200." I said, "What do you mean, they were playing for £100 a game?" He said, "Well now, it's £200, my cousin was 22 in front with two reds left and he's favourite for the game." I said, "Right and?" He said, "He wants to double it." I said, "Well you can't double it at snooker! I've heard of using the cube and doubling up at backgammon, but I've never ever heard of using the cube at snooker." He said, "That's the way they play, they play with the cube at snooker." Well this made me think, this becomes a much more interesting game now, because Kenny went on to explain that a lot of the games don't end up going to the black because, for example, if you are 20-odd in front on the colours and there is only 27 left on the table you might give your opponent the cube. He is probably going to refuse, so you win the game there and then. Very clever, I thought. So I carried on watching the game. The game was now for £200. The guy that Kenny's cousin was playing took the two reds and two blacks and then took the yellow, green and then he decided to play safe on the brown, he scored 21 points, he was only one point behind. I looked up at Ken and said, "Why didn't he give your cousin back the cube after he took the two reds and the two blacks?" Ken replied to me, "No, you can only give the cube before your next shot, not in between a break." Well this made it even more interesting, because this brown was safe. Kenny's cousin got down and played another good safety shot on the brown. Then the guy said to Kenny's cousin, "I give you the cube, I make this game for £400." Even though the brown was safe, Kenny's cousin refused the cube and lost £200 instead of accepting it and making the game for £400. You might ask yourselves why did he do that, well only being one point in front on the colours with the brown pretty safe, he knew he wasn't favourite. With

22 points remaining on the table, he knew he was the underdog and decided to refuse the double. I'll tell you what, what I've noticed is that by adding the doubling cube to snooker it adds so much more interest. Ken told me that on several occasions the cube is given early on in the game when someone feels that he is favourite and is then given back the cube and sometimes the games can get up to £800 a game. The surprising thing is, it's very rare that the game gets completed! Someone will pass and lose their money without the final black going down.

Andy Gus, who is a friend of mine, who I've mentioned before, was playing regular Hold'em and going up to Luton for the competitions. He said to me one night, "Steve why don't we all pop up there, six or seven or us and we can go for the tournament on Thursday." Eight of us decided to go up, including my dad and we took my wife's 4 x 4 as it seated all eight of us. Well all of us, bar one got knocked out within the first hour after the re-buys and the time was only ten o'clock at night. The only one left in was Andy Gus. The prize money went up to £5000, which was quite good for a £25 entry. Midnight came, we were all waiting to go home, but we couldn't as Andy Gus was still in the competition. Two o'clock in the morning, we're still waiting to go home, Gus is still in the competition. By 3.30 am Andy Gus was left in the competition Heads Up with another guy who we didn't know. The other guy said to Gus, "Do you want to make a deal? Shall we split the prize money?" Gus said, "I can't split the prize money, we came up eight of us and my friends have been waiting six hours for me, I've got to win it." Andy Gus proceeded to go all-in on the very next hand and the guy called and Andy Gus won the pot and the first prize. On the way back, Andy Gus said to us all in the car, "Guys what happened, you all got knocked out early?" My Dad said, "Andy, I re-bought six times, then I couldn't re-buy after the first hour!" "Stevie, what happened to you?" Gus said. I replied, "Gus, I stopped, because I re-bought three times and the cards were not going my way." He asked everybody how many times they re-bought. He said, "So let's get this straight, Max you've lost £120, Stevie you lost £80, Mario you lost £80," etc. etc. He asked all of us how much we lost and continued to say "I'll tell you what I'm going to do, you've all waited for me, so in that case because I won the first prize, I'm going to give everybody's money back." I said, "Gus that is very kind of you, thank you very much, I'll give it straight to my two boys." My dad said, "Andy Gus don't give it to me because I am not going to take it." Andy replied "Mr Max you have to take it because if it wasn't for you or Stevie I wouldn't have been coming to Luton tonight, trust me." Dad replied, "Give it to the kids and we'll all be happy." That night Gus gave all seven of us, all the money back that we had lost in the tournament. What a man! I think it came to about £600!

One of the most unbelievable pots I saw at Hold'em was at a Tournament in Luton and the first prize was about £4000, there were only two players left. One player raised, the other one re-raised and the other one went all-in and all the chips were in the middle. They had to turn them on their 'backs' as they always do in tournaments. One player had two Jacks and the other player had Ace, Queen off-suit. Well the two Jacks is marginally favourite over the Ace, Queen, but wait for it, the flop came Jack, 9, 9. So now the two Jacks has got a Full House, three Jacks over two 9s. The Ace, Queen, he hasn't got anything, the turn came, the fourth card, it was a 9. So now the board was Jack, 9, 9, 9. Still no different, the two Jacks has still got the Full House, three Jacks over two 9s and now the Ace, Queen has got three 9s with an Ace, Queen. But listen to this the river card came… It was a 9! So now the two Jacks that had the Full House on the flop has ended up with four 9s with a Jack and the Ace, Queen has ended up with four 9s with an Ace! I mean, to me this is quite an incredible bad beat at Hold'em and I've never ever seen one like this since.

Towards the end of 2002 things had definitely gone quiet on the Five Card Stud poker scene, so I decided to take a trip up to the Vic one night to see if there was any Hold'em, everyone was playing Omaha. I asked the card room manager if there were any spare seats, as it looked quite busy. He said, "I can put your name down Steve and if you'd like to wait 20 minutes I'll get you a seat." I've often had bad experiences waiting for seats so I've always decided not to wait, but I told him to put my name down anyway because if I was to have waited five or ten minutes I would have played. As I was walking around the card room, I saw that there was a spare seat on the £100 Omaha. I asked the card room manager if it was free and he said, "No, the guy has got the seat 'wrapped up', he's probably upstairs having dinner." The chips were still at the table, but they usually put a clear plastic box over the chips so they know the seat is taken. The card room manager then told me that if I wanted to 'play over' I was able to. Play over means I can sit in that seat and it will not cost me any money for the period of time that this person is away from the table as the session fee comes from his chips. I changed up £100 and I decided to play over. As I sat down the dealer dealt out the cards and I was dealt four hole cards, which was very strange for me. I peeped at them all and I saw Ace of Hearts, Ace of Clubs, King of Hearts, and Queen of Clubs. This I'm pretty sure is a good hand at Omaha. I was on the button so I was last to act. There had been a raise in front of me and then a re-raise. I decided to re-raise and my £100 went all-in on my very first hand! There were three callers, the pot was £400. Just before the flop, the guy whose seat I was sitting in came back and said to me, "I'm back can I sit in my seat?" I said, "May I just finish this pot please?" He replied, "No problem." The flop came out 9, 2, 6, rainbow (no suits). There was a side pot, there was some more betting, I wasn't involved in this. The turn came out (the fourth card), a 2. Everybody was all-in. There was £400 in the main pot and about £180 in the side pot. The river card was a Jack. I turned over my hand, all I had was Aces. It was very hard for me to win this pot, as I've learnt at Omaha you really have to improve on the flop. Everybody turned over their cards and I couldn't believe it, my two Aces had held up all the way, which was a very rare thing at this game. I scooped the £400, the guy standing behind me said, "You were very lucky!" I replied to him, "May I ask you a favour? I've just sat down for one hand, I don't want your chair, but please may I play the next hand, just one more hand?" He said, "No problem." The next hand was dealt up and when I looked at my cards, my four cards were King, Queen, King, and another Queen. I had two Kings and two Queens! There had been a raise; I was one from the button, the raise was towards the middle of the table and there had been two or three flat callers. I flat called with this hand and waited until I saw a flop, which I think is the right thing to do. I can't pass this and I definitely can't raise with this hand as I now had £400 in front of me. There were five people in this flop and there was about £60 in the middle. The flop came out King, 4, 4. I had hit a Full House immediately! Everybody checked, it came round to me and I bet the £60, I managed to get two callers. There is now £240 in this pot. The turn came out an 8, everybody checked to me. I bet the pot £240. One person called and the other person passed. There was now £720 in the middle and the guy that called the £240 was all-in. The last card that came out was a Jack, I turned over my cards and showed him my two Kings and with a King 2, 2 on board I had the Full House. He turned over his cards and he had 2, Ace, which made him three 2s. I scooped a pot of £720. This was the second hand I had played! I looked up at the guy whose seat it was and said, "You can have your seat back now, thank you very much." I cashed in and I thought to myself, "Well maybe I can become an Omaha player!" As every Omaha player obviously knows, the difference between Omaha and Hold'em is, Hold'em you can use both of your hole cards, one of your hole cards or you can play the board. At Omaha you cannot do this. You get four hole cards, but you must use two and you must use three from the board. Sometimes, it can get quite technical but I will be honest with you, I wasn't thinking about all of that at the time.

A week later I went up to the Vic again having now got the 'flavour' and I got myself into another £100 Omaha, it was a good action game, so I decided to sit down with £200. I now wanted to learn this game. It is the only game that there seems to be a lot of money around at the moment. I sat down and within 45 minutes I was winning about £450, so I had £650 in front of me. I was on the button and there were three callers in front of me. I had a look at my four hole cards and I had two 5s, an Ace and a 6. The Ace and the 6 were suited. I decided to call the £5. The small blind checked, the big blind also checked. There was about £25 in the middle. The flop came out 2 of Clubs, 3 of Hearts, 4 of Hearts. Lovely hand for me to hit! With the 2, 3 and 4 on the flop, I had 5, 6 in my hand, I had hit the top straight. The small blind came out betting, he bet £25. There were two callers, so straight away I've put those two callers on flush draws, maybe bottom straights, but all I know is I had the best possible hand, I had the 'nuts' as we say at Hold'em or Omaha, that's a hand that cannot be beaten. I called the £25 and raised £125 knowing this. The small blind called the £125 and re-raised £375. The two other people who were in the pot passed. I double-checked my cards just to make sure that I had the winning hand and yes, I had the highest possible straight on board. I decided to call the £375 and go all-in. This was now going to be over a £1400 pot. He called immediately and he said to me, "What have you got?" I said, "I've got the nuts." I'll never forget what he said, He replied, "Is that all?" I said, "What do you mean, is that all, I've got the winning hand, the most that you can have is the same hand as me and we are going to split the pot." He said, "Is it?" He then turned over his four hole cards, before the turn and the river. He had in his hand a 5, 6, so he had the same hand as me, and a 7 and an Ace. Now the Ace and the 7 was of Hearts so if another Heart hit on the board, he would have won with the Flush, if a 6 hits the boards he's now got an even higher straight! This guy is what we would call at Omaha, had the 'wrap around' and he was 'free rolling'. He was a big favourite to win this pot. I couldn't believe it, he had a Flush draw and a higher straight draw and I thought I had the nuts! Well the turn came and it was a Jack of

Spades, the river came and it was a Queen of Diamonds and we split the pot! I couldn't believe it. He looked up at me and said, "You were very, very lucky to split this pot." I said, "You're right, I thought I had the winning hand!" He said to me and I'll never forget it, "You've got to be very, very alert and very aware at Omaha because these situations come up regularly and when you think you've got the winning hand, someone could be drawing to the nuts." The card room manager came around and asked us for the next session fee. I looked up at him and I said, "Cash me in, this game is not for me!" I cashed in winning about £450 and I can honestly say, I haven't played Omaha since. I'm in front at the Vic at Omaha, I've played about six or seven times and I've won on each occasion but on that last visit I've realised I've got a lot of learning to do!

In 2003 we took a vacation to Florida. We stayed at the Grand Floridian Hotel, one of the nicest hotels on the Disney resort. One night I decided to go for a late-night swim and then I sat in the Jacuzzi for about 45 minutes. There was a guy that was opposite me and we started chatting. He was in the real estate business and he asked what I did. I told him and he was very interested in poker. I explained to him a few of the rules and the regulations. He told me a story and I thought I would share it with you. It was about his best man who lived in LA and was a gambler. He said that his friend used to finish work at 5 pm. As soon as he had finished, he would ring his wife at home and tell his wife that he was working late and he would be home at around 10:30–11 pm, as he had a late night at the office. Well you know what he used to do? He used to go straight to the airport and jump on the first plane to Vegas, be in Vegas maybe by 6 pm, go to the nearest casino and gamble for maybe two or three hours, take the plane home and be back home for about 10 pm and then tell his wife that he had been working late! He told me this was going on for many years, but the wife started to become suspicious, thinking that her husband had a girlfriend, because he was doing this three or four nights a week! She decided to get a private detective to follow him from his work and find out where he was going. Well obviously the private detective reported back that her husband was going straight to the airport. This made her even more suspicious, she didn't know what to do. She was now certain that her husband had a girlfriend and he was visiting her and then coming home. On a couple of these so-called late working nights, she started to call him on his mobile telephone to see if she could get any clue where he was. She made up one or two excuses to say that he had to get home quickly, which by the way he did. He then used to take the first plane home from Vegas and get home straight away! She knew he was going to the airport, but she wasn't certain where he was going until one night, she called him on his mobile telephone and she could hear behind him, where he was gambling at the time, was the ringing of bells of the slot machines. She has now put two and two together and made 52 and decided that her husband now had a girlfriend in Las Vegas! She got the same private detective to follow him to the airport, jump on the aeroplane and find out where he was going, which hotel he was staying in and to follow his movements every second of the time. Well of course, the private detective exposed it all! He told his wife that her husband was a compulsive and addictive gambler who didn't even look at the cocktail waitresses when they served him his drinks! Her husband had lost thousands and thousands of dollars every time he had gone to Vegas! There was no other woman involved except a pack of cards and blackjack. I was told she was relieved but she was upset that this had been going on for four or five years! She estimated how much money he had lost in Vegas. She put a stop to his gambling trips and activities. I'm not too sure if they lived happily ever after, because two years later after all his gambling activities had stopped, he was caught having an affair. His excuse, he had too much time on his hands!

I've said to my wife that gamblers very rarely have affairs. I know many gamblers that rush to the betting shop every day or rush to a poker game every night rather than have a girlfriend. I can say this because I know many untold gamblers.

I popped one day to go and see Cos the Jeweller, the Cos that always used to come and play poker with us on many occasions. I had to go and pick up a ring from him. I asked him why didn't he play poker with us anymore? He said, "Steve, trust me it's cheaper to go out every Friday night to a Taverna, drink a bottle of Scotch, have a great meal, than play poker with you!" I said, "Fair enough Cos, but I'll still call you next time when there is a game." He looked up and said, "Ok… you can do that." I picked up the ring it looked very nice. I said, "Cos, how much do I owe you?" He said, "To you Steve, £350… are you a gambler?" I said, "Well Cos, you could call me that." He said, "Well you know I'm a gambler." I said, "I know that!" He said, "I'm willing to flip a coin, double or nothing, right now for the £350." I looked at him and I said, "Cos I'm not that much of a gambler!" He said, "Come on Steve, £700 or nothing for the money you owe me." I knew Cos was being serious because he was an out and out crazy gambler as I've said before, but

I wouldn't do it. He then looked at me and said, "Since you don't want to do that, have you got ten pence on you? I'll play you penny up the wall, double or nothing." I said, "Cos can't I just pay you for this ring and leave!" He said, "No, you've taken plenty of money off me in the past, double or nothing, penny up the wall!" I said, "Cos have you got any cards here?" He said, "I might have a pack in the back." I said, "Well I'm willing to give you a £350 squeezy, double or nothing right here and right now." You might be asking yourself, well isn't that the same thing as tossing a coin or penny up the wall, it's 50–50 isn't it? Well yeah, you are right, it is 50–50. It's an even money chance, whether he tosses a coin up or if it's a squeezy, but the difference on a squeezy is I always feel, I'm slightly favourite, I don't know why, but I feel I am. If he would have produced the cards I would have squeezed him for the £700, but I wasn't prepared to flip a coin or play him penny up. He actually declined to go and get the cards and play me at the squeezy and he then said to me, "Steve, I know you and I know your squeezys, you are too lucky!"

One night me and Dad popped out to one of the West End casinos and we bumped into a guy named Dennis Watts. Now Dennis Watts was around in the Aspinall days when the big poker games were happening, we hadn't seen him for maybe 20 years, he hadn't changed a bit! He was so pleased to see me and Dad, we sat talking for about an hour, about the old poker games and the old players. He told us that French Alan was now in Miami and was doing extremely well, better than ever but he is still working running his very big company. Not that he had to because French Alan was now in his early 60s and was always comfortable. He told me that he sees Paulo, the Italian Prince from time to time and Israeli Simon, who used to play regularly at Aspinalls. Dad said to Dennis, "Still gambling Dennis?" He replied, "Still losing money in the casinos after 30 years but it's good for the grandchildren." I said, "What do you mean Dennis?" He said, "Well at the end of every month, I always keep a record of exactly how I'm doing in the casino and if I'm losing £3000 at the end of the month, then I give £3000 to three of my grandchildren, a thousand pounds each." So I said, "Wait a minute Dennis, you've got it wrong here, you mean to say if you're winning at the end of the month, you give the winnings to your grandchildren?" He said, "No, not at all Steve, I never win!" I said, "If you never win, how comes you're always giving money to your grandchildren at the end of the month?" He said, "I can't stop gambling and I always want to look after the grandchildren. So I've worked out, to punish me in a very nice way if I'm losing £5000 at the end of the month, I spread out an extra £5000 between the three grandchildren." I said, "Dennis, this can be very expensive indeed." He said, "It is, but at least I feel that the grandchildren get some benefit out of my gambling!" So I said, "Can I ask you a question? What happens if you win £5000 at the end of the month?" He said, "If I win £5000 at the end of the month I don't give them anything, trust me Stevie 11 months out of 12 I always lose!"

I'm now going to tell you what a 'sleeper' is in a betting shop. A sleeper is a winning betting slip that hasn't been picked up by the customer. For example a customer walks in and has a £100 bet, the bet wins and he has to collect his winnings but he doesn't go back for his money. I know you might be thinking that's impossible, but it does happen. All betting shops today have sleepers. I'm going to tell you this because you could probably put this in the *Guinness Book of Records.*

All bookmakers in betting shops keep their betting slips for a certain number of months and you might see from the rules and regulations they keep on the wall that they only keep sleepers for maybe three to six months maximum. After that period of time, the betting slip gets destroyed and the money cannot be picked up. The bookmakers feel that they have given ample time for the customer to go and pick up their winnings. Well we had a betting shop in Archway in the early 90s. Someone walked in one day and had an accumulator on the football, six teams and they all won. The bet came to £4800. On the Monday the customer never came and picked up his money, by Wednesday or Thursday Dad enquired to the manager whether the money was picked up and the manager replied that it hadn't, but he would keep the money in the safe for when the customer comes in. A week goes by, the customer didn't come in. Three weeks goes by, no sign of the customer. My dad asked the manager if it was a regular punter, the manager replied that he does come in every other week, but they haven't seen him since. My dad didn't think anything of it. He thought that this customer must have been on holiday. After two or three months the money was still there to be picked up and my dad received a phone call in the office, it was from the customer that had won the £4800. He said he would be picking it up within the next couple of weeks. My Dad said that it wouldn't be a problem and that whenever he popped into the shop to make sure that he had the winning slip and the money would be there. Another month went by, he didn't come in to collect his money. Another three months went by and still he hadn't been in to collect his money. Now the betting shop was sorting out all its sleepers, so my dad said to the manager that we would have to keep that sleeper on the side, because the customer had phoned him and said that he would be popping into the shop and since it's a large amount of money it's best not to destroy it because he has been in touch with us. Six months went by and the customer phoned my dad and said, "Max I've been in and out of the country, I know I've got to pick up the money, is it OK if I could pick it up in the next couple of weeks?" My Dad replied, "Not a problem, it will be there for you." Dad then took his telephone number, just in case Dad had to call the customer for any reason and another six months went by, nothing, the customer hadn't rang my dad. My Dad called him, it's now coming up to a year! The guy said that he would be in within the next couple of weeks to pick up the money and that he had been very busy but was it still OK to which my dad replied, "It is, but hurry up and pick up your money! We don't want to keep on holding that money in the shop." (By which time the money had gone back to the office, had gone to the shop and it had been used as a float for other shops etc. etc.) My Dad said, "Make sure you give me a call the day before you want to pick it up and I'll make sure it's there." Another year went past! Dad hadn't phoned him and he hadn't phoned Dad! What with one thing and another Dad told me he phoned him once. The guy's answer phone was on so Dad left a message, he didn't reply. Dad phoned him seven or eight months later, again the guy never returned my dad's call. Now this was a sleeper that looked like it wasn't going to get paid. Well, the guy phoned a year later, which was possibly about two and a half years after the bet and said, "Hi Max I don't know if you remember me but I had a bet in your Archway betting shop. Is it possible that I come down on Monday and pick up the money?" My Dad said, "Yes by all means, but where have you been?" He said, "I've been very busy. I've been in and out of the country and I know that my money is safe with you as we have had contact in the last couple of years but I will be in on Monday." Monday came, the customer never turned up! Dad phoned him a week or two later, again the answer phone. Dad then phoned him a couple of months later, the same thing. Well I'm going to tell you the ending to this story because you are not going to believe it. Ten years later! Yes, ten years later! In the year 2003 my dad received a phone call. It was a call from a bookmaker who Dad had known for the last 30 years named Stewart. He said, "Max how are you? Haven't seen you for a long time, I've moved houses and I was cutting the grass one day and next door to me was a guy that had a bet with you and he hasn't picked up the money." Dad said, "Try and refresh my memory Stewart." He said, "It was a football bet at Archway." Dad said, "Stewart I've tried to get hold of the guy a dozen times, in the end he used to return my phone call six months later. I used to get the money down to the shop, the guy never showed up to pick up the money, I got fed up!" Stewart said, "Max, he wants me to ask you if it is possible for him to take you out for dinner and produce the betting slip to pick up his money?" Dad said to Stewart, "Stewart if he produces the betting slip with the winning bet on it, I will bring him his cheque, but I don't believe we'll ever meet!" Another 4 weeks went by and Dad received a phone call from Stewart and they all went out for dinner and the guy produced the betting slip and Dad paid him his money! The customer said, "Max I know you don't have to pay me, none of the 'big boys' or any other bookmaker would possibly pay me this bet ten years after I had it and I told this to Stewart but Stewart said, I know Max and if you produce the slip, Max will pay you." Stewart asked him why he hadn't been to the shop to get paid. He said, "To tell you the truth after I was in and out of the country so much I genuinely forgot and then me and my wife moved house and I found the slip and I realised that I didn't have to get paid by law." That night Dad gave him a cheque for £4800, ten and half years after this punter had had the bet! This had to be the longest sleeper in history of betting!

I went one night to a Jewish Relief Charity and it was raising money for the Jewish people in need. I was asked to go as it was a charity event and I met a lot of the old guys that I used to play poker with. One guy came up to me and said, "I've heard that from a couple of guys here you are a poker player? Well I can get you into a game and it's a big game." I said, "Well put me in, but do they play Five Card Stud?" He replied, "They will play any poker game you want." I said, "Well if they play Five Card Stud put me in, if they play Hold'em still put me in but I am not playing Seven Card Stud or any of the other poker games." We started chatting for five or ten minutes and we swapped names and numbers. He also told me that the guy he knows who runs the games is a guy named Nicky G. I said, "Well pass my number on to Nick and tell him to call me." An hour went past. The same guy came back up to me and his words were to me, I'll never forget them, "You had better change your name!" I said, "Excuse me?" He said, "If you want a game of poker, you had better change your name." I said, "Why's that?" He said, "Well I rang my friend Nicky G and I told him that I had a customer for him that wants to play poker." He then replied to me, "Bring him down." I then told him your name. He then said, "Don't bring him down! That Steve used to play poker with my dad (Peter G) in 1982 in Aspinalls and my dad said that he was too good, so what chance have we got?" I said to him, "So I take it I can't go?" He said, "You are dead right, you can't."

I walked into a very big electrical store in Finchley and there were a couple of Greek guys that owned it. I heard that they played poker sometimes and I thought I would go in there and see if I can get myself into the games. The owner, I recognised from years ago. He didn't recognise me as I had shaved my head in the last couple of years and I looked totally different to the way I did up to about eight years ago. So when I was talking about poker, he told me that they play on a regular basis. He told me that they played Five Card Stud and I said, "That suits me fine, that's the game I love to play." He asked me my name, I told him my first name, without my last name obviously. He then asked me who my dad was. Not because I think he recognised me, but I think it was just out of conversation that went on for 20 minutes. I said to him, "I don't think you know my dad." He said, "Well tell me who he is?" I was a little bit reluctant to say just in case he then knew who I was and I couldn't get in the game. He started to smell a rat. I looked at him and I said, "OK the games up, I'll tell you who my dad is but before I tell you his name, I want to see if you can guess." Now meanwhile there were three or four people listening to this conversation as we were at the back of the shop. I said, "The first clue is my dad is probably one of the best Five Card Stud player that's ever lived." The guy looked at me and said, "Well I do know one player who is the best Five Card Stud poker player…" He then paused, he looked at me in the eyes and said, "Are you Max's son?" I replied, "You've got it in one!" He said, "I've known your dad for 45 years. You can't come to our games, but you are welcome to come for a coffee and I would love to see your dad!"

Many people always ask me, what do you reckon Steve, you and your Dad have won at poker throughout the years? I always reply the same answer, I couldn't tell you. All I can tell you is that we've been on great holidays and really enjoyed life. Poker has given me a chance to travel around the world, Australia, Europe and live in LA for a couple of years with all expenses paid through poker. Probably all the money I've earnt playing poker, we've spent it but enjoyed it and we will carry on spending.

There was a couple of little sayings that I was told when I was about 17 years old and I think one of the sayings were so powerful at the time that it actually stopped me gambling on what we call the 'lucky games'. It really made me have control on any gambling activity that I did throughout my life. The guy who told me this was a compulsive gambler and I had a chat with him one night over a coffee and he said, "Steve I'm going to offer you this advice because I know you're out there playing poker and you're always in the gambling environment but remember this… 'It's surprising in life how little money you need… If you don't gamble!'" I looked up and said to him, "Hold it one second, if I want to go to Stringfellows every night having champagne and caviar, what are you talking about, I could go through fortunes." He looked at me and replied, "Did you hear what I said? I'll repeat it… 'It's surprising in life how little money you need if you don't gamble!' Now Steve you can go to Stringfellows every night, drink your champagne, go out for dinner every night, do what you want to do. What can you spend, but if you gamble there's not enough money that you could earn to supplement your desire to win!" I thought about that on the way home and it really did have an effect on me. This was coming from a man who had done a lot of money gambling. So I thought to myself, if I can get myself into poker that I can make money why lose it in the casinos, why not spend it having a good time. Sure, I know my dad's gambled but he will say and I will agree with him, the only reason he's been one of the biggest ever winners at poker, is because he is a fearless gambler.

Another one was from a bookmaker as he was speaking to my dad. Dad asked him, "John how did you do over Ascot?" He said, "Max we done our brains," (which means they lost a lot of money). By the way, no one ever feels sorry for the bookmakers, but John was saying that they had an absolute disaster. He continued to say, "Max to tell you the truth, I don't mind." My dad replied, "I'm sure you don't John but if you lost a lot of money, it's not good for business is it?" John replied, "Max it was a lot of money but I figure in life if I go skint tomorrow, I'll be levels or evens on the day." I looked up and said, "John what do you mean?" He said, "Steve I've come into this world with nothing and I'll end up going out of this world with nothing, it's what we do in the meantime that counts!"

The other interesting saying was one that I heard from Reggie. Reggie said to me many times in the past, "Stevie, Stevie, Stevie, don't worry about anything in life because everything floats to the right level." I said, "What do you mean Reggie?" He said, "Everything levels out, if you are meant to have money in life, you are going to get it and if you're not meant to have money in life and you've got it, you will end up losing it. If you're meant to have money in life and you lose it you will get it again." Reggie was baffling me, but I know what he means now. Everything floats to its desired level and there is nothing that you can do. Some people are luckier in life than others, we know that, if we accept the way life pans out for us, we'd all be a lot happier.

There was a lady playing slots in Vegas a few years ago and she won the million dollar jackpot. Her and her sister the next day went out a brought a brand-new Cadillac and they were killed on the motorway driving back from Vegas to LA. So it just makes you think doesn't it? If they didn't win the jackpot would they still be alive? I believe life has many corners and many turnings, some we can't control and some we can.

The other funny interesting saying is, "Never educate a mug!" which means if you've got a mug at the table or at anything that you're playing and you are winning money off him, never teach him how to play! And at poker, never bluff a mug and professionals know why!

We went on holiday a year ago and at the hotel we were staying was a table tennis table, that's right a ping-pong table. Me, I've played ping-pong half a dozen times in my life when I was about nine years old on a dining room table. I was never really any good. I used to play my mum, but while on holiday, I started playing a lot. I was with my boys and we had a few games, within five or six days of us being there, my two boys could keep the ball quite well on the table and I was improving too.

What's this all got to do with gambling you are probably asking yourselves, well I'm coming to it. When we got home the boys wanted a table tennis table, so I went up to the local shops and ordered one, it wasn't expensive and we played for a week or two but we weren't getting much better and then we sort of got fed up with it. I spoke to a friend of mine that used to play poker and he told me he was quite a good table tennis player, so I said, "Well I'll tell you what we'll do, you give me the right start or handicap at table tennis and we can always play poker afterwards." I was always looking for an angle. He said, "Forget the poker, I'll never play you poker but I'll play you table tennis." Anyway we agreed on the right start that he had to give me and he then won £200 off me. I said to him that he would have to give me a bigger start. He then said, "I can't give you much of a bigger start because this is a game I want to stay favourite at beating you Steve, you can have your usual 13 start up to 21 for any amount." Well I had to find an angle didn't I! How was I going to beat him next time? That angle never came the next week because I lost another £200 playing table tennis with the same 13 start. It was only by chance that I was driving to Barnet High Street one day that

I drove past the Barnet Table Tennis Centre, it had been there for 35 years. I popped in there and I was introduced to a Hungarian guy called 'Urfi'; that was his nickname. This guy was a pretty good player, just to let you know he is ranked in the Top 10 in England. It was like music to my ears because he taught private lessons. For the next two weeks, I had one to one lessons with Urfi and I would say that I had improved by five or six points straight away. The next time I played this guy around my house table tennis, I took £600 off him. Well I'll tell you now, I'm still playing this guy table tennis. I'm now giving HIM 13 start for £100 a game, so far he is £6000 behind with me at table tennis! But the funny thing is my two boys have continued to play and have lessons, I now play two or three times a week. My oldest boy finished second in the U13s in North London and my youngest finished 12th and we are probably the most improved table tennis players in London in the last year. That's a fact and I'm 42, they are 10 and 8! My Dad always said to me, "You've got to pay to learn." I always have but I've paid the minimum! I even play another table tennis English ranked player name Eli for £5 a game, he gives me a big handicap. I know I can't win but what I'm doing is I'm losing £5 a game with him, but I'm winning £50 or £100 a game somewhere else. You've got to look for the edge, haven't you?

2003 also saw the closure of the Empress Club. That's right, the Empress Club in Haringey had been opened for the last 50 years, but now the Empress Club doors have finally closed. Instead my dad acquired a betting shop licence and it will now be a betting shop. It was quite sad when the Empress closed. As you now know, in the old days it used to have some of the best poker games there was in London at the time. People used to come from all around London and queue up to play my dad and Vellie. Once they knew Max and Vellie were on the table, there used to be an eight handed game with ten people waiting! They knew it was a value game. Nowadays, everything has changed. As I've said, you can log onto the internet and you can play poker, you can even log onto one of the biggest sites in the world at the moment that's turning over £50 million a week and you can bet, you can lay and be the bookmaker on certain sites! Everything has changed. There is not the cash that there used to be in the old days. You can sit in your own armchair, bet a team, lay a team, buy and sell prices on the football or any other sport on the internet. You can make money without leaving home. Gambling has changed. I pop to the Vic now and again, I always make a rule that if there is no seat available, I don't put my name down and wait. If there is a seat available I sit down for an hour or two. If I'm losing after the first hour, I go home. If I'm winning after the first hour I play for an extra hour. Why I do that, first of all I don't really understand the game I'm playing, Omaha is not my game but with a bit of poker sense you've got a chance but you've got to turn the odds into your favour, otherwise you're a million to one! Also in today's gambling there are books that can tell you, how to play, what to play, when to play, percentage books, there is even a book on 'tells', telling you how to watch certain opponents when they are playing, whether they have got the winning hand or the losing hand. Me, I'm from the old school, I always had to pick up everything the hard way. My dad always tells me that he never watched for tells, he used to play his own game. I would safely say now that Five Card Stud Strip Deck is dead. Stavros is at the Vic most nights of the week. My Dad, well he just doesn't play anymore. There is not a game around that would give him a buzz like Five Card did. He still pops up the Vic when there is a big festival on but things are not the same. As for me there is very little Five Card Stud. Sure we have a game every two weeks but then if I win a couple of times on the trot then there are no games for a couple of months.

A couple of sayings that I'd heard, they were from my headmaster at my first school. He used to say, "In life if you have one friend you are a lucky man, if you have two or three you are a very lucky man, if you have more than three… Then you are a fool boy!" If you think about that carefully he is not wrong is he? And the other one was "Where there's a will there's a way, where there's a 'will'… there's relations!"

I've recently found three internet sites that play Five Card Stud, yep that's right, in the last three or four months I've been playing Five Card Stud but wait for it, it's not a 32 card deck, it's a full deck of 52 cards. It's a pot limit game, there is a small ante from each of the players and the low card opens. It's only $100 table but sometimes there can be $1500 or $2000 on the table but the structure is correct. It took me about three or four days to get used to playing full deck but I'm showing a tremendous profit. I sit at home and I play for a couple of hours. You do need quite a lot of patience at 52 card poker but patience is something I've got, you get quite a lot of what I call tourist players that come on line and throw $100 or $200 away. So now I don't wait for the phone to ring for me to be invited to a Five Card Stud game because the phone hasn't rung for years. I'm quite happy, I play three or four nights a week on the internet. It's a game I feel very comfortable with. Don't get me wrong I've shown a profit at Hold'em but for me it's like wearing old slippers, they're comfortable. When I played on the internet before, you can search the web while you are playing but you can't do that at Five Card Stud because you have got to concentrate at all times on the past cards and on every single move that's going on. I'll be even happier if the games get bigger. But as you now know me if there is a game of Five Card Stud, I want to get in it. I was always told that a full deck is a little bit slow and boring as I've said to you earlier on in the book, but I must admit, I really enjoy it. It suits the tight player but the tight aggressive player. Sometimes you are committed in pots and you have to carry on and bet the pot, no matter what you have. It can be quite a dangerous game, having said that, I'm winning and maybe I was born to play Five Card Stud!

One night I was playing heads up Pot Limit Five Card Stud on the net, I had about $1800 in front of me; my opponent had about $1200. It was going one way then the other, he sure was a tough cookie to crack, every time I set a trap he checked with me, few times I bluffed him, he called, I had to look to catch him in one pot, but it wasn't happening. I typed in a message for him online, that within ten minutes I was going to bed, he agreed that we would stop, we were about evens and then this happened.

He opened with a Queen for $4, I raised $8 with a Jack showing, and by the way I'll tell you I've got, a King in the hole. He called my $8 and he re-raised the pot. I waited about ten seconds and then I called. To tell you the truth I put him on Queens backed up or an Ace in the hole. The second card came out, 2 to him, he's now showing Queen, 2, and a King to me, showing Jack, King, lovely!! I checked there was $72 dollars in the pot. I really felt that he would bet the pot and then I was going to skin him. He checked with me! No problem I thought I'll catch him on the next card. The third card came out (the one before the last) 2 to me, I'm now showing Jack, King, 2 and Jack to him, he's now showing Queen, 2 Jack, now for sure I thought he was going to bet the pot. I checked, he then checked again! This for me was going from bad to worse, somehow I've now managed from trying to skin him and win the maximum to looking like winning only $36 off the guy! The last card came out, 3 to me, I'm now showing Jack, King, 2, 3 and 3 to him. He's now showing Queen, 2, Jack, 3. In my mind I felt I have messed it all up but I came out and I bet the pot $72. He thought for about 15 seconds, I said to myself "Serves me right, I got greedy and it has back fired on me" but listen to this… he called the $72 and raised $216. I couldn't believe it, I immediately called the $216 and raised $648, he called me straight away and showed me

Queens, I then showed him my Kings!!! He had lost just under $900 in one pot after playing so well for 3 1⁄2 hours! As Lancey Howard once said in the movie *The Cincinnati Kid*, "It was about making the wrong move at the right time!"

At the beginning of this book, I did say to you that I was going to make up a table of eight players who I consider the strongest Five Card Stud Strip Deck players that have ever lived and as you now know I've played with many. I've also consulted my dad on this one because if I've played with thousands of players he has played with ten times more, so I would say we are quite qualified to do this. I'll go through each player at a time and I'll tell you the reason why I'm putting that certain player in. I won't put them in any order but these are my strongest players.

First of all, I'll put my dad in. As I've said to you he is one of the strongest Five Card Stud poker players. Short-handed (two to six players), he is exceptionally strong and unbeatable in the long run, even on a full table. But let me tell you the reasons I've put him in. My dad has the ability to play the same super aggressive game at all times and build tremendous pots, also from being an underdog in many pots, to turning the pot upside down, looking like losing it and then winning it! This is a major asset at Five Card Stud or at any poker game, I cannot stress that fact enough. When you reach a certain level but play a super strength game at all times you will be strong at any game you play. One of the coolest, if not the coolest poker player that has ever lived and many agree. You could walk into a poker room and you would not know by his emotions, actions or style of play whether he was winning or losing. The bigger the game the better, tremendous bluffer, very good caller and an exceptionally strong better. He will eventually catch you in a pot in the course of the evening and you will lose your money. The only weakness that I would say my dad has is that on an eight-handed games he still plays too aggressive, I've told him this but whether he can adjust I don't know. That's the reasons I've put my dad in.

Second player I would put in is Stavros. The reason I've put Stavros in is because first of all, if it wasn't for my dad and Stavros, Five Card Stud would have died a long time ago! Between the two of them when they were playing, everybody knew there was action in town. Stavros' major asset at Five Card Stud is he too is able to build fantastic pots. Stavros has a great ability to change his game. Stavros also has the ability to read someone's game and change his own game accordingly. This is a great asset at poker, whereas my dad would just steamroll over everybody, Stavros thinks how a certain player plays and then adjusts his own game, a great Five Card Stud player. The weakness Stavros has, is sometimes when the cards are not going his way, he can lose a lot of money and he may steam or chase, but at Five Card Stud Stavros is a big winner.

The next player I would put in would be French Alan. French Alan is one of the greatest Five Card Stud poker players that has ever lived and was exceptionally very good at a full table of eight players. There possibly wasn't a better player on a full table. He wasn't keen on playing short-handed, especially when my dad was at the table, but eight players, Alan was mustard and he used to play some tremendous pots. A very good reader of cards, a very good bluffer and overall a very strong player. Any weaknesses about Alan? Maybe towards the later years he used to play roulette and that would sometimes affect his judgement on the poker table, but that's not taking anything away from him. He's a very big winner and a tremendous player.

The fourth player I would put in and this would be a surprise entry was a player that I used to play with at the Empress Club and his name was Fiddis. The games we used to play in the late 70s weren't big but I'm putting in players who I consider and my dad considers very strong at the game. It doesn't matter if it was only £100 or £200 table or £10,000 table. We know money talks at poker but I'm talking about the actual game and I'm sure if I gave Fiddis £10,000 to sit down with, he would hold his own and be quite comfortable in that game. Even though he might not be able to afford it, we are talking about pure ability. Fiddis, who I haven't mentioned before was a very strong Five Card Stud poker player and I would have my money any time with him on any size game.

The fifth spot I would give to Mansour. Mansour won the 1991 No Limit Texas Hold'em (the big one) in Vegas. Even though I don't think he was as strong as the ones I've mentioned, don't be mistaken he could quite easily win money off any of them and his ability to play poker is fantastic but Mansour had a lovely style and flair about him when he used to play. He used to have some tremendous pots and battles with my dad at the Barracuda in the old days. He was a good reader of cards and a good judge of a player, so my fifth spot would go to Mansour. If there was a weakness in his game I would say it might be the length of time he was playing Five Card Stud with the top class players, but that's not taking anything away from Mansour, a top player.

My sixth spot would go to Paulo the Italian Prince. Paulo was a very strong poker player and a very good gambler, during the pot, he was a good reader of cards, a good reader of players, a good reader of circumstances. He had good money control and very rarely lost his cool. The weakness Paulo had, I feel, is that sometimes if a mistake was made by a dealer or something was irritating him on that night, he wouldn't play to his top level but again, I would say a very strong player.

The seventh spot, I'm going to put in is a guy named Derek Webb. The reason is, he is actually a very strong all round poker player and at Five Card Stud his ability to play the game is quite remarkable. At Five Card Stud from what I remember, I've never seen him lose! Very tight, very Karabina as we say, but a very big winner. I've also mentioned that Ben Roberts is one of the world's best poker players and he is, but he is not on this table because when Ben has played Five Card on a handful of occasions, he seems to play quite a nervy game indeed. This is very unlike Ben because at all other games he is world class, but Derek who is a top player at all the other games can very comfortably sit down with all these players. I would definitely have a share with Derek, I've never seen him lose his cool, and I've never seen him chase his money, a very strong player.

The last spot in number eight, I would have to give to a player called Maverick. Maverick was the guy that used to host a game when Dad went down there with Fossis one night, they were raided by the police. I've never seen Maverick play more than a handful of times in my life, but Maverick was one of the strongest Five Card Stud poker players and his strengths were, they used to call him the statue. Every time he used to make a bet at the end he never used to move his hands or have no emotion on his face. He had completely no 'tells' Maverick, Dad tells me was a great player who never cracked at the poker table, hardly spoke, never smiled, a big winner. Maverick has died now, a world-class player.

It was difficult to put down eight players, as there are three or four other players I will mention because of their ability at Five Card Stud. One is Sonny from the Spinner days, still playing Five Card Stud to this day, strong player. There are no moves that you are going to pull on Sonny. He knows every move in the book and as I told you a great player at full deck.

Another player is Michael Skryne, he won a lot of money in the 70s, playing at the Curzon House, a great Five Card Stud poker player. Israeli Simon at Aspinalls, the one that had the discrepancy with me on the pot when I first played, a very strong Five Card Stud poker player.

Italian Gino. I would have a share with him any day.

Another guy called Bambos Xanthos, he is now playing at the Vic in the Omaha and Hold'em cash games and tournaments. Bambos' strength at the moment is tournament play. A great tournament player but he would still love to play Five Card Stud, even today if there was a game, he would be first in line, a very strong player with a lot of flair. I respect his game and it was very difficult for me not to put him in on the final table because of his knowledge.

I think that about wraps up the players. If I've missed anybody out there that plays Strip Deck, I'm sorry. I do want to make a little mention to Velli from the old days, not that he could ever get on the top three tables of any Five Card Stud but trust me when I say this, Velli could sit down at any table and two things would happen. The game would get ten times bigger and the game would liven up so much that even the Karabinas as we say would end up losing and chasing their money. That was the ability of Velli, but the problem was Velli would still lose . . . However the game would sure have a lot of fireworks.

Do I put myself amongst these players? That's up to you to decide, you've read my book. I can say one thing though, if there was a spare seat and there was only seven players sitting down and one of them was missing, I would have to ask myself would I sit down and play with them. The answer would be and I'll answer you honestly, yeah I would, but and there is a but, I've always maintained in life and especially at poker if there were seven professionals sitting at the table and I had to take the final seat, I would take it but I will only probably take it for a couple of hours and I would see which way the cards were falling! If I had to be truthful with you, if I could see the cards not falling my way, I would probably leave and not chase my loses. That's the makeup of me as a Five Card Stud poker player. If I were winning, I would build on my winnings and stay for the rest of the night even against the best in the world. I suppose it's like any sport, whether it be soccer, tennis or anything. If two teams or two players are very evenly matched, it would be down to the run of the ball, the luck on the day. Many people have said to me in the past, I'm a very lucky poker player, I've always explained to them that luck over the year evens out. It's what you do with the cards, whether you maximise your winnings and minimise your loses. May I hasten to add, if I heard that these players were all sitting down together on a poker table I would just have to be at this game, I wouldn't want to miss it for the world. Still value, I always like a little bit of value on the poker table, it sure would be a great game to be in. My assets are, I know how to maximise the pots I win, minimise the pots when I'm the underdog, protect and build on my winnings and it's hard for other players to get me involved unless I'm favourite in the pot. Then you have to try and outdraw me. The weaknesses I have? You'll have to ask the players that have played with me in the last 30 years and have all lost money! I have had the privilege of playing all of these players mentioned, except Maverick and Michael Skryne and have won most of the time!

I remember 30 years ago, Dad saying to me on the way home from the Empress on a Sunday afternoon, "Boy, never rely on poker for a living, make sure in life you get a proper job, come into the business." I never really knew what he meant as I'd seen him winning many, many times at the poker table but I think now 30 years later, I now know. There are players out there that play poker full time and they make money. Me on the other hand, I feel the reason I've made money at poker was I've had a comfortable cushion, I've been in the family business. I've played poker to win, yes, but if I've lost or there have been no games for six weeks, it wasn't the be all and end all and I now understand what my dad meant. My boys say to me today, "Dad I'd love to play poker like you and earn money and go to Vegas, travel in LA." I look up at them and say, "Boys be in a proper business, don't rely on poker to make your living, it's too difficult!" They always reply, "Well Dad, you've made plenty of money playing poker throughout your years, haven't you?" I said, "Yeah, but it takes a special person to be a poker player with a very special temperament." Well everybody that's known me in all the years I've played with know I've only lost my cool once at a poker table and never ever have I chased my money when losing.

If someone came to me in this day and age and said they wanted to be a poker player I would say to them, exactly what Phil Hellmouth once said (and he is one of the finest tournament players there is), "It's a tough way to make an easy living!" My boys say they would like to learn to play, sometimes I let them play very small Hold'em games on the internet but I don't encourage it. My wife says to me, they shouldn't be playing but I always remember 30 years ago, when my mum wasn't keen on my dad taking me to Charlie Chester's casino at 15 years old on a Saturday night. My dad's way of thinking was that if you're involved in gambling when you're very young and you see others lose their money and you see what goes on in the gambling world you soon wise up. I'm not too sure, I don't know, I can't answer that because for me going to casinos at 15 years old worked as I've never played more than £20 or £30.

As I said to you before, if my dad won we all used to win so why play myself? With other people that have got involved in gambling from a young age, they've stayed in the gambling circle and lost money. Then on the other side of the coin you've got the older ones that don't start gambling until they are in their twenties. There's no hard fast rules as to whether you start gambling at ten, like I did or 30 like a few people I know who I've mentioned in this book. There is not an answer to whether you are going to be a gambler and there is not an answer as to whether you are going to be a winner or a loser. My suggestion is if you really do want to be a poker player, like when my dad said to me many years ago, to get down to the Empress and play with a small amount of money, you will soon learn the game after six months. My advice would be to go with a small amount of money and go and play the cash games at the Vic, restrict your losses because you will probably lose for the first three to six months. If you carry on losing after that then that's not the game for you, but I would say go to the Vic because they have got some of the strongest players down there and you will soon learn the game, that's if you are clued up that is. My training ground was at the Empress, they were possibly the best Five Card Stud poker players in the UK at the time. The best poker players at the moment can be found at the Vic and sometimes you can find some very good ones on the small games, you don't have to play in the big ones. You can sit on the £50 table, round of each Omaha and Hold'em and you will soon learn the game. Mind you, it will cost you to learn, but as I've said several times before, make sure it costs you the minimum!

I can now say officially that Five Card Stud Strip Deck is dead. The casinos don't play it, the private games for me have dried up. My Dad doesn't go to Cyprus to play poker any more, Stavros is at the Vic. All the players have dispersed. If we go back 30 years ago when my Mum used to take us up to the casino on a Sunday afternoon and I used to sit on my dad's knee watching him play poker, with me picking up tips on how to play, without even me knowing it. I'm now playing on the internet and do you know what? My boys come and sit on my knee and watch me play, asking me questions. I heard recently that my youngest son who is ten, was sneaking a pack of cards into school and playing Hold'em for money. I wasn't happy and I did have a strong word with him. He looked at me and said, "Dad, the apple doesn't fall far from the tree!" Just makes you think, doesn't it?

Milton Keynes UK
Ingram Content Group UK Ltd.
UKHW010057060224
437294UK00008B/435